"*On Hallowed Ground* is a beautiful portrait of the place where we honor [our] fallen comrades." —*Bookpage*

"Poole's book tells the stories of many of those buried in 70 sections across these rolling hills just across the Potomac from Washington, D.C. *On Hallowed Ground* is part history lesson, part tourist guide, part mystery novel." —*USA Today*

"In *On Hallowed Ground*, Robert Poole has given us a well-researched look at Arlington National Cemetery, tempered with warmth and reverence. In very readable, journalistic style he also reviews our nation's history, as Arlington is a microcosm of the American story." —*ARMY*

"Here is an intriguing history of a true American shrine . . . Many veterans are apt to say that Arlington National Cemetery proves that the federal government can do something right—and Poole certainly underscores that sentiment." —*Proceedings*, **U.S. Naval Institute**

"Vivid, compelling, filled with rich and unexpected detail, *On Hallowed Ground* tells the little-understood story of Arlington National Cemetery and in the process chronicles how we have honored—and sometimes dishonored— those who gambled everything on our behalf. Robert M. Poole is a fine storyteller and this is a great story." —**Geoffrey C. Ward, author of** *The Civil War* **and** *The War: An Intimate History, 1941–1945*

"Improbably gripping and often deeply moving, *On Hallowed Ground* chronicles both the evolution of our national cemetery and the profound ways in which treatment of the war dead reflects a nation's soul. Readers interested in political, social, or military history from the Civil War on will want to read this book." —**Caroline Alexander, author of** *The Endurance* **and** *The War That Killed Achilles*

"Most Americans, especially most historians, think they know all about Arlington Cemetery. They respect what it represents, and revere the heroes resting there. But only Robert Poole has brought to life all the historic figures, from privates to presidents, who made this national shrine and populate its rolling hills. *On Hallowed Ground* is a memorable combination of historical research, firsthand reporting and sensitive writing—a definitive work that should last as long as the eternal flame at John Kennedy's grave site."

— **Ernest B. Furgurson, author of** *Freedom Rising:*
Washington in the Civil War

"A prism for appreciating American military sacrifice from the time of the Civil War through the present wars in Iraq and Afghanistan. Robert M. Poole not only captures the history of a venerable American institution but with it the politics of commemoration and reconciliation. Absolutely first-rate."

— **Paul Dickson, coauthor of** *The Bonus Army*

"Robert Poole has coupled superb storytelling with meticulous research and produced a gem. *On Hallowed Ground* is by turns illuminating, informative, and enormously readable. In the future you will never think of Arlington Cemetery without recalling the tales contained in this marvelous book."

— **Robert Timberg, author of** *The Nightingale's Song*
and *State of Grace: A Memoir of Twilight Time*

"In his stirring, evocative style, Robert Poole blends Arlington's untold story with America's own story, as Robert E. Lee's home, a prize of war in a divided nation, evolves—through wars and peace—into America's most hallowed ground." — **Thomas B. Allen, coauthor of** *The Bonus Army*

ON
HALLOWED
GROUND

THE STORY OF
ARLINGTON NATIONAL
CEMETERY

ROBERT M. POOLE

WALKER & COMPANY
New York

LIBRARY OF CONGRESS CATALOGING-IN-PUBLICATION DATA

Poole, Robert M.
On hallowed ground : the story of Arlington National Cemetery / Robert M. Poole.
p.   cm.
Includes bibliographical references and index.
ISBN-13: 978-0-8027-1548-7 (hbk.: alk. paper)
ISBN-10: 0-8027-1548-6 (hbk.: alk. paper)
1. Arlington National Cemetery (Arlington, Va.)—History.   2. Arlington (Va.)—Buildings, structures, etc.   3. United States—History, Military—Miscellanea.   I. Title.

F234.A7P66 2009
975.5'295—dc22
2009022677

Visit Walker & Company's Web site at www.walkerbooks.com

First published by Walker & Company in 2009
This paperback edition published in 2010

Paperback ISBN: 978-0-8027-1549-4

1 3 5 7 9 10 8 6 4 2

Interior design by Adam Bohannon
Typeset by Westchester Book Group
Printed in the United States of America by Worldcolor Fairfield

CONTENTS

PART III: THE NATION'S CEMETERY

Show me the manner
in which a nation or a community cares for its dead and
I will measure with mathematical exactness the tender sympathies of
its people, their respect for the laws of the land,
and their loyalty to high ideals.

WILLIAM GLADSTONE

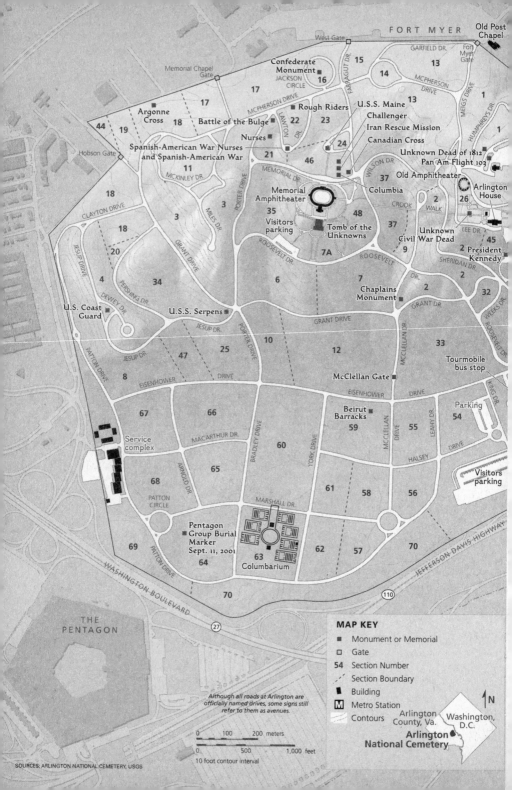

Arlington National Cemetery

N

Superintendent's lodge

Administration buildings

Employee parking

Women's Memorial

President Taft

Visitors center

Administration building

M Arlington Cemetery

Arlington County, Virginia

Washington, D.C.

Monuments and Memorials	Section	Date of Dedication
Unknown Civil War Dead	26	1866
McClellan Gate	33	1870
Spanish-American War Memorial	22	1902
Spanish-American War Nurses	21	1905
Rough Riders Memorial	22	1906
Confederate Monument	16	1914
U.S.S. Maine Memorial	24	1915
Argonne Cross	18	1921
Tomb of the Unknowns	48	1921
Canadian Cross of Sacrifice	46	1925
Chaplains Monument	2	1926
U.S. Coast Guard Memorial	4	1928
Nurses Memorial	21	1938
U.S.S. Serpens Memorial	34	1949
Unknown Dead of 1812	1	1976
Iran Rescue Mission Memorial	46	1983
Beirut Barracks	59	1984
Battle of the Bulge	21	1986
Space Shuttle Challenger Memorial	46	1987
Pan Am Flight 103 Memorial	1	1995
Space Shuttle Columbia Memorial	46	2004
Pentagon Group Burial Marker	64	2005

Presidents and Family	Section	Date of Interment
Robert Todd Lincoln	31	1926
President William H. Taft	30	1930
President John F. Kennedy	45	1963
Robert F. Kennedy	45	1968

Military and Politics		
James McCubbin Lingan	1	1812
General Philip Kearny	2	1812
General Philip Henry Sheridan	2	1862
General George Crook	2	1888
Revolutionary War Veterans	1	1890
General Arthur MacArthur	2	1892
General Nelson Miles	3	1912
William Jennings Bryan	4	1925
John Wingate Weeks	5	1925
General John J. Pershing	34	1926
General Henry Arnold	34	1948
General Claire Lee Chennault	2	1955
General George Marshall	7	1958
Admiral William F. Halsey	2	1959
Admiral William D. Leahy	2	1959
John Foster Dulles	21	1959
Medgar Evers	36	1959
General Daniel James	2	1963
General Omar Nelson Bradley	31	1978
Admiral Hyman Rickover	5	1981
General Maxwell Taylor	7A	1986
Colonel Gregory Boyington	7A	1987
General James Dolittle	7A	1988
Ronald Brown	6	1993

The Supreme Court		
Justice Oliver Wendell Holmes	5	1935
Justice Hugo Black	30	1971
Chief Justice Earl Warren	21	1974
Justice William O. Douglas	5	1980
Justice Potter Stewart	5	1985
Justice Arthur Joseph Goldberg	21	1990
Justice Thurgood Marshall	5	1993
Chief Justice Warren E. Burger	5	1995
Justice William J. Brennan, Jr.	5	1997
Justice Harry A. Blackmun	5	1999
Chief Justice William H. Rehnquist	5	2005

Exploration and Space		
Commodore Charles Wilkes	2	1877
John Wesley Powell	1	1902
Robert E. Peary	8	1920
Adolphus W. Greely	1	1935
Matthew Henson	8	1955
Richard Byrd	2	1957
Lt. Commander Roger Chaffee	3	1967
Colonel Virgil I. Grissom	3	1967
Colonel Francis R. Scobee	46	1986
Captain Michael J. Smith	7A	1986
Colonel Donn F. Eisele	3	1987
Colonel James B. Irwin	3	1991

Medicine		
Jonathan Letterman	3	1872
Juliet Opie Hopkins	1	1890
Walter Reed	3	1902
Jane Delano	21	1919
Anita Newcomb McGee	1	1940
Ollie Josephine B. Bennett	10	1957
Lt. Col. Albert Bruce Sabin	3	1993

Science and Engineering		
Major Pierre Charles L'Enfant	2	1825
George Westinghouse	2	1914
Admiral Grace Hopper	59	1992

Sports		
Abner Doubleday	1	1893
Dwight Davis	2	1945
Spotswood Poles	42	1962
Joe Louis	7A	1981

PROLOGUE

It was a beautiful day for a funeral. The last of the cherry blossoms drifted on a cool breeze, which carried the scent of cut grass and wet stone over Arlington National Cemetery. Somewhere in the distance, the early morning mowing subsided, soon to be overtaken by the all-day crack of rifles, the rattle of horse-drawn caissons, and the mournful sound of Taps floating among the tombstones.

Along Eisenhower Drive, as far as the eye could see, the grave markers formed into bone-white brigades, climbed from the flats of the Potomac River and scattered over the green Virginia hills in perfect order. They reached Arlington's highest point, where they encircled an old cream-colored mansion with thick columns and commanding views of the cemetery, the river, and the city beyond. The mansion's flag, just lowered to half-staff, signaled that it was time to start another day of funerals, which would add more than twenty new conscripts to Arlington's army of the dead, now more than 300,000 strong.

This day at Arlington—May 10, 2005—would be much like any other, with funerals taking place from morning until evening. Most of the ceremonies would be small affairs honoring the aging veterans of World War II and Vietnam.

Other burials would be for young combatants returning from Afghanistan or Iraq, now headed for Section 60 of the cemetery, where their numbers had grown in recent years. Every funeral, run by specialty units from the uniformed services, was made memorable by the solemn ritual and the attention to detail that crisply pressed young soldiers, sailors, marines, airmen, or coastguardsmen brought to the assignment—carrying caskets, firing salutes, slow-marching in formation, driving caissons, folding flags, and offering comfort to friends and family around the grave.

No other nation goes to the effort the United States does to recover and pay tribute to its war dead, a military tradition older than ancient Athens. There, in 431 B.C., selected warriors were returned from the Peloponnesian battlefield with great ceremony, each tribe represented by a dead fighter borne home in a cypress coffin, with one empty bier representing all of the missing, "that is, for those whose bodies could not be recovered," wrote Thucydides. "The bones are laid in the public burial place, which is in the most beautiful quarter outside the city walls. Here the Athenians always bury those who have fallen in war."[1]

The historian might have been describing Arlington. Since the time of Thucydides, societies have developed countless ways of honoring their war dead—by building monuments to those they could not recover, by elevating one unknown warrior to stand for all who sacrificed, by designating holidays for decorating graves with flowers, by establishing national cemeteries on foreign soil to recognize those who died far from home.

Thousands who sleep at Arlington today were brought there by the Civil War, a national trauma so unexpected and so extensive that, five years after Appomattox, recovery teams were still combing old battlefields around Washington to find, identify, and reinter thousands of casualties from both sides. Learning from the mistakes of that war, the United States created a national cemetery system, with Arlington at its heart, and slowly developed expertise in treating its war dead with exquisite care. That tradition continues, as the United States dispatches specialty teams around the world to recover its dead from active theaters of conflict, as well as those from earlier wars.

★ ★ ★

It was such an effort that finally brought the members of Breaker Patrol, 3rd Reconnaissance Battalion, 3rd Marine Division, to Arlington for a long-delayed homecoming on May 10, 2005—exactly thirty-eight years after they disappeared in Vietnam: They were Navy Petty Officer 3rd Class Malcolm T. Miller, Marine 2nd Lt. Heinz Ahlmeyer Jr., Marine Sgt. James N. Tycz, and Marine Lance Cpl. Samuel A. Sharp Jr. All had died in a fierce fight for the high ground near Khe Sanh on May 10, 1967. While their wounded comrades were evacuated by helicopter, it was too late for Miller, Ahlmeyer, Tycz, and Sharp—left behind but not forgotten. Years after the war ended, forensic teams returned to the battlefield in 2002 and 2003 and recovered thirty-one bone fragments, some teeth, and enough supporting evidence to make positive identifications of the four men. Corporal Sharp was the first to reach home, where he was buried in his native California a few days before the Arlington ceremony. He would be remembered at Arlington, where four caskets stood ready for burial in Section 60—one for Miller, one for Ahlmeyer, one for Tycz, and one for unidentifiable remains representing all of the dead from Breaker Patrol.

The fourth casket containing commingled bones was on its way down to Section 60 from the chapel at Fort Myer. You could gauge its progress by the rattle of drums drawing closer, setting the pace for a slow parade of two hundred mourners, a Marine rifle platoon in dress blues and white trousers, a Marine band in gold braid and scarlet, and, bringing up the rear, a squadron of Rolling Thunder—Vietnam veterans on Harleys. This mismatched procession streamed down the hills in brilliant sunlight, turned left on Marshall Drive, and came to a halt on Bradley Drive, where the earth was laid open to make four new graves.

Six burly marines from the burial detail drew the fourth casket from a silver hearse, marched it across the grass, and stopped by the last grave. While the drums rolled, the body bearers hoisted the last casket above their shoulders and held it up to the sky for a final tribute. They eased it onto a catafalque. When the Marine Band struck up the Navy Hymn, the casket team lifted away the flag, pulled the edges tight, and began to fold it with exquisite care. A Navy chaplain began to murmur the familiar words of comfort, but these were snatched away by the sounds of life intruding from all around the cemetery, in the drone of commuter traffic just outside the stone walls, in the whine of jets straining up from Reagan National Airport, in the thump of helicopters lumbering to and from the Pentagon. No matter how solemn the rituals at Arlington, life continued asserting itself from outside. And even in the cemetery, the living formed a link with all of the dead who had gone before—by speaking their names, by recounting their acts of duty and valor, by suspending the other imperatives of life for a few minutes of ritual and reflection. These acts convey a sort of immortality upon the dead, who continue to live as long as they are remembered.

Out among the tombstones, the long journey of Breaker Patrol was drawing to its conclusion. A firing party unleashed a three-rifle volley, a lone bugler stepped forward to sound Taps, and the honor guard began folding the last flag, pulling the fabric taut, creasing it, gathering it, and passing it down the line until it formed a tight blue triangle. With a sharp salute, the flag passed to a gunnery sergeant, who cradled it like a baby, marched it across the turf, and presented it to a chaplain. The chaplain, in turn, passed it to a retired Marine commandant acting as next of kin for all of those in Breaker Patrol.

Last of all, the motorcycle vets padded onto the grass and knelt, one by one, at each of the caskets to retire their MIA bracelets. Dressed in faded jeans and camouflage, the bikers looked incongruous among the spit-and-polish crowd that day, but when they stepped up to a grave, stood straight, and snapped off a salute, you could see that they had been soldiers too, and some of them were crying.

With minor modifications, Arlington's rituals would be familiar to Thucydides or to Homer, who places the climactic scene of his *Iliad* not in battle but during a lull in the fighting, as Hector's body is carried home by his father and prepared for a grand public burial.[2] The old pattern endures at Arlington, where friends, family, and comrades gather to give thanks for a warrior's sacrifice, to honor the military virtues, and all too often to make bearable the most unbearable loss of all, the death of a young combatant cut down in the prime of life. The age-old rituals ease the grief, if only for a moment, in a flourish of ceremony, with brass bands, a blaze of rifle salutes, and flags streaming their battle ribbons from the old wars in Mexico, Germany, Guadalcanal, Belleau Wood, and all the others that link today's warriors with those who marched into combat before them.

Every conflict the United States ever fought is remembered in ceremony and stone at Arlington, none more so than the Civil War, which gave the cemetery its most recognizable traditions. The three-rifle volley signaling the end of a cease-fire; the haunting tune we know as Taps, described as the most beautiful of all trumpet calls; the horse-drawn caissons for transporting dead soldiers from the front; the elaborate honors reserved for unknown soldiers—all of these originated in America's bloodiest conflict.[3]

The scars from that war remain etched deep in Arlington's topography, which also tells the story of the nation's recovery and healing, of a young country's growing realization of its power, of its willingness to exercise that power on the world stage through two world wars, the Korean conflict, the Cold War, Vietnam, and subsequent hostilities, each with its flashes of glory, its moments of doubt and agony, and its added burials for Arlington, which continues to grow; from an initial 200 acres established in 1864, the national cemetery covers 624 acres today.

Few images linger in the national imagination as vividly as this hallowed ground, with its ghostly white tombstones, its deep green turf, its gnarled trees alive with songbirds and cicadas. Almost four million people visit the place each year, to pay homage at President Kennedy's eternal flame on the hillside, to watch the silent, solemn changing of the guard, to walk among the scientists, explorers, jurists, writers, spies, actors, criminals, generals, admirals, and thousands of ordinary citizen-warriors resting at Arlington.

For many visitors, a pilgrimage to Arlington is a devotional act—to seek out a buried relative, to pay respects to a treasured friend, to leave a promised beer or cigarette at the tomb of an Army buddy, to brush off a wife's grave and bring her up to date on the latest headlines. Sisters come to Arlington with photographs of brothers now gone forever; girlfriends bring bouquets and balloons; someone hangs wind chimes in a dogwood, which ring with music when the limbs shiver. A marine's parents drive down from Pennsylvania, unpack their lawn chairs, set them up in Section 60, and pass a spring afternoon with their son, recently killed in Iraq. They speak to his tombstone as if it is the most natural thing in the world. It is at Arlington, where other pilgrims do the same thing every day.

Do the tombstones speak back? Of course they do. Each one tells a story. The marker on James Parks's grave, up in Section 15, speaks for a slave born at Arlington who found his freedom there, stayed on, and saw the world around him utterly transformed. In Section 3, a tombstone marks the resting place of Lt. Thomas Selfridge, a twenty-six-year-old Army pilot who fell to earth at nearby Fort Myer, where he helped inaugurate the age of aerial warfare. Just across the way in Section 8 lies Rear Adm. Robert E. Peary, the explorer who claimed the North Pole in 1909 but failed to credit his associate, Matthew Henson, the African American guide who got him there. Henson finally won recognition in 1988, when he was disinterred, conveyed to Arlington, and buried with high ceremony. Other tombstones speak for the Revolutionary War soldier who died at the hands of a mob while defending the First Amendment; of one-armed John Wesley Powell, explorer of the Colorado River; of one-legged Daniel Sickles, Civil War general, ambassador, congressman, scoundrel. Famous generals from Fort Myer—among them John J. Pershing, George C. Marshall, and Omar Bradley—walked among these tombstones in life, a sobering exercise even for non-generals, and returned to lie among them in death, surrounded by the men they sent into battle. Less prominent are the inhabitants of Arlington's Section 27, where a sea of weathered stones preserves the memory of slaves and freedmen named George Washington, Robert Lee, Bertsey Murray, Selina Brown, Moses Jackson, and thousands of others, segregated in death as they had been in life. Like all of the dead at Arlington, they have stories to tell if you will listen.

New chapters are added daily, as new tombstones appear, twenty-five or so per day, five days a week, all year long. They continue the narrative of war, loss, growth, and remembering, which began long before there was any honor attached to burial at Arlington. That was when a promising colonel named Robert E. Lee lived in its cream-colored mansion, surrounded by a contingent of slaves and 1,100 acres of choice plantation land. If not for him, there would have been no Arlington National Cemetery.

PART I

DISUNION

I

LEAVING ARLINGTON

Col. Robert E. Lee finished a fateful round of interviews and rode away from Washington, D.C., crossing the Long Bridge to Alexandria on April 18, 1861. It was a beautiful spring day, with the trees in young leaf and the Potomac River reflecting a benign sky, but there was no joy in Lee's journey home. He had just turned down a major Army promotion, and now, headed back across the river, he struggled with a momentous decision: should he remain in the Army, which he had served faithfully for thirty-two years, or should he resign his commission to avoid the coming war, which threatened to break apart the country he loved?

The conflict between North and South, brewing for months, would trap Lee between his loyalties to the Union and allegiance to his family, his neighbors, and his home in Virginia, where the Lees had shaped events since 1641. "All the Lees had been Americans," wrote Douglas Southall Freeman, Lee's biographer, "but they had been Virginians first."[1]

Lee brooded over these matters as he crossed the bridge that day, determined to stay with the Union if Virginia remained loyal, to leave if Virginia joined the growing list of southern states plunging toward rebellion. He hoped that some last-minute compromise would avert the conflict, but this was not to be: unbeknownst to Lee, a convention meeting in Richmond had voted to secede the day before and announced its decision at noon, as Lee made his rounds in Washington.[2]

The capital had already begun preparations for war. Workers on Pennsylvania Avenue piled sandbags on the piazza of the Treasury Building, where iron bars had been hastily plugged into the windows. Others sweated in the building's dim basement, stacking barrels of flour for an expected siege. Union troops guarded the White House, newly occupied by President Abraham Lincoln. Next door at the War Department, government clerks mustered in the courtyard for volunteer duty, fumbling with unfamiliar weapons and adding to the city's sense of doom. One lonely Navy sloop patrolled the Potomac River; from his office window President Lincoln could glimpse it bobbing like a clockwork toy in the distance. Women and children made plans to flee the city.[3]

This flurry of activity had been sparked when federal forces surrendered Fort Sumter to Confederates in South Carolina a few days before, prompting President Lincoln to call up 75,000 troops to defend the capital. Volunteers and regulars from Massachusetts, Pennsylvania, Minnesota, and Kansas answered his summons and began trickling into Washington as the spring season unfolded. They set up camp in the Capitol building, where they barricaded the doors with tubs of cement and slept on the floor of the old House chamber. Like the country itself, the building was a work in progress. The new House and Senate wings were not yet finished, and the Capitol's truncated dome described an iron skeleton on the skyline. New troops patrolled the city's thoroughfares and river crossings, set up artillery pieces, established their pickets, and scrutinized the Virginia hills for signs of trouble.[4]

Lee rode past them, crossed into Virginia, and turned up the road from Alexandria to Arlington, the 1,100-acre family estate dominating the rolling green landscape just beyond the river. The very sight of Arlington seemed to gladden Lee, who affectionately referred to the place as "our dear home" or "old Arlington" in correspondence.[5] It was there, he said, "where my attachments are more strongly placed than at any other place in the world."[6] It was easy to see why: Arlington floated in the hills like a Greek temple, sheltered by old oaks and sprawling elms. Looking as if it had been there forever, it peered down from its eminence upon the raw, half-finished capital at its feet.

Although Lee's father, Henry "Light Horse Harry" Lee, had been a commanding presence in the formative years of the United States—a friend and
comrade of George Washington, a hero of the Revolution, a governor of Virginia, a member of Congress, a champion of the Bill of Rights—he had left his
son and family with very little aside from his legend. The elder Lee spent im-
petuously in land speculation, drew little income, and was finally imprisoned
for debt. He fell into ill health. He abandoned the family for the West Indies,
where he lived for several years. He was returning to Virginia in 1818, still broken and poor at age sixty-two, when he died at Cumberland Island, Georgia.
His son Robert, who had been six when his father sailed away, was eleven
when word of his death reached home.

This straitened legacy, combined with Robert E. Lee's career as a professional soldier, had kept him functionally homeless for most of his adult life.
Living out of trunks, sleeping in tents, lodging in a succession of borrowed
houses, he finally found a home in Arlington—along with a web of domestic,
moral, and business entanglements—when his wife, Mary Custis Lee, inherited a life interest in the estate, along with 196 slaves and a portfolio of scattered Virginia properties, upon the death of her father in 1857.[7]

That father, George Washington Parke Custis, was the grandson of Martha
Washington and also the adopted son of George Washington. Custis had become the designated heir to the Arlington plantation from his biological father,
John Parke Custis, who had been an aide-de-camp to General Washington.
The elder Custis died in 1781, before his son was a year old, at which point
Washington took charge of the boy. After George and Martha Washington
died, Custis was left holding not only the land at Arlington but also some seventeen thousand acres that included two forested islands and two plantations
of some four thousand acres each; known as White House and Romancock,
both farms were located on the Pamunkey River in eastern Virginia.[8]

G. W. P. Custis, a dilettante who dabbled at painting, public oratory, experimental sheep farming, milling grain, ferry operations, real estate development,
and a hundred other business schemes that went nowhere, determined to build a
grand dwelling for himself on the Potomac River. He began construction on a
wing of the house in 1802, and in 1804 hired George Hadfield, an important
English architect originally commissioned to supervise the building of Washington's Capitol, to design his Arlington House. Construction resumed that year,
proceeding in fits and starts until the home was finally finished in 1818. Inspired

in part by the Temple of Hephaestus in Athens, the Custis mansion displayed the clean lines and balanced appearance of a neoclassic edifice, anchored by a prominent central hall, and offset with low wings spreading to the north and south. Perched on a hill with a view clear down to the river, the mansion was meant to be seen, a symbol of its owner's refinement and taste.

"It is visible for many miles," a British visitor wrote, "and in the distance has the appearance of a superior English country residence beyond any place I had seen in the states." But he added, "As I came close to it, I was woefully disappointed."[9] The mansion's thick Doric columns, which appeared to be marble when seen from a distance, turned out to be rough stucco, with dark veins painted in to fool the eye. And once you passed Arlington's majestic portico and crossed the threshold, the rooms inside were dark and cramped—and all out of proportion to the mansion's external promise.

Robert E. Lee felt the weight of family obligation when Mary Anna Custis Lee inherited the plantation, and he acquired the dubious honor of serving not only as Arlington's master but also as the chief executor of his late father-in-law's tangled will. The mansion and surrounding grounds at Arlington had fallen into decline during Custis's final years. The big house leaked, the slaves were restless, the fields were sodden and unproductive. Beginning in 1857, Lee took an extended leave from his Army duties and set about putting the place in order. Using as many of Arlington's sixty-three slaves as he could press into service, Lee drained and fertilized the fields, planted oats and corn, restored the fences, attacked encroaching brush, laid the foundations for a new barn, repaired the gristmill, roofed the mansion with new slates, and shored up its rafters.[10] He made the dank old house more family-friendly, installing its first water closet and wood-burning furnace.[11] Mrs. Lee's garden flourished with jasmine, honeysuckle, moss roses, and the colonel's favorite, the delicate Safrano rose, which Lee made a ritual of gathering before breakfast, leaving a rosebud for each of his daughters at the table.[12] Arlington began to feel like home.

It was a mixed blessing. "I am getting along as usual, trying to get a little work done and to mend up some things," he wrote his second son, William Henry "Rooney" Fitzhugh Lee, in 1858. "I succeed badly."[13] Never run for profit in Custis's lifetime, the Arlington plantation had been subsidized by his working farms at White House and Romancock in previous years. This triangular arrangement ended with Custis's death. His will left those subsidiary plantations to Lee's second and third sons, Rooney and Robert, with Arlington intended for George Washington Custis Lee, the eldest heir, upon the death of Mrs. Lee. With the division of the three properties, each thus had to become self-sufficient. To accomplish this, the slaves had to work harder—that, at least, was the view of Robert E. Lee, who felt that his late father-in-law had been too indulgent with workers, allowing them to coast through his declining years. Some slaves, bristling at Lee's more demanding style, tried to escape after he took charge.[14] On at least three occasions, he hired agents to chase them down and put them in jail until they could be returned to Arlington.[15] In one instance from 1859, the antislavery *New York Tribune* reported that Lee supervised the whipping of three escapees—including a woman stripped to the waist—and poured brine into their wounds.[16] The story was quickly picked up and disseminated in other papers—much to the distress of Lee, who coldly dismissed the charges. "The *New York Tribune* has attacked me for my treatment of your grandfather's slaves, but I shall not reply," he wrote to his son Custis at the time.[17] The story would resurface to haunt Lee many years later, after the Civil War. Lee seemed to dispute the account. "There is not a word of truth in it, or any grounds for its origins," Lee wrote a friend. "No servant, soldier, or citizen, that was ever employed by me can with truth charge me with bad treatment."[18] Yet the particulars in the slave's account were confirmed by multiple witnesses and by the public record. Who told the truth? It is impossible to know, but this much is documented: Lee sent agents to capture Arlington's runaway slaves on at least three occasions, he had them thrown in jail to await transport back to Arlington, and he had troublesome slaves banished to other plantations, where they would be out of his sight and farther from the temptations of freedom.[19] Such treatment, while not as salacious as the whipping scene, is no less repugnant, and it provides insight into Lee's dubious moral inheritance at Arlington.

On an intellectual level, Lee deplored the institution of slavery, which he believed to be "a moral & political evil in any Country."[20] At the same time, he supported the extension of slavery in the territories, and, like many of his contemporaries, he viewed blacks as inferior to whites. He believed that African Americans were ill prepared for citizenship. On a personal level, he felt duty-bound to protect the Custis family property—slaves included—until his father-in-law's estate could be settled and properly divided. Given the messy nature of Custis's business affairs and the conflicting requirements of his will, this would take years to unscramble. Custis had, for instance, flamboyantly left his four Lee granddaughters legacies of ten thousand dollars each, but with no funds to pay for them. His estate was ten thousand dollars in debt when Lee stepped in as executor. In one part of the will, Custis suggested that money for the legacies could come from selling land; a few paragraphs later, that the legacies be paid from operations on the Romancock and White House estates. To complicate matters, Custis directed that his slaves should be freed within five years of his death, after the debts of his estate had been cleared. Lee made a choice. Instead of selling land, he intended to keep the slaves in bondage until they could work off their late master's debt and pay the bequests for the Custis granddaughters.

"He has left me an unpleasant legacy," Lee told his eldest son, George Washington Custis Lee, in 1859.[21] The moral burden was onerous, as were the complications of farm and family life. After a few years on leave at Arlington, Lee longed for the simplicity of soldiering. "I am no farmer myself, & do not expect to be always here," he wrote a cousin.[22] He told another relative that he felt "very much in the way of everybody" at Arlington.[23] Having restored the old place to a respectable degree, whittled down Custis's debts, planned for his daughters' legacies, and placed Romancock and White House on a functioning basis, Lee declared provisional victory and decamped from Arlington in February 1860 to rejoin his cavalry unit in Texas. The slaves were not yet liberated, but it appeared to Lee that they soon would be.

Within a year, however, events pulled Lee back to Washington, where the Civil War was about to break upon the nation. Texas had seceded in February 1861, declaring itself an independent republic and ejecting Union forces—including Lee's cavalry regiment. Six other states from the Deep South had already joined the Confederate States of America. With his native Virginia still on the fence, Lee made a slow and sorrowful journey across the country, wrestling with the hard choices he would face at home.

"If Virginia stands by the old Union," he told a friend as he prepared to leave

Texas, "so will I. But if she secedes . . . then I will still follow my native state with my sword, and if need be with my life."[24] He expressed similar sentiments in a letter to his son Rooney: "Things look very alarming from this point of view," he wrote from Texas. "I prize the Union very highly & know of no personal sacrifice that I would not make to preserve it," he wrote—but then added a portentous caveat: "save that of honour."[25] At other times, he expressed the unrealistic notion that, in the event of war, he might quit the Army and sit out the storm at Arlington. "I shall resign and go to planting corn," he said.[26]

These conflicting impulses were still stirring in Lee when he arrived home from Texas on March 1, 1861, in time for dinner. "Found all well," he noted in his diary.[27] Within days he went to see his old commander and mentor, Lt. Gen. Winfield Scott, by then general in chief of the U.S. Army. The two soldiers, friends since serving together in the Mexican War, met privately in Scott's office for three hours. They must have frankly discussed secession fever, the prospects of war, and the possibility that Lee would take command of U.S. forces in the field. Scott had nothing but admiration for this fellow Virginian, whom he considered "the very best soldier I ever saw in the field."[28] Yet the details of their crucial meeting were never revealed: neither man spoke about what transpired between them that day.

By April 18, as Union troops prepared Washington's defenses and Virginia moved toward secession, Lee was summoned to meet with Scott again. That same day he was invited to see Francis P. Blair Sr., a close friend and advisor to President Lincoln. Lee met Lincoln's friend first, calling at the pale yellow townhouse since known as Blair House, just across Pennsylvania Avenue from the president's mansion. Lincoln had apparently authorized Blair to offer Lee command of the Union forces that day. If he accepted, Lee would be head of a powerful army staffed with colleagues he knew from West Point and the Mexican War. He would be promoted to major general. He would be at the pinnacle of his career, with the ample resources of the federal government at his command. If Lee was tempted by this momentous proposal, he did not show it, taking no more than a few seconds to absorb Blair's offer. Then he declined it.

"Mr. Blair," Lee said, "I look upon secession as anarchy. If I owned four millions of slaves in the South I would sacrifice them all to the Union; but how can I draw my sword upon Virginia, my native state?"[29] Years later Lee recalled that he had turned down the command "as candidly and as courteously as I could" before leaving Blair House, crossing Pennsylvania Avenue, and climbing the worn stairs to the War Department to keep his appointment with General Scott.[30]

Seen together, the elderly, rotund general and the elegant, middle-aged colonel made for an odd couple indeed. Sitting behind a desk in Washington had swollen the commanding officer's six-foot-five-inch frame to operatic proportions, aggravating the gout that occasionally confined him to a wheelchair. Scabrous and cloudy-eyed, he was nearing the end of his career just as his understudy, at age fifty-four, was reaching his peak. Not yet the familiar graybeard of the war years, the Robert E. Lee of 1861 might have been an advertising poster for military recruiters. He was, said one eager young lieutenant, "the handsomest man in the army."[31] Powerfully built, Lee carried himself with the easy dignity and soldierly bearing that had earned him perfect marks for deportment as a West Point cadet. Even three decades later, Lee stood with his back as straight as a door, his hair and moustache thick and dark, his chin clean-shaven. The picture of ruddy good health, Lee seemed taller than his five-foot-eleven-inch height. His eyes, a depthless brown that appeared black in some lights, shone with calm intelligence, and a touch of sadness.

Lee briefed his old friend on Blair's offer, and on his response to it, which prompted an explosion from General Scott. "Lee, you have made the greatest mistake of your life," he growled, then softened his outburst with a postscript: "But I feared it would be so."[32] Accounts of their subsequent conversation vary, but it seems likely that Scott offered Lee some fatherly advice that day: if the younger man was ambivalent about remaining in the Army, he should resign right away. Otherwise, he might find himself compromised by fast-breaking developments. If he was ordered into action against Virginia, Lee would have to resign under orders—anathema for any professional soldier. Without resolving the issue, Lee and Scott said goodbye for the last time.

Still undecided and troubled, Lee made his final call in Washington that day, stopping to see his brother Sydney Smith Lee, who found himself in a similar quandary. Like his brother, Smith Lee was a federal officer, and he was resolved to resign his Navy commission rather than attack Virginia. Talking things over, the brothers decided that neither would act until they knew the outcome of the Virginia secession debate in Richmond. Even if the convention opted for disunion, voters still had to ratify the decision in a statewide referendum. That bought some time. With that glimmer of hope before them, thin though it was, the brothers agreed to stay in federal service until they discussed the matter again. At that, Robert E. Lee crossed the river to Arlington, where he would await news from Richmond.[33]

It came swiftly. Running errands in Alexandria the next day, April 19, Lee learned that the Virginia convention had voted overwhelmingly to secede, which prompted a flood of excitement in the old port city. One enthusiast had already hoisted the Confederate Stars and Bars over the Marshall House Tavern, and when Lee visited a pharmacy to settle a bill that day, he encountered a citizen celebrating the prospect of secession. This prompted a gentle rebuke from Lee. "I must say that I am one of those dull creatures that cannot see the good of secession," he said. As soon as Lee left the store, the pharmacist recorded his remark in a ledger.[34]

The lights blazed on the hill at Arlington that Friday, when the family convened to face the crisis together. Lee paced the garden alone. He resumed pacing among the shadows on Arlington's broad portico with its grand view of Washington just across the way, where the capital's lights shimmered in the dark. As the night lengthened, he continued his deliberations upstairs, pacing alone in his narrow bedroom. The floorboards creaked as Lee walked to the north, to the south, and back again, retracing his steps and telegraphing his anguish to family members listening below. At one point Mary Lee, sitting in the downstairs parlor, heard the creaking stop. Then Lee resumed pacing.

"Nothing here is talked or thought of except our troubles," one of Lee's daughters wrote to another. "Our poor country & our Fathers & brothers need all our prayers."[35] Tension permeated the house on the hill. George Upshur, a four-year-old relative visiting that night, burst into tears as the anxiety built around him. "Cousin Mary Lee and other ladies of her family were greatly excited," he recalled. "I recollect that I began to cry and was put in the large room on the left . . . Peering out of the window, I could see Cousin Robert pacing up and down among the trees, and wondered why he was out there."[36] Another witness who remembered that night was James Parks, an Arlington slave born on the estate, who recalled how Lee seemed to age before his eyes. "He looked

fine—keen as a briar—tall and straight," said Parks. "He walked backward and
forward on the porch studying. He looked downhearted. He didn't care to go.
No . . . he didn't care to go."[37]

But he did go, of course. Perhaps his conversation with General Scott, followed by the avid secessionists he had met in Alexandria, convinced Lee that
there was no point in waiting for the Virginians to ratify secession, which
seemed inevitable. After midnight Lee stopped pacing, sat at his desk, and
wrote out two letters. When they were done, he scraped back his chair, made
his way down the narrow stairs at Arlington, and found his wife waiting.

"Well, Mary," he announced, handing the papers to her, "the question is settled. Here is my letter of resignation and a letter I have written General Scott."[38]

The first letter, dated April 20, 1861, and addressed to Simon Cameron, the
U.S. secretary of war, was written in Lee's clear, firm hand. It was brief and to
the point: "Sir," it said. "I have the honour to tender the resignation of my commission as Colonel of the 1st Regt. of Cavalry. Very resply your obt servt, R. E.
Lee, Col. 1st Cavalry."[39]

The second letter, to General Scott, shed more light on Lee's thinking. Referring to their April 18 interview, Lee hinted that he had taken Scott's advice
to heart and felt "that I ought not longer to retain my commission in the Army,"
he wrote. "I therefore tender my resignation, which I request you will recommend for acceptance."

> It would have been presented at once, but for the struggle it has cost me to
> separate myself from a service to which I have devoted all the best years of my life
> & all the ability I possessed.
>
> During the whole of that time, more than 30 years, I have experienced
> nothing but kindness from my superiors, & the most cordial friendship from my
> companions. To no one Genl have I been as much indebted as to yourself for
> uniform kindness & consideration, & it has always been my ardent desire to
> merit your approbation.
>
> I shall carry with me to the grave the most grateful recollections of your kind
> consideration, & your name & fame will always be dear to me. Save in the
> defence of my native State, I never desire again to draw my sword.
>
> Be pleased to accept my most earnest wishes for the continuance of your
> happiness & prosperity & believe me most truly yours
>
> R. E. LEE[40]

After dealing with these professional obligations, it is likely that Lee got some sleep before sitting down to write more letters that day. The second round of correspondence went to key members of his family. Lee felt the need to explain to his brother Smith why he had resigned without further consultation. "The question which was the subject of my earnest consultation with you on the 18th instant has in my own mind been decided," Lee announced in his April 20 note.

> *After the most anxious inquiry as to the correct course for me to pursue, I concluded to resign, and sent in my resignation this morning. I wished to wait till the Ordinance of Secession should be acted upon by the people of Virginia; but war seems to have commenced, and I am liable at any time to be ordered on duty which I could not conscientiously perform. To save me from such a position, and to prevent the necessity of resigning under orders, I had to act at once, and before I could see you again on the subject, as I had wished. I am now a private citizen, and have no other ambition than to remain at home. Save in defense of my native State, I have no desire ever again to draw my sword. I send you my warmest love.*[41]

Lee's brother would shortly follow his example by resigning from the Navy. Their sister, Anne Lee Marshall, was in a more delicate position. Living in Baltimore, she was married to an ardent Union sympathizer, and she was the mother of a U.S. Army captain who would soon be drawn into the war. Robert E. Lee wrote to ask for her understanding, if not her forgiveness, as their own family was forced to choose sides in a conflict that would estrange them, just as it would scar and sometimes break thousands of other families on opposing sides.

"The whole South is in a state of revolution, into which Virginia, after a long struggle, has been drawn," he wrote Anne Marshall that day. He told his sister that he had no choice but to quit the Army.

> *With all my devotion to the Union, and the feeling of loyalty and duty of an American citizen, I have not been able to make up my mind to raise my hand against my relatives, my children, my home. I have, therefore, resigned my commission in the Army, and save in the defense of my native State (with the sincere hope that my poor services may never be needed) I hope I may never be called upon to draw my sword.*

I know you will blame me, but you must think as kindly as you can, and
believe that I have endeavored to do what I thought right. To show you the
feeling and struggle it has cost me I send you a copy of my letter of resignation. I
have no time for more. May God guard and protect you and yours and shower
upon you everlasting blessings, is the prayer of

Your devoted brother,
R. E. Lee[42]

Once Lee made a decision, he was never one to dwell upon what might have been. But his break from the familiar rhythms of Army life, and his foreboding over the troubles that war would rain down upon his family, strained even Lee's legendary composure. A service comrade noticed this about the time of Lee's resignation.

"Are you not feeling well, Colonel Lee?" asked the friend.

"Well in body but not in mind," Lee answered. "In the prime of life I quit a service in which were all my hopes and expectations in this world."[43] For the first time in his adult life, Robert E. Lee was out of a job. He must have worried, if only briefly, that he was destined to follow his father's path from early promise into late disgrace. But unlike the elder Lee, the younger one had prospects. Long before Virginia's secession convention, Lee had received an offer from the Confederate secretary of war, L. P. Walker, who had written in mid-March offering him command as a brigadier general, the highest rank then available in Confederate service. There is no record that Lee ever answered Walker.[44] But even then Lee must have known that he was destined to join the conflict if war broke out; this, despite his often-stated desire to put down his sword and take up his plow, a self-conscious refrain running through his prewar correspondence. The truth is that, with both Union and Confederacy competing for his services, Lee was ensured a command on one side or the other. And so his life as a citizen-farmer was destined to be a brief one, lasting all of two days.

With little fanfare, Lee emerged from Arlington on Monday, April 22, and climbed into his carriage.[45] Dressed in a black suit and a black silk hat, he disappeared down the long gravel driveway, past the greening fields where slaves bent to their work, and down past the brown Potomac with its silver countercurrent of shad pushing upstream to spawn, right on schedule. Lee made his way downstream toward the Alexandria train station, which bustled with passengers and buzzed with war talk. He pressed through the crowd and boarded the car for Richmond, where he had been summoned for an interview with Gov. John Letcher. There on April 23, 1861, Lee accepted command of Virginia's military and naval forces, with the rank of major general.[46]

From that moment Arlington was lost.

2

OCCUPATION

When Lee rode away from Arlington in April 1861, he left behind not only a choice piece of real estate but also one essential to Washington's defenses. It did not take a military genius to appreciate the strategic importance of the old plantation, where the heights climbed more than two hundred feet above the surrounding countryside. Any artillerist occupying that position could easily harass troopships plying the Potomac River, blow up the capital's bridge crossings, and lob shells at the most tempting target of all—the White House, its roof peeking from the green fringe of trees just across the river.

There was no way that war planners in Washington were going to cede the high ground of Arlington to enemy forces, and within days of her husband's departure, Mary Custis Lee received notice of the Federals' intent. A young Union officer friendly to the family came rushing into the Arlington mansion in early May, urging Mrs. Lee to prepare for her evacuation. "You must pack up all you value immediately and send it off in the morning," Lt. Orton Williams told her. Since he was one of Mrs. Lee's many cousins and worked as secretary to Lt. Gen. Winfield Scott, she took the warning seriously.[1]

That night she and her daughters supervised some frantic packing by slaves, who put the family silver in boxes for transfer to Richmond, crated the papers of George Washington and G. W. P. Custis, and arranged Lee's files in a separate box. Mrs. Lee gathered up some Washington memorabilia for shipping, stowing the larger pieces—his campaign tent, a punch bowl, and crates of Washington's Cincinnati china—in the mansion's basement.[2]

After the night of organizing her escape, Mary Lee tried to get some sleep, only to be awakened just after dawn by Orton Williams, who returned with word that the Union advance upon Arlington had been delayed.[3] Although he stressed that occupation was inevitable—merely postponed—Mrs. Lee took the respite as an excuse for lingering several more days at the home she had known since childhood.[4] She wrote newsy letters to her daughters, gossiped with visiting friends, and lamented the pushiness of South Carolina and other states so eager for war.[5] She savored the time remaining at Arlington and sat for hours in her favorite roost, a garden arbor to the south of the mansion, where spring flowers were making a luxuriant start on the season. Their promise of renewal seemed mockingly out of place as the country hurried toward conflict.

"I never saw the country more beautiful, perfectly radiant," she wrote to Lee. "The yellow jasmine in full bloom and perfuming the air; but a death like stillness prevails everywhere. You hear no sounds from Washington, not a soul moving about."[6]

In that lull before the clash, General Lee sat stranded at a desk in Richmond, feverishly mobilizing Virginia's forces, organizing his blankets and camping kit for what he expected to be a long season afield, and worrying about his wife's safety. Effectively immobilized by arthritis, she had grown feeble in recent years, which only heightened her husband's concern. He tried to prod her into leaving.

"I am very anxious about you," he wrote on April 26. "You have to move, & make arrangements to go to some point of safety . . . War is inevitable & there is no telling when it will burst around you."[7]

A few days later he wrote again: "When the war commences no place will be exempt . . . You had better prepare all things for removal, that is the plate, pictures, &c. & be prepared at any moment. Where to go is the difficulty."[8]

The newspapers added credence to Lee's fears. On May 10, the *New York Daily Tribune* reported that a volunteer regiment of New York Zouaves would soon "encamp on Arlington Heights" under the command of Col. Elmer E. Ellsworth. "His men are at once to erect tents and prepare for out-door life," said the *Tribune*. "At this prospect they are delighted."⁹ A few days later, the same paper revealed that General Scott was planning to place "a powerful park of artillery" on the hills of Arlington.¹⁰

Lee nudged his wife once more. "You had better complete your arrangements & retire further from the scene of war," he wrote. "It may burst upon you at any time. It is sad to think of the devastation, if not the ruin it may bring upon a spot so endeared to us. But God's will be done. We must be resigned."¹¹

By this time Lee almost certainly knew that Arlington would be lost—at least in the war's early stages. He had made no provision to hold the heights there, choosing instead to concentrate his limited troops on a line some twenty miles to the south of Washington, near an important railroad junction at Manassas, Virginia. With that in mind, he boosted the state's militia from 18,400 troops to 40,000 in a matter of weeks, shored up Virginia's coastal defenses, and scoured the country for field artillery pieces.¹² He consulted with an obscure colonel named Thomas J. Jackson—not yet Gen. Stonewall Jackson—about raising forces in the Shenandoah Valley.¹³ He coordinated the defense of Harper's Ferry with Gen. Joseph E. Johnston, a prickly but esteemed colleague who had recently resigned as quartermaster general of the Union Army. Amid these developments, Lee heard the distant rumble of northern newspapers, which were training their big guns on him—labeling him an ingrate and a traitor "in the footsteps of Benedict Arnold!"¹⁴

Reality was taking hold. With the capital braced for an attack, President Lincoln called for another 43,000 troops in May.¹⁵ The rhetoric grew warmer with the weather. Former Army comrades who had admired Lee now turned against him. None was more outspoken than Montgomery C. Meigs, a fellow West Point graduate who had served amicably under Lee in the engineer corps but who now considered him a traitor who deserved hanging. "No man who ever took the oath to support the Constitution as an officer of our Army or Navy . . . should escape without the loss of all his goods & civil rights & expatriation," Meigs wrote that spring. Singling out Lee, Joseph Johnston, and Confederate president Jefferson Davis, Meigs urged that they "should be put formally out of the way if possible by sentence of death & executed if caught."¹⁶

Meigs and Lee never met on the battlefield, but Meigs proved to be one of Lee's most implacable foes in the months and years ahead. He stepped into the quartermaster's post on May 15, after the incumbent, General Johnston, went south with Lee. Meigs, a demon for hard work and efficiency, quickly began to mobilize for a conflict he viewed as a life-and-death struggle for the nation's soul. Born in Georgia but raised in Philadelphia, Meigs had a strong sense of duty, a flair for the dramatic, and a well-earned reputation for honesty in an arm of the service plagued by corruption and mismanagement. Tall and straight-backed, he projected an intimidating, no-nonsense image, a man with a firmly set jaw, hooded eyes, and the bulging forehead his contemporaries took as a sure sign of braininess. His fearsome appearance sometimes frightened his own wife. "He looks so dreadfully stern when he talks of the rebellion that I do not like to look at him," Louisa Meigs confided to a relative.[17] His own mother conceded that, when young, Meigs had been "high tempered, unyielding, tyrannical . . . and very persevering in pursuit of anything he wants."[18] Those traits would serve him well in his new job.

Toward the end of May, even Mary Custis Lee had to concede that the gathering storm could not be avoided. She supervised servants while they took down the curtains, rolled up the carpets, and packed up the wine cellar. She bequeathed care of the family cat, a big yellow male named Tom Tita, to George Clarke, a slave who appreciated Tom's mousing skills. Her motivation in leaving Arlington, she told a daughter, was to spare her husband further apprehension. "I would have greatly preferred remaining at home & having my children around me," she wrote, "but as it would greatly increase your Father's anxiety I shall go."[19] Then she made an eerily accurate prediction: "I fear that this will be the scene of conflict & my beautiful home endeared by a thousand associations may become a field of carnage."[20]

She took a final turn in the garden, entrusted the keys to Selina Gray, a much-respected slave who served as Arlington's housekeeper, and followed her husband's course down the long, winding driveway. Like others on both sides of the conflict, Mrs. Lee believed that the storm would pass quickly and that she could return to Arlington in a few weeks. In reality, it would take twelve years.[21]

One month to the day after Lee took command in Richmond, the voters of Virginia were presented with a referendum for secession. To nobody's surprise, they ratified the ordinance by an overwhelming margin—more than five to one.[22]

Within hours of that mandate, on May 23, 1861, columns of Union forces streamed through Washington and made for the Potomac River. They gathered at major bridge crossings and boat landings as night descended. Then at precisely two A.M. on May 24, some 14,000 troops began crossing the river into Virginia.[23] They advanced in steamers, on foot, and on horseback, and in swarms so thick that the slave James Parks, watching from Arlington, thought they looked "like bees a-coming."[24]

Col. Daniel Butterfield of New York, who would soon father a bugle tune known as Taps, rode at the head of his 12th New York Infantry Regiment, the first column across the Long Bridge.[25] The moon lit their way, rippling the Potomac in opalescent streaks, flashing on new bayonets, shining on the silently marching boys from Michigan and New Jersey who followed the New Yorkers across. Col. Elmer E. Ellsworth, commanding the 1st New York Zouaves, piled onto a steamboat with his men and sailed toward Alexandria. This dandified regiment of firemen-soldiers was hard to miss, decked out in their red pantaloons, tasseled caps, and white spats and brewing for a brawl. Up on the heights of Arlington, Lee's mansion brooded over this opening movement of the war, cast in cold silver light.[26]

It took most of the night for the soldiers to complete their crossing, whereupon they spread along the roads, established cavalry pickets at the bridges, secured major railroad junctions, and began digging entrenchments.[27] A Union wave spilled into Alexandria to establish control over the port. Arlington changed hands without a whimper. The Union soldiers who took the heights had instructions from General Scott to leave the Lee family alone if any were still in residence. None was. Maj. Gen. Charles W. Sandford, commanding the combined New York militia, found the heights undefended and the family vanished. A score of slaves remained, having nowhere else to go and bewildered about their sudden change of status, which placed them somewhere between their promised freedom and their residual duty to old masters. To guarantee the mansion's security, Sandford moved into Arlington House and established his headquarters there.[28]

Despite the best efforts of General Sandford, nobody could shield Arlington from the vicissitudes of war, which began to transform the plantation from its first day of occupation. Thousands of men in blue were already settling into the rhythms of camp life when the sun rose over Arlington on May 24. Just behind the big house, a tidy village of tents sprouted; soldiers stoked breakfast fires; messengers scuttled across the portico of the mansion with papers from the War

Office. Junior officers lounged on the mansion's front steps, smoking, gossiping, and drinking in the incomparable sight of a springtime capital in full bloom.[29]

By early June, the Confederate capital was relocated to Richmond from Montgomery, Alabama, when Virginia formally joined the Confederacy. This required Lee to transfer his command to the new government. He became a brigadier general and chief military advisor to Jefferson Davis, the Confederate president.[30]

Meanwhile, the Arlington plantation was being made over into a citadel, with new roads carved into the hillsides and breastworks burrowed into the heights. The air thumped to the sound of axes as some of Arlington's massive oaks were tumbled, clearing a field of fire for artillery.[31] "All that the best military skill could suggest to strengthen the position has been done," a newspaper reported after several days of Union occupation, "and the whole line of defenses on Arlington Heights may be said to be completed and capable of being held against any attacking force."[32]

The attack never materialized, unless one counts the fusillade of reproach that Mary Custis Lee poured down upon those now occupying her property.[33]

"It never occurred to me," she scolded General Sandford, "that such an outrage as its military occupation to the exclusion of me & my children could ever have been perpetrated by any one . . . I am left homeless & not even able to get or send to Alexa. [Alexandria] where my funds are deposited to obtain means for my support . . . The whole country is filled with men, women, & children flying in terror."[34]

Unlike her stoic husband, who favored understatement over hyperbole, Mrs. Lee had inherited her father's flair for the dramatic, which grew more pronounced under stress. Her pen flew across the pages of her letters, the words slanting harder as she warmed to her outrage. She underscored key points with a slash of the pen.

There was plenty for her to lament in that first springtime of war. With her husband away, her children scattered, and her health eroding, Mary Custis Lee lived a rootless life, moving from one relative's house to another, trying to stay ahead of the conflict. She was cut off from the home where she had been raised, where her marriage had taken place, where she had borne six of her seven children, and where her parents were buried. Robert E. Lee was greatly attached to Arlington, to be sure, but for Mary Custis Lee the riverside farm was a part of her essence.

Lee tried to understand. "I sympathize deeply in your feelings at leaving your dear home," he wrote Mary on the first day of Arlington's occupation. "I have experienced them myself & they are constantly revived. I fear we have not been grateful enough for the happiness there within our reach & our heavenly father has found it necessary to deprive us of what He had given us. I acknowledge my ingratitude, my transgressions & my unworthiness & submit with resignation to what He thinks proper to inflict upon me."[35]

Lee continued to preach in subsequent letters.

"No one can say what is the future," he wrote a few days later, "nor is it wise to anticipate evil . . . There is no saying when you can return to your home or what may be its condition when you do return . . . [36] I am sorry to learn that you are so anxious & uneasy about passing events . . . Our private distresses we must bear with resignation like Christians & not aggravate them by repining."[37]

But Mary Lee continued to repine. Nobody could stop her.[38] She would not accept the loss of Arlington. Meanwhile, life had to go on. By mail, Mrs. Lee tried to keep Arlington's cycle of planting and harvesting going forward through a farm manager who still lived on the estate. She continued to agonize about the George Washington artifacts locked away at Arlington. And she felt responsible for the bondsmen who remained there. She acted as if she was still in charge, writing to Union officers to arrange for slaves to continue living on the plantation, where they grew food and flowers for the market, buried their friends, and lived among an extended family network. Some maintained ties across the river in Washington, which required military passes for those who rowed over for conjugal visits. Toward the end of May, Mary Lee appealed to General Sandford to continue these arrangements. "You have a beautiful home & people that you love & can sympathise perhaps even with the wife of a 'traitor & a rebel,'" she wrote.

> I implore you by the courtesy due any woman & which no brave soldier could deny to allow my old coachman by whom I send this letter to get his clothes, to give some letters to my manager relative to the farm & c, to give my market man a pass that will enable him to go and return from Washington as usual, where his

family reside. My gardener Ephraim also has a wife in Washington and is
accustomed to go over there every Saturday & return on Monday. My old cook
has also a wife in the neighborhood, to allow the servants to go on with their
usual occupations unmolested by the soldiers & protected by your authority, also
to allow my boy Billy whom I only left at home to complete some work in the
garden to come to me with his clothes as I cannot use my carriage without his aid
& to permit my maid Marcellina to send me some small articles that I did not
bring away.[39]

By the time this letter passed through military lines and arrived at Arlington, its intended recipient had been replaced by Brig. Gen. Irvin McDowell, an Ohio native, a West Pointer, and one of Lee's many friends still serving the Union. McDowell, whose sense of propriety matched Lee's, went to extraordinary lengths to accommodate his new enemy. He acceded to Mrs. Lee's requests about the slaves, offered her safe passage to Arlington if she wanted it, posted guards to protect her overseer's house, and pledged that her home would remain "as little disturbed as possible."[40] In a further gesture of respect, McDowell had his tent pitched on the lawn at Arlington, where he preferred to sleep rather than intrude upon the hospitality of absent owners. His office consisted of an unvarnished table and a plain chair set under the trees, a Spartan arrangement that impressed more than one war correspondent.[41] "He declined occupying his friend's house," the Washington *National Republican* reported with approval, "and gave strict orders that the most severe penalties should be inflicted upon any person, officer, or private found guilty of . . . defacing the grounds."[42]

Selina Gray, the formidable Lee slave who held the keys to the mansion, reinforced McDowell's orders. She patrolled the property brandishing a ring of keys like a weapon, warning soldiers to keep their hands off the family's possessions.[43] But neither she nor General McDowell could effectively monitor the thousands of men encamped at Arlington that spring. With no battles yet to fight and time on their hands, they found other diversions—they shot the farm overseer's pet chickens and rabbits, threatened slaves, and broke into the mansion's locked rooms for a look around.[44] John Chapman, Company K, 25th Pennsylvania, penciled his name on a beam in the attic, where his scrawl remains visible to this day. Another warrior slouched in a bedroom with his feet on the furniture, a scene immortalized in a sketch, "The Civil War—Roughing

It at Arlington."[45] Other marauders rifled through boxes for war souvenirs, making off with some of the irreplaceable George Washington relics, including pieces of Mount Vernon china. Upon discovering these treasures were missing, Selina Gray promptly reported the losses to McDowell, who collected the remaining artifacts and sent them to the Patent Office in Washington for safekeeping, where they remained for the rest of the war.[46]

Such gentlemanly behavior was not unusual at this stage of the Civil War, which remained civilized in its opening months. Until the real bloodshed began, new soldiers acted as if they were on holiday, enjoying the camaraderie of life in camp and the thrill of artillery practice, which rattled the mansion's windows and echoed down the river. A few jittery Union men took potshots at an experimental observation balloon as it loomed threateningly above Arlington, much to the dismay of Professor Thaddeus Sobieski Coulincourt Lowe, who was flying on behalf of the Union.[47] Despite such moments of excitement, the early months of the Civil War were calm ones, with room for brother officers to treat one another with exaggerated courtesy, even across enemy lines. This was about to change.

The heat of summer built in Washington, producing the menacing black clouds and rumbling storms characteristic of the season. Horace Greeley, the prominent editor of the New York Tribune, added to the atmospheric disturbances with calls for a Union attack on the Confederate capital, where the insurgent Congress was convening in July. "Forward to Richmond!" his newspaper thundered. "Forward to Richmond!" boomed other papers and politicians, taking up the call for a quick end to the rebellion. "Forward to Richmond!" cried the soldiers in blue who shouldered their muskets and tramped down the drive from Arlington, General McDowell leading the way. With flags rippling and brass bands glinting in the sun, they headed south for Manassas, gateway to the Confederate capital.[48]

James Parks watched them go. Before the month ended, he heard the shudder of big guns announcing the first major engagement of the Civil War on July 21, 1861. That is when some 32,000 Federals under McDowell ran headlong into 32,000 Confederates under Gen. Pierre G. T. Beauregard just outside the village of Manassas. McDowell's troops got the upper hand that morning.

"We drove them for several hours," McDowell reported, "and finally routed them" across a creek known as Bull Run. But the battle turned later that day, when Generals Joseph Johnston and Thomas J. Jackson pounded into the fray with 10,000 reinforcements. Jackson, holding one end of the Confederate line, earned his nickname, "Stonewall," that Sunday. The Rebel counterattack shattered Union resolve. In the confusion of the afternoon fight, inexperienced Federals fired into their own lines, miscarried orders, and finally fell apart. The bluecoats raced for home, leaving a trail of haversacks, cartridge cases, and dashed expectations in their wake, and there was nothing General McDowell could do to stop them.

"The larger part of the men are a confused mob, entirely demoralized," he reported from Fairfax Courthouse that afternoon. "Many of the volunteers did not wait for authority to proceed to the Potomac, but left on their own decision," he wrote the next day, as the extent of the rout became depressingly evident.[49] Although the casualties from Manassas were shocking for the time—with 418 Union killed, 1,011 wounded, 1,216 missing; 312 Confederates dead, 1,582 wounded, 12 missing—they were infinitesimal compared to the slaughter to come.[50]

Back at Arlington, Selina Gray had heard the thud of artillery tolling the hours of July 21 and wondered who was winning. Like others in the capital, she worried that the fighting might surge north and roll over her in a mighty wave. She remained awake all night, listening for the rumble of guns and watching for telltale flashes of light on the horizon. She was dressed to flee at a moment's notice, grateful that there was a full moon to illuminate her exodus, if it came to that.[51]

The morning brought not the sight of Rebel regiments overrunning the capital but the sorry spectacle of the Union's humiliation. In the drizzle of that Monday, a panic-stricken Gen. Ambrose E. Burnside galloped up to Willard's Hotel in Washington, handed his horse to a groom, and went inside. Someone noticed that the general had lost his hat.[52]

Embarrassed and exhausted soldiers straggled alone or in ragged groups back to their camp at Arlington. Covered in soot and soaked from the rain, these scarecrows flopped down on the wet grass and promptly fell asleep, just as their comrades were doing on the sidewalks and lawns of Washington that day, the next, and the next.[53]

General McDowell passed among his bewildered men, and returned to his tent on the Arlington hillside. There he began the dreary business of writing the reports of his inglorious campaign. Over the scratching of his pen, he might have heard the unmistakable sizzle of a career about to go up in flames—his own. The same politicians and editors who had clamored for a quick strike at Virginia now blamed McDowell for the debacle; this, despite the Ohioan's insistence beforehand that his raw recruits were unprepared for such an offensive. Now he was labeled incompetent, and it was whispered that he had been drunk throughout the melee at Bull Run.[54] "It was one of the best planned battles of the Civil War," Gen. William T. Sherman concluded later, "but one of the worst fought."[55]

McDowell was made subservient to Gen. George B. McClellan, the bantam Napoleon who replaced him as commander of Union forces in Virginia—and who would soon absorb Winfield Scott's duties as general in chief as well. Although McDowell was no longer in charge of Union operations in Virginia, he kept his tent at Arlington and continued working there. His influence was waning as 1861 drew to a close. With McDowell and Scott in eclipse, the old plantation was losing two friends who had tried to make the terrible business of war a bit less brutal.

In his own way, so did George McClellan. He insisted on protecting Confederate property, much to the consternation of Army colleagues including Gen. Montgomery Meigs, Gen. William T. Sherman, and other realists who favored total war. McClellan and others wanted to avoid offending loyalists in the South, an attitude that also made him reluctant to take a stance against slavery. In his view, the war was being fought not to emancipate slaves but to preserve the Union, which was also then President Lincoln's view.

When McClellan took command of Union forces at Arlington, he seldom worked there, preferring to keep house across the river in Washington. He lobbied the War Department for more troops and supplies, restyled his command as the Army of the Potomac, and ringed Washington with a new system of forty-eight forts, batteries, and earthen redoubts.[56] He drilled his troops to perfection, preened at the head of numerous parades, gave frequent champagne-and-oyster luncheons for influential friends, and made elaborate preparations for an offensive that was much discussed but painfully slow to start.[65] Over the misgivings of President Lincoln and the War Department, McClellan proposed to strike Richmond from the side instead of the front. Rather than approaching through Manassas, he would sweep down the Chesapeake Bay and westward up the riverine approaches to the Confederate capital. This crab-wise advance, took the war away from the capital's doorstep, coincidentally relieving pressure on Arlington.

Nonetheless, the grounds around the mansion were soon flattened by the passage of a thousand boots, and more of the magnificent oak forest disappeared with the first chill of autumn 1861, as soldiers from Indiana and Wisconsin waded into the woods, brandished their axes, and built winter quarters on the heights, where a raw collection of log stables, cooking houses, and cabins outfitted with mud chimneys appeared on the skyline. These western soldiers of the Iron Brigade, whose ranks included farmers from Scandinavia, Germany, and Ireland, were unimpressed by the anemic eastern landscape, which one of them described as "cussed poor country . . . I would not live here if i [sic] had the best farm in the country."[57]

While Union troops settled in at Arlington that winter, Confederate president Jefferson Davis dispatched Lee to shore up the coastal defenses of South Carolina, Georgia, and northern Florida. From his outpost in South Carolina, Lee informed his daughter Mildred that he had grown a white beard. "It is much admired," he reported in a Christmas letter in 1861. "At least much remarked on."[58] He folded some violets into a letter to his daughter Annie and regretted that he could not deliver them in person. Lee's thoughts turned toward happier times, and he meditated upon the fate of Arlington.

"Your old home, if not destroyed by our enemies, has been so desecrated that I cannot bear to think of it," he wrote a daughter.[59] Once more he counseled Mary Lee to accept the loss of Arlington. "Our old home, if not destroyed, will be difficult ever to be recognized," he wrote from Coosawhatchie, South Carolina, on Christmas day.

> Even if the enemy had wished to preserve it, it would almost have been impossible. With the number of troops encamped around it, the change of officers, &c., the want of fuel, shelter, &c., & all the dire necessities of war, it is vain to think of its being in a habitable condition. I fear too books, furniture, & the relics of Mount Vernon will be gone. It is better to make up our minds to a general loss. They cannot take away the remembrances of the spot, & the memories of those that

to us rendered it sacred. That will remain to us as long as life will last, & that we can preserve.[60]

Twice in this period of his exile, Lee broached the idea of buying Stratford Hall, his birthplace and boyhood home on Virginia's Northern Neck, to replace the loss of Arlington. But he soon dropped that idea, and after this flurry of holiday letters, Lee rarely mentioned either home for the remainder of the war. He was resigned, perhaps, to the new reality. Certainly he had greater troubles to occupy him as 1862 commenced and the nation got down to the real business of fighting.

Gen. George McClellan amassed troops for his Peninsula Campaign against Richmond, while Union forces began to menace the coastal defenses around Charleston and Savannah. Lee scurried in to defend the coast, recruiting local volunteers, and building up fortifications at strategic points along the shore. "Our works are not yet finished," he reported to the Confederate adjutant from Savannah in January. "Their progress is slow. Guns are required for their armament, & I have not received as many troops from South Carolina & Georgia as I at first expected." He pleaded for more troops and guns.[61]

While this drama unfolded in South Carolina, Lee received news about the disposition of his father-in-law's estate, unsettled since George Washington Custis's death in 1857. A Virginia court had finally examined the estate's papers and ordered Lee to disburse the unpaid balance of his daughters' legacies and to emancipate slaves from the Arlington, Romancock, and White House estates by the end of 1862. Lee had planned to sell Smith Island on the Atlantic coast to raise money for the legacies, but shortly after the war broke out, Union forces had seized that strategically important property, just as they had the Arlington Heights. "No sales of land can now be made," an exasperated Lee wrote Mary in January 1862. "The enemy is in possession of Smiths Isd., & what I am to do with the negroes I do not know." Their liberation would have to wait.[62]

Meanwhile, two of those family slaves continued to travel with the Rebel general. They were Perry Parks, a young Arlington servant who acted as Lee's launderer and valet, and a cook known only as Meredith—most probably Henry Meredith or one of his children from the White House estate. In newsy letters to the family, Lee mentioned both men, conveyed their regards, and reported on their health. And as cold weather approached, he diplomatically informed Mrs. Lee that he had given his servants the new socks she had knitted for him. "As I found Perry in desperate need, I bestowed a couple of pairs on him, as a present from you," he wrote. "The others I have put in my trunk and suppose they will fall to the lot of Meredith . . . Meredith will have no one near to supply him but me, & will naturally expect that attention."[63]

Back at Arlington, some of the slaves had difficulty adjusting to the presence of so many troops on the old farm, and to the inevitable onset of age. Arlington's elderly coachman Daniel had grown feeble and short of breath; the gardener Ephraim suffered from typhoid fever;[64] Selina Gray was reported to be worn out and forlorn.[65] Others simply drifted away to take their chances in Washington or lands beyond.

Their masters were gone, to be sure, but the slaves remaining at Arlington lived in a peculiar limbo, like the thousands of largely illiterate field hands displaced by fighting or escaped from their masters in the opening stages of war. Slaves from Confederate states who arrived behind Union lines were termed "contrabands," a grotesque legal convention that treated runaway slaves like horses, pigs, or other enemy property.[66] Initially unprepared to care for these refugees, some Union forces mistreated them; others tried to ignore them; still others developed a rough affection for them. When a contraband died at Arlington, a Wisconsin soldier mourned his death, noting, in the casually racist language of his day, that the decedent had been "treated . . . more as a companion than a nigger" by the regiment.[67] In more elegant terms, another member of the Iron Brigade expressed genuine admiration for the refugees: "The contrabands are the only people we can depend upon," he wrote. "They tell us where the Secesh are—never lie to us—wish us God speed—and are of great use to us."[68]

The Union eventually recruited former slaves in their war effort: the blacks dug entrenchments, buried horses, made bricks, drove wagons, grew food—and generally got paid for it. As both armies crisscrossed Northern Virginia and more slaves streamed north across the Long Bridge, Union forces often assumed responsibility for their well-being—in part, to keep them from helping the enemy, in part for humanitarian reasons. More than a few contrabands were surprised, upon finally reaching Washington, to be ushered into the Capitol

Prison, not because they were accused of any crime, but because that was one of the few places Union forces could offer them food, shelter, and protection in a crowded city seething with Confederate sympathizers and racial tension.[69]

Although a few of Arlington's house servants had been given the rudiments of education, most of the estate's slaves were illiterate, unskilled, and poor when they got their first glimpse of the Promised Land. Until they could support themselves as free men and women, the slaves of Arlington became wards of the Union Army, under orders issued in 1862. In one of his last acts as secretary of war, Simon Cameron decreed that Union officers had the obligation to care for the slaves, an act of charity that would profoundly shape the future of Arlington.

"The Secretary of War directs that such of the old and infirm negroes of the Arlington estate, Va., as may be unable to provide for themselves, be furnished such articles of subsistence as the officer commanding at Arlington, for the time being, may approve & order," Adjutant General Lorenzo Thomas wrote on Cameron's behalf. "The estate, which is now in the possession of the Government, was, it is understood, charged by its former owner—the late Mr. Custis—with the care of these old people who have no other means."[70]

With a stroke of his pen, Simon Cameron had solved the problem that had been vexing Lee in faraway South Carolina—*What I am to do with the negroes I do not know.* More significantly, the document asserted the Union's first claim on Arlington, a sense of ownership that would deepen as the war ran its long, sanguinary course.

3

"VAST ARMY OF THE WOUNDED"

THROUGH THE FIRST YEAR OF THE CIVIL WAR, MARY CUSTIS LEE LIVED A precarious existence, nursing her arthritic condition and fretting over the famous husband she had not seen since April 1861. Two of her sons had also joined the Confederate Army, with a third soon to follow. They would be on the firing line when Federal troops renewed their campaign for Richmond in the spring.

Uncertain about where the season's fighting would erupt, Mrs. Lee finally settled on her son Rooney's White House plantation as 1861 drew to a close. The farm, a four thousand–acre spread nestled among the pines on Virginia's languorous Pamunkey River, had been an important family holding since Martha Washington's day. Located some twenty miles northeast of Richmond, the property seemed to offer a reasonable haven from the war. Placed well away from Manassas, it was situated far north of the James River, the most likely aquatic approach to the Confederate capital. Surrounded by two daughters, a daughter-in-law, her only grandson, relays of visiting relatives, a few servants, and a thousand family associations, Mrs. Lee felt safe on the plantation, which provided a transitory sense of well-being. She rode out the winter, writing letters, knitting socks, and collecting the news that drifted down from the Potomac. Most of it was disheartening.

Letitia Corbin Jones, one of Mrs. Lee's many cousins, had managed a recent reconnaissance at Arlington, probably gaining access through her brother Roger, a Union officer. She reported to Mary Lee in an undated letter, which appears to be from early in the war. "I write dear Cousin feeling that you would like to know what I could tell you about Arlington," Miss Jones wrote. She continued:

> The Thefts & depredations there have been going on from the beginning . . . You may be sure that whatever we can do for your interest, we will do, but I fear it will not be much . . . Everything had been ransacked—I suppose there was not a paper or a letter, that had not been pried into—the Loft was in dire confusion—at one time the Soldiers used to sleep up there . . . Selina [Gray, housekeeper] searched in vain for your handsome parlor curtains—but they were gone—and now, no doubt they are adorning some of the Yankee's houses . . . The Union people say that they are in fine Spirits & that the South is nearly subjugated & that the war will soon be ended.

She closed by reporting that federal authorities planned to use Mrs. Lee's house as a hospital—a rumor never realized.[1]

"I do not allow myself to think of my dear old home," Mrs. Lee wrote a friend that spring. "Would that it had been razed to the ground or submerged in the Potomac river than [to] have fallen into such hands . . . Poor Virginia is pressed on every side."[2]

Indeed it was. The federal army had grown from 16,000 to 670,000 in the past year. Some 60,000 Union troops had interposed themselves between Manassas and Washington, while others were scoring wins on the western front. Better equipped and numerically superior to the Confederates, the Union had won recent victories in Kentucky under an obscure general named Ulysses S. Grant. About the same time, Rebels had been forced to abandon western Tennessee, and they had lost Fort Columbus, their most advanced position on the Mississippi River. In the East, Gen. George McClellan had been methodically amassing troops and supplies for his springtime advance on Richmond. Then, according to Abraham Lincoln's new secretary of war, the real fighting could commence.

"We have had no war," Edwin M. Stanton told a sympathetic editor as 1862 began. "We have not even been playing war."[3] That would change under Stanton, a shrewd, robust, snub-nosed, magnificently bearded Ohio native who spoke of sweeping aside the rebellion with "fire & sword." Stanton's Old Testament combativeness, coupled with his superhuman work ethic, endeared him to President Lincoln.

Stanton and Lincoln prodded the cautious Gen. George McClellan to move his troops down the Potomac River and out into the Chesapeake Bay that April. The time had arrived for the Young Napoleon's much-anticipated Peninsula Campaign. With a force that grew to 100,000, McClellan slogged his way toward Richmond, rolling back a force of 80,000 Confederates as he went. Rebels abandoned Yorktown on May 4, Williamsburg on May 5, and Norfolk on May 9. At the other end of the peninsula, Robert E. Lee, monitoring developments from his office in Richmond, realized that the Union tide was aimed straight for Mrs. Lee's refuge on the Pamunkey River, where that tributary swirled into the York River.

"I do not pretend to know what they will attempt or what they can accomplish," Lee wrote his wife that spring. "One of the probable routes . . . is up the Pamunkey. Should they select that, their whole army & c. will land at the White House. To be enveloped in it would be extremely annoying & embarrassing, and I believe hundreds would delight in persecuting you all for my . . . sake . . . I think it better, therefore, that you should all get out of the way."[4] It was time for Mrs. Lee to move again. On her way out of her son's house, she posted a note on the door:

> Northern soldiers who profess to reverence Washington, forbear to desecrate the home of his first married life, the property of his wife, now owned by her descendants.
>
> A Grand-daughter of Mrs. Washington[5]

With her daughters Annie and Mildred in tow, Mrs. Lee made her retreat, this time to a friend's house in Hanover County, a few miles to the northwest of the Pamunkey River estate. It was not long before McClellan's army took over the White House plantation, transforming it into a bustling depot. The old farm became, in the words of a correspondent traveling with the army, "a fair rival of New York, Philadelphia, or Boston in the extent of its coastwise commerce. Steam and sail vessels continually arriving and departing, extensive wharves, with cargoes constantly unloading, . . . and all the hubbub and confusion of a large port."[6] The estate's pine forests were cut for lumber, which workers hammered into coffins—much in demand, not because of fighting but because typhoid fever, yellow fever, and other diseases had joined McClellan's march up the peninsula.[7]

Amid his preparations, McClellan still found time for chivalry. He ordered his troops to respect Rooney Lee's White House property—and he meant it. As his predecessor Irvin McDowell had done at Arlington, McClellan established his headquarters outside and posted guards around the house to discourage scavengers.[8] When one of his officers shot a Lee family pig, McClellan confined the soldier to his tent until he wrote a letter of apology.[9] And when advancing Federals overtook Mrs. Lee again, surrounding her new sanctuary in Hanover County, McClellan had her brought to his headquarters, offered his condolences, issued traveling papers, and dispatched her through his lines for Richmond. Her carriage traveled under a flag of truce.[10]

The fraternity of officers who had studied at the U.S. Military Academy and fought the Mexican War together was still capable of such gestures. But a growing number of hard-liners in the Union war effort—among them Montgomery Meigs, William T. Sherman, and Edwin M. Stanton—had little use for such gallantry. In Secretary Stanton's view, total war would bring the crisis to a speedy conclusion.[11] His brand of realism would trump McClellan's gentlemanly code as the war dragged on and the bloody reality of the conflict became apparent.

Meanwhile, Mary Custis Lee made it safely through the blue ranks and into Confederate territory, where her husband was waiting to greet her. He was shocked by her transformation. In the fifteen months since he had seen her, she had become, at age fifty-three, an old lady. She would soon be confined to a wheelchair.[12] Lee settled her in Richmond, where she remained through most of the war, and went out to face Gen. George McClellan, whose troops were pressing close to the Confederate capital—so close, in fact, that by the end of May, Union soldiers could hear the city's church bells pealing in the dusk.

★   ★   ★

The chimes were soon interrupted by the bark of muskets and the wallop of artillery, which ushered in a furious season of fighting for control of Richmond. The first of these battles, known as Seven Pines or Fair Oaks, opened on May 31, 1862, producing 11,000 casualties in a single day. One of those casualties would change the course of the war: when Confederate Gen. Joseph E. Johnston was severely wounded that evening, Robert E. Lee took his place as field commander of Confederate forces in Northern Virginia, an assignment he would keep for the rest of the conflict. After a year of watching from the sidelines, Lee plunged into the fray.

Restyling his force as the Army of Northern Virginia, he took the fight to McClellan, chasing him across the swamps and rivers of the peninsula as spring turned to summer. He stripped Richmond's defenses to beef up his own lines, divided his forces in the face of McClellan's superior numbers, and attacked against the odds.

In a week of engagements around Richmond known as the Seven Days, which commenced on June 25 and ended on July 1, Union and Confederate forces remained in almost uninterrupted contact, often fighting at close quarters, with the result that 35,984 men were killed, wounded, or captured in a single week. The Federals lost 15,849, the Confederates 20,135. The Rebels had the worst of it, to be sure, but Lee had made Richmond secure, shattered Union confidence, and driven McClellan from the peninsula.[13]

One of the lasting legacies of that muddy summer was the soldier's lullaby we know today as Taps. Though details of its origins differ, the song is usually credited to Brig. Gen. Daniel A. Butterfield, a New Yorker commanding the 3rd Brigade of the Union's 5th Army Corps. As McClellan retreated and Butterfield gathered his men in camp on the James River, he grew irritated at the army's standard lights-out tune known as "Scott's Tattoo," named for the former army chief Winfield Scott and in use since 1835. It signaled soldiers to prepare for the day's final roll call. Butterfield found the tune too harsh, "not as smooth, melodious and musical as it should be." So in July of 1862, he summoned Oliver W. Norton, his twenty-three-year-old bugler, and asked him to make changes in the song as the brigadier listened. Freely admitting that he could neither read nor write music, Butterfield made his alterations by ear, putting his bugler through the paces until the tune sounded right. Norton took up the story:

After getting it to his satisfaction, he directed me to sound that call for Taps there-after in place of the regulation call. The music was beautiful on that still summer night, and was heard far beyond the limits of our Brigade. The next day I was vis-ited by several buglers from neighboring Brigades, asking for copies of the music which I gladly furnished.

Thus was born the famous twenty-four-note call, known as "Butterfield's Lullaby" or Taps, which spread throughout the Union Army, crossed enemy lines, and was entered in the Confederate Mounted Artillery Drill manual by 1863. The new tune was first adapted as a funeral song in the summer of the Peninsula Campaign. As opposing armies exchanged artillery fire near Harri-son's Landing, an unknown Union cannoneer was killed that July. Comrades prepared to bury him and fire the customary three-volley salute at graveside. But with enemies in such close proximity, Capt. John C. Tidball of Battery A, 2nd Union Artillery, feared that an outburst of musketry at close quarters might trigger more bloodshed. So he called for his bugler and asked him to sound a soothing new lights-out tune known as Taps, which seemed a fitting farewell gesture—and the first recorded instance of the melody being played over a soldier's grave. The practice caught on at funerals and spread informally through the Army, but it took decades for the song to become official—it ap-pears in the U.S. Army Infantry Drill Regulations for the first time in 1891.[14]

With deaths mounting on the peninsula, hope for an easy war faded in Wash-ington. "We have had a terrible reverse on the Peninsula," Montgomery Meigs confided to his father as McClellan hurried his army out of Lee's reach.[15] The season's events made it clear that the nation was, to borrow Edwin Stanton's phrase, "playing war" no longer. This reality was attested by a Confederate col-onel's description of the scene from the Peninsula Campaign, as the fog lifted following the Battle of Malvern Hill. The morning revealed "an appalling spectacle . . . Over five thousand dead and wounded men were on the ground in every attitude of distress. A third of them were dead or dying, but enough were alive and moving to give the field a singular crawling effect."[16]

That scene would be repeated at intervals in the months ahead—at the Battle of Second Manassas, at Antietam Creek in Maryland, in the tangled woods around Chancellorsville, below the heights of Fredericksburg, Virginia—as blue and gray armies traded blows, each striving for a knockout punch. Most of the victories of 1862 went to Lee, culminating in the frigid weeks before Christmas at Fredericksburg, where the armies massed along opposite banks of the Rappahannock River. There Lee watched thousands of Union soldiers cross the river and charge uphill where his men, entrenched above town, mowed down wave after advancing wave of Federals. Caught in the open between the river and the town, Union troops lay flat on the ground to avoid getting hit. "At one point the exposure was absolute," a Federal officer recalled, "and stillness as absolute was the only safety. A slight barrier was afterward formed at this point by a disposal of the dead bodies in front, so that the dead actually sheltered the living."[17] Observing the slaughter, Lee was at once delighted and disgusted. "It is well that war is so terrible," he famously said that day. "We should grow too fond of it."[18]

A few days later, Lee celebrated another Christmas in camp, where his thoughts once more turned to home and family. Things were going so well that he even indulged the hope that he might spend a future Christmas at Arlington, as in the old days. "I have pleased myself in reminiscences to day, of the many happy Xmas' we have enjoyed together at our once happy home," he wrote to his daughter Mildred. "Notwithstanding its present desecrated & pillaged condition, I trust that a just & merciful God may yet gather all that He may spare under its beloved roof. How filled with thanks & gratitude will our hearts then be!"[19]

Lee had reason for optimism as 1862 wound to a close. Despite horrific losses, his ragtag army had accomplished a lot with very little, while in Washington, President Lincoln was still frustrated with the Army of the Potomac. The president had shuffled through one commander after another—from McDowell to McClellan to John Pope and back to McClellan again; then to Ambrose Burnside, who was soon to be replaced by Fighting Joe Hooker, who would, in his turn, flame out to make room for yet another temporary commander. Meanwhile, the federal war debt was soaring—it was $600 million at last count—and new enlistments were sorely needed to replace casualties.[20] Lincoln's cabinet quietly discussed the possibility of recruiting black soldiers, a proposal the president resisted in this early phase of the war.

Neither side had anticipated the war's cost in blood. More than 100,000 soldiers, Union and Confederate, would be killed, wounded, or captured in the eastern campaigns of 1862, as the armies fought back and forth between Washington and Richmond. Even before the casualties climbed into the tens of thousands, Lee was protesting that he lacked manpower for burying the dead.[21] Meanwhile, citizens and military planners in Washington watched with growing distress as the war's human wreckage became evident. Newspapers printed long gray columns listing casualties each day, which lengthened with the fighting. Friends and relatives scrutinized the papers for some word of missing loved ones.[22] Some anxious mothers and fathers even made the long journey to Washington to search for a familiar face in the city's crowded hospitals and temporary morgues.[23]

From the opening shot of the Peninsula Campaign, Washington was swamped with a tide of the wounded and dying, who arrived from the front by the hundreds, packed so closely on transport ships that the men hardly had room to roll over; when one did, the jostling set off a chain reaction of groans from stem to stern. Trains rattled into the capital with a similar cargo of broken fighters.[24]

The poet and war nurse Walt Whitman was waiting to greet the first hospital ships when they arrived from the front. They usually came in the night, ghostly white steamers emerging at the Seventh Street wharves. One night, Whitman found them docked in the rain. A few sputtering torches cast the scene in spooky light as, one by one, the men were lifted off, carried ashore on stretchers, and laid on the ground, there to await transfer to one of the city's improvised hospitals. "The pale, helpless soldiers had been debark'd and lay around on the wharf," Whitman wrote. "The rain was, probably, grateful to them; at any rate they were exposed to it . . . All around—on the wharf, on the ground, out on side places—the men are lying on blankets, old quilts, &c., with bloody rags bound round heads, arms, and legs . . . Quite often they arrive at the rate of 1000 a day . . . The wounded are getting to be common, and people grow callous."[25]

Desperately short of hospital space, Washington made do with temporary fixes. The Capitol building was outfitted with cots, which filled the House and Senate chambers and overflowed into the Rotunda. Iron beds were stacked in the Patent Office, where the sick convalesced among the glass display cases of inventors' models. Hotels were transformed into hospitals, as were a synagogue, a clutch of mansions on Minnesota Row, Georgetown College, the former Republican campaign headquarters, the Odd Fellows Hall, the Smithsonian Castle, and no less than thirteen churches; in the latter, bells were silenced in deference to those recuperating under the rafters. New hospital tents and whitewashed pavilions were hastily constructed on Judiciary Square, along the Washington Mall, and on the heights of Meridian Hill. Other war casualties—including those with no hint of mental impairment—were housed in the insane asylum. At least twenty-two hospitals came into being as a result of the Peninsula Campaign, which transformed the nation's capital into a city of fifty thousand patients. This vast army of the wounded, in Whitman's phrase, was "more numerous in itself than the Washington of ten or fifteen years ago."[26]

Modern sanitary practices were unheard of at this stage of the war. The new Armory Square Hospital, while convenient to the wharves and the train depot, overlooked the Washington Canal, a sluggish open sewer linking the Potomac River with its Eastern Branch tributary.[27] At these and other military hospitals, amputation was the preferred treatment for serious wounds. Performed by hard-pressed and often incompetent surgeons, the procedures were frequently botched and had to be redone. "Many of the poor afflicted young men are crazy," Whitman wrote. "They have suffered too much."[28]

After surgery, a doctor's assistant might sponge down the operating table with cold water before a new patient was brought in and laid out to be probed, sawed, or sliced with instruments wiped off—but not sterilized—from the previous operation. Surgeons explored wounds with their bare fingers, honed their operating knives on their boots, and moistened sutures with spit before threading silk through a needle. If a soldier survived battle, and the painful journey from the front, and the brusque attentions of army doctors, he remained a prime target for gangrene, pneumonia, diarrhea, typhoid, smallpox, measles, malaria, and the other fatal diseases haunting army camps and hospitals—indeed, sickness and infection would kill many more Civil War soldiers than bullets.[29]

The country, which had never before faced death on such an enormous scale, was as poorly prepared for burying its soldiers as it had been for giving them proper hospital care.[30] On the front lines, where commanding officers were responsible for disposing of the dead, thousands of soldiers were interred in plots laid out near battlefields.[31] One could mark the progress of the war by the sudden appearance of these rough-and-ready cemeteries, which sprouted overnight among the blasted trees, abandoned wagons, and shell-cratered fields around Washington and Richmond. If the dead could be identified by letters in their pockets or notes pinned to their uniforms, their graves were marked with crude wooden headboards noting the soldier's name and company. In the haste of the moment, names were often misspelled or incomplete; even this scanty identifying information, scrawled in pencil or crudely carved on markers, weathered and became indecipherable in time. Fallen officers and soldiers from well-to-do families were usually shipped home, with expenses borne by relatives.[32]

Many others went to their graves anonymously. In this age before dog tags, two out of five Civil War fatalities were fated to be unknown soldiers.[33] If time allowed, a comrade might record a few descriptive details of an anonymous corpse for the quartermaster's files. "Dead of gunshot wound of bowels," one such burial report read, "age unknown, regiment, rank, and company unknown . . . light brown hair, light complexion, blue eyes, 5'6"."[34] Such fragmentary notes were useless when, years later, grieving relatives came looking for a lost soldier, who would have been tumbled into a mass grave with scores or even hundreds of others, their tomb marked by a single headboard recording the number of dead and the dates of the action that killed them. Others simply lay where they had fallen in battle, left to the elements as the fighting rushed to another point.[35] There was little time for ceremony.

Nor was there much hope of a dignified burial for the unfortunate warrior who died in Washington's hospitals—in part because government expenses were so tight and personnel so scarce, in part because Washington's hot, humid climate required that the dead be disposed of quickly.[36] There was no refrigeration to preserve remains, and the new science of embalming was too expensive for the farm boys, immigrants, and small-town youths who did most of the fighting. They left the hospitals as they had entered them—penniless— and far from friends and relatives who might have provided them a better send-off.[37]

The quartermaster's office, which took charge of burials around Washington, made contracts with undertakers to dispose of the dead. These contractors collected bodies, hauled them away, provided a shroud, crammed them into cheap coffins, buried them, and erected a wooden headboard—all for $4.49 per soldier.[38] With trade booming, some of the capital's undertakers had trouble keeping pace with demand. Citizens grumbled about the stench, and when the uncollected bodies piled up, irate notes flew from hospitals to the War Department.[39] In a typical message, a surgeon at Harewood Hospital gave an assistant quartermaster a tongue-lashing for leaving a dead soldier moldering in his ward for three days:

> The body of John Northrop, late Priv. of Co. I 188th Regt. N.Y. Vols. of whose death you had the usual notice on the 8th inst. not having been taken away by friends for Private Burial, you will please have interred on the 11th inst. at 2 p.m.[40]

In addition to these delays, which were for the most part unavoidable, it became clear that contractors handled their dead soldiers with less care than they would accord a load of turnips bound for market: they cut corners to save money, dug shallow graves to save time, slapped coffins together with gaps between the thin pine planks, and sometimes rolled a serviceman in a blanket and buried him with no casket at all. Even in a capital inured to the cruelties of war, though, some assaults on human dignity surpassed endurance. When residents living near the Judiciary Square Hospital awoke to find a neighborhood lot filled with the naked bodies of soldiers awaiting their appointment with the undertaker, protests were raised. Such incidents gave rise to indignant newspaper articles and to complaints from relief societies, which campaigned for better treatment of the nation's soldiers, living and dead, during that hectic year of 1862. Chaplains rallied at the Washington YMCA to call attention to another scandal: ordinary soldiers were being sent to their graves with no religious rites to mark their passage. The War Department would eventually correct this oversight, even if it meant that a lone, overworked minister had to dash around the cemetery all day murmuring a few lines of scripture over forty or fifty fresh burials.[41]

With deaths from the Peninsula Campaign filling Washington's private graveyards to the bursting point, Congress responded with a new law creating the first military cemeteries on U.S. soil.[42] On July 17, 1862, President Lincoln signed the omnibus bill, which empowered him to purchase new cemetery grounds "whenever in his opinion it shall be expedient . . . for the soldiers who shall die in the service of the country."[43] As a result of this legislation, fourteen military cemeteries came into being by the end of 1862, among them plots at

the Military Asylum, later known as the Soldiers' Home, in Washington, D.C.;
in Alexandria, Virginia; and in Annapolis, Maryland. Eleven other national
cemeteries were opened in Kansas, Illinois, New York, Kentucky, and other
states; most were situated on military posts or adjacent to supply depots.[44]
New York's Cypress Hills National Cemetery, in Brooklyn, was established ex-
pressly for Confederate prisoners of war, their guards, and Union soldiers who
died in the city's hospitals.[45]

The Soldiers' Home in Washington was a soothing place to spend eternity.
Situated on three hundred acres in the hills skirting the city, the reserve afforded cool breezes, sweeping views, and a refuge from the push and shove of
war. Some 150 disabled warriors, many of them veterans of the Mexican campaign, lived on the site, shuffling between the main residence building, an infir-
mary, and a dining hall—all set in deep, peaceful shade. The government had
purchased the place with funds furnished by Gen. Winfield Scott, the durable
old Mexican War hero, who had demanded a $100,000 tribute from local
authorities when his army seized Mexico City in 1847.[46]

By the time of the Civil War, the Soldiers' Home had become a favorite destination for city dwellers in need of fresh air—most famously for President Lincoln, who began commuting the three miles between the White House and his
suburban retreat in the summer of 1862. There he would relax at the Anderson
Cottage in the evening, sitting on the porch in his slippers, reading aloud from
Shakespeare and other favorite books, swapping yarns with visiting friends, and
finding some relief from the pressing business of war—relief, but no escape.
Even in these shaded hills, he slept among the fresh graves of soldiers he had sent
to their deaths. Week after week the wagons, piled with caskets, creaked into the
cemetery, where workers were kept busy digging, burying the dead, and setting
new headboards in place. The graveyard was filling.[47]

So too was the capital, which bloomed from a village into a small city in the
war years. Many of the newest citizens were soldiers, officers, and government
workers, but the war also triggered a flood of black refugees into Washington.
In April 1862, when President Lincoln signed the first Emancipation Proclamation, freeing just those slaves in the capital, about 14,000 blacks lived in
Washington; of these, about 4,200 were the fleeing slaves known as contra-

bands. By the war's end, the capital's black population would swell to as many as 40,000.[48] This later surge—made up of slaves sweeping into the capital on foot, in buggies, and in farm wagons—was the result of Lincoln's second, and more famous, Emancipation Proclamation of January 1, 1863, which liberated some three and a half million slaves in Confederate states.[49]

As that historic New Year's Day approached, a group of former slaves crowded into a schoolhouse in Washington to celebrate their imminent freedom. An elderly man named Thornton rose to explain how Lincoln's announcement would change old ways: "Can't sell your wife and children any more! . . . No more dat!" Thornton declared, his speech rendered in minstrel's vernacular by a journalist. "Goin' to work, I feel bad. Overseer behind me! No more dat! No more dat!"[50] Many of the able-bodied went to work for the federal war effort, first as civilian laborers or teamsters, or later as members of the newly formed U.S. Colored Troops, segregated army units that helped tip the momentum of war in the Union's favor.

About the same time, almost unnoticed, Robert E. Lee summoned a justice of the peace in Spotsylvania County, where he was camped for the winter at Fredericksburg, and went over the papers that finally freed his family's slaves, in accordance with his late father-in-law's wishes. Given Lincoln's sweeping Emancipation Proclamation of 1863 and the reality that many of the Lee slaves were already living within Union lines, one might wonder if the general's gesture was a needless formality. But Lee was nothing if not punctilious, even amid the distractions of war.

"I desire to do what is right and best for the people," Lee wrote his wife that December, referring to the slaves. "Any who wish to leave may do so . . . They can be furnished with their free papers & hire themselves out . . . Those at Arlington & Alexandria I cannot now reach. They are already free & when I can get to them I will give them their papers." Like other men of his day, Lee took a paternalistic view toward blacks, which caused him to worry about how they would fare without masters. "The men could no doubt find homes," he wrote, "but what are the women & children to do?" Without resolving that question, he made it clear that any slaves remaining on Lee family property would be expected to work, with the net proceeds of their labor set aside "for their future establishment."[51] In the deed conveying their liberation, Lee scrupulously listed each of the 196 slaves by name, along with their places of residence, and ordered that they be "forever set free from slavery." He signed the deed of manumission on December 29, 1862, beating Lincoln's historic declaration by barely three days.[52]

That winter, when Lee was not basking in the glow of his recent military triumphs, he took a moment to assess his own financial prospects. They looked anything but promising. His wife was living in a rented house in Richmond. His enemies occupied family properties at Arlington and Smith Island. Their White House home had burned to the ground as Union forces withdrew from the peninsula. Only the Lees' Romancock plantation remained largely untouched by war, at least for the moment. Lee's meager investments in Virginia bonds and railroad stocks would soon be worthless. And now the slaves were going. Even though he disapproved of slavery, the pernicious institution had made possible his family's sprawling land holdings and the earnings flowing from them. That affluence was dissolving, along with the old certainties of Virginia's aristocratic order, in which the Lees had been leading actors. "I have no time to think of my private affairs," he confided to Mrs. Lee that winter. "I expect to die a pauper, & I see no way of preventing it."[53]

With nothing to lose, Lee would become all the more dangerous in the months ahead. He provided thousands of new casualties for the hospitals and cemeteries as the campaign of 1863 unfolded. Emboldened by his success at Chancellorsville in May, but still desperately short of food and supplies, he risked an offensive into Pennsylvania that summer, when both armies squared off near the village of Gettysburg in July. As many as 50,000 Union and Confederate soldiers were killed, wounded, or captured in three days of fighting, with Rebels suffering almost 60 percent of the losses. Lee barely escaped across the Potomac River with his reduced and mangled army.[54] After the bloodbath of Gettysburg, the Union would gain the upper hand. Robert E. Lee, who had begun to feel the twinges of a heart condition that would eventually kill him, no longer seemed invincible. On his long retreat from Gettysburg, he got the news that his son Rooney, a Confederate cavalry officer, had been captured and jailed by Union forces. And Lee would soon be facing a new Union commander—Gen. Ulysses S. Grant—who was not afraid of him.

Meanwhile, blacks continued streaming into Washington, where about a thousand had been settled in a squalid freedmen's camp within sight of the Capitol. The congested neighborhood of shacks and tiny row houses became a breeding ground for disease and disappointment, hardly the paradise the refugees had dreamed of finding along the Potomac. Although military officials and the newly formed Freedman's Relief Association provided food, shelter, clothing—and even schooling—for some of the former slaves, no agency could keep pace with the torrent of new arrivals.

Poor sanitation and crowded conditions led to an outbreak of typhoid fever in Duff Green's Row, a squalid street situated near the site of today's Supreme Court building. Infected refugees were placed in quarantine there, while those who showed no sign of sickness were removed to an army camp at Twelfth and O streets, on the northern edge of the city, which became a new freedmen's camp. It was described as a mud hole, with one end of the site situated in a former brickyard, the other in an old cemetery. With barracks crowded, some of the refugees had to make do with tents. The camp's water, drawn from wells that were drying up, triggered a massive outbreak of dysentery.[55]

The refugee population reached an estimated ten thousand by the spring of 1863. Freedmen improvised as best they could. Some moved into the former slave pens in Alexandria. Others built shanties from scrap lumber and tarpaper on Capitol Hill. A rickety line of huts, which came to be known as Murder Bay, appeared along the fetid Washington Canal. Outsiders were shocked by what they found in such neighborhoods.

"I have just visited the freemen in their cabins," said one visitor. "Their sufferings are most heart rending. The weather is cold; they have little or no wood. Snow covers the ground; and they have a scanty supply of rags called clothes . . . Government gives them very, *Very* small allowance of soup. Many will die."[56]

Many did. Most of the black refugees had little resistance to scarlet fever, smallpox, and whooping cough. Infants and children were especially susceptible. Illness claimed at least five lives each day among Washington's black refugees—probably many more.[57] "Exactly how many, no record ever told," wrote historian Constance McLaughlin Green.[58]

After medical authorities expressed concern over conditions in refugee camps, Lt. Col. Elias M. Greene, chief of the quartermaster's Washington Department, was called to investigate. In May 1863, he proposed a fix that would bolster the war effort, improve living conditions for former slaves, and enlarge the Union presence at Arlington, already a bustling Federal encampment.

Without mentioning Robert E. Lee by name, Greene urged the War Department to establish a new freedmen's camp on those lands south of the Potomac that had "been abandoned by rebel owners and are now lying idle." He meant Arlington, of course, and its rich bottomlands. The unused outbuildings and slave quarters on the Lee property, Greene wrote, could easily accommodate new residents desperately in need of shelter.[59]

"The houses are left standing," Greene argued. "There are enough to provide quarters for from 500 to 750 field hands with a very small outlay for additions and improvements." Why not move the former slaves to Arlington?

The force of contrabands, males and females, now idle in this city & a dead weight on the Government can be employed to a very great advantage in cultivating the above lands, raising corn & millet, and cutting hay . . .

The families need not be separated, as they can still be united and may be fully as well provided for as their present quarters in this city and at less expense. Besides this there is the decided advantage afforded to them of the salutary effects of good pure country air and a return to their former healthy avocation as field hands under much happier auspices than heretofore which must prove more beneficial to them and will tend to prevent the increase of diseases now prevalent among them. I also propose establishing a large vegetable garden South of the Pòtomac to be cultivated by the younger Contrabands and others of them who are unable to do heavy field work. The proceeds of such labor would be considerable . . .

The arrangements I propose will not only in my opinion conduce to the sanitary & moral improvement of the Contrabands, but it will save the Government an immense amount of money . . . I respectfully suggest that the matter should be decided within the next forty-eight hours. It will be absolutely necessary to commence any farming operations for the present season otherwise it will be too late to plant.[60]

Secretary of War Edwin M. Stanton approved Greene's proposal on the spot, and on May 22, 1863, Maj. Gen. Samuel P. Heintzelman issued General Orders No. 28, directing Greene to take responsibility for all contrabands in

Washington, D.C., and Alexandria, to seize Arlington and "all rebel lands, farm houses and tenements thereon, at present abandoned by their owners . . . situated south of the Potomac and within the lines of his command," and to put able-bodied freedmen to work cultivating "said lands . . . in such a manner as may be most beneficial to the Government."[61]

Freedmen began moving to Arlington that spring. There they would live under the joint patronage of the quartermaster's office and the American Missionary Association. The first wave of a hundred former slaves, including some who had belonged to the Lees, filed into the fields and began sowing wheat and planting potatoes. Some lived in surplus army tents while a village of simple frame duplex houses took shape along the Potomac River.[62] This new Freedman's Village, where the streets were named for famous generals and political figures, was formally dedicated on December 4, 1863. A correspondent from *Harper's Weekly* wrote approvingly about the settlement. It was "quite lively, having a large number of children in it . . . The principal street is over a quarter of a mile long, and the place presents a clean and prosperous appearance at all times."[63]

It would grow to a community of fifteen hundred, with a hospital, two churches, a home for the aged, and schools for both children and adults. The latter were trained as seamstresses, blacksmiths, wheelwrights, and carpenters. The idea was that the village would provide a temporary haven for freedmen until they found jobs and established their own homes elsewhere.[64] Some did move on, but many refugees stayed at Freedman's Village for decades, raising children and even grandchildren on the fringes of the old plantation.

The new settlement at Arlington was applauded by those who believed that slavery was a sin and Lee a traitor. "One sees more than poetic justice in the fact that its rich lands, so long the domain of the great general of the rebellion, now afford labor and support to the hundreds of enfranchised slaves," wrote a visiting journalist, who also found hope and enthusiasm among the "dusky faces" she encountered in Freedman's Village.[65]

Within a few weeks of establishing the new community at Arlington, Lt. Col. Elias Greene declared it a success. "The Arlington Estate is one of the largest and most fertile of the abandoned farms, has a full supply of good water, [and] is remarkably healthy," he wrote. "And being well within the lines of defenses, it secures the safety of the contrabands . . . The crops are in fine condition and the farms promise to be very remunerative."[66]

Despite Greene's glowing report, not all of those living at Freedman's Village enjoyed the experience. Toiling in the fields and workrooms under military discipline seemed, for some, scarcely preferable to slavery. The fresh vegetables freedmen grew were requisitioned for sale in Washington, while many of the farm workers were expected to live on army rations. "Don't feel as if I was free," said one woman after a few years in Freedman's Village. " 'Pears like there's nobody free here."[67] Established residents were suspicious of new arrivals, distrusted as disease-ridden, dirty, and discontented.[68] And in the patronizing fashion of the day, missionaries and well-intentioned Union officers took moral responsibility for villagers, hectoring their charges on the importance of cleanliness, godliness, and other virtues. "You must be industrious," admonished the Rev. Dr. J. George Butler, preaching to a gathering of Arlington freedmen. "I do not wonder that so many of you do not love to work," said the Lutheran minister. "But when you look over all this grand land—the cities and factories and farms—at all its great wealth—and ask where it came from, there is but one answer. It is the reward not of indolence, but of industry . . . Your race can never become manly except they work industriously."[69]

Many took Butler's advice, prospered, and established successful lives in Freedman's Village. Others left Arlington as soon as they could, creating new communities in Alexandria that thrive to this day. But the majority of black refugees who made it to the Washington region preferred to stay in the capital. Life could be precarious there, to be sure, but it was less regimented than Arlington—and perhaps more secure for the long term.[70]

What if the Confederates won the war and Robert E. Lee returned to reclaim his plantation? Where would that leave the blacks who lived there? To avoid this eventuality, the federal government, having firmly established its physical presence on the Lee estate, moved to make its legal title secure.

With little fanfare, Congress had laid the groundwork for seizing the title to Arlington early in the war. Just as the Peninsula Campaign heated up, lawmakers enacted legislation allowing for direct taxes in the "insurrectionary districts" in June 1862. Amended in February 1863, the statute was meant not only to raise much-needed revenue for the war effort but also to punish those supporting the rebellion. It enabled federal commissioners to assess and collect taxes on real estate in Confederate territory; if those taxes were not paid in person, the commissioners were empowered to sell the land. Acting under that law, the authorities levied a tax of $92.07 on the 1,100-acre Arlington estate in 1863. Mrs. Lee, stranded in Richmond by the fighting and by deteriorating health, dispatched a cousin to pay her tax bill. But when Philip R. Fendall presented himself to the commissioners in Alexandria, they informed him that they would accept the money only from Mrs. Lee. They sent him packing and set the date for selling Arlington: January 11, 1864.[71]

The Potomac River was covered with ice that day, with no boats running and carriages scarce. Although the auction was well attended, arctic conditions seemed to chill the bidding. The sole offer for Arlington came from the federal government, which tendered $26,800 for the estate, something less than its assessed value of $34,100.[72] The new owners intended to reserve the property "for Government use, for war, military, charitable, and educational purposes," according to the certificate of sale.[73]

Because the auction was prominently reported in local papers, it is certain that the Lees knew about it, but nowhere in their voluminous correspondence does this milestone appear to be mentioned directly. General Lee may have cryptically referred to the sale a few weeks after the event, when he wrote to Mary on February 6, 1864. "I am glad you have not been discouraged by the notice of the papers," he wrote then, perhaps a reference to Arlington, perhaps to reassure his wife about the condition of his army.[74] It had been an especially harsh winter, with hundreds of his men barefoot and more than a thousand without blankets. Rations were scarce, desertions mounting.[75] Faced with these realities, Lee had little time to mourn the loss of Arlington.

For her part, Mary Lee, who after several months of separation had been briefly reunited with her husband a few weeks before, was shocked to see how the war had aged him; now she refrained from burdening him with unpleasant intelligence from home. She sent him socks, family news, and encouragement on the front, where Lee's heart condition sent new spasms of pain down his left arm. He kept busy, badgering the Confederate quartermaster for beef, shoes, and other supplies, while pleading with President Jefferson Davis for reinforcements. Lee expected the new Union commander, Ulysses S. Grant, to concentrate his forces for an all-out assault as soon as the weather allowed.[76]

★ ★ ★

This was precisely what Grant had in mind. On May 4, 1864, his army crossed Virginia's Rapidan River and pressed to the south with 119,000 men. His objective was not Richmond but Lee's army, now reduced to a force of 62,000.[77] As soon as Grant was across the river and into the tangle of scrub oak and briars known as the Wilderness, Lee launched a furious attack, driving into the Union line and setting off a series of battles that would be among the bloodiest of the war. For more than a month the generals fought their way south, with Grant trying to force his army between Lee and Richmond, and Lee maneuvering to interrupt the blue tide. The Battle of the Second Wilderness raged down to Spotsylvania Courthouse, then spread to North Anna River, Cold Harbor, Riddell's Shop, and Petersburg. There the Forty Days' Campaign finally sputtered to a halt on June 14, leaving a seventy-mile trail of dead horses and charred fields behind. By then, Grant had crossed the James River, just to the south of Richmond. The campaign had cost him 50,000 killed, wounded, or captured. Lee's casualties were less—some 32,000—but that amounted to half his army. Lee could not afford the depletion. Grant could.[78]

After the first clash that May, the inevitable backwash of wounded and dying soldiers piled into Union-controlled Fredericksburg, a transshipment point where the injured—both Federals and Confederate prisoners—were borne into churches, stores, and shell-pocked homes to await treatment. Others were dropped in the street, shoulder to shoulder and head to toe, lying so thick on the ground that one cavalry patrol was forced to find another route through town. Many of the men died before they could be treated; others starved in place before provisions could reach them. When the lines of transportation reopened to the north, the thousands of injured men who had been languishing in Fredericksburg were collected on hospital transports and trains for the return trip to Washington. There, as in past seasons of fighting, the wharves and depots overflowed once more with the wounded. By May 21, 1864, the *Washington Chronicle* reported the arrival of eighteen thousand new patients, a piece of news confirmed by the ambulance wagons jostling through the capital's streets day and night.[79]

Even as Washington blossomed with the promise of another spring, new battalions of injured soldiers lay dying in the city's hospitals. They quickly filled the national graveyards. The Alexandria National Cemetery was approaching its limit of one thousand burials, as was the Soldiers' Home, with its eight thousand graves. With the Union focused on winning the war, little attention was paid to caring for the dead. Burial mounds eroded and caved in at the Soldiers' Home; pools of standing water spread over the graves; headboards rotted and disappeared in the mud. "The few remaining up [had] become so obliterated by exposure to the weather that it was with difficulty many names could be read," an assistant quartermaster reported. "In some places hardly a trace was left, but for an unsightly stake, to indicate the graves of the departed."[80]

Meanwhile, the corpses piled up in Washington faster than the quartermaster's harried laborers could dispose of them. A stench of death hung over the city, pervasive as wood smoke, prompting a new wave of complaints from war-weary citizens. In desperation, federal officials began scouting for new burial grounds. They settled on Arlington.

4

FIRST BURIALS

A MONTH BEFORE ARLINGTON OFFICIALLY BECAME A NATIONAL CEMETERY, the burials began there. It was an act of improvisation born of necessity to process the war's carnage before it became a public health or a public relations nuisance. More than a touch of vengeance was involved too, courtesy of Brig. Gen. Montgomery C. Meigs.

While some details of Arlington's transition from plantation to cemetery remain obscured by the confusion of war and the passage of time, there is no doubt about the first soldier laid to rest on the Lee estate: That honor belongs to Pvt. William Christman, twenty-one, of the 67th Pennsylvania Infantry, buried on May 13, 1864, just as Lee and Grant plunged into their blistering Forty Days' Campaign. The private's grave was situated in a poorly drained sector of Arlington, down among the low hills skirting what was then the Alexandria-Georgetown Pike. This far corner of the estate was out of sight of the mansion, where Union officers lived and worked. Not wishing to have the view marred by new graves, they directed the first burials well away from the house.[1]

James Parks, the family slave who had witnessed Lee's departure in 1861, was still living at Arlington when the initial wave of war casualties appeared there. He went to work digging the cemetery's first graves, struggling to keep pace with the long rows of coffins that appeared each morning, stacked in the hills "like cordwood," as he recalled it.[2] These burials took place in the Lower Cemetery, which describes a location as well as the social status of those destined for the potter's field, the place meant for poor enlisted men such as Private Christman.

Like others who would join him in the Lower Cemetery, Private Christman was felled by disease instead of a bullet. He developed measles and died of peritonitis in Washington's Lincoln General Hospital on May 11, 1864. A farmer newly recruited into the army, Christman never knew a day of combat. He was committed to the earth on May 13 with no flags flying, no bugles playing, and no family or chaplain to see him off. A simple pine headboard, painted white with black lettering, identified his grave, just like the marker erected for Pvt. William H. McKinney, a Pennsylvania cavalryman buried on that same Friday the thirteenth.[3] They were joined the next day by Arlington's first battle casualty, Pvt. William B. Blatt, 49th Pennsylvania Infantry. Wounded in the Wilderness fighting and transported to Washington, Blatt died on his way from the wharf to Armory Square Hospital on May 13.[4] All three were from modest backgrounds, as were the other soldiers who soon filled the Lower Cemetery: Alvah Kirk from New York, Artemus Sweetland from Vermont, Lyman E. Besse from Maine, Peter Rawson from New Jersey, Moses Hatch from Massachusetts, and Levi Reinhardt from North Carolina.[5]

Reinhardt, a wounded Rebel prisoner who died in Washington's Carver General Hospital, was buried alongside his enemies at Arlington, just as hundreds of other Confederates would be in the last years of war. Several hundred freedmen, who lived and died nearby, would join them in the Lower Cemetery, as would the U.S. Colored Troops who had been fighting for their freedom as well as their lives; the blacks would lie a few rows away from Christman, Reinhardt, and the others, but in the manner of the times, they were scrupulously separated by race.[6]

Officers got better treatment. Less than a week after Private Christman came to rest in the Lower Cemetery, the first Union officers were given prominent burial close by the Lee mansion. The first of these, Capt. Albert H. Packard of the 31st Maine Infantry, was interred on May 17, 1864. He was placed at the edge of Mrs. Lee's garden, about a hundred paces from the mansion, with its sweeping views of the river and capital. Packard, shot in the brain during the Wilderness fighting, miraculously survived his journey from the battlefield to Washington's Columbian College Hospital, where he died on May 16. Buried the next day, he occupied a part of the grounds where Mrs. Lee had enjoyed reading in warm weather, surrounded by the scent of honeysuckle and jasmine.[7] Before the middle of June, six other officers were sleeping on the hillside with Packard, their graves guarding the garden's eastern border.[8]

The placement of these tombs illustrates a bit of strategic maneuvering by Meigs, who planned to make Arlington uninhabitable for the Lees after the war—unless they wished to live among ghosts.[9] Meigs also knew that planting Mrs. Lee's garden with prominent Union officers would make it politically difficult for anyone to disinter these heroes of the Republic.[10]

The old estate made a logical site for new burials in any event. Since January 1864, the Union believed that it held clear title to the property. There was still plenty of open land there, and it was convenient to Washington's hospitals, yet at a discreet distance from the capital's population. And there was precedent for a cemetery on the estate. Members of the Custis clan had been buried there, as had the family's slaves, and after them the many contrabands and freedmen who found their way north during the war.

It is clear that Meigs had formed a master plan for Arlington before he sought permission to make it the nation's preeminent graveyard. A week in advance of its official designation as a burial place, he was already referring to the "new cemetery" and describing how it would handle the growing traffic of interments from Washington.[11] In one often-repeated account of the cemetery's origins, Meigs and President Lincoln get joint credit for the idea. According to this story, which seems rooted in Meigs family lore, the moment of inspiration came on May 13, 1864, as Meigs and Lincoln were visiting Arlington on a carriage ride. Their outing was interrupted when the general noticed a crew loading a dozen dead soldiers into wagons from an Arlington hospital for burial at the Soldiers' Home. He stopped the presidential carriage and ordered the dead to be buried on the spot, and thus began Arlington National Cemetery—so goes the legend.[12]

Yet files from the Office of the Quartermaster General cast doubt on this time-honored story. The record shows that the first military interments at Arlington came from hospitals in Washington, not from one on Lee's estate; that the first burials were sent to Arlington not en masse but in small shipments over a number of days—two on May 13, six on May 14, seven on May 15, two on May 17, four on May 27, one on May 29, two on May 30, one on June 8, one on June 9, and one on June 13; and finally, that the only hospital operating at Arlington when Meigs and Lincoln are supposed to have visited was Abbott's Hospital, a fifty-bed facility that treated the residents of Freedman's Village—not white soldiers such as Christman, Blatt, and others in Arlington's first colony of burials.[13] The most likely explanation is that Meigs and his fellow officers hit upon the Arlington idea, put it into practice under the exigencies of war, and sought bureaucratic approval after the fact—not the first time a military officer would request authorization for something he had already done.[14]

Private Christman had been in the ground for barely a month when Meigs moved to make official what was already a matter of practice at Arlington. "I recommend that . . . the land surrounding the Arlington Mansion, now understood to be the property of the United States, be appropriated as a National Military Cemetery, to be properly enclosed, laid out, and carefully preserved for that purpose," Meigs wrote to Secretary of War Edwin M. Stanton on June 15, 1864. Meigs proposed carving a two hundred–acre parcel out of the property—more than a fifth of the plantation—for the new graveyard. He also suggested that Christman and others recently interred in the Lower Cemetery be separated from the contrabands and slaves and reburied closer to Lee's hilltop home. "The grounds about the Mansion are admirably adapted to such a use," he wrote.[15]

Edwin Stanton, whose disdain for Lee matched Meigs's, endorsed his quartermaster's recommendation on the day it was put forward. "The Arlington Mansion and the grounds immediately surrounding it are appropriated for a Military Cemetery," Stanton ordered. "The bodies of all soldiers dying in the Hospitals of the vicinity of Washington and Alexandria will be interred in this Cemetery. The Quartermaster General is charged with the execution of this order. He will cause the grounds, not exceeding two hundred acres, to be immediately surveyed, laid out, and enclosed for this purpose, not interfering with the grounds occupied by the Freedmans [sic] camps."[16]

Then Stanton signed the historic order in his bold, back-slanting hand.

Loyalist newspapers applauded his action. "This and the contraband establishment there are righteous uses of the estate of the rebel General Lee," the *Washington Morning Chronicle* reported. "The grounds are undulating, handsomely adorned, and in every respect admirably fitted for the sacred purpose to which they have been dedicated. The people of the entire nation will one day, not very far distant, heartily thank the initiators of this movement."[17]

Meigs visited the new cemetery on the morning of its creation, touring the place with Edward Clark, the engineer and architect he assigned to survey the property. On that tour of Arlington, Meigs was incensed to find that his orders to cluster graves around the Lee mansion had been ignored: most of the new burials were still being placed in the Lower Cemetery. "When the season permits it the bodies lately interred there . . . will be removed to the National Cemetery at Arlington," he told Brig. Gen. D. H. Rucker, the officer in charge of the quartermaster's Washington Department.[18] It is clear that he meant for Private Christman and others to be reburied closer to the mansion. Yet it was an order Meigs found devilishly hard to enforce. "My plans for the cemetery had been in some degree thwarted," he recalled later.

> It was my intention to have begun the interments nearer the mansion, but opposition on the part of officers stationed at Arlington, some of whom used the mansion and who did not like to have the dead buried near them caused the interments to be begun in the Northeastern quarter of the grounds near the Alexandria road.
>
> On discovering this by a visit I gave special instructions to make the burials near the mansion. They were then driven off by the same influence to the western portion of the grounds . . . On discovering this second error I caused the officers to be buried around the garden.[19]

Meigs blamed Gen. Rene E. DeRussy, who had his headquarters at Arlington, for subverting his plans. To make sure this did not happen again, Meigs moved to evict DeRussy and his staff from the mansion, replacing them with two full-time chaplains who would oversee day-to-day operations at Arlington.[20] The appointment of chaplains also served another purpose—to quell public criticism of the military's slapdash approach to burials. "The Quartermaster's Department is, I think, unjustly blamed for interring the soldiers without appropriate ceremonies," Meigs wrote Edwin Stanton on June 16, 1864. "It has not the appointment or employment of chaplains," Meigs protested. "Its officers are occupied with their appropriate duties, and cannot be present at the cemetery constantly. The interments are going on all day."[21]

Meigs then suggested a solution. If chaplains set up residence at Arlington, they could "take charge of the whole conduct of the interments, and perform appropriate religious services over all persons interred therein."[22] Stanton quickly approved the plan.[23] DeRussy was out and Meigs's chaplains were in, along with Capt. James M. Moore, a loyal lieutenant from the quartermaster's corps. Moore and his family moved into the mansion to keep an eye on the cemetery. These administrative shifts proved to be critical in the evolution of Arlington, which would gradually become less important as a strategic military site and more so as a national symbol of the martial virtues—duty, honor, and sacrifice.

Once Meigs had his new bureaucratic arrangements in place, Mrs. Lee's garden began to fill with graves. Union captains and lieutenants joined the handful of officers already sleeping on the hilltop, one felled by a shot to the chest, another by a thigh wound, an arm wound, a face wound, a shoulder wound, a knee wound. Others died of diphtheria, typhoid, or dysentery; others from the shock or infection from amputation. One died from drinking bad whiskey.[24]

The most curious garden burial was marked by a short, square stone with no identifying name, merely the number 5232. Beneath it three amputated legs had been interred, all from Union soldiers treated at Judiciary Square Hospital in May 1864. One of the legs belonged to James G. Carey, a private in the 106th Pennsylvania Infantry, who not only survived his operation but lived until 1913; the fate of the second solider, Arthur McQuinn, 14th U.S. Infantry, is unknown; the third, Sgt. Michael Creighton, a native of Ireland in the 9th Massachusetts Infantry, survived his amputation for two weeks but died on June 9, 1864. He was interred in the Lower Cemetery the next day, separated from his left leg by more than half a mile, which makes him the only person at Arlington with two graves.[25]

In a capital where surgeons performed amputations throughout the Civil War, it is unknown why the legs of Creighton, McQuinn, and Carey were chosen for this peculiar but honorable burial. Unlike most others in Mrs. Lee's garden, none of these three was a commissioned officer, which places them in a distinct minority.[26] Most amputations were buried in unmarked mass graves or burned. Why was this trio singled out? Perhaps their symbolism mattered more than their individual identities, another rebuke for the

Confederate general who had caused so much Union suffering. The gesture could not have been an afterthought—someone had to label the remains, transport them from the hospital across the river, record the particulars in a ledger, ready a marker for the grave, and bury the legs in the garden. Like much else that transpired at Arlington in those days, there is no official explanation for it, just a worn white stone rooted in the grass, one of three thousand graves appearing in Arlington's inaugural year as a military cemetery.[27] By the end of that year, some forty officers' graves had filled the garden, while most other burials were destined for the Lower Cemetery or to a new section just west of the mansion.[28]

That last autumn of the war produced thousands of casualties, but few were felt more bitterly at home than the death of Lt. John Rodgers Meigs, a son of the Union quartermaster. Lieutenant Meigs, twenty-two, was shot on October 3, 1864, while on a night scouting mission for Gen. Philip Sheridan in Virginia's Shenandoah Valley. Accounts varied, with Sheridan saying that Lieutenant Meigs had been killed by Confederate guerillas disguised as civilians; Rebels claimed later that Meigs had fired on them first. Whatever the cause, Lieutenant Meigs was dead. He was returned with solemn honors to Washington, where President Lincoln, Edwin Stanton, and other dignitaries joined General Meigs for the funeral. Meigs mourned the loss of his "noble precious son," saw him buried among relatives in a Georgetown cemetery, and braced for the final clash of the conflict, which now seemed infinitely less benign than the "great & holy war" he had foreseen at its outset.[29]

The war was almost over. Lee's army had eroded from 60,000 to some 28,000 men by the time fighting renewed with the springtime. Abandoning their entrenchments around Petersburg and Richmond, the Confederates made a dash to the west, where Grant blocked the retreat. Lee surrendered at Appomattox, Virginia, on April 9, 1865. The rest of the Confederacy collapsed soon afterward.

Lee slowly made his way home to Richmond, where his wife and daughters had lived through the last years of war. He arrived on April 15, 1865—the very morning on which President Lincoln died—to join his family at 707 Franklin Street, a borrowed house in a burned-out city now occupied by Union troops.

Lee handed his faithful warhorse, Traveller, to an attendant, acknowledged cheers from the street, and closed the door behind him.[30]

His future looked bleak that spring. In the four years—almost to the day—since he had bid farewell to Gen. Winfield Scott and turned south, Lee had lost almost everything. Arlington, which held thousands of graves, was gone. He owned no other home. His investments, moderate at best, had dwindled. He was without a job, a prisoner of war on parole, stripped of the right to vote or to hold public office. And shortly after arriving in Richmond, he received the unsettling news that his old commander in chief, Confederate president Jefferson Davis, had been captured while trying to flee the country. Arrested in Georgia, Davis was brought back to Virginia, thrown into military prison at Fort Monroe, and clapped in irons.[31] There were rumors that Davis would be tried and hanged for his part in the rebellion.[32] Lee faced the same fate. Less than a month after Appomattox, he received word that he, Davis, and other Confederate leaders had been indicted by a federal grand jury—for treason.[33]

Among Lee's adversaries, none seemed keener to make an example of him than Meigs, still indignant over the death of his son six months before. "The rebels are all murderers of my son and the sons of hundreds of thousands," Meigs fumed as word of Lee's surrender reached him. "Justice seems not satisfied [if] they escape judicial trial & execution . . . by the government which they have betrayed attacked & whose people loyal & disloyal they have slaughtered." If Lee and other Confederate leaders escaped punishment because of clemency, then Meigs hoped that Congress would banish them from American soil.[34] He was not alone in these views, which were strongly held by radical Republicans on Capitol Hill and by some newspapers. At least one of the latter resurrected the old charge about Lee's whipping Wesley Norris and an unnamed cousin, both slaves, who had escaped from Arlington before the war.[35]

But with the prospect of national reunion in sight, other leaders were happy to follow the late President Lincoln's model of malice toward none and charity for all. General Grant was one of these. Relentless in battle but magnanimous in victory, he believed that Confederates would become useful citizens if treated generously. And from the time of Appomattox, Lee set an example for his former comrades in arms, urging them to put the war behind them, go home, and rebuild their broken country. "All should unite in honest efforts to obliterate the effects of the war and to restore the blessing of peace," he wrote.[36] This attitude reassured Grant, calmed some of the raw anti-Union feeling in the South, and probably saved Lee from prosecution. The treason charges against him quietly disappeared, almost certainly because Grant interceded on his behalf with President Andrew Johnson.[37]

While the Confederate general avoided the spectacle of a trial, he found it difficult to regain his citizenship. His application for a presidential pardon, heartily endorsed by Grant, was postponed for weeks, then months, then years. Lee continued to wait for the presidential reprieve, which never came. The delay might have been intentional, as penalty for his role in the insurgency, or it might have been an honest mistake caused by bureaucratic error. Lee's oath of allegiance, signed on October 2, 1865, disappeared into the State Department files for more than a century, finally resurfacing in 1970, when a researcher discovered the document, duly notarized and fixed with Lee's faded signature, in a dusty box of documents at the National Archives. With this legal requirement finally met, Congress restored the general's citizenship in 1975. President Gerald R. Ford signed the legislation in ceremonies at Arlington, attended by Robert E. Lee IV and other family members.[38]

The Lees would spend the postwar years trying—or at least hoping—to regain possession of Arlington, a struggle that continued their long-distance battle of wits with Meigs. Mrs. Lee, less fatalistic and more outspoken than her husband, felt a growing sense of outrage about changes at Arlington. The ink was barely dry on the Appomattox surrender when a cousin wrote to Mrs. Lee on May 15, 1865, urging her return to the plantation. "It is thought well for persons who have property in that part of the state to be near at hand, that they may take possession as soon as it is vacated . . . I trust dear Cousin you will be back ere long at Arlington too. I can not believe that you will be defrauded out of it."[39]

Neither could Mrs. Lee, who often gave voice to her feelings, in contrast to her self-possessed husband. "I cannot write with composure on my own cherished Arlington," she admitted to one friend.[40] She seethed over the placement of Union graves: "They are even planted up to the very door without any regard to common decency[41] . . . My heart will never know rest or peace while my dear home is so used & I am almost *maddened* daily by the accounts I read in the paper of the number of interments continually placed there . . . If *justice & law* are not utterly extinct in the U.S., I *will have* it back."[42] Such outbursts probably did the Lees more harm than good, fueling adverse comment in the press and hard feelings among radical Republicans who had no sympathy for leaders of the rebellion.

For his part, Lee understood this political reality and kept his ambitions for Arlington hidden from all but a few advisors and family. He conferred quietly with lawyers about reclaiming the property, a matter he was willing to investigate but not to press openly. "I have not taken any steps in the matter," he cautioned a Washington attorney who offered to take on the Arlington case for free, "under the belief that at present I could accomplish no good." However, he encouraged the sympathetic lawyer to research the case.[43] To his elder brother Smith Lee, the general admitted that he wanted to "regain the possession of A." and particularly "to terminate the burial of the dead which can only be done by its restoration to the family. I have made no application on the subject waiting for the action of President Johnson upon my application to him to be embraced in his proclamation of Amnesty."[44]

While Arlington remained in limbo, the family searched for a new place to live. Seeking relief from the visitors thronging their Richmond house, they escaped to Derwent, a friend's country estate, where they lived through the blazing summer of 1865 in a weather-beaten farmhouse. The place was stuffy and uncomfortable, but it gave them some rest, and time to consider where they might resettle. Lee fielded correspondence, and took long rides on Traveller. Toward the end of the summer, he agreed to a position as president of Washington College, a tiny school with forty students and a staggering debt in Lexington, Virginia. The college, set deep in the Shenandoah Valley and far from the prickly entanglements of Richmond or Washington, seemed ideal to Lee, who needed honorable work as well as a home. Washington College provided both.[45]

As students returned that autumn, the Lees settled at Lexington and unwrapped some of the silver plate and paintings they had salvaged from Arlington. When they unrolled carpets rescued from the plantation, the rugs were too long and had to be folded at one end to fit their new home.[46] Lee found the place comfortable and his work absorbing, but his wife continued to miss her old property on the Potomac. "I long for the old scenes & old haunts," she repined to a cousin. "I cannot take root in a new soil—I am too old for that."[47] She still held out the hope that Arlington's dead could be disinterred, buried elsewhere, and her family home restored.[48]

Although this dream was unrealistic, key members of the clan made discreet visits to the old estate in the closing months of 1865 to see for themselves how the war years had changed Arlington and to gauge whether it might be put in livable condition again. The most detailed reconnaissance came from Mary Lee, thirty, the family's eldest daughter and by all accounts the most adventurous one. While visiting friends in Georgetown she ventured over the river for a bittersweet homecoming. "It seemed like a dream to be looking quietly once more on the old familiar Scenes & under such different auspices," she reported to her mother that winter.

> We proceeded along a perfect road through a Country so changed that had I not known where I was I should have never identified it in the world. Not one single tree, not a bush, is standing on either side of the road. The heights from the river . . . are lined with fortifications & barracks & freedmans [sic] villages & back in the Country as far as the eye can reach the perfect desolateness extends. Where the Arlington tract commences large placards are stuck over both sides of the road "Government Farms—Do Not Trespass" . . . On the Height the graveyard commences & extends almost to the little stream . . . The vegetable garden with its old brick wall & ivy looked just the same, the only thing that did . . . The flower garden is entirely altered, made smaller in every way . . . surrounded by a white paling . . . Round the paling were the row of graves of which you have heard. The front looked very desolate, all grown up with church mint & aspens & ailanthus . . . Not saying who I was, I was not allowed to enter many of the rooms . . . I went into the parlour, in which nothing was standing but the old sideboard, with broken doors . . . One of the mantels was also broken . . . I was forbidden to enter Papa's office . . . Upstairs I was permitted to go into my own dressing room "to see the view." There was nothing in it, nor the hall. I saw several of the servants in the distance but not wishing to be recognized did not speak to them. Thornton . . . Cornelius . . . & Dandridge I think & Robert. The graveyard commences from the road as it descends the hill & stretches out . . . acre after acre . . . I returned that way over the long bridge to see as much as I could & had I not been so unwell I would have gone over again.

*It was a very trying visit, more painful even than I had expected . . . It was a
beautiful bright nice day and the view was lovely but the whole face of the country
so utterly changed that turning my back on the house I could have scarcely
recognized a feature of it.*[49]

Her letter offered little hope for returning to Arlington, in marked contrast
with a contemporaneous assessment from her uncle Smith Lee, who visited
the estate in the late autumn or winter of 1865 on what he thought was a clandestine inspection. After touring the house and grounds, he concluded that
the place could be made habitable again and reported this to his brother in
Lexington.[50] Smith made the mistake of sharing his views with the cemetery's
superintendent, who dutifully sent them to the quartermaster general—along
with the mystery visitor's identity.[51]

"A brother of Genl. Lee (Smith Lee) in a recent visit to Arlington, remarked
to the Superintendent, 'that the house could still be made a pleasant residence,
by fencing off the Cemetery, and removing the officers buried around the garden,'" Capt. James M. Moore wrote his superiors on December 11, 1865.
Moore, detailed by Meigs to look after the cemetery, took occasion to suggest
more burials around the mansion, in keeping with his commander's goal "to
more firmly secure the grounds known as the National Cemetery, to the Government by rendering it undesirable as a future residence."[52]

Shortly after this memorandum made the rounds, word of Smith Lee's visit
leaked out. Then, in an instance of poor timing for the Lee family interests,
one of Mrs. Lee's eruptions appeared in the press. She intended getting Arlington back, the *Philadelphia Press* reported, even if she "is obliged to live in the
black quarters." Other newspapers noted that she had been lobbying President
Johnson for the return of Arlington.[53] "But among other obstacles she will
probably encounter is the fact that 12,000 Union soldiers have been buried
upon its soil," the Philadelphia paper warned that winter. "Sixty brave officers
sleep their last sleep in the grounds which surround the family mansion . . . It
is of course impossible that the nation can surrender the graves of so many of
its defenders to the leader of armies they volunteered to oppose."[54] One sentence
in this news item—the one referring to brave officers—was underlined in the
heavy blue pencil Meigs often used for annotating records, and the clipping
placed in the quartermaster's files.[55]

Meigs, the consummate bureaucrat, had outmaneuvered Lee, the consummate strategist, for possession of the high ground at Arlington. To ensure that he kept it, Meigs took the offensive as the winter of 1866 began, urging Edwin Stanton to make sure the government had sound title to Arlington. "I respectfully recommend that the title be investigated by the legal advisor of the Government and that then if not perfect, steps be taken to make it entirely secure," Meigs wrote. "A portion of this estate has been set aside as a National Military Cemetery and in it a large number of interments have taken place. Inquiries have been made lately of members of Congress by their constituents, the bodies of whose kindred repose in this cemetery, suggesting a fear that the United States may yet restore to the original possessors, the land consecrated by these remains."[56] Meigs would return to this refrain again and again in the years ahead.

For the present, he arranged for reinforcements in the cemetery, where the army of the dead would continue to grow, keeping James Parks and other gravediggers busy at their shovels for months to come. Between December 16 and December 27, 1865, for instance, quartermaster's crews disinterred 297 soldiers from the wartime graveyard at the Augur Hospital in Alexandria and reburied them on the Lee plantation.[57] Other crews made similar forays into the capital, where they cleared temporary cemeteries and transferred the remains to Arlington. Simultaneously, Meigs dispatched Capt. James Moore into the Virginia countryside to locate and rebury tens of thousands of Union soldiers from battlefields within a thirty-mile radius of Washington, from Manassas to the Rappahannock River of Virginia.[58]

Moore's squads would take years to accomplish this gruesome assignment, given the rushed nature of wartime burials and the chaotic state of the battlefields. Conditions at Spotsylvania and the Wilderness were typical. "Hundreds of graves on these battlefields are without any marks whatever to distinguish them," Moore reported, "and so covered with foliage that the visitor will be unable to find the last resting place of those who have fallen until the rains and snows of winter wash from the surface the light covering of earth and expose their remains." To further confuse matters, Union skeletons were mingled in trenches with Confederate bones; skulls and femurs were disembodied and scattered; burial records were often nonexistent. Little wonder that few of the dead could be identified: of 5,350 Union fatalities Moore's crews uncovered at Spotsylvania and the Wilderness, only 1,500 could be named. Most of these unknowns would be reburied in new battlefield cemeteries close to where they had fallen, but more than 2,000 would be packed up and returned to Arlington, where Meigs had reserved a place of honor for them.[59]

There was no way to make sense of the unspeakable losses the Civil War inflicted, but it was possible in the aftermath to impose some semblance of order—and a degree of solace—by accounting for the loyal soldiers and sailors lost in the recent tragedy and by giving each a decent burial. Who were they? Where had they fallen? How could friends and loved ones find their graves? Meigs mobilized the peacetime army to answer these questions, beginning at Arlington. There the first phase of the restoration process took place, beginning a five-year program to honor hundreds of thousands of Union dead by mustering them in new national cemeteries across the nation.[60]

Until Lee's surrender at Appomattox, Meigs had been preoccupied with winning the war—which for him meant supplying troops with food, weapons, boots, mules, and other essentials. Now that it was over, Meigs called in burial reports from quartermasters throughout country, tallied them up, and discovered documentation for only 101,736 burials—about a third of the 341,670 estimated Union war deaths. Faced with this deficit, Meigs renewed his order in October 1865. Special recovery crews from the quartermaster's department, headed by Capt. James Moore in the east and by Col. Edmund B. Whitman in the west, began to comb through old battlefields in Virginia, Maryland, and Pennsylvania, in Tennessee and Kentucky, down through the Mississippi valley, across Georgia, and into crowded graveyards of infamous Confederate prison camps at Andersonville, South Carolina, and Salisbury, North Carolina. Traveling with clerks, letterers, painters, and lumber for new headboards, the teams gradually converted temporary graveyards into permanent national cemeteries, scattered from Maryland to Texas. There were seventy-four in existence when the reburial program finally ended in 1870.[61]

By this point, the campaign to recover the dead had consumed more time than the war itself.[62] Costing $4 million, the program proved to be a lavish mission, but the results exceeded expectations, accounting for 315,555 of the total 341,670 Union fatalities. The remaining casualties were thought to be lost in private cemeteries or obscure battlefield plots Meigs's scouts had been unable to penetrate.[63] "Such a consecration of a nation's power and resources to a *sentiment*, the world has never witnessed," said Quartermaster Edmund Whitman, summarizing the unprecedented care which the United States devoted to those who never returned from the war.[64]

While the recovery program went forward, Meigs kept his officers busy collecting field reports for a comprehensive Roll of Honor, which attempted to list the name, rank, unit, and final burial site for each serviceman killed in the conflict. When the last names were printed in 1872, the Roll of Honor ran to twenty-seven paperback volumes, eagerly snapped up by friends and family who had lost loved ones in the war. This printed series, although peppered with misspelled names, duplication, and gaping omissions, remains one of the most complete records of Union burials, and a tribute to Meigs's diligence. Publishing such a roster at government expense was the least a grateful nation could do for grieving relatives, Meigs thought. "All care for the dead is for the sake of the living," he wrote.[65] "I do not believe that those who visit the graves of their relatives would have any satisfaction in finding them ticketed or numbered like London policemen or convicts . . . But if he finds his . . . ancestor's name and position in full therein inscribed he will be satisfied that a grateful country had done due honor to the solider."[66]

Decades after the war, government clerks were still trying to assess its human cost by collecting hospital records, muster rolls, casualty lists, and other official documents in a Washington office, where information about each Union veteran was distilled on an individual index card. Army scriveners were poring over these cards upstairs at Ford's Theatre in 1893 when the accumulated weight of people and paper brought two floors crashing down in a cloud of dust, adding another twenty-one casualties to those killed by the Civil War, according to historian Drew Gilpin Faust.[67] At least five of the victims, who had survived the shot and shell of battle only to be dispatched by the accident at Ford's, were buried with honors at Arlington that summer.[68]

When General Meigs finally received word, on September 21, 1866, that recovery crews had gathered in the last of the unknowns from Manassas and other nearby battlefields, he asked that a large shipment of them be sent to Arlington for reburial. He set laborers to work excavating a huge pit just to the southwest of Mrs. Lee's garden. Twenty feet deep and twenty around, it was to be a mass grave, which the quartermaster intended as Arlington's first memorial to unknown soldiers.[69]

A reporter came to witness the mass burial. "A more terrible spectacle can hardly be conceived than is to be seen within a dozen rods of the Arlington mansion," the Washington *National Intelligencer* reported. "Down into this gloomy receptacle are cast the bones of such soldiers as perished on the field and either were not buried at all or were so covered up as to have their bones mingle indiscriminately together. At the time we looked into this gloomy cavern, a literal Golgotha, there were piled together, skulls in one division, legs in another, arms in another, and ribs in another, what were estimated as the bones of two thousand human beings."[70]

Meigs put the number at 2,111. When the burials were done that September, workers sealed the vault and Meigs designed a stone sarcophagus to cover it. He included an inscription, which was carved into the face of the monument:

Beneath this stone repose the bones of two thousand one hundred and eleven unknown soldiers, gathered after the war from the fields of Bull Run, and the route to the Rappahannock. Their remains could not be identified, but their names and deaths are recorded in the archives of their country; and its grateful citizens honor them as of their noble army of martyrs. May they rest in peace!

—September, A.D. 1866.[71]

The solemn gray memorial, a boxy structure surmounted by a quartet of Rodman guns and a crown of round shot, launched Arlington's long tradition of honoring unknown soldiers, a military ritual that would be refined with each new war.[72] By his placement of this monument, Meigs was erecting another barrier to the Lees' return. Other motives—including a sense of duty and a particular passion for design—also may have inspired his gesture, typical of much that the quartermaster initiated on the Lee estate.

The abstract concept of honor found physical expression in these busy postwar years, in which Meigs gave vent to his aesthetic urges at Arlington. This was nothing new for the quartermaster, who was fascinated by design and architecture. Like Lee, he had joined the elite engineer corps after West Point, but unlike Lee, Meigs continued to design and build things, putting his stamp—and quite often his name—on prominent public structures all over the capital. He supervised designs for the National Museum on the mall, the multiturreted red brick edifice now known as the Arts and Industries Building of the Smithsonian Institution; for the Cabin John Bridge, the world's largest masonry span when completed in the 1860s; and for the Washington Aqueduct, which conveyed fresh water to the capital before and after the war. Meigs also supervised the expansion of the Capitol building in 1853, with its new dome and statue of Freedom, a project jointly commissioned by Meigs and a Mississippi senator named Jefferson Davis. Perhaps his best-known design was the Old Pension Building, now the National Building Museum, with its grand atrium, its frieze of Union soldiers marching off to war, and its fifteen million bricks; this made it the world's largest brick building when completed in 1887, earning it the derisive nickname "Meigs's Old Red Barn." After Gen. Philip Sheridan toured the sprawling building with its proud designer, Sheridan could find only one fault: "It is fireproof," he joked to his old friend.[73]

If such criticism discouraged Meigs, he did not show it. After the war, he turned a creative eye upon Arlington, where the rolling hills and grand views offered an irresistible canvas for his artistic impulses. Before many others, Meigs viewed Arlington as an important element of Washington's future landscape design.[74] In 1870 he even consulted Frederick Law Olmsted Sr., the country's preeminent landscape architect, about the look of Arlington. Olmsted counseled restraint. Arlington, he said, should be "studiously simple . . . to establish permanent dignity and tranquility" and to guard against "ambitious efforts of landscape gardeners."[75]

Meigs largely ignored this advice. His own sense of design was rooted in Victorian tradition and enhanced by the flourishes of the Gilded Age, which caused Arlington's austere hills to sprout with new ornamented monuments, layer-cake mausoleums, hefty stone markers, granite urns, and any number of obelisks. Not all of these were placed there by Meigs, but they were the reflection of an exuberant time when bigger meant better—before official standards constrained the size or taste of markers in the cemetery. If his family could afford it, a lowly lieutenant's tombstone could overshadow and outweigh a colonel's marker in the next row. Several stone angels materialized around the Lee mansion, one brandishing a trumpet; another, an anchor; another, a spray of roses. Officers had their military exploits chiseled into the lids of their crypts; one soldier had accomplished so much and was so cramped for space that he was forced to end his own epitaph with an anticlimactic "etc." Most idiosyncratic was the marker chosen by Major Gen. Wallace F. Randolph, an artillery officer who had a twelve-hundred-pound Napoleon cannon hauled to Arlington to indicate his resting place. Such eccentricities were tolerated at Arlington until the twentieth century, when new regulations were finally imposed—to preserve space as well as aesthetic standards.[76]

When General Meigs finished his monument to the Unknown Civil War Dead, he focused on other embellishments at Arlington, where he raised the Temple of Fame to George Washington and famous Civil War generals; established a wisteria-draped amphitheater large enough to accommodate five thousand people; designed the Sylvan Hall, composed of living maples laid out in the pattern of a cathedral nave; and erected a massive red arch at the cemetery's entrance. The arch honored one of the war's least effective—but most popular—generals, George B. McClellan. Like much of what Meigs built, the McClellan Arch was ornate in the Victorian style, with flourishes of gold leaf and effusions of patriotic poetry carved into the gate:

ON FAME'S ETERNAL CAMPING GROUND THEIR SILENT TENTS ARE SPREAD AND GLORY GUARDS WITH SOLEMN ROUND THE BIVOUAC OF THE DEAD

This poem, thought to be one of Meigs's favorites, was rendered in bold block letters, as was the name MCCLELLAN, which strides across the gate's massive lintel. Meigs had his own surname chiseled into a column by the arch—it is one of the first things one sees upon entering the cemetery.

Meigs's feelings for Arlington grew more proprietary with the years. He sketched his own design for the amphitheater's rostrum, chose new plantings for the mansion's borders (*Caladium esculentum* and canna), and even dictated the formula for plastering the cracked columns on Lee's house (one part Portland cement, two parts "clear, sharp sand"). The columns, he wrote, "should be cemented to resemble those of the Parthenon, which is the accepted canon of Grecian Ionic order."[77] Nothing escaped the quartermaster's notice. When the grapevines languished around one building, he urged gardeners to enrich the soil with a mixture of soup skimmings and crushed bones. The final ingredient was mentioned without a hint of irony.[78]

5

A QUESTION OF
OWNERSHIP

ROBERT E. LEE NEVER RETURNED TO ARLINGTON. HE MAY HAVE GLIMPSED it from Alexandria, probably for the last time, in February 1866. "I did not approach Arlington nearer than the railway which leads to the city," he reported to a cousin. "I know only too well how things are there."[1] Lee had come back to Washington reluctantly, summoned to give testimony before a joint congressional committee on Reconstruction.

He tried to avoid reopening old wounds, but when members pressed the general for his views on black enfranchisement, Lee's answer revealed that four years of war had done nothing to change his views about African Americans. "They are an amiable, social race," he said. "They like their ease and comfort, and, I think, look more to the present-time than to the future . . . My own opinion is that, at this time, they cannot vote intelligently, and that giving them the right of suffrage would open the door to a great deal of demagogism, and lead to embarrassments in various ways."[2]

Lee's testimony, disturbing by today's standards, attracted little criticism, except in the *Chicago Tribune*, which excoriated the old general for his slipperiness and recalcitrance. The *Tribune* concluded that "Gen. Lee is either an uncommonly ignorant man or that he is a very costive witness." It continued:

> Congress and the people of the loyal States should exclude the rebels from positions of power until a political party can be created at the South which shall know the definition of treason. Gen. Lee's testimony makes it plain that such a party can only be formed of the colored population. The whites, slave-holders and poor trash alike, are indoctrinated with the belief that rebellion is not a crime but is a virtue in the individual, if the State, which is but the aggregate of individuals, gives its sanction to it. How long, in the ordinary course of things, can a Government exist, when half its territory is controlled by men who believe it is their duty to take up arms against it whenever they see a chance of overthrowing it?[3]

Although Lee tried to steer clear of such controversy on his two-day visit to the capital, he remained mindful of the resentments his presence rekindled. "I am considered now such a monster," he wrote of the Washington visit, "that I hesitate to darken with my shadow the doors of those I love lest I should bring upon them misfortune."[4] The same reticence likely kept him from visiting his old home.[5]

Despite this, Lee still clung to the hope that Arlington might be returned to his family—if not to Mrs. Lee, then to their eldest son, George Washington Custis Lee, designated as Arlington's heir in his grandfather's will.[6] During this and later visits to Washington, Lee quietly huddled with Francis L. Smith, his trusted Alexandria lawyer, to explore the subject of redeeming the estate. Their last known consultation, which produced little hope, came in July 1870. "The prospect does not look promising," Lee reported to Mary after the meeting.[7] The question of Arlington's ownership was still unresolved, along with Robert E. Lee's citizenship, when he died, age sixty-three, at Lexington, on October 12, 1870.[8]

By this time the scars of war were beginning to heal, but not for all of those who had faced Lee in battle. Union authorities barred Confederate mourners from the nation's first official Decoration Day at Arlington on May 30, 1868.

Timed to coincide with the blooming of spring flowers, the celebration was established to honor the nation's war dead. The event, organized by the Grand Army of the Republic, a Union veterans group, had been the brainchild of former Maj. Gen. John A. Logan, an Illinois congressman and radical Republican known for his combativeness and fiery oratory.[9] Decoration Day, he wrote, would be set aside for "cherishing tenderly the memory of our heroic dead, who made their breasts a barricade between our country and its foes . . . We should guard their graves with sacred vigilance."[10]

Hundreds of politicians, spectators, and old warriors answered Logan's summons, crossing the river to Arlington, where the gnarled oaks sprouted new leaves and the hills were thick with new grass for the occasion. The mansion's columns were draped in mourning and bristling with flags. Military bands played hymns, cannons boomed their salutes to the dead, poetry was declaimed especially for the occasion, and patriotic prayers echoed among the graves. ("We come to mourn over a great national calamity," the Rev. C. B. Boynton intoned, "which partially and temporarily rent our Republic asunder, drenched the land with blood, dug it over for graves, and brought the death and shadow upon thousands of homes."[11]) A one-legged general solemnly read Lincoln's Gettysburg Address to the crowd. Another general, James A. Garfield—soon to be elected President Garfield—made a long speech from the portico of Lee's mansion, where the Virginian had paced alone just seven years before; for all that had transpired since, a century might have passed.[12]

"What other spot so fitting for their last resting-place as this, under the shadow of the Capitol saved by their valor?" Garfield asked, invoking the memory of the soldiers and sailors buried around him. "Here, where the grim edge of battle joined; here, where all the hope and fear and agony of their country centered; here let them rest, asleep on the nation's heart, entombed in the nation's love!" Without mentioning Lee by name, Garfield reminded his listeners of the Confederate's leading role in the rebellion: "Seven years ago, this was the home of one who lifted his sword against the life of his country, and who became the great Imperator of the rebellion. The soil beneath our feet was watered by the tears of slaves, in whose hearts the sight of yonder proud Capitol awakened no pride, and inspired no hope . . . But, thanks be to God, this arena of rebellion and slavery is a scene of violence and crime no longer!"[13]

As Garfield spoke, a contingent of children, brought across from the Soldiers' and Sailors' Orphan Asylum in Washington, squirmed in their best Sunday clothes by the mansion's steps. "And here are the children," said Garfield, gesturing toward them, "little children, to whom the war left no father but the Father above. By the most sacred right, theirs is the chief place today. They come with garlands to crown their victor fathers. I will delay the coronation no longer."[14]

At this the war orphans formed lines, marched around Mrs. Lee's garden, and spread blossoms over the graves of officers Brig. Gen. Montgomery C. Meigs had given a place of honor there; then the crowds trailed the children to the Tomb of the Unknown Civil War Dead, which was hung with garlands and flags; then out through the cemetery to decorate all of the graves—except those belonging to several hundred Confederates at Arlington. This ceremony of remembrance, known as Memorial Day since it was declared a national holiday in 1888, has been repeated in all the years since.[15]

Friends and families of the Confederate war dead chafed at the restrictions placed on them at Arlington. They also envied the care and expense their former enemies lavished on the Union dead, while the graves of their own sons and husbands remained neglected in many northern cemeteries. With no government resources for reburial and memorial operations, southerners organized ladies' memorial associations, local volunteer groups that took responsibility for maintaining Confederate graves at home and for recovering thousands from battlefields in the North. In 1871, the Ladies' Hollywood Memorial Association of Richmond won permission to bring Virginia's dead home from Gettysburg, which added almost three thousand new Confederate graves to the Richmond cemetery; in May 1872 the ladies collected the remains of eighty-nine Confederates from Arlington for reburial in Richmond; more than a hundred Rebels from North Carolina were removed from Arlington in October 1883, placed in black caskets, and conveyed through Alexandria, heralded by church bells throughout the city. Returned to Raleigh, they were led through the streets by a military band, honored in state at the rotunda of the capital, and accorded final honors in the Confederate section of the city's Oakwood Cemetery.[16]

With the urgency of the war years receding, there was finally time for making such adjustments at Arlington, which was gradually being transformed from a cemetery of convenience into a shrine for national heroes. Veterans campaigned to have federal regulations relaxed so that all of those who had served in the Civil War, along with their dependents, would be eligible for burial at Arlington and other national cemeteries. Ever conscious of budget constraints, General Meigs opposed the liberalized standards, arguing that legislation of 1862 and 1866 explicitly limited burial privileges to those who had died in battle or in military hospitals. It would be impractical, he reported in 1869, to provide "suitable burial places throughout the country for the many hundreds of thousands of veterans that might avail themselves of such right were it found to exist."[17]

Although this view won support from the War Department, it was stoutly disputed by Gen. William T. Sherman, then general in chief of the Army, who argued that all national cemeteries should be open to all Civil War soldiers, active or retired. "Surely, when practicable these cemeteries should be devoted to the burial of soldiers for all time to come," Sherman wrote. This expansive view eventually won out over Meigs's more restrictive one. Under pressure from the Grand Army of the Republic, Congress voted in March 1873 to extend burial privileges at Arlington and other national cemeteries to all honorably discharged Civil War veterans. They would be buried at no cost, provided with a headstone, "and their graves shall receive the same care and attention as the graves of those already buried," the legislation decreed.[18] In later years, these standards would be broadened to embrace the veterans of all wars, not just those who had served in the Civil War.

Still a work in progress, Arlington was hardly a place of rest in the decades following the war: Confederates were carted away, their remains jumbled and confused with other bones during the transfer; Federal dead and former slaves were imported from nearby battlefields and cemeteries; Union families came from far away to disinter relatives; agents scoured Arlington's markers for the names of long-missing soldiers—not only to ease the suffering of their survivors, but also to secure a percentage of pensions due to war widows.[19]

Veterans lobbied the War Department to have comrades disinterred and moved to more prominent graves at Arlington. One such request came in 1871, when a committee of African American soldiers petitioned the War Department to relocate hundreds of U.S. Colored Troops to the high ground around Lee's mansion—up from the Lower Cemetery, where black soldiers had been buried unceremoniously among the poor white warriors and former slaves.[20]

General Meigs, who still kept a firm grip on developments at the national cemetery, fielded the request and advised against the transfer. "I regret always to move a body once interred in the National Cemetery, believing that the dead, once decently buried, should have rest," Meigs told William W. Belknap, then secretary of war. "As for the disinterment and removal now proposed, I think that there are objections to it in sentiment as well as in the expenses." He continued:

> If the colored people generally prefer to have their comrades, who fought for them, taken up again and scattered among the whites, it can be done . . . I believe that hereafter it will be more grateful to their descendants to be able to visit and point to the collected graves of these persons, than to find them scattered through a large cemetery and intermingled with another race. The records show that there are in Arlington Cemetery 3,757 contrabands or refugees and 343 colored soldiers.[21]

The War Department agreed, and the U.S. Colored Troops stayed in the Lower Cemetery, a short distance from the slaves and freedmen who had unwittingly pioneered the way to Arlington.[22]

For her part, Mrs. Lee continued to obsess over the loss of her home in the years following General Lee's death. "Her thoughts were ever in the past at Arlington, always Arlington," recalled her youngest daughter, Mildred.[23] Instead of brooding over the situation, Mrs. Lee took action. Within weeks of her husband's death in 1870, she petitioned Congress to form a joint committee, which was asked to examine the federal claim to Arlington, disclose the number of graves there, and "report . . . on what terms a suitable spot for a cemetery can be purchased in the neighborhood, and the probable cost of removing the bodies to the new place of sepulture . . . The committee shall take the statements of Mrs. Lee in order to identify her property with greater certainty, to discover the extent of her losses, and they shall report all facts necessary to a settlement upon the principles of substantial justice."[24]

This resolution, introduced by the gallant but politically tone-deaf Sen. Thomas Clay McCreery, a Kentucky Democrat, provoked a torrent of protest in the Republican-dominated Senate. "That resolution is . . . repugnant to my notions of justice," boomed Sen. George Franklin Edmunds, a Vermont Republican. Despite this warning shot, McCreery not only plunged ahead with Mrs. Lee's petition but also took occasion to eulogize the Confederate general, comparing him to the military giants of the Old World—the Warwicks, the Marlboroughs, and the Wellingtons. "But who among them all had more genius and less ostentation than General Lee?" McCreery asked his stunned colleagues, several of whom had worn the Union blue. "Was he not a hero? Was he not a Christian? Was he not a gentleman? The widowed partner of his bosom still lives and in her behalf I implore your justice. I do not ask for anything else." [25]

But the Kentuckian asked for a great deal more—far more, indeed, than the Senate was prepared to consider. "Now what is the character of this proposition?" asked Sen. Waitman Thomas Willey, a Republican from West Virginia. "It is that the Congress of the United States shall deliberately inquire whether the remains of the sacred dead should not be disturbed in their repose and scattered we know not where. Is there anything more insulting to the sense of the country and to the sense of the Senate?" [26]

For more than an hour, colleagues answered Willey's question in the negative. Sen. Charles Sumner, Republican of Massachusetts, recalled that he had been present at the birth of Arlington National Cemetery in 1864, when the late Edwin M. Stanton had signed orders establishing the burial ground. [27] It had been Stanton's express intention, Sumner declared, to put the property beyond the Lee family's reach. "He said he meant to bury those dead there in perpetual guard over that ground," Sumner said, "so that no person of the family of Lee should ever dare to come upon it unless to encounter the ghosts of those patriots. It was in that spirit that that ground was set apart. Now, as I understand, it is proposed to take up those remains and to give over the ground to the family of the traitor." [28]

Sen. James Warren Nye, a Nevada Republican who had been particularly close to President Lincoln, described Mrs. Lee's petition as "an insult to all the dead who fell in the mighty struggle for the Union . . . Disturb these dead, and for what? To make room for a traitor's widow." [29]

A battered McCreery tried to withdraw his resolution—to no avail. His opponents insisted on a vote, and the Senate rejected the petition, fifty-four to four. In the process, the debate helped to elevate Arlington's status: from a potter's field created in the heat and desperation of wartime, the cemetery was becoming something grand, a ground hallowed in the national imagination, symbol of sacrifice and honor. Senators wanted the place preserved for "the sacred dead," "the patriot dead," "the heroic dead," home of "martyrs" and "patriotic graves."[30] Nobody was going to yield that piece of ground without a fight. Meigs's preemptive occupation of Arlington was working.

The old plantation the Lees had known became less recognizable with each passing year. Carved up for various uses during the war, Arlington remained so after it, with the four hundred–acre Freedman's Village and government farms sprawling through the bottomlands, a semicircle of forts guarding heights to the north and west, and, of course, the two hundred–acre cemetery dominating the plantation's heart, where the old forest disappeared and graves took its place.[31] Although the number of troops at Arlington declined in the postwar years, a strong contingent of soldiers stayed on at Fort Whipple; one of six Civil War forts at Arlington, Whipple was eventually renamed Fort Myer, which covers 256 acres of the original property today.[32]

The cemetery continued to grow, with more than sixteen thousand graves in place by 1870. Weeds moved in, the mansion leaked, and burial mounds sagged as coffins decayed. Wooden headboards rotted and fell away. The Grand Army of the Republic, which had become a powerful voice for veterans, complained about Arlington's slovenly appearance, and the quartermaster's department responded, refilling slumped grave plots, buying burros to pull new mowing machines, tidying paths among the tombs, and patching up the old house, which would continue to spring leaks for years to come.[33]

By the mid-1870s, the first white marble headstones began to appear at Arlington, where they replaced the wooden grave markers from the war years. The old wooden headboards had been cheap, costing about $1.25 to $1.50 each, but they had to be painted regularly and lasted no more than five years. With his usual attention to detail, Meigs calculated that it would cost $1 million a decade to replace the wooden headboards at Arlington and other national cemeteries. He suggested a solution: outfitting each tomb with new tablets made from galvanized iron, at a cost of about two dollars each; they would last for decades instead of years, saving replacement and maintenance expenses.[34]

"One of these will be placed at the foot of every grave and will remain when the wooden headboards decay and perish," Meigs proposed. Several hundred of the iron markers were produced at the Rock Island Arsenal in Illinois and set up in various national cemeteries, but they proved to be unsightly and difficult to read, and they won little praise from anyone but the frugal Meigs, who blocked the adoption of costly marble or granite replacements for several years.[35]

"I am still of the opinion that the best monument for this purpose yet contrived is the small rectangular block of cast iron, galvanized to protect it from rust," Meigs wrote in his annual report of 1868. "It is not costly, it is easily transported, is not an object of plunder. With wages of stone cutters at $5 a day, the cost of 320,000 headstones properly lettered would be a very great charge upon the treasury."[36]

Even as the old wooden headboards decayed and fell away, Meigs held out for his metal markers until 1873, when pressure from the Grand Army of the Republic prompted Congress to appropriate $1 million for a nationwide headstone replacement program. The legislation called for "durable stone of such design and weight as shall keep them in place when set." It was left to Secretary of War William W. Belknap to develop a design, which was soon announced. The new tombstones would be fashioned from granite or white marble, cut four inches thick, ten inches wide, and a yard long; markers in northern latitudes were made taller by six inches to withstand frost; each tombstone, slightly rounded on top, displayed an incised shield with a grave number, the name of the deceased, his rank, and his home state. Since the first of these markers appeared at Arlington, few modifications have been made to their simple, elegant design. Belknap also decreed a design for the individual tombstones of unknown soldiers, sailors, and marines, who received granite or marble blocks six inches square, two feet six inches tall, and planted so that six inches of stone appeared above ground; each would be inscribed with a number keyed to the cemetery's registry. By late in 1873, the quartermaster had arranged contracts for the first of Arlington's new headstones, which ground crews began planting with the spring of 1874. The headstone replacement program, like the reburial campaign before it, made a vital point—that Union servicemen had lived and died in a noble cause, which earned them a place of honor in the nation's cemeteries.[37]

The same was not true for the freedmen, slaves, and Confederates who remained segregated at Arlington. There was no provision for replacing their grave markers in the legislation of 1873, which was construed to apply only to the Union dead. Meanwhile, the Lower Cemetery suffered from neglect: the grass ran rampant, graves collapsed, and so many headboards rotted that the cemetery superintendent suggested in 1877 that they be tossed out entirely, without replacement. Relatives could find loved ones from records in the cemetery office, said James Gall Jr. "The grounds would be much improved in appearance and the cost of maintaining them materially reduced," he told superiors. His idea was overruled by the War Department, but it would take several years before Arlington's freedmen, slaves, and Confederates received their own permanent headstones, which were thinner and less substantial than those in the main cemetery.[38]

Just downriver on the plantation, a thousand former slaves were still living in Freedman's Village after the war, making their temporary refuge into a permanent community. Many had no other place to go. Although barred from owning houses at Arlington during the war years, many managed to buy them afterward; many rented plots of five and ten acres for a nominal fee. A platoon of thirty soldiers from the 107th Regiment of the U.S. Colored Troops kept order in the village, while preventing outsiders from harassing residents.[39] Former slaves such as James Parks continued to live and work at the cemetery, where he would prepare the ground for the famous and the obscure for decades to come.[40] Other freedmen worked as cemetery gardeners, laborers, and teamsters. Many grew their own produce for markets in the capital, as they had done in plantation days.[41]

One prominent black family even managed to peel off a 17 1/2-acre parcel from the Lee estate as soon as Union victory was ensured. In a case that got a good deal of attention in its day, William Syphax, an Arlington native and a messenger for the Department of the Interior, petitioned President Andrew Johnson for title to the land. In his appeal, dated May 11, 1865, Syphax argued that Arlington's first master, George Washington Parke Custis, had given the land to his mother, a former slave named Maria Syphax, at the same time that he freed her.

"In the year 1826, the late Mr. G. W. P. Custis manumitted my Mother and her children," William Syphax wrote, "and at his death my father became free by the terms of Mr. C's will. At the time my mother was freed Mr. Custis gave to her, for the use of herself and heirs, a small parcel of land . . . lying on the outer boundary of the Arlington tract, where my parents continue to reside . . . My parents have no written evidence of this gift of land made to them by Mr. Custis, but can establish, by parol evidence, the facts herein alleged."[42]

This narrative evidence proved convincing: Maria Syphax was, in the terms of those times, a mulatto with strong Caucasian features; unlike most other slaves, she had been raised in the Custis mansion, playing with Mary Custis (later Mrs. Robert E. Lee); she had been singled out for preferential treatment by George Washington Custis, who freed her and her children three decades before arranging to free his other slaves. He had given property to no other slaves, and for years had allowed the Syphax family to use their corner of Arlington as if they owned it. Within the Syphax clan, it was understood that Maria had been not only a slave of George Washington Custis—she was also his daughter, from a union with a household servant of Martha Washington's named Airrianna Carter.[43]

It took a year for the Syphax case to work its way through the federal bureaucracy, but the petition was finally granted on June 12, 1866, when President Johnson signed legislation awarding the small Arlington tract to Mrs. Syphax. Newspapers, happy to poke fun at Custis family history, had a field day with the story. "It happens that this colored man (Charles Syphax) is a half-brother to Mrs. General Robert E. Lee, and grandson of George Washington Parke Custis, who was a stepson of George Washington!" reported *Frank Leslie's Illustrated Newspaper*. "That is quite a parentage, is it not? . . . It is also asserted that Mrs. General Lee has, in all, some forty half-brothers of the same sort in and around Washington."[44] Forty was probably an exaggeration, but there were, in fact, more than a few children of mixed race on the Arlington plantation, with many claiming ancestry in the Custis line. "We're all colors, from white to dark brown," said one such descendent. "Nobody's black."[45]

If Mrs. Lee worried about this aspect of family history, she kept her own counsel. Her views on race, like her late husband's, were far from simple. She held a strong prejudice against African Americans, whom she derided at one time or another as lazy, idle, and untrustworthy. They were the "pets" of northern do-gooders, she said.[46] Yet alongside these beliefs, she maintained tender feelings about many of those blacks she knew, exchanging news with former servants who had emigrated to Liberia and inquiring after the fortunes of those remaining at Arlington. Her correspondence with Selina Gray, the former housekeeper who had watched over the mansion since 1861, is particularly affectionate.

Like others who had lived at Arlington, Mrs. Gray knew of Mrs. Lee's attachment to her home and kept her apprised of changes there. "It is a most lovely place now," Selina Gray wrote in 1872, but "so changed you wold hardly know it . . . The whole of it is rented to the freemen. They have little huts all over that beautiful place . . . Your things at the time of the war was taken away by every body." One artifact of old Arlington remained, however: a rosebush Mrs. Lee had planted by her mother's grave in the hills behind the house. Mrs. Gray clipped a bud from the plant and folded it into her letter that autumn, along with this wish: "I trust I may see the day yet when you all will have Arlington."[47]

Mrs. Gray betrayed no hint of bitterness toward her former owner, although she admitted that she "under went a great deal to stay at Arlington as long as I did having so many inferior persons to contend with . . . But I am very happy that I have got a comfortable home of my own now . . . a bout half way to Alexandria. We have 10 acres of land."[48]

Whether the two women met again is unknown, but Mrs. Lee did manage a farewell visit to Arlington, early in June 1873.[49] Accompanied by a friend, she rode up the long hill in an open carriage at eleven A.M. and toured the estate until two P.M., stopping from time to time to take in the scene. She never emerged from her coach, but asked for a drink of water at the Arlington spring; someone brought it to her, along with a handful of flowers. Then she was driven away.[50] "My visit produced one good effect," Mrs. Lee wrote a friend later that week. "The change is so entire I have not the yearning to go back there & shall be more content to resign all my right in it."[51] She died in Lexington five months later. She was sixty-five.

With her death, Mrs. Lee's hopes for Arlington lived on in her eldest son, George Washington Custis Lee, now thrust into the role of family leader. For Custis, who was nothing if not dutiful, regaining the estate was a matter of filial obligation, as well as enlightened self-interest: He had no inheritance beyond the Arlington property, now encumbered by thousands of graves, a crumbling manor house, a military outpost, a refugee village, and what seemed to be an unshakable federal claim of ownership.

Diligent, handsome, coolheaded, and exceedingly reserved, Custis was the image of his father, whom he had been content to follow from his earliest days.[52] Trailing Robert E. Lee to West Point, Custis graduated first in the class of 1854 (while his father was superintendent); entered the engineer corps (as his father had done); resigned his commission at the outbreak of the Civil War (after his father's example); and followed his father to Richmond in 1861, when both joined Confederate service. Assigned as a military aide to Jefferson Davis, Custis yearned for a battlefield appointment but endured the war years without one, doing what was expected of him and rising to the rank of major general. In addition to his staff duties, Custis served as the family's acting patriarch in his father's absence, shipping blankets, clothing, bridles, and camping equipment to the general; keeping track of Mrs. Lee and his four sisters when fighting threatened to maroon them; dispensing funds to relatives; writing checks for his father's rent on the Richmond house; consulting lawyers and business associates when the general was unable to do so; and helping to settle the confused estate of George Washington Custis as the war crashed around the Confederate capital.[53]

When the fighting was over, Custis followed his father in peace, moving to Lexington, Virginia, with his parents in 1865. There, age thirty-three, he was appointed professor of civil and military engineering at the Virginia Military Institute. When the elder Lee died in 1870, Custis moved across town to replace him as president of Washington and Lee College, where he remained for twenty-seven years.[54]

Through it all Custis suppressed his own ambition, maintained a terse correspondence with family, veterans, and college associates, and disappeared for weeks at a time, when it was said that he was suffering from arthritis, boils, dysentery, typhoid fever, and other ailments; it was rumored that these absences might have been caused by drinking. More likely Custis was suffering from depression, which began to haunt him at West Point and dogged him for years afterward.[55] The intensely private Custis remained a lifelong bachelor. Often housebound in his later years, he left few clues about the man behind the stiff, soldierly form glimpsed in family photographs and official correspondence.

Custis resumed the campaign for Arlington within months of his mother's funeral, returning to Congress with a new petition. This time the appeal went forward without Mrs. Lee's inflammatory suggestion that Arlington be cleared of graves. Instead, he asked for an admission that the property had been taken unlawfully, and requested just compensation for it. No sum was specified in his request of April 6, 1874, but he offered to convey Arlington's title to the United States in exchange for a settlement.[56]

His closely argued petition, which bristled with judicial precedents and ran to six thousand words, strongly suggests that he was still getting advice from Francis L. Smith, the family lawyer who had previously counseled Robert E. Lee on the subject of Arlington. The document asserted that the federal government had designed its 1864 tax auction to grab the Lee estate for the bargain price of $26,800. At the time the wartime tax was levied on Arlington, Custis asserted, his mother had been "absent from her home and with a line of flagrant war separating her from it." Although she had dispatched an agent to pay the tax, federal commissioners had refused her money. This rejection, Custis now claimed, citing recent Supreme Court rulings, invalidated any government title to Arlington: Mrs. Lee's good-faith *attempt* to pay the tax was the same as if she *had* paid it.[57]

"Your petitioner has been deprived of his property without due process of law, and not only without just compensation, but without *any* compensation whatsoever," Lee argued in his Senate appeal. Lee acknowledged the realities at Arlington: "As Congress has devoted it to the purpose of a national cemetery, and naturally desires to preserve in their graves, under the guard of the Federal authority, the remains of those who lost their lives in the service of their country, your petitioner is willing to avoid litigation, by the release of his title to the estate upon the payment of a just compensation."[58]

Referred to the Judiciary Committee, Lee's proposal languished there for months. Congress remained sharply divided along regional lines, and Montgomery Meigs was still very much in charge as quartermaster. Spurred by Lee's Senate initiative, Meigs urged the secretary of war to make sure that the government's title stood up to scrutiny. "The Adjutant General can probably report more fully as I have understood that under instructions of the late E. M. Stanton, then secretary of war, he took some measures to obtain perfect record of the title," Meigs wrote in January 1875. "The Cemetery should not pass out of possession of the country."[59] Meigs still fretted about Senate Bill 661 months later, worried that it might eke through Congress and "interfere with the United States' tenure of this National Cemetery—a result to be avoided by all just means."[60] He need not have worried. Lee's petition died quietly in committee, attended by no debate and scant notice. He retreated to Lexington to fume about the occult ways of Capitol Hill—"not a pleasant place for me to go," he confided to a friend.[61]

Custis Lee might have given up then and there if not for signs that the hard feelings between North and South were beginning to thaw. The War Department, yielding to an appeal from Confederate veterans, eased its restrictions on their participation in Decoration Day at Arlington.[62] The department also gave permission to southern memorial associations to provide new headstones for several hundred Rebels remaining at the national cemetery.[63]

By the mid-1870s, it was also clear that a decade of Reconstruction—a serious impediment to North-South reconciliation—was on the verge of collapsing from a combination of southern obstinacy and northern indifference. Throughout the old Confederacy, the hard-won gains of African Americans were in tatters. Although national troops had been dispatched to enforce voting rights and to protect black citizens from violence, the deployments were scarcely sufficient for the mission. More than three thousand blacks and their white supporters were killed by the Ku Klux Klan and other terrorists between 1866 and 1876. In one such incident, on April 13, 1873, a heavily armed white gang, led by former Confederate officers, stormed the courthouse in Colfax, Louisiana, and killed more than sixty black men deputized to protect local officials. Although three of the vigilantes were eventually brought to trial and found guilty in federal court, their conviction was overturned by the Supreme Court in 1875. They were never punished. By this time federal troops had been withdrawn from most southern states, where black citizens would continue to be intimidated, prevented from voting, and routed from office into the early twentieth century. This happened because the impetus for reconciliation of North and South proved greater than the commitment to full citizenship for black Americans.

With few exceptions, southern whites resented the years of federal rule and made their voices heard. They helped to sway the tightly contested presidential election of 1876, in which Rutherford B. Hayes of Ohio, a Union general wounded in the war, promised to reunify North and South. He pledged to appoint a southerner to his cabinet and promised to withdraw federal troops from South Carolina and Louisiana. When the disputed presidential election was thrown into Congress in that centennial year, an electoral commission was appointed to resolve the matter. Hayes won the White House by a single electoral vote, in large part because of his conciliatory gestures toward the South.[64] It was not known at the time, but Hayes privately sympathized with the Lees. Having visited Arlington in 1866, when he was a congressman and the cemetery was new, Hayes sensed the enormity of the family's loss. "Lee—his is the severest punishment of any Rebel," Hayes confided to his wife in May of that year. "Expelled from such a paradise, and it made a graveyard for twelve thousand Rebel and loyal dead!"[65]

Sworn in as president in March 1877, Hayes hardly had time to unpack his bags before Custis Lee revived the campaign for Arlington. This time he took the battle to the circuit court of Alexandria, Virginia. In the three years since his fruitless appeal for a congressional solution, Lee had hardened his legal position: Instead of compensation for Arlington, he now asserted his ownership of the property and asked the court to evict all trespassers who had occupied it as a result of the 1864 tax auction. These he named as defendants: Frederick Kaufman, superintendent of the cemetery; Capt. Richard P. Strong, the Army officer in charge of Fort Whipple; and hundreds of freedmen still living on the old plantation. Since Lee's suit of ejectment was filed in Alexandria, where the family had deep roots and could expect congenial treatment, the federal government moved swiftly to have the case shifted to federal court. On a writ of certiorari from Charles Devens, the U.S. attorney general, the Arlington suit was removed to the U.S. Circuit Court for the Eastern District of Virginia in July 1877, where Judge Robert W. Hughes, a lawyer and newspaper editor appointed to the bench by President Grant, took over the case.[66]

Devens, a thrice-wounded Union officer and national commander of the Grand Army of the Republic, filed a motion to dismiss Lee's suit. His argument: the government had lawfully acquired Arlington by an act of Congress and presidential order, had held the estate for more than ten years, and was using it "as public property of the United States . . . in the exercise of their sovereign and constitutional powers, as a military station, and as a national cemetery." These uses had been clearly set out in the certificate of sale, Devens argued, and the court had no jurisdiction to consider Lee's case.[67]

Months of legal maneuvering ensued, with briefs flying, hearings scheduled, precedents cited. Judge Hughes finally rendered an opinion in March

1878. The case would go forward, he ruled. "The right of every citizen to a judicial determination of a controversy affecting his liberty or property . . . will not be denied at this day in this country," he wrote.

> The courts are open to the humblest citizen, and there is no personage known to our laws, however exalted in station, who by mere suggestion to a court can close its doors against him . . . It is a cardinal tenet of the Constitution that the judiciary are an independent branch of government, not to be controlled in its dispensation of justice by interference from other departments, and not only empowered but bound to administer the right without fear, favor, or affection.[68]

Hughes ordered a jury trial. Lee's suit, argued by Francis L. Smith and a team of lawyers, turned upon the legality of the 1864 tax sale—exactly the argument Custis Lee had put to the Senate in 1874. After a six-day trial, the jury held for Lee on January 30, 1879. By requiring the "insurrectionary tax" to be paid in person and by refusing payment from Mrs. Lee's agent, the government had deprived Custis Lee of his property without due process of law. "The impolicy of such a provision of law is as obvious to me as its unconstitutionality," Hughes wrote. He explained:

> Its evil would be liable to fall not only upon disloyal but upon the most loyal citizens. A severe illness lasting only ninety or a hundred days, would subject the owner of land to the irreclaimable loss of its possession . . . It might happen by accident that government, desiring a piece of land belonging to a loyal citizen engaged in its military service, might in time of war order his command to a distant and protracted service, rendering it impossible for him to "appear in person before the tax commissioners . . ." and thereby bring on a sale of it for taxes, at which sale it would itself have the power to obtain the land irreclaimably. The familiar expedient employed by King David toward Uriah would here be repeated.[69]

The government appealed Hughes's decision to the Supreme Court, which ruled for Lee again. On December 4, 1882, Associate Justice Samuel Freeman Miller, a Kentucky native appointed by President Lincoln, wrote for the 5-to-4 majority, holding first, that the U.S. Circuit Court had jurisdiction to try the Arlington case, and second, that the 1864 tax sale had been unconstitutional.[70]

"Can not the courts give remedy when the citizen has been deprived of his property by force, his estate seized and converted to the use of the government without any lawful authority, without any process of law, and without any compensation, because the president has ordered it and his officers are in possession?" Miller asked. "If such be the law of this country, it sanctions a tyranny which has no existence in the monarchies of Europe, nor in any other government which has a just claim to well-regulated liberty and the protection of personal rights."[71]

On the second question, regarding the legality of the 1864 sale, Miller held that the jury had ruled correctly. Mrs. Lee had attempted to pay the federal tax. She had been refused. The sale was therefore invalid, "as if the tax had already been paid or tendered," Miller ruled.[72] "What is that right as established by the verdict of the jury in this case?" Miller asked. "It is the right to possession of the homestead of the plaintiff . . . It is absolutely prohibited, both to the executive and the legislative, to deprive any one of life, liberty, or property without due process of law, or take private property without just compensation."[73]

The Lees had retaken Arlington. This left few options for the federal government—now declared to be trespassing. It could abandon Fort Whipple, roust the residents of Freedman's Village, disinter almost twenty thousand graves, and vacate the property—or it could buy the estate from Custis Lee, if he was willing to sell.

He was. Both sides agreed on a price of one hundred fifty thousand dollars. Congress quickly appropriated the funds.[74] Lee signed papers conveying the title on April 24, 1883, which placed the federal claim to Arlington beyond dispute.[75] The man who formally accepted title to the property was none other than Secretary of War Robert Todd Lincoln, son of the Civil War president so often bedeviled by Custis Lee's father. If the sons of such enemies could bury their differences at Arlington, there might be hope for national healing.[76]

With Arlington's ownership settled, the federal government moved to consolidate its hold on the Lee estate. The army established a permanent presence at

Fort Myer, which was transformed into the nation's premier cavalry facility with the arrival of Maj. Gen. Philip H. Sheridan in 1887. The renowned Civil War cavalryman, newly appointed to command the Army, expanded the stables at Fort Myer, installed fifteen hundred horses there, and pressed them into duty for funerals, parades, and other occasions of high ceremony in the capital.

The neighboring cemetery, originally designed to cover two hundred acres, continued to grow as veterans aged and died, and Arlington—once the last stop for destitute and unknown soldiers—became *the* place for burial. Eminent Union generals, among them George Crook, Philip Kearny, Abner Doubleday, and William Rosecrans, helped pave the way to Arlington's heights, where they competed for prominent burial space around the Lee mansion. By the late 1800s, more than 19,000 servicemen had been laid to rest in the nation's cemetery.

More land was needed for new graves, a development that ultimately doomed Freedman's Village.[77] This ragged community of blacks, still clinging to the bottomlands of Arlington after two decades, had outstayed its welcome on the old estate. Since the onset of war, the federal government and various missionary societies had helped to keep the refugees alive, doling out rations, shelter, clothing, training, spiritual instruction, and jobs for the former slaves. One twenty-nine-year-old government laborer, Jerry Savage, was even outfitted with a wooden leg at the village hospital when he lost his own to frostbite.[78] Another refugee, Comilius Camey, age sixty-five, was feeble, friendless, and homeless when he was found wandering in Washington and sent to Arlington for sanctuary in the postwar years.[79] Other settlers made the most of their new homes at Arlington; some built additions to their houses; still others built new homes by the river. They planted vines and fruit trees, dug wells, erected chicken houses, and welcomed a second and third generation into their families.

"The population appears to be quiet and law-abiding, and free from the vice of drunkenness," an assistant quartermaster reported in the 1880s. He counted 124 dwellings, three shops, two churches, a schoolhouse, and a population of 763. The community gave every evidence of becoming a permanent fixture at Arlington.[80]

But the settlement was never meant to be more than a brief shelter on the road to self-sufficiency. The war was long over by the 1880s, and many of the freedmen's once-trim cottages had fallen into decay—something of an embarrassment for a new capital city striving to be modern. "The village is a picturesque jumble of shanties, few of which are worthy of the name of houses," the *Washington Post* reported in December 1887.[81]

The village did nothing to help African Americans, an unsympathetic visitor wrote after the war. "It has but encouraged his habits of idleness and dependence, and it would seem far better to abandon it as soon as possible, and thus relieve the country of the heavy load of taxation which its support renders necessary."[82]

Just as the federal effort at Reconstruction ran out of steam in the 1870s, compassion for Arlington's freedmen seemed to waver as the hard work of peace continued. The blacks remaining at Arlington were a daily reminder of how little progress had been made. With no other place to go, freedmen begged for work around the cemetery, where they dug graves, drove wagons, set headstones, and earned between $1 and $1.75 per day.[83] They haunted the old estate at all hours, tilling their meager plots and looking decidedly unmilitary—this on a site recently designated as a military reservation encompassing the national cemetery, Fort Myer, and other lands from the original 1,100-acre plantation.[84] Although able-bodied residents worked hard and treasured their family life, some freedmen complained when they were not given jobs around the cemetery[85] and protested to the War Department when they were asked to work ten-hour days.[86]

"We beleave it to be a violation of the Law and, an injustice to the laboring man," an Arlington hand wrote anonymously to the quartermaster in 1869. "Besides very ill convenience some of us have familys in the city and cannot go home after quitting for it is too late in the evening and too early in the morning for to get over hear in time to go to work . . . Hear I will close hoping you will give it ameadate notice."[87] When this appeal landed on his desk, Brig. Gen. J. C. McFerran, a deputy quartermaster, did just that. Fuming that the petitioner had gone around him, the general won permission to fire any laborer who complained again. "I am satisfied we can get men who will gladly and willingly work ten hours per day," McFerran assured his superiors.[88] What became of the protesting workers remains unknown, but it was clear that the War Department, which had protected and cared for the residents of Freedman's Village for so long, was losing patience with them.

Tolerance for the freedmen reached the breaking point in November 1887. The nights were growing chilly in the Arlington hills, and each morning revealed gray smoke coiling from the scattered cottages of Freedman's Village, where shivering residents stoked breakfast fires and struggled to warm their thinly planked homes.

From the Lee mansion where he lived and worked, Arlington Superintendent J. A. Commerford, himself a wounded Union veteran, took in the tableau of puffing chimneys, inspected the wooded hills around his headquarters, and experienced a *Eureka!* moment: Arlington's old trees had been going up in smoke, one log at a time, right under his nose. "For the past year," he reported to the quartermaster, "some of the colored people who live on the reservation have been in the habit of entering the cemetery during the late hours of the night for the purpose of getting wood for fuel . . . It has been suggested that the most effective way of preventing such thefts is to cause the removal of these people from the reservation."[89] Commerford provided no evidence for his accusation, but he probably needed none. Even without substantiation, his argument carried the day.

The War Department needed more land and welcomed any pretext for evicting the residents now considered to be squatters at Arlington. Lt. Col. George B. Dandy, newly appointed as deputy quartermaster, seized Commerford's complaint and bucked it up the line to Brig. Gen. Samuel B. Holabird, who sent it forward to his superiors with an endorsement: "In violation of paragraph #138 Army Regulations, amended by General Order #26, Adjutant General's Office, 1883, civilians are residing upon the Military Reservation, upon which the Arlington National Cemetery and the Military Post at Fort Myer, Va., are located. This occupation has continued many years, and since the title of the land passed to the United States by purchase, May 18, 1883, no steps have been taken for the removal of these occupants, mostly colored people. In consequence of the complaints now made, it would seem to be proper that they [the freedmen] should be ordered to vacate their holdings, giving them sufficient time for moving their property to prevent suffering."[90] Within days, Holabird received permission to eject the freedmen. The eviction orders, issued on December 7, 1887, cited pertinent army regulations: "No civilian will be permitted to reside upon a Military reservation unless he be in the employ of the government . . . no permission will be given any one to cultivate any portion of a Military reservation." The freedmen were given ninety days to gather their possessions and get out.[91]

This announcement, coming as a most untimely Christmas present, produced a predictable wave of consternation among village residents, now facing homelessness at the worst time of year. Some complained to the *Washington*

Post, which reported a general "feeling of uneasiness . . . among the colored people of Freedman's Village occasioned by the order of the Secretary of War."[92] A resident named Thomas Owens, who told a *Post* reporter that he had bought his house at Arlington for fourteen dollars in 1868, still paid the equivalent of thirty dollars a month in free labor at Fort Myer. Lucy Harris, informed of the eviction order, rooted around in her papers and came up with a receipt showing that she had paid the quartermaster fifty dollars for her house on October 31, 1868. Now she wondered "if it were really true that they were going to be turned out of house and home," the *Post* reported. The *New York Herald*, still a voice for beleaguered African Americans, took up their cause, warning that Arlington's "poor, helpless colored men, women, and children shall be driven out of their little homes next February in the bleakest part of the winter— homes in which they have lived undisturbed for nearly a quarter of a century."[93] It was clear that the eviction plans threatened a new controversy over property rights at Arlington.

Facing that prospect, Secretary of War William C. Endicott did what any seasoned bureaucrat would do: he stalled for time without reversing his decision. He tried to soften the blow by letting it be known, through a reporter at the *Alexandria Gazette*, that the freedmen could stay in their homes until warm weather arrived. And he announced that those owning houses would be allowed take them apart and move them.[94]

This gesture did little to mollify the freedmen. "Nearly all of these houses are so constructed, and in such a condition of decay, as to be useless to take down and move away," said John B. Syphax, a respected community leader and the first African American elected to the House of Delegates, Virginia's legislature.[95] Chosen to speak for his neighbors and relatives, Syphax ably outlined their case to the secretary of war. For more than twenty years, he wrote, freedmen had occupied this corner of Arlington, paying rent, buying houses, working hard, and treating the place as home. They were encouraged to do so by a succession of federal authorities. "Agents representing the government fully impressed upon the people the idea that in some way they would come to possess a valid claim to this part of Arlington," Syphax argued. The residents had put down roots, he wrote:

> About nine years ago, Lieut. R. P. Strong, then commanding at Fort Myer, gave
> permission to erect a brick church on the reservation, costing nearly two thousand

dollars, and, here again, they were made to believe that their stay would be indefinitely prolonged; therefore, several houses were built, and the spirit of improvement again revived . . . Many began to plant trees, and make such other improvements as their scanty means would permit . . . Coming from the shades of the past, these people have proven, in their new condition of self reliance, more thrifty, and less vicious than could be reasonably anticipated . . . I know not what may be the purpose of the government, or the pleasure of the Honorable Secretary in the premises, but if it be to take this property wholly for National use, I most respectfully ask that an appropriation be recommended of not less than three hundred and fifty dollars a-piece for each owner of a house . . . Twenty-four years of residence at Arlington, with all the elements involved in this case inspire the hope that full and simple justice will be done to the weakest members of this great Republic.[96]

The lessons of Custis Lee's recent Supreme Court victory had not been lost on John Syphax or his constituents. If they could not prevent the evictions at Arlington, at least they might expect compensation for their property. The War Department took the point. Two days before Christmas 1887, General Holabird ordered his men to survey the village, record any improvements, and assess the value of each holding. He authorized the purchase of land held by "unauthorized citizens or others as squatters or for residence, under the color of any permission or otherwise." Then he ordered that the freedmen's occupation of the village be "made to cease and desist."[97]

The first wave of black residents pulled up stakes in the spring of 1888—most of them with trifling payments for their Arlington property. Lucy Harris received $35 for her house; Martha Smith, a former Custis slave, got $40.34 for hers, along with $3 for the trees and vines she had planted. Her neighbor James Parks, who occupied half of a duplex built in the first days of Freedman's Village, received $13.20 for his home, while his brothers Lawrence and William were paid $63.09 and $78.09, respectively. The unfortunate William Winston, lot 83, got nothing at all. Members of the Mt. Olive Baptist Church were paid $1,040 for their brick building, which provided seed money for the replacement they would soon raise down the road in Alexandria. The War Department's total assessment for the village amounted to $10,936—or $103 per household, far less than the $350 figure John Syphax had proposed. Congress provided $15,000 to cover payments and some moving expenses for displaced villagers. Many years later, in 1900, lawmakers authorized another $75,000 to reimburse freedmen and their heirs for the "contraband" taxes they had been required to pay during and after the war for the support of their impoverished neighbors.[98]

Most freedmen had disappeared from Arlington by the 1890s, with the last holdout departing just as the old century gave way to the new. All that remains of their presence are the timeworn headstones of their friends and relatives in the contraband cemetery: Mary Mack, Citizen; Tuda Simms, Civilian; Anna Ross, Citizen; Elija Hawkins, Civilian; Moses Jackson, Citizen; Child of T. B. Fladroy, Civilian; and hundreds of others who sleep in tidy rows at the far margins of Arlington.

With the freedmen out of the way, the national graveyard had room to grow. It added 142 acres in 1889 and another 56 acres in 1897, bringing the total to just over 400 acres—double the size that General Meigs had envisioned when he first sketched out the boundaries in 1864.

Meigs watched with pride as Arlington made the transition from pauper's ground to field of honor. He instituted decorative improvements, lavished attention on the graveyard's gates and roads, and made sure that old comrades were buried in grand military style. When he was not fussing over designs for Arlington, Meigs put his itchy pencil to work sketching plans for bowling alleys and billiard tables for army posts, where peacetime troops had time on their hands. It was cheaper, Meigs thought, "to amuse soldiers than punish them for faults resulting from ennui and want of interesting employment for leisure hours."[99]

Looking to his own future, Meigs incorporated Arlington into family plans, commandeering a prime corner of the cemetery for himself and his relatives. His wife, Louisa Meigs, was the first to be buried there, in 1879, occupying a hilltop plot alongside Meigs Drive. Here, just to the west of Lee's mansion, where gnarled oaks spread their branches wide to the breezes, Mrs. Meigs was joined by the general's father, numerous in-laws, and four of their children, including Lt. John Rodgers Meigs, their beloved son killed in the Civil War. As quartermaster, Meigs had expressed reluctance to disturb anyone's grave, but he did not hesitate to break this rule where his own relatives were concerned, digging them up from Washington churchyards and transferring them to his corner of Arlington. By the 1880s, the Meigs clan far outnumbered any Lees remaining on the estate.[100]

Even in this moment of triumph, however, the old quartermaster's influence was waning. When an assassin's bullet claimed the life of President James A. Garfield in 1881, Meigs lost a sympathetic executive in the White House and, by extension, his protection in the higher reaches of the War Department. Power passed to Vice President Chester A. Arthur, who lacked his predecessor's wartime experience and showed no particular sympathy for Meigs. The new president ordered the quartermaster's retirement, in part to make room for others long overdue for promotion. Still vigorous at age sixty-five and protesting that he was "not too old to have lost all desire to be useful," Meigs surrendered his army post in 1882—the same year of the Supreme Court's ruling for Custis Lee. These developments must have proven keenly disappointing for Meigs, a diligent officer who had served with distinction for forty-six years and who had so ardently resisted the Lees' claims to Arlington.[101]

Set adrift for almost six months, Meigs eventually found new work, boosted by highly placed friends on Capitol Hill. In August 1882, Congress named him to design and oversee construction of the new Pension Building in Washington, a sprawling nine hundred thousand dollar project that would absorb the general's creative attention for another five years. As was his practice, Meigs left his mark on the new building by incorporating busts of himself, his wife, and his father in the interior cornice work, among the likenesses of American Indians who glared down on visitors far beneath them. When Meigs was not immortalizing himself, he plunged into the capital's thriving scientific community, serving as a regent of the Smithsonian Institution and a member of the National Academy of Sciences. He gathered for regular round-table discussions with the astronomer Simon Newcomb, the artist-naturalist Titian Ramsay Peale, the aviation pioneer Samuel P. Langley, and the Smithsonian secretary Joseph Henry, who used his scientific expertise to concoct a powerful alcoholic punch Meigs particularly enjoyed.[102]

As he grew older, Meigs made frequent visits to Arlington, where his family's graves anchored Section 1, Row 1 of the cemetery. He designed his last monument with typical thoroughness. Resting over his wife's grave, it would be a massive gray boxlike sarcophagus, elevated on a pedestal of brown fieldstone and built on the same imposing scale as his earlier shrine to the unknown soldiers of the Civil War. In words carved into the face of the stone, it would celebrate the

highlights of Meigs's public career: QUARTERMASTER GENERAL, SOLDIER, EN-
GINEER, SCIENTIST, PATRIOT.

All was in readiness in January 1892 when Meigs, seventy-five, died in his
Washington home after a brief bout with the flu. After funeral services at St.
John's Church on Lafayette Square, he made the final journey to Arlington in
high style, accompanied by an Army band and an honor guard of 150 foot soldiers decked out in their best uniforms. He rode away on clouds of praise.
"The Army has rarely possessed an officer who contained within himself so
many valuable attainments, and who was entrusted by the Government with a
greater variety of weighty responsibilities or who has proved himself more
worthy of confidence," read the General Orders from the War Department.[103]
A caisson bearing his flag-draped casket rattled across the river, up the long
slope to Arlington, and across the meadow of tombstones he had so assidu-
ously cultivated. With muffled drums marking time and guidons snapping in
the winter wind, the procession passed Mrs. Lee's garden and came to a halt on
Meigs Drive. There, in a plot that James Parks had just cleared for the general,
the rifles barked their last salute, Taps sounded over the tawny hills again, and
soldiers in blue eased Montgomery Meigs into the ground.[104] His burial instructions were precise: workers were directed to seal his tomb with hydraulic
cement and leave him to await the Resurrection.[105]

With Meigs's death, the old order shifted. Lee and Grant were long gone.
So was Jefferson Davis. So was Gen. John A. Logan, father of Memorial Day.
Gone too were the generals whose names recalled the bloody work of Manassas, Chancellorsville, Gettysburg, and other battles: Hood, Thomas, Hooker,
Jackson, McClellan, Stuart, Sheridan, Burnside, Meade. Even the durable
William T. Sherman had joined the silent ranks by February 1891, barely a
year ahead of Meigs. One of Sherman's pallbearers that winter was Confederate Gen. Joseph E. Johnston, eighty-four, who had stood bareheaded in the
cold at Sherman's funeral in St. Louis out of respect for his old adversary. "If I
were in his place and he standing here in mine," Johnston said, "he would not
put on his hat." Johnston caught cold and died in short order.[106] Such displays
of magnanimity helped soften hard feelings between North and South. But as
the historian Edmund Morris has observed, it took a new war to heal scars
from the old one.[107]

PART II

REUNION

6

"A SPLENDID LITTLE WAR"

THE NEW WAR WAS SPARKED BY THE FIERY EXPLOSION OF THE U.S.S. *MAINE* in Havana harbor on the night of February 15, 1898. More than 260 American sailors, marines, and landsmen were lost in the blast and its aftermath, which came at a delicate moment in Spanish-American relations. The second-class battleship had been summoned to Havana to evacuate Americans if the unrest between Cuban colonists and Spanish authorities roared out of control. The *insurrectos* had been seeking autonomy from Spain for decades, through peaceful protest, armed resistance, and occasional rioting. As strife continued to roil the island in the 1890s, newspapers such as the *New York Journal* of William Randolph Hearst and the *New York World* of Joseph Pulitzer agitated to expel Spain, free the Cubans, and enlarge U.S. interests in the region, just as other imperial powers—among them Britain, Germany, Belgium, France, and Italy—were extending their reach into other parts of the world. The cause of the *Maine's* explosion was unknown but that did not matter to those clamoring for war.[1]

While Navy divers began the grim business of recovering the burned and mutilated bodies from Havana Harbor, President William McKinley remained reluctant to mount an invasion of Cuba. The former Union major, who had lived through the carnage of Antietam and other Civil War actions, counseled restraint until a board of inquiry could establish the cause of the *Maine*'s sinking. Meanwhile, as Hearst and Pulitzer agitated for war and the first *Maine* victims were given temporary burial in Havana's Colon Cemetery, McKinley tried to soothe jingoists in Congress, explored diplomatic initiatives with Spain, and sought to dampen militants within his own administration, where his assistant secretary of the Navy, Theodore Roosevelt, was spoiling to punish Spain for "an act of dirty treachery."[2]

McKinley demurred. "I don't propose to be swept off my feet by the catastrophe," the president told a Senate confidant. "The country can afford to withhold its judgment and not strike an avenging blow until the truth is known."[3]

Just in case, though, the nation prudently cranked up its rusty war machinery, with McKinley hoping it would not be needed. The regular Army, shrunken to a force of less than 30,000 by peacetime, made hasty plans for boosting troop strength and appointing officers, while the navy scoured European ports for surplus ships. Congress approved $50 million for war preparations on March 8, 1898. When the bill was reported to the House of Representatives that day, a Rebel yell pierced the decorum of the chamber and all eyes turned to its source, a wiry little man with a pointed white beard who stood all of five feet two inches in his boots—Rep. Joseph Wheeler, sixty-one, a Democrat representing the Eighth Congressional District of Alabama.[4]

The diminutive congressman, first elected in 1891, was known as "Fighting Joe" Wheeler from his days as a hard-hitting Confederate lieutenant general of cavalry. Ranging from the Mississippi across Georgia and up through the Carolinas, Wheeler joined in more than two hundred engagements, had sixteen horses shot from under him, was wounded three times, and earned the respect of both William T. Sherman, whom he had plagued incessantly, and Robert E. Lee, who placed Wheeler on a par with J. E. B. Stuart as a cavalry officer.[5]

After the war and Reconstruction, Congressman Wheeler worked as hard to reconcile North and South as General Wheeler had labored to thrash his Union enemies.[6] At the mere suggestion of a new conflict, Fighting Joe was one of the first to volunteer for army service. Within a day of the *Maine* explosion, the Alabaman dashed off a letter to President McKinley. "In case of any trouble with Spain," Wheeler wrote, "remember that my tender of services is on file at the War Department." Wheeler also made sure that the Associated Press and other news organizations knew that he was ready to saddle up again.[7]

McKinley, who embraced sectional reconciliation as a goal of his administration, knew that the reformed Confederate's loyalty was genuine.[8] He filed away the congressman's letter until the *Maine* investigation could run its course, which it soon did. On March 25, 1898, messengers arrived at the White House with a report from the board of inquiry. The board's findings proved to be tantalizingly inconclusive: The doomed battleship had touched a mine. This had set off two shipboard magazines, which caused the *Maine* to explode and sink. But the report found no evidence that Spain or its agents had planted the mine or was responsible for the tragedy.[9] Despite this, the nation's fever for war—stoked by sensationalist newspapers, by expansionists on Capitol Hill, and by growing public desire to avenge the *Maine* disaster— could not be chilled. Congress declared war on April 19; McKinley ordered a Cuban blockade on April 22; Spain declared war on April 23; and McKinley summoned Fighting Joe Wheeler to the White House on April 26.[10]

The president offered the veteran cavalryman a commission as major general of volunteers—one of only fifteen positions of that rank. It was an appointment calculated to make other southerners feel welcome in the new war. "General," McKinley told Wheeler, "I have sent for you to ask if you want to go, and if you feel able to go." Wheeler was not only willing but eager to wear the Union blue again.[11] "I replied that, while I was sixty-one years old," he recalled, "I felt as strong and capable as when I was forty, or even much younger, and that I desired very much to have another opportunity to serve my country."[12]

Wheeler went home to pack for the Spanish-American War, while McKinley doled out other key military appointments—including a new set of major general's stars for Fitzhugh Lee, another former Rebel officer and the nephew of the late Robert E. Lee. Fitz Lee was particularly well acquainted with conditions in Cuba, where he had served as U.S. consul general since Grover Cleveland's administration, monitoring the unsettled conditions that had led to war. Indeed, it could be said that Lee was inadvertently responsible for the new conflict—or at least the excuse for it—for it was he who summoned the *Maine* to Cuba to show the colors and to evacuate stranded Americans if need be.[13]

The news that these two prominent Confederates would be fighting under the old flag won almost universal praise. "There is no longer a North or a South in the old sense," the *Indianapolis News* reported. "It is but a memory."[14] The *New York Tribune* commended McKinley's conciliatory gesture: "Even a year ago such appointments . . . would have been almost impossible. A common enemy has removed the last vestige of proscription. The southerner is as anxious to defend the country as the northerner, and some anxiety is expressed in the south lest the war end before the old Confederates have the chance to march under the Stars and Stripes."[15]

No soldier yearned more to do so than Fighting Joe Wheeler. After some quick drilling in Georgia, he disembarked with his troops in Cuba and led almost a thousand men into the first major land action of the Spanish-American War. On June 24, 1898, Wheeler urged his troops through the sweltering jungle from Siboney and into the hills at Las Guasimas, where they were soon engaged in a brisk exchange with well-entrenched Spaniards.[16] The defenders finally gave way to a dogged American assault, prompting the old Confederate to forget where he was: "We've got the damn Yankees on the run!" Wheeler whooped.[17]

Such outbursts of enthusiasm were as music to those serving under Wheeler. Among them was Lt. Col. Theodore Roosevelt of the Rough Riders, who had given up his post in the McKinley administration to organize his famous volunteer regiment; he pronounced his pugnacious little general "a regular game cock."[18] Another officer, watching disparate companies fighting as one in Cuba, noticed how the experience erased regional and racial distinctions: "White regiments, black regiments, Regulars and Rough Riders, representing the young manhood of the North and the South, fought shoulder to shoulder, unmindful of race or color, unmindful of whether commanded by an ex-Confederate or not, and mindful only of their common duty as Americans." The officer who said this was Lt. John J. "Black Jack" Pershing, who had earned his derisive nickname while commanding African Americans of the 10th Cavalry in the Indian Wars. Rejoining the unit in Cuba, Pershing led them into fierce fighting on San Juan Hill and around Santiago. Not only did his Buffalo Soldiers hold their own there—five of them earned the Medal of Honor.[19] Even so, it would take half a century and two more wars to desegregate the armed forces of the United States.[20]

The Spanish-American War ended quickly. Spanish forces withdrew from Cuba on July 17, 1898, ending four centuries of colonial rule and giving the United States a new foothold in the Caribbean. At the same time, American troops seized Puerto Rico with little resistance; Commodore George Dewey routed Spain from the Philippines; Guam was ceded as U.S. territory; and Hawaii was annexed to round out America's holdings in the Pacific. Summing up, John Hay, then U.S. ambassador to Britain, marveled at the ease with which these acquisitions had been snapped up. "It has been a splendid little war," he wrote to his friend Theodore Roosevelt in July 1898, "begun with the highest motives, carried on with magnificent intelligence and spirit, favored by that fortune which loves the brave."[21]

In a matter of months, the United States had established itself as a world power with a new stake in international affairs, a condition that would exact unimagined responsibilities, and a great deal of blood, in the century to come.[22]

Both Hay and Roosevelt might have considered the Spanish-American War considerably less splendid if more of their countrymen had perished in it— but relatively few did. Of more than 375,000 in uniform for the war and its aftermath in the Philippines, 460 died fighting, while 5,200 were killed by malaria, dysentery, typhoid, and yellow fever. In the Philippines, where occupation by U.S. forces precipitated an indigenous insurrection between 1899 and 1901, another 4,300 Americans died. Compared to the enormous slaughter of the Civil War, which claimed some 620,000 lives on both sides, the death toll from the new conflict seemed infinitesimal.

Nonetheless, if nothing else the Civil War had taught that each fatality was a loss to be reckoned, a name to be recorded, a comrade to be buried with appropriate ceremony. This attention to detail grew out of the massive federal effort to recover and reinter almost 300,000 of the Union dead between 1865 and 1870. That program set new standards for diligence and raised public expectations for those who had sacrificed all for the nation.[23]

Few better understood the importance of honoring fallen warriors than President McKinley, who had seen battle firsthand and realized the agonies of losing comrades among the Civil War's thousands of unknowns. In that conflict of long marches, moving fronts, and hurried battlefield burials, months or years had elapsed between the deaths of soldiers and the effort to recover them, a major factor in the extraordinary number of Civil War graves without names on them. To avoid this outcome in the new conflict, McKinley ordered specialized teams to Cuba and Puerto Rico as soon as the fighting ended, so that each battlefield grave could be quickly found, fixed with a marker, and if possible its occupant identified.[24] Less than a week after the guns fell silent on

San Juan Hill, Congress appropriated funds to disinter and repatriate the remains of all Americans who died in the war.[25] This recovery program set a significant precedent for the United States, which for the first time pledged to bring dead servicemen home from overseas instead of burying them on foreign soil if their next of kin requested repatriation.[26]

Brig. Gen. Marshall I. Ludington, the quartermaster who oversaw the global repatriation effort, realized the historic importance of the new policy, "probably the first attempt in history where a country at war with a foreign power has undertaken to disinter the remains of its soldiers . . . and bring them by a long sea voyage to their native land for return to their relatives and friends, or their reinterment in the beautiful cemeteries which have been provided by our government."[27]

To begin the homecoming process, the War Department dispatched D. H. Rhodes, a landscape gardener at Arlington and inspector of national cemeteries, to provide a full accounting of the dead from America's splendid little war. Arriving in Cuba in August 1898, hot on the heels of departing Spaniards, Rhodes slogged over a hundred miles of backwoods trails, and through swamps and abandoned hospital camps, surveying gravesites every day for five weeks. It took some detective work, since most graves were crudely marked with sticks, stones, broken tiles, bits of tin, strips of boxes—whatever was handy at the time of burial. "In many cases," Rhodes said of the burial sites, "these had become covered with vines, weeds, grass, etc., rendering the grave difficult to be found, even when only a few feet distant." Working across the island, Rhodes discovered 654 graves of U.S. soldiers and civilians associated with the war, clearly marked the sites, and kept meticulous notes for each. He managed to identify 141 of the dead on the spot from well-marked graves, interviews with army comrades, uniform insignia, and, in more than a few instances, from ginger ale bottles containing slips of paper identifying the deceased—probably left by burial crews.[28]

"In each case where a grave or trench was found unmarked, or where a temporary marker had become totally obliterated," Rhodes reported, his crews put up "a headboard with the words 'Unknown United States Solider' and the proper grave number, in order to identify and preserve this spot as that of a grave." When Rhodes finished his Cuban mission, he sailed on to Puerto Rico, identified and marked graves there, and returned to Washington in October 1898 to await further orders.[29]

They arrived with the New Year. By early February 1899 Rhodes was bound south again to oversee the return of remains from Cuba and Puerto Rico. Traveling with a team of forty-six undertakers, foremen, and laborers, Rhodes began disinterring warriors from graves he had identified the previous autumn. When the dead had been cleaned, placed in new zinc-lined caskets, and loaded onto army transports for the journey home, Rhodes sailed on to the Philippines, where he would direct disinterment operations for another two years.[30]

When the repatriation program ended a few years later, the vast majority of those who died in the Spanish-American War were reburied with their identities intact. Only one in seven from the Caribbean theater (13.6 percent) was unidentified—a great improvement over the Civil War record, in which 42.5 percent of all war dead went to their graves without names.[31] Virtually all of those recovered from the Pacific theater from 1899 through 1902 were identified, in part because Rhodes had by hard experience developed proficiency in the melancholy art of exhuming and identifying the dead. In 1901, for instance, when he shipped 1,073 Americans home from the Philippines, only 15 of them were unknowns; for each of these he prepared a careful report, including sketches and maps pinpointing not only the cemeteries from which they had been recovered but also the precise locations of individual graves.[32] Rhodes improvised use of the "burial bottle" to preserve the identity of the dead through disinterments and transfers. His comrades wrote out the name, rank, and organization for each deceased serviceman, corked the paper in a bottle, and wrapped it into a blanket containing the remains to preserve the dead soldier's identity.[33]

In the next war, Rhodes's bottle would be replaced by a simple but revolutionary piece of equipment—the dog tag. Stamped with the name, rank, and serial number of its bearer, the metal tag would speed identification and reduce errors. The inspiration for the dog tag is usually credited to Charles C. Pierce, an Army chaplain who helped recover the dead from the Philippines during the time that Rhodes worked there. The two men, working under separate commands, did not always get along, but by trial and error they developed practices that would improve methods for honoring America's dead.[34]

★　★　★

While Pierce and Rhodes sweltered in tropical morgues, President McKinley began a frantic campaign at home, where he was trying to end the war which he had never much wanted to start. The Treaty of Paris, signed on December 10, 1898, spelled out formal peace terms for Spain and the United States, but the agreement required Senate approval, along with a payment of twenty million dollars for acquisition of the Philippines. Ratification was by no means certain; a formidable coalition of conservative Senate Democrats and isolationist Republicans opposed the measure. To drum up crucial support for the treaty and to express his gratitude to those who had helped win the recent war, McKinley boarded a special train in Washington and headed south for the Peace Jubilee, a victory tour he kicked off in Atlanta on December 14, 1898.[35]

How would this city of long memories, reduced to ashes by Gen. William T. Sherman, receive a president who was not only a Republican but also a former Union major? The answer came roaring up from the Atlanta rail station on that biting cold morning as McKinley's train chugged into view, screeched to a stop, and thousands of citizens cheered their welcome. The cheers exploded into thunder, punctuated by Rebel yells, when the first passenger bounded from the train and the crowd recognized the chipper form of Fighting Joe Wheeler, back from the wars. He would remain at McKinley's side, providing legitimacy for the visiting President throughout his travels in Georgia.[36]

Saluted by cannons and flag-waving children, this incongruous pair—one lugubrious and heavy with dignity, the other fidgeting like a terrier—made its way up the steps of the Georgia state house, where McKinley addressed a joint session of the legislature that afternoon. The president stunned his audience with an unexpected promise: from now on, he pledged, the federal government would take responsibility for the hundreds of neglected Confederate graves in northern states, long an irritant for the family and friends of those who had died in faraway battles, prison camps, or enemy hospitals.[37]

"Every soldier's grave made during our unfortunate Civil War is a tribute to American valor," McKinley told the packed House chamber that day. Frequently interrupted by cheering and applause, he continued:

> And while when those graves were made we differed widely about the future of the government, these differences were long ago settled by the arbitrament of arms—and the time has now come ... when in the spirit of fraternity we should share with you in the care of the graves of Con-

federate soldiers. The cordial feeling now happily existing between North and South prompts this gracious act, and if it needed further justification, it is found in the gallant loyalty to the Union and the flag so conspicuously shown in the year just passed by the sons and grandsons of these heroic dead . . . Sectional feeling no longer holds back the love we feel for each other . . . The old flag again waves over us in peace with new glories.[38]

Here was proof that McKinley's message of reconciliation was authentic, and its effect on those who heard him was electrifying. "When the President referred to the care of the graves of the Confederate soldiers," the *New York Times* reported, "a wild cheer went up from every throat in the . . . Southern audience, a cheer that echoed and reached through the chamber until it was taken up by the crowds outside . . . One Confederate veteran, now a venerable legislator, had passed forward until he was leaning against the Speaker's desk, hanging on every word the President uttered. When the reference was made to the Confederate dead this old man buried his head in his arms and, while cheers rang out, cried like a little child."[39]

The nation was reunited again, at least on the surface—a status that would soon manifest itself on Arlington's green hills, where Confederates from Washington's scattered cemeteries would be gathered in, reburied, and celebrated. In the meantime, President McKinley continued his tour, combining flattery for southern fighting spirit with an appeal for the Treaty of Paris. Only by ratifying the peace accord, he argued, could the nation honor those who had fought in the recent war. His southern audiences listened attentively and repaid McKinley's goodwill. The president's winter charm offensive, combined with strenuous lobbying and some well-aimed promises of patronage, paid off in Washington: On February 6, 1899, the Treaty of Paris squeaked through the Senate on a vote of fifty-seven to twenty-seven, just one more than was needed to seal the peace. Last-minute conversions by Sens. Samuel D. McEnery of Louisiana and John L. McLaurin of South Carolina clinched the deal.[40]

A few weeks later, on April 6, 1899, just as spring began to smooth the scars of winter in the capital, the first wave of dead soldiers from the Spanish-American

War—336 in number—arrived for burial at Arlington, a solemn reminder that even short, agreeable wars required payment in blood.

With government offices shuttered for the afternoon and flags lowered to half-staff throughout the city, the 4th Artillery Band, brushed and buttoned into their best red coats, formed ranks on a high hill at Arlington just southwest of the Lee mansion and launched into the first soothing strains of "Nearer, My God, to Thee," welcoming home the warriors disinterred from Puerto Rico and Cuba over the winter. Two newly opened acres, still fragrant of freshly turned earth, had been laid out in straight trenches to receive the dead, their last stop on a long passage that had begun, for most, in high hopes and excitement the previous spring.[41]

President McKinley led his cabinet and ranking military officers to the graveside at two thirty P.M. that day. They stood bareheaded as thousands of citizens crowded into the cemetery, some of them scrambling into Arlington's trees for a better look at the long, long rows of flag-covered boxes, arranged with military exactness and attended by an escort of cavalry troopers, artillery units, marines, and infantry reservists, all with medals gleaming and uniforms ironed to a knife's edge. Cannons from nearby Fort Myer rumbled tribute every half hour. The parents of an infantryman named John O'Dowd pressed through the multitude, broke into the open, placed a spray of roses on their son's casket, and melted into the crowd again. A military chaplain read the Episcopal service; a Catholic priest, trailed by three acolytes, blessed the raw, red earth; and silence settled over Arlington. It was broken by a booming three-volley artillery salute; Taps quavered over the hills; army comrades crumbled clods of dirt over each new grave; the president and his entourage put on their hats and departed the cemetery. As dusk came down, Arlington's laborers went to work, letting the heavy caskets down for the last time, a task that would take them two or three days to finish.[42]

With minor variations, this ritual would be repeated at Arlington in successive months, which stretched into years, as hundreds of soldiers, sailors, marines, and civilians found their way home from the scattered theaters of the Spanish-American War. A new shipment of the dead arrived in May 1899, another in December of that year, more in 1900, still more in 1912.[43]

President McKinley and all of Washington turned out to greet 150 dead warriors from the wreck of the *Maine*, who arrived from Cuba on December 28, 1899. The capital was blanketed in snow when caissons met the funeral train and set out for Arlington under cavalry escort. The fresh snow muffled the sound of horses' hooves as the *Maine* men were conveyed to a new section of Arlington with a commanding view of the Lee mansion, the frosted pines fringing it, and the broad Potomac beyond, swirling with chunks of ice. Only seventy-four of the new arrivals could be positively identified; the other seventy-six went to their graves as unknowns. All were seen off by comrades and shipmates—a battalion of marines in scarlet coats and spiked hats, cavalry from Fort Myer with winter capes flapping in the wind, sailors from the U.S.S. *Texas*, the *Maine's* sister ship, in thick blue jackets. The *Maine's* old commander, Capt. Charles D. Sigsbee, presided over the ceremonies at Arlington that day, assisted by the ship's chaplain, the Rev. John P. Chidwick, who had plucked many of his shattered and dying shipmates from Havana Harbor just the year before.[44]

"With head bared to the wintry blast, this best-beloved of naval priests read the memorial service of his faith, consigned the dead, blessed the ground, repeated the Lord's Prayer, and concluded with a fervent appeal for the repose of the souls of the departed," the *Washington Post* reported. When Chidwick was done and the last notes of Taps faded, as if on cue a pair of gray-haired women moved deliberately down the line of flag-covered caskets, closely scrutinizing each one for a name. They told a reporter they were looking for their sons. They never found them, and the unnamed women vanished that day, just as their boys had done.[45]

Thirteen years would pass before the rest of the *Maine's* victims could be recovered from the wrecked ship and reunited at Arlington, where they were gathered in the shadow of the vessel's mainmast, salvaged from Havana Harbor. Brought to Washington, raised at Arlington, and recast as a war monument in 1915, the mast became the centerpiece of the U.S.S. *Maine* Memorial. The shrine, designed by architect Nathaniel Wyeth, son of the artist N. C. Wyeth, celebrated the individuals who slept around it, as well as the event that led the United States to war.

President McKinley made good on his promise to assume the care of Confederate graves in the North, which closed the circle in his crusade for reconciliation.[46] Even as the Spanish-American War dead were being repatriated through 1898 and 1899, Confederate veterans explored Civil War cemeteries around Washington to locate the graves of old comrades. They found Rebel tombs slumping, matted with weeds, and marked by rotting headboards, or by the same thin tombstones as those issued to former slaves and civilian employees of the quartermaster's department.[47] Veterans identified 128 Confederate graves at the Soldiers' Home Cemetery in northwest Washington; another 136 were scattered through Arlington. All were teetering in a sad state of neglect— a sore point among those who had worn the gray.[48]

One of these, a Washington-area physician named Samuel Edwin Lewis, asked McKinley to have the Rebels disinterred and removed to a plot at Arlington, where they would form the advance guard of a new Confederate section. Lewis argued that segregating former adversaries within the national cemetery not only would be appropriate but "would doubtless also be gratifying to many good people of the North." McKinley promptly agreed, letting it be known that he would back legislation authorizing the initiative.[49]

With this encouragement, two former Civil War enemies rolled up their sleeves and went to work on the legislation. Brig. Gen. Marcus J. Wright, a Tennessean who had fought for Confederates in the western theater, drafted a bill for the reburial program, while Sen. Joseph R. Hawley, a Connecticut native brevetted major general of Union volunteers, introduced the measure on Capitol Hill.[50] Their bill provided two thousand five hundred dollars for disinterring Confederates in the Washington area and furnishing each with a new pine coffin and a prominent plot at Arlington, hard by recent burials from the Spanish-American War. In the brotherly spirit of those times, this legislation sailed through Congress without objection. President McKinley signed the bill into law on June 6, 1900, and the first interments were made the next year.[51]

Under the new statute, the secretary of war was directed to provide Confederates with "proper headstones" at Arlington, which meant that for the first time they would have marble or granite markers equal to those erected over Union graves. The Rebel tombstones, like the Union ones, would be thirty-six inches tall, ten inches wide, and four inches thick, but unlike the Union markers, which were rounded on top, each Confederate stone came to a point. A popular myth, repeated down through the years, held that Confederate markers had angular tops to discourage Yankees from sitting on them; in truth, the pattern was probably intended to give southerners' tombstones a distinctive look, so that they could be distinguished at a glance. Like the design for Confederate markers, the pattern of burials in the new section was also unique: instead of being arranged in the long, regimented lines characteristic in other parts of Arlington, the Confederate tombstones were planted in concentric circles, forming ever-widening rings around a central point, like ripples on a pond. In this and other ways, the design reflected the South's ongoing struggle to find its proper place in the nation, while standing proudly apart from it.[52]

Once unwelcome at the national cemetery, grizzled southern veterans realized how far they had traveled when they arrived to celebrate Memorial Day at Arlington in 1903. There they walked among the neatly tended graves of more than 400 reburied comrades, marked by gleaming new tombstones and decorated with fresh flowers from the White House, courtesy of none other than Theodore Roosevelt, the nation's new president. Old Confederates reciprocated the gesture, marching over the hills to Mrs. Lee's garden, where they left a floral tribute at the tomb of the Civil War Unknowns, their message spelled out in a display of blossoms: "In the Spirit of Fraternity." The phrase, borrowed from McKinley's Atlanta speech, was heartfelt, but it would take generations to cleanse the last dregs of bitterness from the Civil War.[53]

The old animosity, always simmering just beneath the surface, boiled over again in 1906. The occasion was a funeral at Arlington, where Fighting Joe Wheeler, McKinley's partner in reuniting North and South, was to be buried. Having retired to live with a sister in Brooklyn, Wheeler lost his last battle to pneumonia at age sixty-nine. He was given a hero's send-off in New York, where some sixty thousand spectators braved a cold January rain to bid the little general farewell. They stood six deep and bareheaded along Broadway to watch Wheeler's casket pass by, draped in both Confederate and Union flags and trailed by the black horse, now riderless, that had served him through the Cuban campaign. Among the honorary pallbearers was Gen. Frederick Grant, son of the late president.[54] After services at St. Thomas's Episcopal Church on Fifth Avenue, Wheeler's remains were returned to the caisson, conveyed to Jersey City, and transferred to a train for Washington.[55]

There an honor guard of Spanish-American War veterans was waiting for him. They kept vigil through the night at St. John's Episcopal Church, to be relieved by regular Army sentinels the next day. Men from both wars crowded across Lafayette Square for afternoon services, which became so full of well-wishers that the overflow spilled into the streets. Milling about out-side, former enemies murmured greetings, recalled old battles, and shuffled into line when Wheeler emerged for his last parade, a solemn mingling of aging men in blue and gray, of gleaming horses and creaking leather, inching along Penn-sylvania Avenue, across the river, and up the slope to Arlington. Each mourner wore a white carnation in memory of the late President McKinley, who had handed out such flowers to White House visitors, and who had made it possi-ble for these old foes to march together again.[56]

In the low-slanting light of that winter afternoon, Wheeler was laid to rest with full military honors—and with a final dash of controversy. Most of his old comrades from the Confederacy endured the afternoon's ceremonies with-out complaint, but several felt compelled to stay away in protest. In a final show of loyalty to the old flag, Wheeler was buried in a Union section of the cemetery, where he would lie among such famous enemies of the South as Philip Sheridan, George Crook, and Edward Ord. Their graves held the terri-tory in Section 2, southeast of the Lee mansion and beyond the view of the new Confederate section.[57]

This struck some diehard Rebels as a betrayal. "Ex-Confederates Angry," read the New York Times headline on the eve of Wheeler's funeral. "The Confederates say that Wheeler's fame was won chiefly as a Confederate soldier," the paper's correspondent wrote, ". . . and that his brief experience in the Spanish war should not overshadow that part of his record which made him famous." Despite this, Wheeler's family went forward with his funeral plans, which placed him among Union men who had come to admire the pint-sized general and his instinct for national healing. His grave would be marked by one of Arlington's tallest obelisks, which still casts its long shadow over neighboring tombstones.[58]

7

L'ENFANT'S GRAND VIEW

By the dawn of the twentieth century, Arlington had matured into something more than a Civil War cemetery; it had become a national symbol for sacrifice and honor, a rallying point for veterans, for ordinary visitors, and for solemn ceremony. And for those with an eye for landscape, it was seen as valuable open space in an increasingly cramped capital, an extension of the engineer Pierre L'Enfant's grand vision for Washington.

The brilliant French soldier and engineer fought alongside George Washington and Alexander Hamilton in the Revolutionary War. He had befriended and impressed both men with his energy and talent. Brevetted a major of engineers in the American army, L'Enfant made the United States his adopted country and won Washington's commission to create a new capital alongside the Potomac in 1791.[1]

L'Enfant pored over maps with Thomas Jefferson and James Madison, explored prospective building sites with President Washington, and picked a location for the nation's new Congress House on Jenkins Hill—"a pedestal waiting for a monument," in L'Enfant's phrase. Over the objections of both Jefferson and Madison, L'Enfant placed the President's House more than a mile

away, emphasizing not only the splendid river views but also the modest standing of the executive branch in the new republican order. He sited the Capitol
so that it would gleam in the afternoon sun and offer a wide prospect to the
Potomac, down through a mile-long park L'Enfant called Grand Avenue; this
space would become the National Mall. Between streets, shady avenues, and
traffic circles, L'Enfant sketched in parks and public spaces, which covered almost two-thirds of his plan for the city, giving it a welcoming, wide-open aspect. He persuaded President Washington to enlarge the capital so that it
could grow, as L'Enfant put it, "proportioned to the greatness which . . . the
Capitale of a powerful Empire ought to manifest."[2]

His plan, submitted to President Washington in August 1791, was magnificent, but implementing it proved difficult for the temperamental Frenchman,
who had little patience with small-minded people who failed to share his vision.[3] When a powerful landowner built a new house where L'Enfant intended
to place New Jersey Avenue, the engineer indignantly demolished the structure, earning a scolding from the president of the United States. "In future,"
President Washington told his old friend, "I must strictly enjoin you to touch
no man's property without his consent."[4]

Deaf to diplomatic suggestion and impervious to criticism, L'Enfant continued building like a man possessed, digging canals, raising aqueducts, opening a
quarry, and erecting new bridges without waiting for permission to do so. He seldom worried about cost. He eventually billed the government $95,500 for his
services, which Congress had estimated to be worth $3,000. After less than a year
on the job, L'Enfant was encouraged to find work elsewhere. He did, but the pattern was set: he would continue to win commissions, dream big, and watch his
schemes crash on the shoals of his own extravagance and unbending aesthetic
standards.[5] Bitter, aging, and all but forgotten in the capital he had fathered,
he stalked the halls of Congress, looking for the big payoff that never came.
He was surprised at this fate. "I had . . . fortune, friends, and relations who
generously supplied all my wants," he wrote late in life. "They are no more—
all have perished and with them my fortune and friends."[6]

One friend remained, however—Thomas Digges, an old patron who was
pained to see the great designer facing his last years in such lonely, threadbare
condition. He invited L'Enfant to live on the family estate at Green Hill,
Maryland, which the Frenchman had designed in better days. Still sketching
away on new projects, he died there, leaving an estate valued at forty-six dol-

lars. He was buried in the Digges family plot with nothing to mark his grave but a red cedar, a few miles downriver from the imposing city he had envisioned but never could manage to build.[7]

L'Enfant might still be sleeping in obscurity if not for a group of well-placed architects and city planners who rediscovered the engineer and restored his reputation as the twentieth century opened. One of these was Daniel H. Burnham, the visionary designer who helped launch the "city beautiful" movement with his plans for the White City, centerpiece of Chicago's Columbian Exhibition in 1893.[8] Burnham had grown alarmed at the haphazard development of Washington, a worry shared by Sen. James McMillan of Michigan, chairman of the Senate District of Columbia Committee; Charles F. McKim, a prominent New York architect who supervised restoration of the White House in 1902; Frederick Law Olmsted Jr., landscape designer and conservationist; and Glenn Brown, secretary of the American Institute of Architects, the influential professional organization, which had recently moved to Washington and taken over historic Octagon House.[9]

Burnham and company could see that the late Frenchman's plans for Washington had been swept aside as the capital matured, sprawled, and began to swallow the nineteenth-century city of grand vistas and carefully placed buildings. By 1900, the Treasury Department was blocking the Pennsylvania Avenue axis L'Enfant intended to link the White House with Capitol Hill; the Library of Congress had taken over space L'Enfant had foreseen as parkland; the Washington Monument was built a few hundred feet out of kilter, away from the point at which L'Enfant had sight lines intersecting from the White House and the Capitol; the War and Navy Building boxed in the executive mansion from its western side, casting the president's quarters in shadow and interrupting the intended reach of New York Avenue; and the great gray hulk of the Pennsylvania Railway depot squatted across the National Mall, now cluttered by railroad sheds and hissing trains. New government buildings were under construction on both sides of the mall, threatening to encroach upon the space L'Enfant had envisioned as the cool, green nucleus of his design. The reform-minded architects dusted off L'Enfant's old plans, enlarged upon them, and used them to thwart future assaults on the federal city's aesthetic integrity.[10]

Their blueprint for the future, unveiled as Washington's second century began, came to be known as the McMillan Plan to honor the senator who introduced legislation for a new federal parks commission.[11] Published in 1902, the plan would shape the city's development for years to come: It proposed a regional park system with an expanded National Mall at its heart, relocated the Pennsylvania Railroad depot from the Mall to the new Union Station northeast of the Capitol, sketched plans for a new government office complex to be known as the Federal Triangle, opened public spaces on land reclaimed from the Potomac River, and envisioned a Lincoln Memorial to anchor the southern terminus of the mall and pay homage to the man who saved the Union. The plan also endorsed the long-proposed—and yet unbuilt—Memorial Bridge to provide ready access to Arlington and connect Lincoln's monument to Lee's mansion, symbolically pulling North and South together again.[12]

Their vision did not stop at the river but crossed into Virginia with guidance for future development at Arlington National Cemetery and Fort Myer, joined by history and both notable for their natural beauty. Both were popular destinations for residents and an intrinsic part of the capital's overall landscape, in the view of those distinguished designers considering the future.

"The interest excited by the drills at the cavalry post, the superb views from the heights, and the feelings of patriotism awakened by the vast field of the hero dead . . . all call for such a treatment of the entire reservation as shall not diminish but rather enhance the effect produced on the visitor," the panel reported. Then the group took aim at the jumble of oversized tombs proliferating in the officers' section at Arlington, which was decried as pretentious.[13]

Instead of erecting such grandiose tombs, the McMillan Commission urged, Arlington should strive for a look of dignified simplicity, such as that evoked by the plain white tombstones marking the graves of enlisted men and former slaves in the Lower Cemetery. "Nothing could be more impressive than the rank after rank of white stones, inconspicuous in themselves, covering the gentle, wooded slopes, and producing the desired effect of a vast army in its last resting place," the report said. "Those spaces reserved for . . . officers and their families, however, exhibit all the heterogeneous forms which disturb those very ideas of peace and quiet which should characterize a spot sacred to the tenderest feelings of the human heart. In particular, the noble slopes toward the river should be rigorously protected against the invasion of monuments which utterly annihilate the sense of beauty and repose."[14]

Like other recommendations the commission floated that year, the proposed ban on self-aggrandizing monuments would eventually be adopted at

Arlington—but not for decades. In the meantime, the McMillan group and a coalition of city leaders moved to rebury their patron saint, Pierre Charles L'Enfant, on the heights at Arlington, where he would soon have the best view of Washington at his feet.[15]

Cheered on by newspaper editorialists, local historians, and French ambassador Jean Jules Jusserand, Congress voted the nation's long-overdue tribute to L'Enfant on May 27, 1908, when lawmakers approved his transfer to a choice spot at Arlington. For good measure, Congress set aside one thousand dollars for the cost of exhuming the Frenchman and providing him with a headstone befitting his new status.[16] A few months later, Henry B. F. Macfarland, president of the Commissioners for the District of Columbia, the city's congressionally appointed governing body, informed the secretary of war that a new gravesite had been chosen for L'Enfant at Arlington, "in front of the Mansion . . . at the top of the slope, on a line with the monument erected to General Sheridan and the flagstaff . . . overlooking Washington." Macfarland assured the War Department that, in keeping with guidelines from the McMillan Plan, L'Enfant's new marker would be discreet, not a shaft to rival Sheridan's showy plinth, "but rather a monument low in height."[17] Aided by professionals from the American Institute of Architects, Macfarland chose a spot for L'Enfant's new grave a few steps to the east of Lee's mansion, where the Marquis de Lafayette, another Frenchman and Revolutionary War hero, had gazed across the river during a visit in 1825 and pronounced the vista the greatest in the world.[18]

Arrangements for L'Enfant's disinterment were complete by April 11, 1909, when orders went out from the quartermaster to D. H. Rhodes, the Arlington landscape gardener who had repatriated thousands of the war dead from Cuba and the Philippines a few years before.[19] He gathered a team of laborers, assembled the proper equipment, collected a new casket and metal shipping case, and drove into the Maryland countryside, arriving at the Digges farm on April 22, 1909. Accompanied by local officials, a *Washington Post* reporter, and descendants of Thomas Digges, Rhodes found his way to the cedar marking L'Enfant's grave. In the eight decades since the engineer's death, the tree had matured into a "very fine specimen" in Rhodes's practiced view, but it had insinuated its roots into L'Enfant's grave, complicating his disinterment. Rhodes got permission to chop down the tree, accomplished this, and set his crew to digging.[20] As soon as they put spades to earth, it seemed to trigger a celestial reaction: a spectacular thunderstorm rolled in, with sheets of rain and spears of lightning scattering the burial party.[21] Just as drama and disruption had marked L'Enfant's course through life, so it was now.

But not for long. After twenty minutes, the skies cleared and Rhodes's men resumed digging. They found L'Enfant four feet down, reduced to a few inches of discolored mold, two pieces of bone, and one tooth—nothing more. An undertaker cleaned the meager remains and placed them in the casket. Rhodes wrapped the box in a silk American flag.[22] They transferred L'Enfant to a vault in a nearby cemetery, where he would rest until his funeral on April 28, 1909.[23]

On the morning of that day, a military detail arrived to escort the Frenchman to the Capitol Rotunda, where L'Enfant lay in state until noon, an honor Congress had previously conferred upon only eight people, three of them presidents. L'Enfant was the first foreigner to receive the privilege.[24] President Taft and Vice President John Sherman traveled to Capitol Hill to pay their respects, as did Jules Jusserand, the French ambassador. "This impressive ceremony today," he said by way of benediction, "is more than enough to recompense for all that Major L'Enfant did for the country he loved so well."[25]

When Jusserand finished, soldiers bore L'Enfant from the Rotunda, down the long Capitol steps, and out into the April sunlight. They eased him onto a caisson pulled by six bay horses, and the cortege moved down Pennsylvania Avenue, past the White House, through Georgetown, and across the river to Arlington, accompanied by cavalry, two military bands, a battalion of army engineers, and a long procession of mourners who converged on Lee's mansion.[26]

After a brief Catholic service and the sounding of Taps, soldiers prepared to lower L'Enfant into the ground, but before they could do so, a man stepped from the crowd, unpinned a gold medal with a blue ribbon from his coat, and reverently laid it on L'Enfant's casket. The man was Sen. Augustus Octavius Bacon, Democrat of Georgia, and the medal, in the form of an eagle crowned by laurels, was from the Society of the Cincinnati, a fraternal order for French and American officers of the Revolutionary War and their male descendants.[27] L'Enfant had not only been a member of the society; he had designed its original badge, won George Washington's imprimatur for the prototype, and sailed to Paris in 1783 to oversee the first badges cast.[28] Somewhere along the way, L'Enfant had lost or sold his own Cincinnati medal. Senator Bacon had noticed and made amends, and this time the decoration stayed with the Frenchman.[29]

It took another two years for L'Enfant's monument to be finished.[30] Thirty-five architects entered a competition for the design, which was won by William Welles Bosworth of New York. He produced drawings for a chunky Beaux Arts marble shaft decorated with oval panels and draped with swags.[31] Reviewing the design for the American Institute of Architects, president Cass Gilbert and secretary Glenn Brown recoiled at Bosworth's proposal. "I could not approve the design selected by the jury either as a suitable design for the purpose or as the best design of those submitted," Gilbert wrote. Leaving nothing to chance, he and Brown came up with a simpler plan, presented it to Bosworth, and urged him to adopt it. "If a monument had been erected to L'Enfant at the time of his death, by his friends in Washington, it would have been a cemetery monument of that period," Gilbert wrote, suggesting an understated memorial "colonial in type—a table tomb, with the Plan of Washington on top, and the remains in the ground below." Bosworth swallowed his pride and embraced the revision. He produced blueprints for a tabletop tomb precisely like the one Brown and Gilbert prescribed.[32]

That problem was resolved, but one last controversy remained. When plans for the tomb were presented to the quartermaster in November 1910, an alert officer noticed a problem: the architects had erroneously listed L'Enfant's rank as "Major, U.S. Engineer Corps," when in fact the Frenchman had been a captain of U.S. Engineers and brevet major of the Continental Army. Distinctions of rank mattered little to ordinary civilians but carried great weight with military professionals. They knew the difference between temporary titles, such as L'Enfant's majority, and permanent rank; their daily status, not to mention their paychecks, depended upon precision in such things. To make matters worse, L'Enfant's graveyard promotion had already been committed to stone. The monument was scheduled to arrive at Arlington in less than a month, followed by President Taft and a retinue of high-powered officials expected for the springtime dedication.[33]

"Inasmuch as the inscription has already been cut," assistant quartermaster George Ruhlen reported to the secretary of war, "these discrepancies cannot be remedied without disfiguring the monument. For this reason, and owing to the further fact that the circumstances under which the monument is to be placed in Arlington National Cemetery are entirely different from those affecting monuments of other officers interred there, this office recommends approval of the design and inscription in accordance with the copy herewith submitted, this case not be taken as a precedent."[34] The War Department took this face-saving advice, the monument arrived, and the cream of Washington society turned out for a formal unveiling on May 22, 1911. From the portico of the Lee mansion, where chairs had been set up for distinguished visitors, President Taft led the speakers that afternoon:

> All Americans who take pride in the Capital and its development . . . must feel deep gratitude to L'Enfant for what he did . . . and must rejoice that now, 86 years after his death, the time has come when we are paying him just tribute in sight of the city that he designed, in a place full of tender memories for the nation, a beautiful estate dedicated to the patriotic dead, furnishing a terminal—and a proper terminal—for the design of the future of the city of Washington. L'Enfant will now lie here appropriately in state and in rest, with the gratitude of the nation he served so well.[35]

On this day of celebration, Taft avoided mention of the confusion over Captain L'Enfant's rank, just as he did not call attention to the error permanently chiseled into line nine of the engineer's tombstone, which lists the year of his birth as 1755, when in fact he was born in 1754.[36]

Even with these distractions, L'Enfant's arrival at Arlington helped balance the years of neglect he had suffered, while bringing attention to the new breed of architects such as Glenn Brown, who saw it as their mission to civilize the nation's cities. "This is the first tribute to a City Planner and is worth the attention of the country," Brown wrote to the editor of *Harper's Weekly* to generate interest before L'Enfant's tomb was dedicated in 1911.[37] In addition to advancing the ambitions of fellow designers, the Frenchman's ascension also marked Arlington's emerging status as the nation's most esteemed war memorial. Begun as a graveyard for destitute soldiers, it had expanded to receive all Civil

War veterans a few years later. Then it grew to accommodate those who fell in the fight with Spain. And with the reburial of L'Enfant and those who had served in earlier wars, it became the place to honor all of America's conflicts—past, present, and future.

From his new grave overlooking the capital, L'Enfant held the heights for comrades who had fought and bled in the Revolutionary War, as he had done. Just over the hills behind him, another fourteen long-dead warriors, disinterred from Washington and transferred to Arlington in 1905, claimed space for all who perished in the War of 1812.[38] Other graves belonged to soldiers from the Mexican-American War (1846–48). All were mingled in Section 1 of the cemetery—also known as the officers' section—where Montgomery Meigs, Abner Doubleday, John Wesley Powell, and distinguished Civil War veterans already slept. Their close-set tombstones, situated on six rolling acres near the Fort Myer gate, told of the nation's troubled birth, its violent coming of age, and its precarious survival in a hostile world.[39]

One such grave marker, worn and discolored by time, belonged to Gen. James McCubbin Lingan, a Marylander who had fought alongside L'Enfant and Washington in the War of Independence, in which he was wounded and jailed on a British prison ship. He finished the Revolution as one of the war's most respected officers. Years later, he attracted attention for his opposition to the nation's next great conflict, the War of 1812. He never fought in the later war, but he sacrificed everything for it, becoming perhaps the first American to die for the First Amendment.[40]

A few weeks after the United States declared war on Britain in June of 1812, Lingan turned up in Baltimore to defend Alexander Contee Hanson, publisher of the Federal Republican and Commercial Gazette. A Federalist like Lingan, Hanson ardently opposed the new war and forcefully said so in his paper—even after a mob of pro-war Baltimoreans stormed Hanson's office, wrecked the presses, and tore down the building. Hanson defiantly kept printing from another site, informing readers that he would continue to criticize President James Madison's ill-advised war. Goaded into action by the paper's inflammatory stance, Hanson's neighbors took to the streets on July 27 and 28, promising violence. When bricks started flying toward the publisher and his friends, Hanson shot into the mob, killing at least one man and wounding others. The enraged crowd chased him, Lingan, and a handful of supporters into the city jail, where the men sought protection. The crowd broke in, dragged

Hanson and others down the stairs, beat them mercilessly, and left them for dead.[41]

When rioters turned on Lingan, he ripped open his shirt. "Does this look like I am a traitor?" he cried, revealing an ugly bayonet scar from his Revolutionary service. This gesture inflamed his attackers, who beat him to death. They tried to do the same to Henry "Light Horse Harry" Lee, a Revolutionary hero, father of Robert E. Lee, and a defender of Hanson. Beaten to a pulp and left for dead, Lee survived, but he was "as black as a negro, his head cut to pieces without any hat or any shirt but a flannel one which was covered with blood," according to an eyewitness. Crippled and partially blinded, Lee never really recovered. For his part, Hanson played dead until friends managed to cart him away. He survived the war and won election to the U.S. Senate.[42]

Within days of the Baltimore riots, Lingan's broken body was quietly returned to a private cemetery in Georgetown. The chief orator at his funeral was none other than George Washington Parke Custis, an ardent Federalist and master of the newly built Arlington estate. It was said that Custis spoke so movingly that it prompted crying from "old warriors who had almost forgotten how to weep." In the same spirit of delayed homage that led to L'Enfant's enshrinement at Arlington, Lingan's body was recovered from Georgetown in 1908, ushered over the river, and recommitted to earth to the sounds of brass hymns, rifle salutes, and stirring oratory.[43]

That same year, a middle-aged naval commander named Robert E. Peary struggled toward the North Pole, the Arctic grail that had eluded him for more than two decades. Although his previous forays into the ice had claimed seven of Peary's toes and much of his fortune, this time he hoped finally to plant the Stars and Stripes at the top of the world, not only to win fame for himself but also, as he put it, "for the honor and credit of this country."[44] Such patriotic talk was not unusual in those self-assured times, when John Philip Sousa took the Marine Band to play packed houses, the Navy's Great White Fleet toured the world on a prestige-building cruise, and Teddy Roosevelt unashamedly foresaw "a new century big with the fate of mighty nations."[45]

Mighty nations such as the United States established territories in the Philippines and the Caribbean, linked the oceans by means of a new Panama

Canal, and embraced figures such as Peary, who returned to a hero's welcome in 1909, claiming to have reached the North Pole.[46] While these patriotic initiatives unfolded, the country reached into its past to restore the memory of figures such as L'Enfant and ventured abroad to reclaim the patriarchs of key national institutions.

In this nationalistic spirit, Gen. Horace Porter, a famous Union officer appointed U.S. ambassador to France in 1897, devoted part of his European assignment to searching for the lost grave of John Paul Jones, patron saint of the Continental Navy. It took Porter six years to find what he believed to be Jones's grave just outside Paris. The remains were removed, examined closely, and shipped home in July 1905 under naval escort, accompanied by Rear Adm. Charles D. Sigsbee—he of the U.S.S. *Maine* catastrophe. Sailing up Chesapeake Bay in fine July weather, Sigsbee brought his squadron safely through to Annapolis, where Jones was encrypted at the heart of the U.S. Naval Academy, in a chapel tomb described as "one of the most ornamental and elaborate . . . in America."[47] A similar patriotic impulse inspired the retrieval of James Smithson, benefactor of the national museum, in 1904. The Smithsonian Institution assigned its most famous regent, Alexander Graham Bell, to escort Smithson's bones from Italy; President Roosevelt ordered the warship *Dolphin* to accompany the funeral convoy from New York; and the museum's English-born benefactor was seen into a specially commissioned sepulcher, which still guards the entrance to Smithsonian headquarters today.[48] By exalting such figures from the past, the country emphasized virtues considered essential to its future.

Ceremonies for L'Enfant, Lingan, Jones, and Smithson attracted considerable attention in their day, but virtually no controversy. So many graves were being emptied and shifted that the burst of funerary activity came to appear almost normal. The Civil War had hardened the quartermaster's office to moving dead armies from one place to another, while the Spanish-American War had taught that it was possible to recover compatriots from overseas, often under appalling conditions, with efficiency and dignity. Hardly anyone noticed when Congress first considered L'Enfant's disinterment in 1905; the bill sailed through with only perfunctory debate and no hearings.[49] If the cause was patriotic and handled with tact, such moves produced little fuss.

The pause between wars allowed time for such refinements at Arlington, where workers relocated graves, paved new roadways, reseeded grass, and built new stone walls to replace wire fences as the twentieth century began. Down by the river on land once worked by freedmen, the Agriculture Department took over some four hundred acres, plowed test plots, developed new crops, and experimented with plants introduced from abroad. Rows of fresh tombstones appeared in the section of Arlington dedicated to nurses from the Spanish-American War, a part of the cemetery where the women still occupy most of the real estate. Meanwhile, the cemetery's durable gardener, D. H. Rhodes, fine-tuned the landscape around the mansion, digging up Mrs. Lee's garden, grading the ground smooth, and planting new roses as a backdrop for the graves of Union officers. Around the edges, Rhodes created a flower border spelling out the names of famous soldiers in blossoms, a medium he also employed to display a running total of Unknowns at Arlington.[50]

By 1902, the army issued new regulations for its standard headstones, making them more durable, taller, and wider than before. It also adopted more prominent markers for the graves of unknown sailors, soldiers, and marines—in place of the small square stone blocks issued before 1903, the unidentified dead of the future would have standard marble slabs like others at Arlington, with "Unknown" curving across the stone face.[51]

Even in times of peace, however, Arlington was never far from the memory of war or the prospect of a new conflict. The summer of 1908 brought the sound of sputtering airplane engines drifting over the cemetery, which combined with cheers from more than two thousand voices late on the afternoon of September 17. A rickety biplane slid down the tracks at Fort Myer, hovered uncertainly over the grass a few moments, and lurched into the sky at precisely five fourteen P.M.[52]

As the shadows lengthened, John B. McCarthy, a Washingtonian who had been attending a funeral at Arlington, heard the commotion and wandered over to the Fort Myer parade grounds for a look. He gazed up to see Orville Wright, sitting stiffly and wearing a tartan cap, at the controls of a plane swooping over the field in lazy circles. The plane's only passenger, Lt. Thomas E. Selfridge of the Army Signal Corps, sat beside Wright, waved to friends on the ground, and chattered over the propeller's drone.[53]

"The emotions aroused as one watched the craft sailing about so lightly and easily cannot be described," McCarthy recalled. He watched the skies eagerly, as did a crowd of military brass keen on the reconnaissance potential of the new flying machines. The army had pledged twenty-five thousand dollars to anyone who could meet its specifications for the first warplane: It had to fly at a speed of forty miles an hour, cover a distance of one hundred twenty-five miles, carry a pilot and observer safely, and be portable enough to fit on a mule-drawn wagon. Lured by the hope of a government contract, the Wright brothers delivered the first prototype in September 1908. Orville brought the flying machine to Fort Myer for a series of demonstration flights, while his brother Wilbur performed related experiments for prospective customers in France.[54]

The Fort Myer trials were going well. By the time Orville took Selfridge aloft, the inventor had already made a dozen runs over the base, breaking all previous records for sustained flight by staying airborne for more than an hour. This impressed a curious public, as well as military observers such as Lieutenant Selfridge. At age twenty-six, Selfridge was already a pioneering aviator who had flown dirigibles and experimental planes in the months before the Fort Myer trials. Assigned by his service to join Orville for the September 17 flight, Selfridge enthusiastically clambered aboard, throwing off his coat and hat and settling in for the adventure. "He looked as eager as a schoolboy for the test to begin," the *New York Times* reported.[55]

It was Orville's thirteenth flight in the Fort Myer series, a number that proved to be unlucky as well as historic. On the plane's fourth pass over the parade grounds, a propeller blade cracked, the aircraft faltered, and it plunged headlong into the ground. The crowd watched in horror, first gasping, then going dead quiet. With their clothes in tatters and covered with blood, Wright and Selfridge lay in the wreckage, pinned down by twisted wires and shattered framework. Women shrieked, men rushed to help, and cavalry troops galloped across the field to hold back a whirling, panicked crowd. A burly Army officer—the one who assigned Selfridge to the flight that day—fainted with a thump.[56]

In the wreckage of his plane, Wright retained consciousness. Beside him, Selfridge lay perfectly still, crushed under the aircraft engine. Picked from the ruins of the flying machine, they were borne to the post hospital on stretchers. Wright, who sustained a broken thigh, broken ribs, and numerous lacerations, remained hospitalized for months. Selfridge, his skull fractured, died three hours after the crash.[57]

"It came down like a bird shot dead in full flight, describing almost a complete somersault and throwing up a dense cloud of dust," said Maj. H. C. Magoon, then superintendent of Arlington. He had been standing near the cemetery wall and was closest to the plane when disaster struck. "The aeroplane started over the cemetery . . . and I stood aghast, fearing it would alight on the trees. From where I stood I could not see the men when it struck the ground. The machine went to smash in the twinkling of an eye," he told the *Washington Post.* "All that I have told you happened in a few seconds, probably two or three, but it seemed a much longer time."[58]

After an investigation and hardly a pause for doubt, the Army forged ahead with its aerial ambitions. "I see no reason why this accident should give any serious setback to the experiments in aeronautics being made by the Army," said Gen. Luke E. Wright, secretary of war. "When Mr. Wright recovers, if he desires to try again to fulfill the contract, the opportunity will be open to him."[59]

Orville Wright recovered. He went home to his Ohio workshop, made changes to the plane, and returned to Fort Myer in June 1909 with the improved Wright A aircraft. He crawled in, took the controls, and coolly put the machine through its paces. Again and again he flew over the parade grounds, casting a flickering shadow over expectant, upturned faces—this time without incident. Satisfied with the new flyer, the Army accepted delivery of the plane, which it designated Signal Corps Airplane No. 1. It was the first warplane ever produced.[60]

8

KNOWN BUT TO GOD

Lieutenant Thomas Selfridge, the first casualty of powered flight, was buried with full military honors at Arlington, his grave marked by a soaring white obelisk and placed a few hundred yards from where he had fallen to earth in September 1908. The western gates of the cemetery, which opened onto the Fort Myer parade grounds, were renamed in his honor. Shorty after this, an order went out for all Army pilots to wear leather helmets.

Their future, like that of other combatants heading into the new century, would be characterized by conflict waged on a monstrous scale unlike anything known before. The new era of warfare would reach into the sky, rumble across entire continents at record speed, roil beneath the oceans, and finally achieve the promethean power that reduced Hiroshima and Nagasaki to rubble.

A photograph of Selfridge's crash captured the danger and promise of the new century in a single frame: the Wright Flyer lies crumpled in the dust; a crowd rushes toward the wreck; a mounted cavalryman sits straight in the saddle, fixing his gaze on some faraway object; the broken plane lies behind horse and rider; an automobile noses into the scene from the right. Humans stood at the threshold of a realm they had yet to conquer.

As the century opened, warhorse and musket, caisson and sailing ship—all would begin to fade as the familiar equipment of war gave way to flying machines, magazine-fed rifles, water-cooled machine guns, torpedo-equipped submarines, armored dreadnought ships, and massive new field artillery. Powered by internal combustion energy, modern warfare would bring into action bigger guns with more accurate firepower over longer distances than anything achieved in nineteenth century conflicts. The rate of fire, for infantry and artillery alike, would jump markedly. Foot soldiers who managed to get off three rounds a minute in the Civil War could fire fifteen rounds by 1914; heavy artillery pieces, improved with automatic recoil, boosted their rate from three rounds a minute to twenty; new machine guns could spray the battlefield with six hundred rounds in sixty seconds. Smokeless gunpowder, introduced in the Spanish-American War, helped to conceal firing positions, increased rates of reloading, and improved accuracy and distance for small arms as well as artillery units.[1]

All of these innovations would make war less human, more aloof, more destructive, and markedly more degrading for everyone involved. The distance between opposing armies increased, placing the killing on an impersonal level; infantrymen were sent scuttling into trenches to avoid the rain of metal above ground; anyone who ventured into daylight to face his enemy was often killed on the spot—or worse. Thousands of soldiers survived the Great War but lost their eyes, ears, noses, or faces, spending the rest of their days in hiding or wheezing behind painted masks.[2]

Spurred by burgeoning industrial growth, new mass manufacturing techniques, and economic expansion, the arms race grew in Europe, where Continental powers nervously watched their neighbors, added the latest weaponry to their armamentaria, and planned for the worst. Millions were conscripted into the armies of France, Germany, Belgium, Britain, Russia, and other European powers as the Continent moved toward war.[3]

America held back. Memories of the Civil War still lingered, giving "war a lasting bad name in the United States," in the phrase of historian John Keegan.[4] When the storm finally broke over Europe in 1914, the United States remained resolutely neutral, in part because public opinion did not favor intervention and in part because of President Woodrow Wilson, who had beaten William Howard Taft and Theodore Roosevelt in the three-way election of 1912.

All three had experienced war at first hand—Roosevelt, of course, as a swashbuckling cavalry colonel in the Spanish-American War; Taft, as governor of the Philippines during its bloody insurrection, followed by a stint as Roosevelt's secretary of war; and Wilson, whose first memory in life sprang from the Civil War.

"My earliest recollection," Wilson wrote, "is of standing at my father's gateway in Augusta, Georgia, when I was four years old, and hearing someone pass and say that Mr. Lincoln was elected and there was to be war. Catching the intense tones . . . I remember running to ask my father what it meant." The boy learned soon enough. It meant that his father's Presbyterian Church was converted into a Confederate hospital; it meant anxious rumors of General Sherman's approach to Georgia and the smoking reality of his progress across that state; it meant stripped farms, ruined cities, mass graves, and men with empty sleeves on the courthouse square.[5]

"The impressions of horror produced upon him by the Civil War were indelible," wrote biographer Charles Seymour. Wilson's experience made him into an unwavering man of peace, even as the rest of the world was spoiling for war.[6] Appearing for Memorial Day ceremonies at Arlington two years into his first term, Wilson praised the selflessness of Union soldiers and urged his listeners to fight for peace as earlier generations had fought for war.

"I can never speak in praise of war, ladies and gentlemen," he told the crowd at Arlington. "But there is this peculiar distinction belonging to the soldier . . . He is giving everything he hath, even his life, in order that others may live, not in order that he himself may obtain gain and prosperity. And just so soon as the tasks of peace are performed in the same spirit of self-sacrifice and devotion, peace societies will not be necessary . . . We can stand here and praise the memory of these soldiers in the interest of peace. They set the example of self-sacrifice, which if followed in peace will make it unnecessary that men should follow war any more." From the hard lessons of his own youth, Wilson built a grand and impossible vision of a new world without conflict.[7]

He returned to Arlington—and to his high-minded theme—on June 4, 1914. Veterans in blue and gray gathered near the Selfridge Gate, where the 5th Cavalry Band struck up "The Star-Spangled Banner," followed by "Dixie." Old soldiers whipped off their hats for both songs. The crowd of three hundred spectators and veterans had come to celebrate the birthday of Jefferson Davis, to hear the speeches of reunion, and to watch Wilson dedicate the new centerpiece of the Confederate section—a towering bronze monument to peace.[8]

Designed by Moses Ezekiel, himself a Confederate veteran, the sculpture was called "New South" and took the classical form of a woman in laurel crown and flowing robes. Facing Richmond, she held a laurel wreath in one hand, extending honors toward the vanquished Confederacy. Her other hand, resting lightly on a plow, held a pruning hook. Everyone in the crowd—especially Wilson, the clergyman's son—understood the artist's allusion to Isaiah 2:4: "And they shall beat their swords into ploughshares and their spears into pruning hooks. Nation shall not lift up sword against nation; neither shall they learn war any more."[9]

The sentiment was noble, the sculpture magnificent, the moment inspiring. The afternoon sun shone on old enemies tottering among the graves and shaking hands in a show of forgiveness. From his perch on the reviewing stand, Wilson, a pacifist among the warriors, smiled down on the scene. Perhaps if old adversaries such as these could settle their differences, so could others, who might learn from their example. The president rose to make this point, but just as he launched into his message of reconciliation, the sky tuned purple and a storm of Old Testament fury descended on Arlington. Wind-whipped rain threatened to topple Confederate and Union flags on the reviewing stand. Crowds scrambled for cover. The president dashed for his car and, peering out through windows streaming with rain, waited for the storm to clear. When it did not, he was driven back to the White House, away from the sodden cemetery.[10]

That afternoon's storm portended the four-year tempest about to descend on Europe. Within weeks of Wilson's appearance at Arlington, German forces massed for their invasion of Belgium and France. The first wave of Kaiser Wilhelm's army tromped into Belgium on August 4, 1914, and headed for the Meuse River crossings. Expecting a quick, easy war, they received a surprise welcome when a chorus of Belgian artillery and machine gun fire greeted their approach to Liège. Like other Germans, Gen. Otto von Emmich had expected little resistance from Belgium, a mere doormat to be crossed on the way into France. Enraged by the hostile reception, Emmich led five brigades of infantry into the tiny country, where his men proceeded to torch villages, fire into homes, and kill hostages. The violence was necessary, a German officer explained, because "we are fighting for our lives and all who get in the way must take the consequences."[11]

Emmich's troops slogged through Belgium as his comrades to the south gathered for a direct thrust into Alsace. Europe rushed to respond. To meet the combined forces from Germany and Austria-Hungary, which would mobilize more than 22 million troops, Russia raised an army of some 13 million, Britain 9.5 million, France 8.2 million, Serbia 1 million, Italy 500,000, and Belgium 380,000. Before August was half spent, the French had formed defensive lines in the north and east of their country. Across the Channel, the first British Expeditionary Force clattered aboard transports, crossed the water, and put ashore at Boulogne. Russia slowly gathered its strength and took up positions on the Eastern Front. The Great War was under way.[12]

While the first clashes began, President Wilson, watching anxiously from afar, offered to broker a settlement among the belligerents. He might as well have tried to quell Vesuvius. When his American ambassador approached Kaiser Wilhelm with a peace proposal on August 10, the idea was summarily rebuffed. Confident of victory, the Germans were in no mood for mediation.[13]

They advanced through northeastern France during the late summer and fall of 1914, driving the Allies before them. But when the kaiser's army reached within striking distance of Paris, the French rallied and launched a furious counterattack. Forced back across the Marne, the Germans halted along the Aisne River and began to dig a line of entrenchments that would cut across more than four hundred miles of Europe, from the North Sea to the Swiss border. British and French brandished shovels and followed suit, digging their own trenches and settling in for a long, numbing stalemate, which would be punctuated by massive artillery assaults and futile, murderous infantry advances in the months and years to come.[14] Tens of thousands of soldiers would be sacrificed to gain a few yards, only to yield the same ground a few weeks later; then came another round of waiting, another shuddering deluge of artillery, another order to go over the top. "It isn't death we fear so much as the long drawn expectation of it," a British captain wrote of life in this setting.[15]

The first few months of war offered a foretaste of grisly days ahead: from

August through November 1914, more than 800,000 soldiers died—510,000 French, 241,000 German, 30,000 Belgian, and 30,000 British. Russians contributed their own casualties from the Eastern Front—just how many was never known. As the deaths mounted in Europe, letters from the front revealed the brutal character of the new conflict.[16]

"You cannot imagine, beloved mother, what man will do to man," a French soldier wrote in February 1915. "For five days my shoes have been slippery with human brains, I have walked among lungs, among entrails . . . We have no officers left." The writer went missing in action a few weeks later. He was never recovered, but his letters, published anonymously in 1917, spoke for all who lived and died in the trenches.[17]

More than one serviceman spoke of the tenderness with which fellow soldiers cared for comrades dying under unspeakable conditions. One wrote about the rough-and-ready epitaphs the British composed for temporary graves at the front. "Sleep on, Beloved Brother; take thy Gentle Rest," someone chalked over a shallow burial in a part of the trenches where bones protruded from the parapet. Behind the lines, where time allowed for decent burial, Harold Chapin marveled at the kindness fellow soldiers lavished on two dead friends. Writing to his wife in May 1915, Chapin, a lance corporal in Britain's Royal Army Medical Corps, described the preparations for such a funeral:"Their chums were so particular to dig them a *level* grave and a *rectangular* grave and *parallel* graves, and to note who was in this grave, who in that, that my mind, jumping to questions as always, was aching with whys which I wouldn't have asked for the world—almost as if the answer—you take me—would disgrace me for not knowing it already, brand me as lacking some decency the grave-diggers had. O Lord, the mystery of men's feelings."[18]

Just as Chapin's letter was making its way home toward London that spring, the British ocean liner *Lusitania* left New York, crossed the North Atlantic, and steamed into the crosshairs of Kapitänleutnant Walther Schwieger's U-20 submarine, then patrolling off the coast of Ireland. The German captain fired a single torpedo, which slammed into its target broadside. The great ship exploded and began to sink. Schwieger stole away in his sub, and in less than twenty minutes, the *Lusitania* disappeared, taking 1,198 people down with her. Among those killed were 128 Americans.

The attack on the *Lusitania* sparked a sharp response in the United States, especially in northeastern cities reliant on shipping. In New York, thousands poured into Times Square to call for a declaration of war, while newspapers across the country goaded Wilson to retaliate. "The nation which remembered the sailors of the *Maine* will not forget the civilians of the *Lusitania*," the *New York Tribune* promised. The *New York Times* assailed Germany for making war "like savages drunk with blood." Former President Theodore Roosevelt, who had refrained from publicly criticizing President Wilson in the first years of war, broke his silence. The sinking of the British liner, he declared, "was not only an act of simple piracy, but . . . piracy accompanied by murder on a vaster scale than any old-time pirate had ever practiced before being hung for his misdeeds." Roosevelt called on the government to exact punishment. "It seems inconceivable to me that we can refrain from taking action in this matter, for we owe it not only to humanity but to our own national self-respect," he told reporters in Syracuse, New York.[19] In private Roosevelt thundered over Wilson's "cowardice and weakness" while he excoriated William Jennings Bryan, the pacifist secretary of state. "I am sick at heart over the way Wilson and Bryan have acted toward Germany," he confided to his sister Anna Roosevelt Cowles.[20]

In the face of such criticism, Wilson remained above the fray, maintaining the nation's neutrality. He sent a stiff note to the Germans, from whom he requested reparations and an apology. He warned against further U-boat assaults. But he stopped short of breaking off relations or going to war.[21] "There is such a thing as a man being too proud to fight," Wilson famously told a crowd in Philadelphia within days of the *Lusitania* disaster. "There is such a thing as a nation being so right that it does not need to convince others by force that it is right."[22]

Wilson resisted any move toward war, as well as any effort to prepare for a future conflict. On the home front, meanwhile, he floated vague hints that America might run out of patience if pushed too far. "We are not only ready to cooperate, but we are ready to fight against any aggression," he said during Memorial Day exercises at Arlington in 1916. "But we must guard ourselves against the sort of aggression which would be unworthy of America . . . She does not want any selfish advantage over any other nation of the world, but she does wish every nation in the world to understand what she stands for and to respect what she stands for."[23] Wilson maintained this judicious balance, dreaming of peace while hinting at war, through the presidential election of 1916. He was narrowly returned to the White House that November, largely on the strength of returns from the Midwest and West, where isolationist sentiment ran strong and Wilson's campaign slogan, "He has kept us out of war," carried the day.

War fever, which had spiked with the *Lusitania's* sinking, remained low as 1917 began. This was about to change. Boxed in by continued fighting on two fronts and an effective British blockade on the North Sea, Germany began to starve as 1916 ran its course. Food riots broke out, morale flagged, and Germany moved to crack the naval cordon by resuming unrestricted submarine warfare in February 1917. Wilson severed diplomatic relations in reaction, but he still held back from war, which was finally thrust upon the United States a few days later. On March 1, the American public learned of a German plot, detailed in an intercepted telegram from Foreign Minister Arthur S. Zimmermann, to launch an attack on the United States with Mexico and Japan. This was followed on March 18 by U-boat attacks on three American merchant ships without warning. After almost three years of war and millions of deaths, Wilson was ready to choose sides.[24]

"Neutrality is no longer feasible or desirable where the peace of the world is concerned," he told a joint session of Congress on April 2, 1917. "The world must be made safe for democracy . . . It is a fearful thing to lead this great peaceful people into war, into the most terrible and disastrous of all wars," he said. "But the right is more precious than peace, and we shall fight for the things which we have always carried nearest our hearts." Four days later, on April 6, 1917, Congress declared war. From then on, the peace-loving Wilson, an idealist primarily interested in domestic reform, would be known as a wartime president.[25]

Some German military officers airily dismissed the threat posed by green American troops about to enter the European conflict. "They will not even come," Adm. Eduard von Capelle told the German parliament early in 1917, "because our submarines will sink them. Thus America from a military point of view means nothing, and again nothing and for a third time, nothing."[26]

The admiral's prophecy could not have been more mistaken. Protected by convoys, American transport ships delivered the first wave of troops in time for them to march through the streets of Paris with their new commander,

Gen. John J. Pershing, on July 4, 1917. The French greeted the American Expeditionary Force with an outpouring of gratitude: a one-armed brigadier gave a welcoming speech, bands maniacally played "The Star-Spangled Banner" and "La Marseillaise" over and over again, and women wept and dropped to their knees as surprised doughboys marched by. Citizens covered the Americans with so many blossoms that their battalion was said to look "like a moving flower garden" as it marched through the city.[27] When the parade reached the grave of Lafayette, who had hurried to America's rescue in that first war, Pershing reverently placed a wreath of roses on the Frenchman's tomb, stepped back, and turned the oratory over to Col. Charles E. Stanton. Fluent in French, Stanton addressed an already emotional crowd and earned roars of approval with his theatrical closing line: "Lafayette, we are here!"[28]

More doughboys would follow, with no interference from U-boats. The United States drafted 2.8 million men between 1917 and 1918, which brought the strength of the nation's ground forces to some 4 million. By March of 1918, the United States had sent 318,000 troops to France, with a million in the offing. They were sorely needed to replace the ranks worn thin by casualties that spring, when the Germans, sensing their last chance for victory, came out of their trenches for a final, desperate plunge into the heart of France. Opening their offensive on March 21, 1918, the kaiser's men pushed weary British troops back from the Somme, attacked over the Aisne River, and prodded weak spots where British lines tenuously joined those of the French. Inch by inch, the Allies yielded ground all along the Western Front. Yet they put up enough resistance to deny the decisive blow that might have finished the war.[29]

Meanwhile, fresh American troops poured into France at the rate of 250,000 per month. "Rare are the times in a great war when the fortunes of one side or the other are transformed by the sudden accretion of a disequilibrating reinforcement," writes historian John Keegan.[30] The spring of 1918 was such a time, when the accretion of new Allies tipped the balance of power in the long war.

Among the Americans joining the fight that season was Lt. Quentin Roosevelt, a twenty-one-year-old Army pilot and the youngest of the former president's four sons, all serving in France.[31] Less prominent among the flood of new arrivals was an ordinary soldier named Francis Z. Lupo, twenty-three, of Cincinnati. The son of Sicilian immigrants, Lupo made eight dollars a week distributing The Cincinnati Times-Star before he was drafted and assigned to the Army's 18th Infantry Regiment.[32] By mid-July both Private Lupo and Lieutenant Roosevelt found themselves standing between the Germans and Paris as the Second Battle of the Marne began. That four-day action encouraged a German retreat. This opened the Allied counteroffensive leading to the armistice of November 11, 1918, and ending the greatest war the world had known.

When the smoke finally cleared and the losses were counted that autumn, it was estimated that some 8.5 million had died in World War I. Quentin Roosevelt and Francis Lupo were among 116,516 Americans claimed by the war.[33]

Roosevelt, flying his Nieuport 28 fighter near Château Thierry, was killed on July 14, brought down while trying to escape pursuing German planes. Enemy soldiers recovered his body, realized his identity, and fashioned a cross for his grave from his plane's propeller. They turned out a thousand troops for his honors burial near Chamery, a few miles from Rheims.[34]

There was no such send-off for Francis Lupo, who went into battle—his first and last—near Soissons on July 20, armed with his Enfield rifle and a Catholic prayer card. The card, bearing the image of St. Thérèse of Lisieux, read: "I will spend my Heaven in doing good on earth." It disappeared with Lupo, who was last seen charging into the wheat fields under heavy artillery fire with the 18th Infantry.[35] When the four-day battle for Soissons ended, Lupo's 3,800-man regiment had sustained 2,609 casualties. He was one of these, his name added to the list of the missing when he failed to answer the roll on July 21.[36]

Back in Cincinnati, Anna Lupo received the dreaded telegram from the War Department a few days later. Her son was missing and presumed killed. She refused to accept the loss, keeping a photograph of her handsome boy on display at home, lighting candles for him at church, and praying for his return. She even traveled to France with other Gold Star mothers to search for some trace of her son after the war, but never saw him again.[37] He had simply vanished—one of 3,173 Americans missing from the Great War.[38]

In the rambling Roosevelt home in Oyster Bay, New York, the former president met the news of Quentin's death with predictable stoicism. "Quentin's mother and I are very glad that he got to the front and had a chance to render some service to his country, and show the stuff there was in him before his fate befell him," Roosevelt told reporters.[39] It was another story behind the scenes, where a servant found a forlorn Roosevelt rocking in a chair and muttering to himself: "Poor Quinikins! Poor Quinikins!"[40] Roosevelt took the blame for Quentin's loss. "To feel that one has inspired a boy to conduct that has resulted in his death, has a pretty serious side for a father!" he admitted to a confidant.[41]

In public, though, the old lion remained indomitable. When General Pershing sent his condolences and offered to have Quentin's body shipped home, Roosevelt declined the gesture: "Mrs. Roosevelt and I wish to enter a most respectful but most emphatic protest against the proposed course as far as our son Quentin is concerned," he wrote. "We have always believed that 'Where the tree falls, there let it lie.' We know that many good persons feel differently, but to us it is painful and harrowing long after death to move the poor body from which the soul has fled. We greatly prefer that Quentin shall continue to lie on the spot where he fell in battle and where the foeman buried him." There Quentin remained.[42]

Less than a month after the fighting ended in Europe, President Wilson and other leaders began arriving in Paris to arrange permanent peace terms and, at least in Wilson's view, to construct a new world order in which war would cease to exist. While Wilson discussed his plans for the future at Versailles, hundreds of other Americans fanned across the ruined landscape of Europe to process the war's carnage.[43] Theirs was a monumental task—to locate, identify, and reinter thousands of countrymen from the millions of hastily buried combatants, and to do so in a way that restored some dignity to each individual the conflict had claimed.

In Washington the War Department recalled to duty Capt. Charles G. Pierce, the retired Army chaplain who had originated the idea of dog tags and pioneered the repatriation of thousands of dead Americans from the Philippine Insurrection at the turn of the century. Now commissioned as a major in the Quartermaster Corps, Pierce and more than 900 men from the army's Graves Registration Service surveyed some twenty-four hundred makeshift European cemeteries after the armistice of 1918, and identified all but 2.2 percent of the 79,351 Americans killed in combat. The paucity of unknown soldiers is remarkable considering the absence of embalming, the haphazard nature of battlefield burials, and the depredations wrought by intense artillery fire. Reburied and concentrated in fifteen regional cemeteries along the front lines of France, the American dead would remain there until the War Department decided whether to ship them home or leave them in Europe.[44]

As 1919 opened, it became clear that General Pershing and other leaders preferred to let America's war dead remain in Europe, as the Roosevelts had done with their son Quentin.[45] Speaking through his adjutant general, Robert C. "Corky" Davis, on May 6, 1919, Pershing made his views known just as congressional committees took up the question of bringing fallen soldiers home from the war. For one thing, Pershing argued, the French opposed returning America's soldiers for fear that their own families would expect their 4.5 million war dead repatriated to every village and town in France. With so much of the country a vast wartime graveyard, French officials feared the upheaval that disinterring millions would cause. Such a massive operation would also pose unprecedented health risks, prolong France's suffering, and distract from the important work of reconstruction. Pershing, negotiating with the French for permanent American burial sites, conveyed these diplomatic concerns to Washington. At the same time, he and other Army officers worried about the massive expense and logistical difficulties of shipping tens of thousands of American casualties from Europe—a homecoming program that would dwarf the one following the Spanish-American War. Finally, Pershing expressed apprehension over a potential public relations concern: if relatives opened the caskets of their dead sons and husbands at home, families would be in for a shock when they realized how the war had brutalized their loved ones.[46] Pershing's adjutant put it starkly: "Viewing the remains would result in most distressing scenes in view of the fact that the bodies will be in a badly decomposed state and in many cases badly mutilated. In some cases only part of the body could be found."[47]

Back in Washington, Gen. Peyton C. March, the army's wartime chief of staff, shared Pershing's concerns and urged that "steps be taken to give publicity to the difficulties attendant on the return of bodies, with a view to creating a sentiment in favor of having all America's dead left abroad."[48] A few weeks later, Maj. Gen. Frank McIntyre, March's executive assistant, prepared a long news release enumerating the reasons that America's war dead would be better left in Europe. Citing the Roosevelt family's example, McIntyre argued that there was no greater honor than to bury each soldier "where he fell, fighting the foes of civilization, upon a battlefield in France . . . What can be a better testimonial to the valor and devotion of her dead sons . . . than that the Nation should secure and maintain in perpetuity vast cemeteries in France—cemeteries which, in themselves, with their thousands of graves, will arouse sentiment and emotions in pilgrims of future generations, which mere monuments can never do?"[49]

This stirring rhetoric did little to soothe the grief for mothers such as Anna Lupo, who clung to the hope that her son would return, or for Mrs. L. Mantel of Fairfax, Minnesota, who simply wanted her boy's body brought home. "He was my only son I had," Mrs. Mantel wrote to Newton D. Baker, secretary of war, in December 1919. "I want him to rest on his home soil poor boy," she wrote. "Pleas send his body home to us as soon as you can and tell me . . . how bad he was hert and if he had a chance to say eny thing be for he died oh if I could of bin with him . . . it want seem so hard on me."[50] Another mother, writing from Brooklyn, gave Robert Lansing, secretary of state, a tongue-lashing for leaving her son overseas. "You took my son from me and sent him to war . . . My son sacrificed his life to America's call, and now you *must* as a duty of yours bring my son back to me."[51]

Many such letters poured into Washington in the months following the armistice. War widows and mothers of servicemen reprised the role women had performed after the Civil War, when they had organized memorial associations to provide civilized treatment for the war dead. They did so again, goading leaders to honor the fallen, filling the front rows at public hearings, stalking the halls of Congress—trying to clean up the mess their men had made. Less philanthropic urges also flourished in this period, as American undertakers organized the Purple Cross and lobbied for the speedy return of war dead in "a sanitary and recognizable condition." Their professional journals shamelessly anticipated a windfall from massive repatriation of the dead.[52]

These appeals, the craven with the altruistic, soon swayed deliberations in Washington, where policy makers reached a compromise on repatriations just as the first anniversary of the armistice approached: On October 29, 1919, the War Department announced that dead servicemen could be returned from Europe to any relative who requested it, with the government bearing expenses for transport and for burial in one of the national cemeteries; families also had the option of interring their loved ones in private graveyards.[53] Fallen servicemen remaining in Europe would be transferred to one of eight newly established American cemeteries—Brookwood in England, Flanders Field in Belgium, and Aisne-Marne, Meuse-Argonne, Oise-Aisne, Somme, St. Mihiel, and Suresnes in France. Congress quickly approved $5 million for repatriation expenses. Most

Americans requested that their loved ones—more than 46,000—be returned for burial.[54] The homecoming project, begun in November 1920, continued until July 1922, when the last wave of World War I dead were put to rest.[55] Some 5,800 were buried in national cemeteries, 5,241 of those at Arlington.[56] Another 30,000 stayed in Europe, where they lie today in exquisitely maintained military cemeteries on lands ceded to the United States by allies.[57]

Of the thousands brought home for burial, perhaps none has been more celebrated or more visited than the serviceman now enshrined on the heights of Arlington National Cemetery as the Unknown Soldier of World War I, an individual who stood for all of those lost in the twentieth century's first great conflict. Although his tomb evolved into one of Arlington's most revered sites, the Unknown Soldier might still be buried in Europe if Gen. Peyton C. March, the army's chief of staff, had gotten his way.

March discounted the idea of honoring an anonymous warrior when the suggestion was proposed to him in October 1919 by Brig. Gen. William D. Connor, commanding officer of American forces in France. Impressed by French plans to bury their *poilu inconnu* under the Arc de Triomphe, Connor urged a similar program for one of the American war dead. March, never one for diplomatic subtlety or imaginative gestures, dismissed Connor's suggestion with little discussion.[58] The idea languished until Armistice Day a year later, when thousands turned out for emotionally charged ceremonies in London and Paris to honor unidentified warriors from each country.[59] Inspired by the European example, a New York editor named Marie M. Meloney renewed General Connor's ill-fated proposal in November 1920.[60]

"There is in this thing, the way England has done it, the essence of democracy, and the soul of a people," Mrs. Meloney, editor of the *Delineator* magazine, wrote to General March. "It is the kind of thing which should have found birth in America. I want you to do the fine, big human thing that no one else in America has initiated. It is not sob-sister stuff . . . It is a big strong influence in the future . . . It brings patriotism home to men in a personal way."[61]

March rebuffed her suggestion, just as he had Connor's a year before. "The problem of Great Britain and France in this matter is entirely different from ours," March wrote. "I was informed on my recent trip abroad that there were still over one hundred thousand unidentified and missing British soldiers, and their unidentified soldier is the representative of a tremendous class." By contrast, he pointed out, the number of unidentified and missing Americans (then 4,221) was "very small and constantly growing smaller." It was probable, he wrote, that the Graves Registration Service would soon know the names of many more soldiers, making it impossible to guarantee the anonymity of anyone selected as an unknown. Finally, March wrote, even if such an unknown could be found, there was no suitable place to put him. "We have no national arch like the Arc de Triomphe, or national building like Westminster Abbey in which has been interred countless bodies for centuries." If Congress approved a memorial for the unknown, however, March indicated that he would support it.[62]

Prodded by public sentiment, Congress did just that. Within days of Mrs. Meloney's approach to General March, the *New York Times* proposed that the government select an unknown for special honors. "His tomb should be a shrine for the Americans of all the States and all the lands under the flag. And that shrine should be in the National Cemetery at Arlington, where the bravest lie, men of the South as well as men of the North, who fought for the Stars and Stripes."[63]

Rep. Hamilton Fish of New York, a distinguished army reserve major recently back from the war,[64] took up the cause, introducing legislation on December 21, 1920, for the "bringing to the United States of a body of an unknown American killed on the battle fields of France, and for burial of the remains with appropriate ceremonies."[65] His bill sailed through the House of Representatives but stalled in the Senate Committee on Military Affairs, blocked by Newton D. Baker, secretary of war. Parroting General March's earlier objections, Baker warned that Fish's gesture was premature. Dead servicemen were being identified daily, raising the possibility that in time, there might be no Unknown Soldier from World War I. Why bury one now, Baker argued, only to suffer the embarrassment of digging him up later?[66]

Baker's resistance crumbled under the growing weight of newspaper editorials, lobbying from the American Legion, importuning from war mothers, and support from popular military leaders such as Gen. John J. Pershing and Marine Commandant John A. Lejeune, both of whom stepped forward to speak for the Unknown Solider.[67]

"I favor the idea," Pershing told the House Committee on Military Affairs on February 2, 1921. "It is a fitting tribute for the nation to pay, not only to its unknown dead, but to all who gave their lives or risked their lives in France. There has been no national expression since the war ended to give the people an opportunity to show their appreciation." Yielding to the inevitable, Nelson Baker reversed course, backed the proposal, and even predicted that the unknown's grave would become "the Westminster Abbey of America's heroic dead."[68]

Once it was clear that Congress intended to adopt legislation, there was a flurry of discussion about where the Unknown Soldier should be buried. One group of legislators proposed placing him in a crypt—originally designed for but never occupied by George Washington—under the Capitol Rotunda.[69] The *New York Times*, abandoning its earlier argument for Arlington, heartily endorsed this new suggestion. "All America finds its way to the Capitol, many Americans never go to Arlington, which, being a military cemetery . . . can hardly be the 'Westminster Abbey of America's heroic dead.'"[70] Rodman Wanamaker, philanthropist and department store magnate, urged Congress to bury the Unknown in Central Park. "Those privileged to leave us to fight for the freedom of the world embarked from the harbor of New York," Wanamaker wrote to the House military committee. "Those who had the privilege of living returned home through this harbor. It was in New York City . . . that the nation's welcome was given to the returning victorious troops, and it is the place above all others hallowed as the shrine for the spirit that never returned . . . Millions and millions of people will constantly be desirous of paying tribute to this hallowed ground who never will be able to visit any other city."[71]

Unimpressed by Wanamaker's logic, and perhaps concerned about converting the Capitol Rotunda into a mausoleum, Congress determined that Arlington was the proper place for the Unknown Soldier, who would rest among thousands of his comrades in the Virginia hills. Legislation authorizing the warrior's enshrinement at Arlington passed on February 4, 1921. By this time, President Woodrow Wilson, enfeebled by a stroke, humbled by the Republican electoral sweep of 1920, and humiliated by the Senate's rejection of his Treaty of Versailles and League of Nations Covenant, had barely a month left in the White House. In his last hours there on March 4, 1921, the president who had so grudgingly sent so many young Americans into battle put his rickety signature to Public Resolution 67, which would bring one of them back to Arlington. Thus began the Unknown Soldier's long journey home.[72]

Clearing Europe's battlefields after the war, the Army had gone to extraordinary lengths to identify dead Americans, reducing the percentage of unknowns to a fraction of their number from any previous conflict. Now the War Department reversed course, issuing orders for the Quartermaster Corps to find an unknown solider who was a combat fatality, buried in France, positively known to be American, and selected "so as to preclude the remotest possibility of future identification as to his name, rank, organization, service or the battlefield on which he fell," according to orders from Brig. Gen. William Lassiter, assistant army chief of staff.[73]

Receiving these instructions in September 1921, a special quartermaster's team in France had just over a month to locate the Unknown Solider, who was to be the honored guest for Armistice Day at Arlington on November 11. While preparations went forward on the home front, officers pored over burial records in Paris, where the Graves Registration Service had prepared extensive files for each of the American dead. Even unknown servicemen were assigned an individual grave number, which appeared in their file, along with particulars of their burial, and in many instances, postmortem dental records. From this archive, the army selected four candidates and four alternates for whom no identifying details were evident in the record.[74] The goal was to ensure the anonymity of the Unknown Soldier, precluding later identification and allowing every grieving family to believe that the repatriated soldier might be a missing loved one.

Lt. Col. G. V. S. Quackenbush, supervising the recovery operation, assigned four specialty teams to unearth a pool of candidates for Unknown Soldier from American cemeteries at Aisne-Marne, Meuse-Argonne, Somme, and St. Mihiel. Each venue had been the scene of fierce fighting during the war. Arriving at these cemeteries, each disinterment detail found a gray steel casket and a wooden shipping crate waiting for them, with all identifying markings removed from the boxes. Each casket was "thoroughly cleaned and polished and put in absolutely first-class condition in every particular," according to orders from Quackenbush, who left nothing to chance.[75]

"Should there be anything found on the body or in the coffin which will tend to identify this particular body, an alternate body, for which the required forms have been prepared, will be then exhumed and similarly searched," Quackenbush directed. "The body will be prepared according to regulations— wrapped in a blanket and placed in a special casket provided for this purpose.

No marks whatsoever will be placed on the body, casket or shipping case. The metallic lining will be screwed down but no asphaltum paint will be used on the rubber gasket. The casket top will then be placed on the casket and the shipping case lid attached by only six (6) screws, which will allow the ready opening of the shipping case when the body arrives at its destination." All four teams did their work, loaded their dead comrades onto trucks, draped each shipping case with an American flag, and converged upon the village square of Châlons-sur-Marne at three P.M. on October 23. Here the final selection of the Unknown was to be made.[76]

With solemn ceremony, the flag-draped shipping boxes were conveyed into the Hôtel de Ville, or City Hall. Flags were drawn from each case, caskets were taken out, and each case turned over to serve as a bier. Recovery teams surrendered the original cemetery files and exhumation forms to an officer who burned the records on the spot to prevent any possibility of later identification. After these preliminaries were completed, the doors to City Hall were opened to receive local officials and townspeople, who streamed in with flowers, lingered before the caskets, murmured blessings, crossed themselves, wept openly, and moved slowly away. When darkness fell that night, guards closed the room and, acting on orders, rearranged the caskets so that it would be impossible to tell their cemeteries of origin. The doors were reopened; a combined detail of French and American sentinels marched in and stood watch until the morning of October 24.

The town square of Châlons filled with dignitaries, curious citizens, and soberly dressed neighbors who came to offer their respects. One of these townsmen, Brasseur Bruffer, who had lost two sons in the war, appeared with a bouquet of white roses. He presented these to Maj. Robert B. Harbold, chief of quartermaster operations in the field, who passed the flowers to Sgt. Edward F. Younger, a twice-wounded veteran of every major American offensive of the war. Younger was given the honor of choosing the Unknown from among the four candidates in the holding room. A French military band struck up a hymn in the courtyard, while Younger entered the room to make his choice. Still clutching the roses, he slowly walked among the caskets. "I passed the first one . . . the second," he recalled. "Then something made me stop. And a voice seemed to say, 'This is a pal of yours.' I don't know how long I stood there. But finally I put the roses on the second casket and went back into the sunlight." The choice was made.[77]

Officers lifted the newly designated Unknown Soldier and carried him into the main hall where a catafalque had been set up, and with the help of a mortician, they transferred the serviceman's remains to a new casket, made of ebony and decorated with silver. The coffin was then sealed and locked.[78] Monsieur Bruffer's roses were placed on the lid, where an engraved plaque described the occupant: "An Unknown American Soldier Who Gave His Life in the Great War."[79]

The Unknown's old casket was returned to the holding room, where bodies were shuffled once more to confound any chance of identification. One of the three remaining candidates was removed from his coffin and put into the one just vacated by the Unknown. As soon as this was done, the three bodies in the holding room were secured in their caskets, returned to their shipping crates, covered with flags, and driven to the Meuse-Argonne Cemetery. There, as the familiar strains of Taps sounded in the waning light, they were buried in Graves No. 1, 2, and 3, Row 1, Block G of the American cemetery, where they remain today.[80]

By caisson and train, through silent throngs and deepening autumn, the Unknown Solider made his slow progress across France, through champagne country and blood-soaked battlefields, around sleeping Paris, and finally down to the great port of Le Havre, where well-wishers crowded the pier, bands played "The Star Spangled Banner," and the cruiser U.S.S. *Olympia*, which had been Admiral Dewey's flagship at the Battle of Manila, waited to receive the Unknown. From the knot of officials crowded at quayside, one Frenchman stepped out, limped across the paving stones on a war-shattered leg, and paused before the Unknown's casket.[81]

"The whole of France bows down with me before your coffin," said André Maginot, minister of pensions and later war minister of France.[82] "Brother from America," he said, "they can take you back to the great land from which you came, but your French family will always piously preserve your memory and the land of France will not forget that it was to it you entrusted your last dreams." Maginot knelt to place his country's highest tribute, the Cross of the Chevalier of the Legion of Honor, on the Unknown's casket, the first of many awards he would receive.[83]

As the afternoon shadows lengthened on October 25, 1921, the Army's body bearers lifted their comrade, marched him up the gangway of *Olympia*, and entrusted him to the care of six sailors and two marines, who took the

Unknown aboard and settled him on the stern, where schoolchildren blanketed his casket with flowers. By three twenty P.M., it was time to go. *Olympia* nosed into the harbor and, escorted by the destroyer *Reuben James* and eight French vessels, turned for home. One of the French destroyers boomed a farewell salute of seventeen guns, fired with sober deliberation and answered by *Olympia* in exact order. It might have been a punctuation mark denoting the end of Europe's long trial and the beginning of hope that some good might come of it.[84]

While *Olympia* and her escort steamed across the Atlantic, teams frantically prepared for the Unknown's homecoming at Arlington. Working against the clock, laborers burrowed twenty feet under one of the plantation's most prominent hills to excavate a vault to the south of the old Lee mansion. Set on massive concrete footings, the chamber opened by way of a connecting shaft to the white marble plaza of the new Memorial Amphitheater, completed in 1920. Here on a broad terrace facing east across the Potomac River, the Unknown's sarcophagus, carved from the same Colorado stone as the Greek-inspired amphitheater, was erected over the hillside vault. The tomb on the hill was simple to the point of austerity, consisting of a rectangular plinth a few feet high, surmounted by a smaller rectangular collar, and crowned with a capstone with curved edges. It was considered a temporary structure until something grander could be built, which would take another decade to accomplish.[85]

Meanwhile, there was the matter of a fitting epitaph. Caught up in the patriotic spirit of the times, the public flooded the War Department with suggestions for an inscription for the new tomb. In the manner of those days, most of these literary offerings were syrupy concoctions, such as the one served up by Anais O'C. Pugh in "The Silent Soldier":

> Oh! Mothers! Daughters! Sweethearts! Wives!
> Greave not, but wipe thy tear!
> Your boy has won, who sleeping lies
> On Yonder sacred bier![86]

Lucia R. Maxwell, describing herself as a Daughter of the Confederacy, confirmed with her poem that sectional feelings had improved:

Lift up your head, Columbia
And fling your banner high;
For its starry fold and stripes so old
Your soldiers will fight and die.[87]

Arthur Pew, consulting engineer for waterworks and sewerage in Atlanta, submitted an original work entitled "A Requiem for the Boys who went to France, and were brought Home only to be re-interred," which was of epic length and reminded readers that,

Bright tho the field of France, Homeland is best.
Here midst thy loving friends, Rest, soldier, rest.[88]

This contribution landed in the adjutant general's office on November 4, 1921—regrettably too late, Brig. Gen. Peter C. Harris informed Mr. Pew, to be considered for Armistice Day ceremonies. His verse was filed away with that of other literary aspirants and mercifully forgotten.[89] The tomb's final inscription would not be unveiled for more than a decade.

As the eleventh hour of the eleventh day of the eleventh month drew closer, soldiers at Fort Myer drilled for the forthcoming ceremonies, fretted over the inevitable peacetime force reductions, and helped to fill new rows at Arlington with a steady stream of dead comrades who had been repatriated from Europe that autumn.

Any casual observer might have noticed a small but significant change in graveside ceremonies at Arlington, where those in uniform no longer removed their hats to honor to a dead soldier, sailor, or marine. Instead, servicemen kept their hats on, or in military parlance, "remained covered," thanks to an eminently practical suggestion from H. Allen Griffith, an Army chaplain who tired of seeing his friends and colleagues die from their gallant behavior at funerals.

"Having for the last eighteen years officiated at a larger number of military funerals," the Rev. Mr. Griffith reported to Secretary of War Nelson D. Baker,

"I have become more and more impressed with the danger incurred by the men standing with bared heads during the services. Large numbers of men, especially in the Soldiers Home, are afflicted with thin locks and bald heads, and in the cold rainy weather, there can be no question but that large numbers have contracted colds that have led to chronic sickness or speedy death. There is nothing military in this old custom of 'hats off,'" he reported, perhaps remembering the late Confederate Gen. Joseph E. Johnston's fatal gesture of respect for Gen. William T. Sherman a few years before.

Griffith suggested that instead of "uncovering" at funerals, those servicemen in attendance might simply salute. In a surprise move for a service known for resisting innovation, Gen. Peyton C. March issued Army Circular No. 286 on March 24, 1920, with new rules for military funerals. From that time, men in uniform were directed to "stand at attention covered," according to March. "During prayer they will bow the head. While the casket is being carried to the grave, and while 'Taps' is being sounded they will stand at the salute. They will salute the passing of the casket in any military funeral at any time or place."[90]

Officers at Fort Myer, eager to acquit themselves at forthcoming ceremonies for the Unknown, began to worry that Arlington's regularly scheduled funerals might throw off their preparations for the big day. Of particular concern, Brig. Gen. William Lassiter warned, was the flood of other dead servicemen being repatriated at the rate of seventy-five to a hundred per week. Each of the returning dead required an individual escort who had to be detached from Fort Myer and sent to the receiving port at Hoboken, New Jersey, to accompany the remains to Washington, where the deceased warrior would be buried at Arlington or returned to his family.[91]

"A shipment is due here on October 21 . . . requiring 69 men as escorts," Lassiter warned the War Department on October 9. "There will be two other shipments that would ordinarily arrive here between that date and November 11, 1921. The Quartermaster General states that the relatives of these last two shipments have not been notified and that the bodies could be held at Hoboken until after November 11." Lassiter proposed that these dead servicemen be detained at Hoboken so that men at Fort Myer could concentrate on training "in order to present a creditable appearance on November 11." His request was granted. The dead piled up in New Jersey without the knowledge of their loved ones, who had already endured years of waiting for their return. In deference to the Unknown Solider, they would have to wait a few weeks more.[92]

Long before *Olympia* reached Washington on the drizzling afternoon of November 9, 1921, her approach could be marked by the dull, distant thud of artillery, as forts and posts down the river saluted her passage and she answered, gun for gun, sailing the same course so many hospital ships had followed in the dark days of Civil War. The salutes grew louder until suddenly *Olympia* broke into view, a gray ship ghosting out of a gray mist and turning slowly upstream for the Navy Yard. At her rails stood silent, dripping bluejackets in rigid lines; at her stern, an honor guard of marines and sailors kept vigil over the flag-draped casket protected by a canvas awning; on shore, a mounted band formed ranks on restless horses; beside them, a regiment of cavalry drew their sabers and stiffened, eyes forward, caps streaming rain. The great ship slid into place at precisely eight bells, announced by the vessel's double chime. *Olympia*'s marine guard filed solemnly down the gangway, turned to face the cavalry, and stood to attention as the boatswain piped the Unknown over the side, his casket borne down the ramp, and back to American soil with all the honors due an Admiral of the Fleet.[93]

The band struck up "The Star-Spangled Banner." Monsieur Brasseur's white roses, shriveled and dried from their Atlantic crossing, stayed with the Unknown as he passed from the care of the Navy into the hands of Army bearers, who slow-walked the casket over slick cobblestones and strapped it onto a waiting caisson. The cavalry escort moved into place, six black horses strained in their harness, and to the tune of "Onward, Christian Soldiers," the caisson clattered down a winding drive lined by marine guards standing like statues in the rain.[94]

The light was fading when the caisson rolled up to Capitol Hill, where body bearers stepped forward, shouldered the Unknown's remains, and trudged up the marble steps. Inside, under the soaring Rotunda dome that had sheltered Lincoln, L'Enfant, McKinley, and other honored figures lying in state, the Unknown's comrades eased him down for the night, with his head pointed toward France, his feet toward Arlington.[95]

From his arrival in Washington, he would never be alone. Sentinels stood watch through two nights, relieved at regular intervals by their comrades. President Warren G. Harding brought flowers, as did Chief Justice and former President William Howard Taft, Vice President Calvin Coolidge, General Pershing, and other dignitaries. Some came bearing fresh roses from England; some, poppies from the bloody soil of Flanders. King George V of Britain sent a wreath with a biblical inscription on the ribbon: "As Unknown, yet well known; As dying, and behold, we live."[96]

When the Rotunda's massive bronze doors opened on the morning of November 10, thousands of ordinary citizens poured through to pay their respects, bringing so many flowers that the growing mountain of blossoms had to be carted off to make way for more visitors and more flowers. The weather cleared. The silent crowds edged four abreast past the Unknown's casket and streamed out of the Rotunda at the rate of a hundred a minute. Soldiers old and young came to honor one of their own, followed by mothers in black, wearing the gold star of those who had lost their sons to war.[97]

Because the Unknown had no name, no home, no rank, and not a scrap of evidence suggesting his identity, he could be claimed by everyone. Mothers who had never recovered their sons from Europe allowed themselves to think that the boy in the casket was theirs.[98] Rich and poor embraced him, as did small-town shopkeepers from the flatlands and farmers from the hills. African Americans, wondering if he had been a brother, came bearing a wreath for him.[99] Some ninety thousand to one hundred thousand made the effort to give their thanks or say farewells in person. A blind man, led by a child, paused before the casket, listened for a whispered cue, and crossed himself. Wounded French soldiers struggled by on crutches and canes, which echoed harshly under the dome; old men and women shuffled between rope lines. Many lingered at the bier, made to move off, and turned for a last look at the flower-covered casket and the fresh-faced guards with heads bowed around it, lit by pale sunlight slanting in from high in the dome. Many left the Rotunda with tears coursing down their faces.[100]

Those planning the funeral march from Capitol Hill had intended for General Pershing, the Army's new chief of staff, to lead mourners through the city and across the river to Arlington on horseback, as grand marshal of ceremonies. He would have none of that. Pershing insisted on walking behind the caisson, content to cover the five miles on foot. At precisely eight A.M. on November 11, 1921, pallbearers emerged from the Rotunda on a mist-shrouded day, brought the Unknown down the Capitol steps, and loaded him on the caisson, just as a field artillery battery, positioned near the Washington Monument, commenced firing the gun that would mark each minute throughout the day, pausing only for the traditional two minutes of silence at eleven A.M.[101]

Rank upon rank formed behind Maj. Gen. Harry H. Bandholtz, commanding the Military District of Washington, who nudged his horse and led the way down Pennsylvania Avenue, followed by the Army band, a drum corps beating quick time, a foot regiment, a mounted field artillery battalion, a squadron of cavalry, and four clergymen. Then came the caisson bearing the Unknown, who was accorded the final honors reserved for a general.[102]

President Harding and General Pershing strode behind the caisson, followed by the Supreme Court, the cabinet, governors, columns of senators and House members, Medal of Honor winners, and white-haired sailors, soldiers, and marines from the old wars. As the cortege turned downhill from the Capitol, former president Woodrow Wilson joined the line, riding in an open horse carriage with Mrs. Wilson and drawing cheers from thousands of spectators lining the streets. He had not been seen in public since March, when he and Harding had ridden along this same street at the latter's inauguration. The once-proud figure, now pale and broken, was a reminder that the casualties of war were not limited to those in uniform. The public obviously appreciated Wilson's gesture, brief though it proved to be. When the procession reached the White House, Harding and Wilson tipped hats to each other and the Wilsons were driven home. Harding peeled off from the parade at this point, along with cabinet officers, Supreme Court members, and other luminaries, who intended to drive to Arlington later.[103]

Pershing, his uniform unadorned except for a single Victory Medal, closed ranks with hundreds of others remaining in the cortege and marched out the length of Pennsylvania Avenue, through Georgetown, over the old Aqueduct Bridge into Virginia, and slowly up the long hill to Arlington, reaching the new Memorial Amphitheater at eleven fifteen A.M. To the strains of a hymn, the casket team gathered up the Unknown, marched him into the apse of the amphitheater, and, while the audience rose in silence, positioned his casket on a bier piled high with flowers. Pershing filed in. War mothers took their places on marble benches. Nurses in gray helped wounded soldiers into seats of honor. Marshal Foch of France, his chest gleaming with war medals, found his place, followed by Britain's Admiral Lord Beatty, Belgium's General Baron Jacques, Generalissimo Diaz of Italy, former British prime minister Arthur J. Balfour, French premier Aristide Briand, and Chief Plenty Coups of the Crow Nation.[104] Technicians fussed with wires behind the podium, nervously testing amplifiers and microphones for the first presidential speech ever broadcast across the country—which brought the Arlington service to thousands of far-flung Americans in New York City, Chicago, and San Francisco at the same time.[105]

President Harding, caught in traffic jamming the Potomac River bridges, took his place in the amphitheater at eleven fifty A.M., just in time for opening ceremonies. With visible emotion, he stood beside the flag-covered coffin and called for an end to war—just as his predecessor had done on previous occasions at Arlington. "Ours are lofty resolutions today," Harding said, his words crackling from loudspeakers set around the amphitheater, "as with tribute to the dead we consecrate ourselves to a better order for the living. With all my heart, I wish we might say to the defenders who survive, to mothers who sorrow, to widows and children who mourn, that no such sacrifice shall be asked again . . . Standing today on hallowed ground, conscious that all America has halted to share in the tribute of heart and mind and soul to this fellow American . . . it is fitting to say that his sacrifice, and that of the millions dead, shall not be in vain. There must be, there shall be, the commanding voice of a conscious civilization against armed warfare."[106]

After leading the crowd in the Lord's Prayer, Harding gathered up the Medal of Honor and the Distinguished Service Cross, stepped over to the Unknown's casket, and pinned them there. These honors were followed by one after another—from Belgium, France, Italy, Romania, Czechoslovakia, Poland. Admiral Lord Beatty came bearing the Victoria Cross, never before awarded a foreigner.[107]

When ceremonies in the amphitheater were done, body bearers hoisted the Unknown onto their shoulders for the last time, marched a hundred yards east to the plaza overlooking the green hills, and situated his casket over the sarcophagus. They stepped back and straightened. The burial service was read. General Pershing walked across the terrace and tossed a handful of soil into the tomb, saluted, and stepped back. Chief Plenty Coups ceremoniously removed his war bonnet, placed it on the tomb, and expressed his hope "for peace to all men hereafter." He was answered by three salvos booming from the saluting battery. Pallbearers stepped forward and tenderly lowered the Unknown into his crypt, where he would rest in French soil brought over on *Olympia*. Monsieur Brasseur's roses remained with him. A bugler sounded Taps, and as the final note died, the artillery spoke for the last time, shaking the hills of Arlington with a resounding twenty-one-gun salute for the soldier "known but to God."[108]

9

A TIME TO BUILD UP

Nothing could redeem a young life lost to war, but the rituals at the Tomb of the Unknown helped ease the grief for mothers such as Mrs. Emmett Digney of White Grange, New York, who took solace from the artillery salutes, the majestic old hymns offered up by brass bands, and the outpouring of sympathy from thousands of ordinary citizens who converged on Arlington in November 1921 to pay tribute to those who never returned from World War I.

"Our government does not know what it has done for the thousands of bereaved mothers in the United States," said Mrs. Digney, president of the National American War Mothers, after the Arlington ceremonies. "I know how I felt when I viewed the bier of the man who represented all of America's fallen sons . . . The thought came to me that in the coffin . . . of one American soldier the hearts of every mother who lost her boy were carried to the final resting place . . . Every mother whose boy died on the field of battle and whose body was interred in a foreign land must feel that the body interred today is that of her boy and glean comfort from that thought."[1]

The world stopped to pay attention at Arlington that day, providing a sense of closure for Mrs. Digney, as it did for thousands of American families reduced by war. For others, though, the flag-waving speeches and the flash of swords had the opposite effect, rekindling memories of brutal fighting, pointless casualties, and comrades gone forever. The burden of remembrance fell especially hard on Lt. Col. Charles W. Whittlesey, thirty-seven, who as an army major had lost more than half of his battalion in the American offensive at Argonne Forest in October 1918. Driving deep into German-held territory, troops from the 308th Infantry Regiment outran their own lines and endured five days of merciless bombardment and machine gun fire—some of it from their own compatriots. Germans offered Whittlesey the chance to surrender; he declined, maintaining his forward position until reinforcements broke through. When the smoke cleared and the roll was called on October 6, the reckoning showed 356 of the unit's 554 soldiers killed, wounded, or captured. The survivors, celebrated by Damon Runyon and other war correspondents, won fame as the "Lost Battalion." Whittlesey was promoted to lieutenant colonel and won the Medal of Honor for gallantry and intrepidity.[2]

After the war, the reluctant hero returned to practice law in New York City, quietly resuming civilian life until November 1921, when he was summoned to Washington to march with fellow Medal of Honor laureates at ceremonies for the Unknown. He fell in with old comrades tramping through the chill streets of the capital and across the river to Arlington, where he saw the honored warrior lowered into the earth, felt the familiar shudder of artillery once more, and heard the silver notes of Taps ringing among the tombstones for the last time.[3]

The sensitive, bespectacled Whittlesey returned to New York, booked passage on the S.S. *Toloa* for Havana, and, when well out to sea at night, leaped overboard to his death. He left letters for family and friends, named an executor, and finally put the war behind him. His body was never recovered.[4]

The war had broken Whittlesey, just as it had wiped out a generation in Europe, brought the Bolsheviks to power in Russia, shattered old alliances, and redrawn political boundaries from the North Sea to the Mediterranean. Within the peace terms imposed on Germany by the Versailles Treaty were imbedded the irritants that would animate Adolf Hitler's rise to power and, all too soon, lead to the next global conflagration.[5]

In the meantime, however, world leaders did what they invariably do after a war: they picked through the ruins, buried their fighting men, welcomed their returning veterans, and struggled to restore some semblance of hope for the future. On the day after ceremonies for the Unknown at Arlington, President Harding convened an international disarmament conference in Washington, where nine leading nations met to stave off the sort of arms race that had helped to spark World War I.[6]

On the eve of the conference, even Gen. John J. Pershing—that most unbending of soldiers, now Army chief of staff—endorsed the peaceful aims of the international gathering. He called for a ban on chemical weapons, which he termed a "cruel, unfair and improper use of science." He favored a limit on arms production, as long as the terms applied to all sides proportionately. And he warned about "nations striding up and down the earth armed to the teeth . . . we may well ask ourselves whether civilization does really reach a point where it begins to destroy itself."[7]

With Europe weary of fighting, most diplomats expected the next war to break out in Asia, where seafaring powers would likely shape the course of events—thus, the emphasis on reducing naval arms among the United States, Great Britain, Japan, France, and Italy. After months of intense discussion in Washington, the five major powers agreed to scuttle their older capital vessels—those battleships and cruisers with the heaviest armor and the biggest firepower—and to limit production of new ones at an agreed-upon ratio. Another treaty called for the United States, Britain, France, and Japan to consult before taking any military action in East Asia, where the world's commercial powers were maneuvering for a share of the China trade. Signed by President Harding and ratified by the Senate in 1923, the treaties briefly accomplished their purpose, providing a decade of peace before the world took up arms and resumed fighting in the 1930s.[8]

The pause between wars at Arlington provided another opportunity for rebuilding and refining the cemetery, which continued as a work in progress as the twentieth century gathered steam.

The old Lee mansion, still the cemetery's most imposing landmark, had fallen into a state of neglect by the end of World War I. Stripped of furniture and paintings, its rooms were for the most part empty, given over to the utilitarian functions of cemetery administration. Arlington's durable gardener and disinterment specialist, D. H. Rhodes, had commandeered one room for office space; in another, the cemetery superintendent received visitors and kept burial records, while a third downstairs chamber was cluttered with battle flags and unsorted mementos from the Union's Civil War campaigns. Little thought was given to preserving the distinctive character of this historically significant structure—a state of affairs that prompted an influential writer to call attention to the matter in her *Good Housekeeping* column, "Letters from a Senator's Wife."[9]

"Whatever our opinions and traditions may be," Frances Parkinson Keyes wrote in the August 1921 issue of the magazine, "we all realize now that Robert E. Lee was one of the greatest generals and one of the noblest men who ever lived. To every American woman the abuse of his home must seem a disgrace; to every Southern woman it must seem a sacrilege." Although married to Sen. Henry Wilder Keyes, a New Hampshire Republican, Frances Keyes was a devoted Virginia native and admirer of the Confederate general. She took inspiration from the recent restoration of George Washington's Mount Vernon estate, just down the Potomac River from Arlington. The success of that initiative, organized by the Mount Vernon Ladies' Association, encouraged Mrs. Keyes to propose similar renovations for the Lee family's homestead. She used her *Good Housekeeping* column to generate interest in the project, and her husband's position on Capitol Hill to recruit an able ally, Rep. Louis C. Cramton, to carry it forward.[10]

Cramton, a Michigan Republican whose father had fought as a Union soldier against Lee, took up the case for Arlington in May 1924, when he introduced legislation to restore the house to its pre–Civil War condition. "The exterior of the mansion is as it was in the old days," Cramton explained in congressional hearings that spring. "The interior is barren and naked. Whenever I have taken any friends . . . I have felt obliged to apologize to them for the condition of the interior, in its barrenness and unattractiveness." Cramton made it clear that he not only hoped to return the mansion to its former glory but also shared Mrs. Keyes's regard for Lee, whom he called "an American who occupies a very high place in our history and in the hearts of our people." Creating a Lee memorial at Arlington "would be tangible recognition by the country, North and South, that the bitterness of other days is entirely gone."[11]

That bitterness had moderated, to be sure, but it was not entirely gone. More than fifty years after his death, Robert E. Lee still exerted a strange power among many who remembered—and could not forgive—his Civil War performance. The prospect that Arlington might be established as a shrine to the Rebel general spurred Sen. Porter H. Dale, a Vermont Republican, to propose that Lee's home be converted into a museum for displaying "trophies and emblems of the Union Army and Navy of the United States during the Civil War." Dale's legislation, supported by the aging veterans of the Grand Army of the Republic, also called for keeping the cemetery's administrative offices in the mansion. After some lively discussion, Dale's bill was referred to the Senate Committee on Military Affairs in February 1926. It disappeared there.[12]

A more serious threat to the Lee memorial came from Charles Moore, the influential chairman of the National Commission of Fine Arts, a federal advisory board of painters, sculptors, architects, and landscape gardeners established in 1910 to evaluate the design and site selection for new buildings and parks in the capital region. Although the board had no real authority, it was soon established as the final arbiter of taste for buildings and grounds in Washington, where commissioners sought to enforce a particular aesthetic, incorporating open spaces, long views, a horizontal construction scheme, and simple, classical lines for buildings—in short, the look that Pierre Charles L'Enfant had in mind when he sketched out plans for the federal city in 1791.[13]

As soon as Moore heard of Mrs. Keyes's plans for the Lee mansion, he strongly objected to making the place a memorial to the Confederate general. Lee already had countless shrines, Moore argued, so why create another? Instead, he urged the quartermaster to emphasize the mansion's architectural heritage, as one of the first Greek Revival homes in the United States, from the days of George Washington Parke Custis. Restoring the interior to the florid Victorian style of the Lees would clash with the clean, cool neo-Greek exterior, Moore believed. He even tried to divorce the family's name from the house—calling it not the Lee Mansion, as most people did, but the Arlington Mansion. "It is eminently proper that the name Arlington Mansion should be applied to the house," he told the quartermaster, "and that it should be refitted both as to the house itself and the grounds immediately surrounding it, as a home representative of the first fifty years of the Republic"—and not, he implied, as the home of the Lees.[14]

In the end, Moore lost his skirmish with the Confederate ghost. Congress passed Cramton's bill extolling the general's "exalted character, noble life, and eminent services" and established the residence as his memorial. The bill, which pointedly referred to the house as the Lee Mansion, authorized the secretary of war to restore the place "to the condition in which it existed immediately prior to the Civil War, and to procure, if possible, articles of furniture and equipment which were then in the mansion and in use by the . . . Lee family."[15]

President Calvin Coolidge signed the legislation in March 1925. Because budgets were tight in the postwar era, it took another four years for Congress to appropriate one hundred thousand dollars for renovations.[16] As soon as the money came through, the quartermaster plunged into the project, dispatching workers to restore mantels and fireplaces, repair sagging floors, replace old hardware and rotten framework, and rebuild crumbling walls within the house. Chandeliers and chimneys were put into working condition; electrical wiring was modernized; General Lee's heating system was torn out and converted to a modern one, placed outside the mansion to reduce the risk of fire. Maj. L. M. Leisenring, an army architect overseeing research for the project, combed through archives and interviewed former slaves to gather authentic information about the mansion and grounds.[17]

An invaluable source for this living history was James Parks, the slave who had been born at Arlington, had grown up there, and had continued working on the estate long after the Civil War. He helped Leisenring locate the conservatory where the Custises and Lees had raised camellias; pinpointed the rooms where G. W. C. Custis had set up his office; recalled how Custis had played his fiddle for dances down by the river; and meticulously described the layout of the stables and slave quarters, which allowed them to be reconstructed with historical accuracy. He provided details about the summer kitchen, the smokehouse, the old vegetable garden, and the covered well from which he and generations of slaves had drawn water for their masters.[18] When project managers found a drawing of the mansion from 1853, they noticed that it depicted balustrades around the upper wings, an architectural element long since missing from the house. Quizzed about it, Parks vividly remembered how, in her more nimble days, Mrs. Lee would climb out of an upstairs window to stroll around the roof on the mansion's north wing: "Miss Mary used to come out from dat window up dere and walk around on dat roof, and she sure gwine to fall and break her neck if dey ain't no fence up dere to stop her," said Parks, his language recorded in the dialect formulaic for those times.[19]

Trusting his testimony, restorers replaced the copings just as he described them. He had established himself as a reliable witness, never prone to exaggerate or to jumble the facts.[20] "He was very careful in answering questions to answer them in accordance with his memory and not to fake any of the information," Leisenring reported. "If he didn't remember . . . he candidly said so, or explained why he was not familiar with the matter . . . I asked him many questions regarding the . . . summer kitchen building. He described it quite minutely and although some of the entrances which he said were there had been filled in, and the stone or brick work stuccoed over, I tore off some of the stucco to verify the location of the doors . . . and found the wooden lintels . . . He had an unusually good memory of things connected with the place of bygone years."[21]

The restoration was just getting under way when James Parks died in August 1929. He was said to be eighty-six years old, and in the phrase of the Washington *Evening Star*, which gave him a page-one obituary, he was the "last of the home folks" from "those far-off days of stately minuets and crinoline and old lace."[22] Affectionately known in his later years as "Old Uncle Jim," Parks had grown up among the Lee children, seen them disappear with the war, walked among Union forces camped on the hills, and witnessed the rise and fall of Freedman's Village. He had dug the first graves for military burials at Arlington and watched the white tombstones proliferate with each new war. He had married at Arlington, fathered twenty-two children there, and sent five of his sons to serve in World War I, from which all returned safely. He vividly remembered President Lincoln's Emancipation Proclamation but credited G. W. P. Custis with his freedom, because that is what Custis had stipulated in his will. Parks had known the mansion when it was new, witnessed its decline, and, here at the last, contributed to its revival, which must have been a satisfying way to close the circle on an eventful life.[23]

His friends at the War Department arranged a memorable farewell for Parks, whose last wish was to be buried at Arlington. He was assigned a prominent grave close by the Fort Myer Gate. More than sixty friends and family members turned out for the ceremony. On a steamy August day, they gathered around his grave as an Army chaplain read the burial service, soldiers snapped off a three-rifle salute, and James Parks returned to his home soil in fine military style. A few months later, a commemorative tablet appeared on his grave, placed there by the American Legion in tribute to the courtly man who had been so much a part of Arlington. "In appreciation of his faithful service the Secretary of War granted special permission to bury his mortal remains in this National Cemetery," the tablet read. "Requiescat In Pace."[24]

Workers brought the Lee mansion slowly back to life. Leisenring explained that the restoration, largely completed by 1934, was meant to give visitors the impression that the family "had gone out for the afternoon and would soon return."[25] This notion was reinforced when the superintendent and gardener moved out of the mansion in 1932 to new offices in the plantation's refurbished stables, a miniature version of the main house with its central hall and symmetrical wings. Removing cemeterial functions from the mansion underscored the building's historical standing and furthered its new role as a memorial to the Lees.[26]

Undaunted by his failure to make the house an architectural specimen of the Custis period, Charles Moore of the Fine Arts Commission turned his attention to Arlington's landscape design, where his influence was more readily felt. Here, emphasizing the mansion's colonial setting, its classical lines, and its superb views down the river, Moore urged the quartermaster to dig up colorful flower beds near the mansion and replace them with grass and boxwoods more in keeping with the cemetery's sober purpose and the early Republican style. He also asked that heavy iron vases in front of the house be "taken out and lost" and recommended colonial-style walkways of brick or gravel to replace paved ones around the house. He railed against a pavilion known as the Temple of Fame, a tin-roofed eyesore the late General Meigs had built with columns salvaged from the Patent Office fire of 1877. After years of resistance, the Army razed the Temple of Fame and Moore's landscape plans gradually took hold at Arlington, where his suggestions reduced clutter, soothed the palette of hillside plantings, and called attention to the house's dignified architectural lines. In the end, Moore's contribution greatly enhanced views of—and from—the heights of Arlington.

Civilians who crossed the river to visit graves or check on progress at the Lee mansion soon found their way to the new Memorial Amphitheater and the Tomb of the Unknown, where no sentries were present to enforce decorum. By 1923 enterprising photographers had set up shop and were charging for pictures. The cameramen irreverently posed subjects around the tomb and even encouraged young ladies to sit on the sarcophagus for portraits. This was just one of the indignities visited upon America's hero of the Great War. Men approached his shrine with their hats on; others stubbed out cigarettes on the marble plaza; some enjoyed picnicking on the nearby hills; others strolled around laughing and talking excitedly, seemingly oblivious to their surroundings.[27]

It was not long before complaints began flowing to the Army brass in Washington. "We do not honor our Unknown as well as those in France do," Maj. R. H. Fletcher wrote the adjutant general in 1922, recalling the Europeans who had inspired America to honor its nameless warrior in the first place. "If our people do not understand," Mabel Brown wrote to General Pershing from Norfolk, Virginia, "could not the tomb be protected against them?"[28]

The answer—from Pershing, from Quartermaster General William H. Hart, and from Secretary of War John W. Weeks—was no. Aggravated by tight postwar budgets and force reductions, Weeks informed a member of the American War Mothers organization that there was no structure for billeting sentries at the tomb and therefore no way to post guards there; it apparently never occurred to him that such barracks might be built or that men from Fort Myer might be encouraged to walk a few hundred yards downhill to Arlington for sentry duty. "It is realized that the placing of an armed sentry at this tomb . . . would lend dignity to the Shrine," Weeks wrote in December 1922, "but in view of the fact above noted, it is regretted that it is not considered advisable to issue instructions to this effect at this time."[29] In a less roundabout explanation, a deputy from Pershing's office dismissed complaints about the Army's stewardship at the tomb, which was placed so far off the tourist track that it did not merit a full-time guard, in the opinion of Brig. Gen. H. H. Bandholtz.

"As is well known," Bandholtz told the adjutant general, "the average visitor to Washington, or the average citizen of the city, can reach the distantly located tomb only with great difficulty, and it is not and never will be visited by the thousands of visitors as is done in England, France, and Italy."[30] Posting a sentry at the tomb, he argued, would "not lend dignity to the shrine, and would . . . work a real hardship on the soldier required to do sentry duty there, and in time this feeling of irritation, transmitted from sentry to sentry, would unquestionably detract from the respect and veneration in which the shrine is now held . . . Furthermore, the average American visitor . . . would probably not even notice the fact that a sentry was stationed nearby."[31]

Despite the opposition of Bandholtz and like-minded officers, the War Department eventually took steps to protect the tomb, largely because the place had become a magnet for visitors who found conditions wanting at Arlington and complained about it. After the *Washington Post* called attention to rowdy crowds and litter around the tomb, the Army erected a picket fence, rousted commercial photographers from the area, and posted a civilian guard there later in 1923. The watchman had "strict orders to keep visitors from the top of the Tomb, and picnickers are not allowed in the vicinity," Quartermaster William Hart reported. But he warned that hired guards could do nothing to prevent visitors from wearing their hats or smoking at the tomb.[32] This changed in 1926, when veterans' groups shamed the War Department into posting armed soldiers to "prevent any desecration or disrespect" at the tomb. A few years later, the sentries, originally assigned to patrol during daylight hours when the cemetery was open, were put on duty around the clock, a practice that has continued without interruption since 1937. With this, what had begun as a reluctant duty became one of the proudest traditions of the service.[33]

Just as the first contingent of sentinels shouldered their Springfields and began patrolling the tomb, Congress came through with funds to construct a substantial new sarcophagus over the temporary one, which had been in place since Armistice Day ceremonies in 1922. The original monument's plain style and unfinished condition—and the government's long delay in completing it—provoked widespread criticism in newspapers across the nation, which prodded lawmakers to set aside fifty thousand dollars for completing the tomb in July 1926.[34] Congress authorized the secretary of war to secure competitive designs. Seventy-four plans were submitted. From these the Fine Arts Commission and other experts awarded the winning design to Lorimer Rich as architect and Thomas Hudson Jones as sculptor in 1929. Their plan was simple to the point of severity. It used the old tomb as a base for a new sarcophagus, an oblong marble box more than thirteen feet long and eleven feet tall. The spare, classically inspired figures—representing Victory, Valor, and Peace—were to be carved on the eastern end of the tomb facing Washington; its western end, at the edge of the amphitheater terrace, was saved for the inscription HERE RESTS IN HONORED GLORY AN AMERICAN SOLDIER KNOWN BUT TO GOD. Side panels were to be decorated with inverted laurel wreaths and Doric columns. None of these visions could be realized until the raw material— three massive blocks of white marble weighing a total of more than eighty tons in the raw—was ordered from the Yule Marble Quarry in Marble, Colorado, the same company that had provided stone for the Lincoln Memorial.[35]

It took a year of trial and error before acceptable pieces of marble could be extracted from the quarry, located near a mountaintop at ten thousand feet. After three attempts, workers finally cut a suitable fifty-ton die block, the main component for the new tomb; it took three more tries to extract the eighteen-ton tomb base, while the third component, a fourteen-ton capstone, was freed from the mountain on the first try and pronounced perfect. Then the massive pieces were shipped by rail to Vermont, trimmed down, and finished smooth before the rail journey to Arlington, where the three separate elements had arrived by September 1931. There a timber A-frame was erected over the old tomb and the new base was hoisted into place and painstakingly lowered onto the amphitheater terrace—whereupon project managers from the quartermaster's office discovered a flaw in the new marble. All work came to a halt for three months while a replacement stone was cut and the pattern was repeated, from Colorado to Vermont to Virginia. While this part of the project dragged on, workers at Arlington focused on another phase of the design, which called for opening views down to the river from the amphitheater terrace. There, where a retaining wall had been built into the side of a hill to form the plaza in 1922, crews demolished the wall, graded a slope to the river, and installed a long flight of marble steps cascading down into the cemetery. This opening provided sweeping vistas across the Potomac, where the newly completed Lincoln Memorial anchored the view from Arlington to the National Mall.[36]

Work on the tomb resumed in December 1931, when the replacement marble base arrived from Vermont. The defective piece was lifted away, the new one fitted in its place, and the massive die block rolled into position over the old tomb. On the last day of 1931, the capstone was sealed over the marble box, ending more than six years of delay. After all the mishaps and waiting, it was at last time for Thomas Hudson Jones to begin carving the decorative figures into the die block, a commission he finished in a matter of weeks. The completed monument was opened to public view on April 9, 1932, with formal dedication ceremonies planned for Armistice Day.[37]

By this time, the national cemetery and capital city had been linked by the long-anticipated Arlington Memorial Bridge, a 2,163-foot-long span distinguished by its graceful stone arches and gilded, muscular equestrian statues at either end: "Valor," "The Arts of War," "Sacrifice," and "The Arts of Peace." Designed by the respected architectural firm of McKim, Mead, and White and opened in January 1932, the bridge finished Washington's riparian landscape in one unified design, extending the National Mall to the Potomac River and linking Lee's newly restored memorial with Lincoln's gleaming marble temple.[38]

The bridge erased some of the distance remaining between North and South, advancing the ongoing work of reunion. But even as this happened, a worsening Depression created new rifts among the survivors of the nation's most recent war.

Hard-pressed veterans of the Great War, disillusioned by the government's delay in paying bonuses promised for their military service, converged on Washington with the spring of 1932 to demand redress. Calling themselves the Bonus Expeditionary Force (BEF), their numbers swelled to as many as twenty thousand by July. Rebuffed by Congress and by President Herbert Hoover, the men and their families milled around the Mall, begged citizens for money, haunted vacant government buildings, and set up dozens of camps around Capitol Hill. Some Washingtonians, accustomed to life in a segregated city, were shocked to see that the BEF, unlike the regular Army, was thoroughly integrated; black and white comrades camped together, messed together, and made their rounds of the capital with little regard for racial distinction. Some crossed the new bridge into Arlington, scrounged food from sympathetic soldiers at Fort Myer, and paid respects at the tomb of their unknown comrade. They may have found it ironic, if not perplexing, that the government was willing to lavish thousands of dollars on the dead from their war but withheld funds for living soldiers who came home from Europe to find their farms ruined, their jobs gone, and their prospects diminished.[39]

Although there is little evidence that the veterans' spontaneous march on Washington had been organized or influenced by Communists, some government leaders believed otherwise, fearing that the ragtag protesters might spark riots and class warfare across the country, as was happening in Europe. As the first wave of the BEF drifted into Washington, Patrick Jay Hurley, the secretary of war, sent messages to the Army's nine regional commanders in secret code, asking them to ferret out the Reds among protesters bound for the capital.[40] The army's new chief of staff, Gen. Douglas MacArthur, held similar views. He thought most of the BEF men were not veterans at all, but imposters bent on making trouble. "There is incipient revolution in the air," he told an aide, Maj. Dwight D. Eisenhower, as the scruffy protesters lingered in the capital that summer.[41] MacArthur was wrong—most of the BEF were simply veterans down on their luck, looking to their government for help, just as thousands of homeless freedmen had done a few decades before. Camping in frayed tents, packing crates, and rough-built shanties around the Capitol, the BEF had outstayed its welcome by mid-July. When Congress recessed without resolving the bonus question that summer, President Hoover determined that it was time for the BEF to go. At his direction, Patrick Hurley issued orders for their eviction on July 28, 1932.[42]

General MacArthur, vowing to "break the back of the BEF," took prompt action, organizing the army to march against civilians.[43] At his command, more than two hundred cavalry troopers saddled up at Fort Myer, swept down through Arlington National Cemetery, and thundered over the new Arlington Memorial Bridge, while infantrymen who usually served as tomb guards and casket bearers took up arms, grabbed their gas masks, and climbed aboard trucks that followed the cavalry across the river. Other infantry units were called up from nearby Fort Washington. With forces in place on the Ellipse by four thirty P.M., the cavalry clattered down Pennsylvania Avenue with sabers drawn, followed by army trucks carrying five tanks and mounted machine guns, with some four hundred infantrymen bringing up the rear, marching in columns, closing implacably on Capitol Hill.[44]

There the army plowed into startled BEF members and curious spectators, scattering citizens before them. Through clouds of tear gas and cries of "Shame! Shame!" MacArthur's men drove thousands of citizens up Pennsylvania Avenue, across the Mall, and over the Eleventh Street Bridge toward Anacostia, where the BEF had its main encampment. Although President Hoover gave MacArthur precise instructions not to pursue veterans beyond the bridge, the general ignored this order, stormed into the BEF shanty town, and set the makeshift settlement aflame.[45] The Bonus Army was broken that night. A few veterans stayed in Washington to nurse injuries from tear gas and rough handling, while most returned to their homes or settled at new camps in Pennsylvania and New York's Central Park. Those who stood their ground were trampled or slashed by cavalrymen.[46]

Two veterans were killed in a related police action just hours before the army's July 28 offensive. In a scuffle with officers along Pennsylvania Avenue, where bricks were thrown from the crowd, William Hushka, a thirty-five-year-old from Chicago, and Eric Carlson, thirty-eight, from Oakland, California, were fatally shot by police. Hushka, a Lithuanian native and a butcher by trade, died on the spot. Carlson clung to life a few days, dying on August 2.[47] Both were buried at Arlington, attended by family, hundreds of fellow legionnaires, and the very soldiers called to eject them from the capital.[48]

Despite the deaths and despite MacArthur's disregard for orders, Patrick Hurley declared the campaign a success. "It was a great victory," he told a midnight press conference while the ruins of the Anacostia camp smoldered. "Mac did a great job," he said, crediting the general at his side. "He is the man of the hour."[49]

The nocturnal assault temporarily relieved tensions in the capital, but as word spread of the army's heavy-handedness at the expense of unarmed men, women, and children, public opinion turned against President Hoover, Patrick Hurley, General MacArthur, and others responsible for the July 28 offensive. The morning after the Washington riots, when Franklin D. Roosevelt read the *New York Times* account of the event, he told an associate that it would not be necessary to campaign against Hoover that year—the incumbent was doing FDR's work for him.[50] When newsreels of MacArthur appeared in movie houses around the country following the riots, audiences booed him as well as the Army.[51] And when Hurley walked onstage at an American Legion convention in Portland, Oregon, in September 1932, he drew jeers from many veterans in the crowd.[52] The nation's economic decline, combined with Hoover's mean-spirited treatment of the BEF, doomed his election that fall. Roosevelt won by seven million votes.[53]

Less than a week after Hoover's humiliation at the polls, thousands of dignitaries, soldiers, and veterans staged what one newspaper called a "monster parade" through Washington before climbing into the hills of Arlington to dedicate the new Tomb of the Unknown on November 11, 1932. Hoover avoided the ceremonies, which had been organized by the American Legion. Instead he dispatched Patrick Hurley to represent his administration. This gave the BEF an opportunity to even the score.[54]

When the lame-duck secretary of war arrived at the Tomb of the Unknown that morning, he found a hundred stone-faced veterans from the American Legion's Victory Post of Washington, D.C., standing at attention on the terrace, where they had just laid a wreath at the tomb. They made no effort to yield their position to Hurley, whom they watched in silence as he placed his own floral tribute and retreated toward the amphitheater. Just as he did, the commander of the Victory Post Drum Corps snapped an order to his men on the plaza: "Right by squads!" he barked. The corps pivoted and, maintaining its columns, tromped down through the cemetery to the thump of drums and the shrill of fifes, headed for the graves of William Hushka and Eric Carlson.[55]

In the packed amphitheater, meanwhile, spectators feared trouble as they settled into their seats, heard the distant drums marking time for the Victory Post parade, and nervously watched Hurley take his place at the rostrum, clap on a pince-nez, and fidget with the notes for his speech.[56]

"Again we stand at the sacred tomb . . . ," he began.

Before he got further, a few veterans scattered through the arena stood up and walked out, climbing over the knees of spectators who remained seated. Hurley resumed speaking, and a few more men and women pointedly left, followed by more at intervals, all synchronized to disrupt Hurley's talk. He forged ahead, pretending not to notice.[57]

The protest had been orchestrated by Raymond Burke, commander of the Victory Post Drum Corps, who explained his group's actions this way. "The men in our drum corps feel that Mr. Hurley cannot express the feeling that caused the Unknown Soldier to lay down his life for this country," he told the *Washington Herald*. "His brutal treatment of the war veterans in Washington . . . clearly revealed that his sympathies are not with the men who fought overseas.[58] Yes, we're of the mob, but we're gentlemen and patriots anyway. We have paid our tribute to the Unknown as sincerely and honestly as we can. Instead of listening to Mr. Hurley, we are now going to the graves of our comrades, William Hushka and Eric Carlson."[59]

Some two hundred men and women followed Burke's drum corps through the cemetery to lay wreaths for Hushka and Carlson that day, as the local remnants of the BEF looked on. Many of them were still jobless, distinguished by their threadbare clothes and broken shoes; some had borrowed money to buy flowers for their dead buddies at Arlington.[60] Although many remained destitute, they remembered Hushka and Carlson on Armistice Day and on the anniversary of the Washington riots, when they returned to Arlington with flowers, talked about the old days, and hoped for better ones ahead. Congress finally passed a veto-proof bonus bill in 1936, awarding $1.9 billion for 3.5 million veterans of the Great War, just as a new war was about to break out.[61]

10

"WE ARE ALL IN IT—
ALL THE WAY"

LONG BEFORE THE UNITED STATES ENTERED WORLD WAR II, PRELIMI-nary skirmishing began at Arlington, where war planners mounted a campaign to occupy part of the old plantation. They met stiff resistance from a small band of aesthetes determined to preserve, protect, and defend the grand view from Lee's hilltop mansion.

The year was 1941, the battleground a four hundred–acre parcel curling around the national cemetery on bottomlands by the Potomac River. Lying just southwest of Memorial Bridge, this stretch of ground had been worked by Lee family slaves before the Civil War, occupied by freedmen during and after that conflict, and transferred to the Department of Agriculture when the last of the freedmen were driven from Arlington in 1900. Since that time, scientists and re-searchers had used the Government Experimental Farm, commonly known as Arlington Farm, for growing plants introduced from abroad and for improving varieties of corn, tomatoes, sugarcane, turf, and other useful plants. By the 1930s, when farm operations were moved to suburban Maryland, it set off a scramble for possession of this vacant quarter of Arlington.[1]

By June 1940, as France fell before German forces and the British were routed at Dunkirk, the United States began laying plans for the new war, which promised to be global in scope and daunting in logistical complexity. Anticipating that his country would be drawn into the conflict, President Franklin D. Roosevelt transferred the Arlington Farm in September 1940 to Fort Myer, where additional troops would undoubtedly be needed to reinforce the capital's defenses.[2] About the same time, Secretary of War Henry L. Stimson and Gen. George C. Marshall, the army's chief of staff, moved to consolidate their burgeoning operations, which had outgrown temporary offices on the National Mall and were scattered around a capital buzzing with new federal agencies, a rising tide of New Deal workers, and rumors of war.[3]

"The matter of office space for the War Department has become one of the greatest urgency," Robert P. Patterson, undersecretary of war, wrote Stimson in November 1940. "There is no question but that the congestion is materially retarding the National Defense program."[4] To find more space, Marshall and Stimson cast their eyes across the Potomac to Arlington Farm. Newly under Army control, convenient to Washington, and unobstructed by traffic, it made a logical choice for the War Department expansion, envisioned as a colony of temporary, two-story frame structures that could be razed when the emergency ended. "To be able to build our temporary office buildings on the Arlington Farm site means everything to us," Marshall told a congressional committee in June 1941. "We can do business if our buildings are placed there."[5]

Congress was ready to give Marshall what he asked for—$6.5 million for his temporary complex at Arlington—until a fearless, farsighted Army officer entered the discussion. Brig. Gen. Brehon B. Somervell, recently placed in charge of construction projects for the quartermaster's office, took one look at Marshall's modest plan, found it lacking in imagination, and reworked it into an audacious vision of the future. Somervell saw little reason to waste money building makeshift structures at Arlington. Why not consolidate the War Department's far-flung offices in one modern, efficient, permanent building that would accommodate all employees and serve the nation for years to come? With this objective in mind, he huddled with department architects, surveyed the Arlington site, and came up with new plans for the War Department. Breathtaking in scope, Somervell's proposal called for raising the world's largest office building at Arlington, where his new facility would sprawl over four million square feet of space, enough room for forty thousand workers. To speed construction, save money, and conserve precious steel for the war effort, Somervell's utilitarian building would be made of concrete, with few concessions to beauty; his initial plan called for a four-story structure with no windows. The footprint of the Arlington site, bounded by roads, rail lines, and training fields at Fort Myer, gave the new building a distinctive, oddball shape: it was five-sided—a pentagon, which would in time describe not the just geometry of the building but the War Department itself, the Pentagon.[6] The price tag was estimated at $35 million, and the general was confident that construction could be rushed to completion in a year's time. Speed was important because the European war was escalating. Having consolidated their gains in Western Europe, German forces invaded the Soviet Union in June 1941, opening a second front.[7]

When Somervell unrolled blueprints for the new building in July 1941, Stimson was impressed by the "practical and simple lines" of the pentagonal design. He endorsed the plan on the spot. As the bill raced through the House, Stimson briefed President Roosevelt on the project and won his approval with only minimal discussion.[8] Less than a week later, on July 28, the full House approved the project as part of an $8 billion supplemental defense bill. Only eleven skeptics voted against the measure, which was soon on its way to the Senate. But scathing comments from those few opponents, who questioned the size and scope of Somervell's project, brought the matter to public attention for the first time, giving a preview of the clash to come.[9]

"We cannot win wars with buildings," said Rep. August Andersen of Minnesota. "I understand that . . . they want these big buildings and large facilities so we can police the world after the war is over."[10]

Rep. Adolph Sabath of Illinois wondered if local congressmen were using the threat of war to secure a pork barrel project for Virginia. "We are giving Virginia a great deal," Sabath said. "When this structure is built we shall have given them the greatest building constructed anywhere by any nation."[11]

Watching from the sidelines, Harold Ickes, Roosevelt's confidant and influential secretary of the interior, made some caustic observations about the House debate. "It is easy to see how this greased pig went through the hands of Congress," he wrote in his diary. "Of course it had the support of Congressman Woodrum [chairman of the House Appropriations Subcommittee on

Deficiencies and Army Civil Functions] ... Woodrum is all for economy except when the State of Virginia is concerned." Ickes also discerned a familiar pattern in White House decision making: Without thinking of the implications, Roosevelt had blithely signed off on Somervell's plans for Arlington. "As is so often the case, instead of seeing how vicious the plan was and what it would do in the way of dislocating the carefully considered plan for ... the protection of Washington," Roosevelt "gave a nod of approval," Ickes complained. On the other hand, Ickes knew from experience that FDR's endorsement meant little. At the right moment, one well-aimed word in the president's ear, and Roosevelt could turn on a dime, upend his decision, and make it look effortless. Ickes made plans to pull the president aside and scuttle Somervell's scheme.[12]

The interior secretary had a vested interest in what happened on the old Lee estate, where he had wrested control of the mansion and surrounding acreage from the War Department in the first year of Roosevelt's administration. That was when, much to the consternation of the military, Ickes had persuaded the president to transfer jurisdiction of the mansion, other monuments, reservations, and related federal assets to the National Park Service—a subsidiary of the interior department—by Executive Order 6166. That order, dated June 10, 1933, left Arlington National Cemetery under War Department control but created what would become a twenty-eight-acre island of park service land at the heart of the property. For the Army, which had held the Lee estate since 1861, this loss of turf was a bitter reversal—one that Army people still grumble about. In FDR's day, officials from the War Department lobbied the president to reconsider the transfer. Ickes got wind of it, swooped down, and persuaded FDR to stand by the decision, which added a prime piece of real estate to the interior secretary's growing portfolio.[13]

His acquisition at Arlington, small though it was, encompassed the most historically significant parts of the property, including not only the Lee mansion, the gardens, and the hilltop grave of Pierre L'Enfant but also the best vista of Washington. The French engineer's outlook, high above the capital, demonstrated at a glance the care and thought that generations of architects and planners had lavished upon the city's landscape design. If Somervell had his way—plopping his chunky colossus at the foot of Memorial Bridge—the look of Washington would be forever altered, blocking the capital's gateway, spoiling the cemetery's verdant calm, and obscuring the parklike views from both sides of the river. Even with war approaching, these aesthetic concerns would enliven the Senate debate over Arlington that summer.[14]

While Ickes worked behind the scenes to torpedo Somervell, the eloquent Gilmore D. Clarke, a highly regarded landscape architect, stepped forward to make the case for Arlington's preservation. As chairman of the Commission of Fine Arts, the federal board responsible for the design and site selection of new buildings and monuments in the capital, Clarke was incensed that the War Department had bypassed his panel before rushing legislation for the new building through the House.

"We are opposed to any building whatever on that Arlington site," he told a Senate hearing that August.[15] "It is proposed to place this 'city' at the very portals of the Arlington National Cemetery, thus resulting in the introduction of thirty-five acres of ugly, flat roofs into the very foreground of the most majestic view of the National Capital that obtains . . . from a point near the Tomb of Major L'Enfant."[16]

Somervell, unfazed by Clarke's concerns, shot back. "My hope is that we can make this a city for the living and not for the dead," he told senators. Then he dragged the ghost of Robert E. Lee into the debate. "If there is anything inappropriate in standing on the steps of the home of the greatest soldier we ever produced in this country and looking at the War Department, I do not know what it is."[17]

President Roosevelt, who had blessed Somervell's plan before controversy overtook it, was conspicuously absent from these discussions—for good reason. Just as the appropriations bill reached the Senate that summer, the president had slipped away for a well-earned fishing vacation in Canada; that, at least, was the cover story. In truth, FDR was secretly meeting with Prime Minister Winston Churchill for the first time, just off the coast of Newfoundland, to discuss war plans.[18] Before Roosevelt left Washington, however, he had recognized that the dispute over Arlington was getting out of hand and moved to quell it, urging the Senate to go forward with building on the Lee plantation but to cut the size of the project in half. This compromise offer, dangling over the proceedings as Roosevelt stole off to Canada, did little to calm those opposed to the project. Indeed, it was becoming obvious that for many in Washington, no War Department building, whatever its size, would be acceptable at Arlington, which had achieved an iconic place in the capital landscape and the national conscience.[19]

To preserve that status, Clarke suggested an alternative site for the new building. Why not place it on the low-lying parcel of land less than a mile south of the Arlington Farm and adjacent to Hoover National Airport? This eighty-seven-acre property, near Hell's Bottom, was surrounded by pawn shops, railroads, and shabby housing, and it was already in possession of the army, which had only recently broken ground for a new quartermaster's depot there. Placed well downriver from Memorial Bridge and the national cemetery, the site would be a far less intrusive venue, in Clarke's opinion.[20]

The Senate rejected this idea. It endorsed the Arlington Farm building site, approving the $35 million Somervell plan as part of the supplemental appropriations bill on August 14, 1941. With the president still abroad, the Senate also ignored Roosevelt's suggestion for shrinking the size of the project. Somervell made plans to begin construction, not realizing that his battle had just begun.[21]

Ickes, disgusted with the lack of congressional foresight, registered his objections with the Senate, the public, and the War Department. The project, he warned, would "spoil the setting of such national symbols as the Arlington Lee Memorial and other monuments." He complained directly to Henry Stimson. The despoliation of Arlington, Ickes prophesied, "would be a black mark against this Administration and a discredit to the Army. And so I, for one, protest."[22] Finally Ickes dashed off an angry letter to FDR, whom he begged "not to permit this rape of Washington."[23]

Ickes's appeal was waiting for Roosevelt, along with a sheaf of negative press commentary, upon his return from Canada on August 17. Despite Somervell's success on Capitol Hill—or maybe because of it—public opinion had turned against the project during FDR's absence. Moved by the arguments of Arlington's defenders, annoyed by Somervell's strong-arm tactics, irked by the Senate's failure to embrace his compromise suggestion, and suddenly focused on the aesthetic arguments for Arlington, Roosevelt abruptly—and breezily—reversed course on August 19, leaving Somervell stranded.

"My present inclination is not to accept that action by Congress," Roosevelt told a White House press conference that day. Part of the reason, he said, was based on his own experience as an assistant secretary of the Navy during World War I. Adopting the mantle of a reformed sinner, the president confessed that he had, in those long-ago days, unthinkingly allowed a gross collection of War Department buildings to be raised on the National Mall, where the unsightly structures intruded on the capital's design. More than two decades later, the temporary buildings intruded still. "It was a crime," the president confessed in his most charming tones. "I don't hesitate to say so. It was a crime for which I should be kept out of heaven, for having desecrated the whole plan of . . . the loveliest city in the world." Arlington, he said, was an essential piece of that plan, with its lofty views "known and loved throughout the length and breadth of the land. And here it is—under the name of emergency—it is proposed to put up a permanent building, which will deliberately and definitely, for one hundred years to come, spoil the plan of the national capital . . . I have had a part in spoiling the national parks and the beautiful waterfront of the District once, and I don't want to do it again." Thus spoke the man who had cheerfully endorsed Somervell's plans barely a month before.[24]

But that was then and things had changed. Where would the new building go? The president had a ready answer—the one suggested by Clarke a few weeks earlier: it would go to the eighty-seven-acre quartermaster's site near Hell's Bottom. With that question settled, Roosevelt decreed that one corner of the new War Department building would overlap a tiny section of Arlington—this, to satisfy the letter if not the spirit of the congressional appropriations bill, which said only that the structure should be built on Arlington Farm but did not specify where or to what extent. Roosevelt threaded that loophole with hardly a pause for breath.[25]

To make sure there were no further misunderstandings, the president summoned Clarke and Somervell to the White House on August 29, piled with them into his convertible, and with his terrier, Fala, perched on his lap, was driven across the river to inspect the new site. Along the way, Somervell made a final pitch for his plan, reminding Roosevelt that the new location would require millions more in money and months more in construction time, given its site preparation requirements. Arlington was still the best choice, the general insisted.[26]

At this point, FDR choked off discussion, firmly and finally asserting civil-

Finished in 1818, the Arlington mansion was once the showplace residence of Gen. and Mrs. Robert E. Lee. The Greek Revival structure, modeled after the Temple of Hephaestus, now sits at the heart of Arlington National Cemetery.

(Courtesy of Library of Congress Prints and Photographs Division)

Mary Custis Lee inherited a life interest in the 1,100-acre Arlington estate upon the death of her father, George Washington Custis, in 1857. By then she was married to Robert E. Lee, a promising—though poor—Army officer from a distinguished Virginia family. Painting from 1830.

(Courtesy of Arlington House, the Robert E. Lee Memorial; anonymous lender)

Having sacrificed Arlington to join the Civil War, Robert E. Lee glares at a photographer who captured this portrait a few days after Lee's surrender at Appomattox Court House in April 1865. By this time, Lee owned no home. He stands on the porch of a rented house in Richmond.

(Courtesy of Library of Congress Prints and Photographs Division)

Union troops occupied Arlington from the opening days of the Civil War. Gen. Irvin McDowell, sixth from left, established his headquarters at Arlington. As an old friend of the Lee family, he ordered his men to respect the property. And in deference to the owners, McDowell slept in a tent on the lawn.

(Courtesy of Library of Congress Prints and Photographs Division)

Brig. Gen. Montgomery C. Meigs, the Union quartermaster who kept Federal troops well supplied with food, weapons, and clothing throughout the Civil War, fumed over the treachery of Lee and other officers who joined the rebellion. "No man who ever took the oath to support the Constitution as an officer of our Army or Navy . . . should escape without the loss of all his goods & civil rights & expatriation." When the capital ran out of burial space, Meigs led the drive to turn the Lees' property into a national cemetery, thus becoming the father of Arlington National Cemetery.

(Courtesy of Library of Congress Prints and Photographs Division)

Pvt. William Christman, a farmer who joined the Pennsylvania infantry, never saw a day of combat in the Civil War. But like thousands of other soldiers, he was felled by disease instead of bullets, dying of peritonitis in a Washington hospital. He was interred at Arlington on May 15, 1864—the cemetery's first military burial.

(Robert M. Poole)

When the Civil War ended, there was finally time for ritual at Arlington, where Section 1 became a prestigious site for officers' graves. With no limit on the size or heft of tombstones, the Officers' Section was soon heavy with oversized markers, soaring obelisks, a gathering of stone angels, and one Napoleon cannon. The 1,200-pound gun marks the grave of Major Gen. Wallace F. Randolph, an artillery officer.

(Robert M. Poole)

Once a hard-hitting Rebel cavalry officer, "Fighting Joe" Wheeler, in front, joined Col. Theodore Roosevelt, far right, and other Rough Riders, when the Spanish-American War broke out in 1898. This time Wheeler wore the Union blue. Named a major general of volunteers by President William McKinley, Wheeler led troops into battle in Cuba—a gesture of reconciliation that helped reunite the nation and won the admiration of Roosevelt, who considered the diminutive general "a regular game cock." Wheeler asked to be interred among Union officers at Arlington.

(Library and Archives of Florida)

With the Civil War, the United States began honoring the unknown war dead at Arlington—a tradition refined with each subsequent conflict. Inspired by the examples of France and Britain, the United States sent specialty teams to recover an Unknown from France in 1921. Comrades conveyed his casket toward the train in Le Havre, where his remains were settled onto *Olympia*, Adm. Dewey's flagship, for the voyage home.

(U.S. Army Military History Institute)

Thousands turn out at Arlington to welcome the Unknown from World War I on November 11, 1921—Armistice Day. Gen. John J. Pershing, promoted to Army chief of staff, crossed the amphitheater terrace and tossed a handful of French soil into the Unknown's grave. The site has become one of the cemetery's most visited shrines.

(Courtesy of Library of Congress Prints and Photographs Division)

World War II, the most destructive conflict in human history, produced more than its share of new heroes—among them a Pennsylvania pig farmer named Alton W. Knappenberger. Finding himself outnumbered by German troops near Anzio, Italy, he plunged into the fight of his life, earned the Medal of Honor, and returned home a reluctant hero. He lived out his days in the Pennsylvania hills, shunning the limelight. In 2008 he joined the ranks at Arlington, one of hundreds of Medal of Honor laureates buried there.

(Army Signal Corps)

A Texas sharecropper's son, Audie Murphy became one of the most highly decorated soldiers in World War II. Thousands remember him today, visiting his grave at Arlington, a few paces away from the Tomb of the Unknowns. His standard-issue tombstone is too small to accommodate a list of his many awards, foreign and domestic.

(Robert M. Poole)

One of the nation's most famous Army officers, President Dwight D. Eisenhower, presides at ceremonies for Unknowns from World War II and Korea on Memorial Day 1958. The new recruits were laid to rest on the amphitheater terrace at Arlington, joining the Unknown from World War I.

Members of a joint service casket team bring President Kennedy's casket from the Rotunda to the Capitol Plaza, where Pfc. Arthur Carlson of the Old Guard keeps a grip on Black Jack, the riderless horse. Nervous in the spotlight, Black Jack jounced his way into national consciousness during the Kennedy funeral—watched by millions in November 1963.

(National Park Service)

Clinging to Old Glory, servicemen prepare to fold the flag at Arlington National Cemetery, where thousands (including President Charles de Gaulle of France and Emperor Haile Selassie of Ethiopia, front row) flocked to see President Kennedy buried in 1963. Kennedy's high-profile funeral transformed the cemetery, attracting some seven million visitors in the years after.

(National Park Service)

Seeking to bury the ghosts of an unpopular war, President Reagan presents the Medal of Honor to the Vietnam Unknown on Memorial Day 1984. Although well-intentioned, the burial of a Vietnam Unknown proved to be poorly considered: More than a decade later, the tomb was opened and its occupant was identified as Air Force Lt. Michael J. Blassie. The tomb remains empty—and it is likely, because of advanced DNA testing, that there will be no more Unknowns.

(Courtesy of the Ronald Reagan Presidential Library)

Assisted by comrades, Army Spec. Bruce Bryant, second from right, suits up for duty as a Tomb Guard at Arlington, where millions come to watch sentinels on patrol. The Old Guard, which has watched over the tombs since 1937, puts an emphasis on flawless deportment, a sharp appearance, and attention to duty in service of one of the Army's proudest traditions.

(David Alan Harvey)

An Army sentinel, armed with a rifle and fixed bayonet, guards the Tomb of the Unknowns, keeping vigil with comrades who lost not only their lives but also their identities in the nation's great wars.

(Richard Nowitz/*National Geographic* Image Collection, image ID 1007282)

Darrell Stafford, chief of the interment department at Arlington, recalls September 11, 2001, when terrorists slammed a passenger plane into the Pentagon, adjacent to the cemetery (right). Stafford and colleagues spent the rest of the year burying those who died in the assault, which plunged the United States into a new kind of war. The conflict, waged on two fronts, continues providing new burials for Arlington.

(Robert M. Poole)

ian control of the military. "My dear general," he said, leaning across to make the point, "I am still commander in chief of the Army!" The general retreated. Gilmore Clarke beamed, and by the time their car arrived at Hell's Bottom, the president was beaming too.[27]

"Gilmore," FDR said, pointing across the dreary landscape, "we are going to put the building over there, aren't we?"

"Yes, Mr. President," Clarke answered.

"Did you hear that, General?" Roosevelt asked Somervell. "We're going to locate the War Department building over there." Roosevelt taunted, Somervell seethed, and the battle of Arlington Farm was over.[28]

Being a good soldier, Somervell saluted and went back to work, plunging into his revised construction project like a man possessed. On September 11, 1941—less than three weeks after his humiliating outing with the president— the general watched crews break ground for the new War Department. A mere seventeen months after that, the Pentagon was finished and occupied on February 15, 1943.[29] Although the building was not where Somervell had wanted, his accomplishment must be considered a miracle of sorts, an outsized vision realized with prodigious speed and efficiency, a metaphor for the nation's ability to mobilize for war.[30]

Despite the fireworks over development at Arlington Farm, it soon filled with neat rows of white frame barracks for thousands of soldiers who came into service after Japan's attack on Pearl Harbor in December 1941. Virtually overnight the bottomlands sprouted new housing, a post exchange, a gym, a theater, drill grounds, and new roads—all part of the South Post of Fort Myer, a military community that would grow through the war years. Each morning, hundreds of soldiers answered reveille, streamed across frosty fields, disappeared into a tunnel under Columbia Pike, and emerged at the Pentagon, where they waged war behind desks, in map rooms, and hunched over typewriters in the cavernous new office building.

Clarke, Ickes, and other preservationists, happy to see the Pentagon shifted downriver, declared victory. They tolerated the construction at South Post because it was understood to be temporary and because the United States had, since the Japanese attack, been wholeheartedly and irreversibly engaged in war—the biggest, costliest, deadliest, and most far-ranging conflict the world had known.[31]

"We are now in this war," Roosevelt announced in a fireside chat two days after Pearl Harbor. "We are all in it—all the way. Every single man, woman, and child is a partner in the most tremendous undertaking in American history."[32]

As in the previous war, America had been slow to take sides, but once forced into the fight, the nation faced the challenge with remarkable alacrity. The Army, consisting of 189,839 soldiers when Adolf Hitler stormed into Poland in 1939, had assembled more than 1.4 million troops by the middle of 1941, enough manpower for eleven divisions. That number grew to 16 million by May 1945, including volunteers and draftees of all services.[33] At the same time, the United States cranked up its factories, providing thousands of new planes, tanks, machine guns, and ships for its allies and its own forces. This flow of materièl, produced in quantities the enemy could not match, eventually shifted the war's momentum and sealed the alliance with Great Britain, where Winston Churchill watched the buildup with admiration. The United States, he declared, was "a gigantic boiler. Once the fire is lighted under it, there is no limit to the power it can generate."[34]

Every bit of that power would be needed for World War II, described by historian John Keegan as "different from all wars previously fought, different in scale, intensity, extensiveness and mechanical and human cost."[35] From its beginning in 1939 until its end in 1945, that war unfolded on a global stage, exploding from the skies, churning over two oceans, scorching the landscape of Europe, shaking the deserts of Africa, cutting a bloody swath through Asia, and pounding a string of Pacific islands—Midway, Guadalcanal, New Guinea, Tarawa, the Marshalls, Mariana, Iwo Jima, Okinawa—on the road to Japan.

The need for a huge manpower pool, which produced the nation's first peacetime draft in October 1940, brought millions of recruits into the armed forces from all levels of society, throwing together farm boys and shopkeepers, bank clerks and plumber's assistants, actors and taxi drivers, Baptists and Catholics, and subjecting them to rigorous training toward a common goal. The barriers of class and birthright began to blur under the strain of long marches, abusive drill sergeants, barracks living, cold rations, and combat. Tempered by shared experience, citizen-soldiers discovered that they had much in common despite differences of region, religion, education, and upbringing.

At the same time, deeply ingrained disparities persisted in the services, which remained segregated throughout the war, with African Americans and citizens of Japanese ancestry isolated in their own units. One of the latter, the Army's 442nd Regimental Combat Team, composed of Japanese Americans, proved its mettle in European fighting. Soldiers of the 442nd suffered an extraordinary 30 percent casualty rate, earned 9,486 Purple Hearts, and won more decorations than any unit in Army history—even as 114,490 of their neighbors and loved ones languished in internment camps at home.[36] The races remained strictly separated at Arlington, as they had been since the cemetery's earliest days.

America's fighting men—the ordinary dogface soldiers, sailors, and leathernecks celebrated by wartime cartoonist Bill Mauldin and correspondent Ernie Pyle—proved themselves capable of extraordinary valor when occasion required it. From its start, the Second World War abounded with these transformative moments, when an ordinary serviceman was thrust into action, achieved the impossible, and emerged as a hero—most often without seeking that status. It happened every day: off the coast of the Philippines in 1945, when the U.S.S. *Fletcher* was hit by enemy fire, a magazine exploded, and a young Navy water tender rushed below decks to douse the flames, saving his ship and sacrificing his life;[37] on Engebi, Marshall Islands, in 1944, when a marine corporal fatally threw himself on a Japanese grenade to save two comrades;[38] in the skies over Bremen, Germany, in 1943, when an Air Corps sergeant, severely injured and partially blinded by shrapnel, manned a gun, fought off fighter planes, radioed for help, and assisted a wounded crewman to safety when their B-17 was forced down in the ocean.[39]

Such deeds—each of which earned the Medal of Honor—were performed by ordinary, unglamorous men "bleeding their way forward," as C. L. Sulzberger of the *New York Times* described it. He was following American soldiers up the boot of Italy during the hard-fought winter of 1944. Landing behind enemy lines on the beachhead at Anzio in January of that year, Anglo-American forces ran into determined resistance from Germany's Tenth Army, which blocked the way to Rome, slowed the Allied advance, and produced a withering stalemate until springtime.[40]

Among the soldiers fighting out of Anzio that winter was Army Pfc. Alton W. "Knappie" Knappenberger, a scrawny twenty-year-old pig farmer from Spring

Mount, Pennsylvania. Fresh to combat, he seemed the unlikeliest of heroes. The son of a long-dead moonshiner and the last of seven children, he stood all of five feet six inches tall, weighed 118 pounds, and had no ambition except to survive the war. He freely admitted his terror at the prospect of battle, unsure of how he would react to enemy fire. He soon found out. Moving up from the hotly contested beachhead at Anzio, Knappie and comrades from Company C of the 30th Infantry Regiment, 3rd Infantry Division, found themselves confronting battle-hardened German forces near the market town of Cisterna di Littoria on January 31 and February 1. Ordered across a snow-dusted field affording no cover, the regiment came under merciless fire from concealed enemy positions, the barrage tumbling soldiers on either side of Knappie and neatly slicing off the head of his best friend. With bullets whizzing around him, Knappie watched, hugged the cold earth of Italy, and crawled slowly forward. Members of his regiment fell away. By February 1, death and injury had stripped the company of its officers, leaving Knappie alone on the ragged front line.[41]

With no superiors to give orders, the Pennsylvania farm boy took the initiative, crawling forward to an exposed knoll where he set up the Browning automatic rifle scrounged from a dead comrade—an upgrade from Knappie's slow-firing standard-issue M-1. As soon as he appeared on the hill, German machine gunners opened fire. Knappie rose to a kneeling posture, calmly took aim, killed two members of the hostile gun crew, and wounded a third. His marksmanship, honed by years of hunting squirrels, rabbits, and pheasants for food at home, clicked into play. When a pair of Germans popped up to lob grenades toward the knoll, Knappie wheeled on them, killing both; their explosives fell short. Across the field, about a hundred yards away, another enemy machine gun commenced firing; Knappie silenced it, provoking a new barrage from heavy antitank and antiaircraft weapons trained on his position. The shells landed short, kicking up dirt. Knappie coolly continued fighting, wounding and killing every enemy he could see, while miraculously avoiding injury. Someone said later that none of the bullets reached him because he offered such a small target. He held his ground, exhausted his ammunition, and scurried toward German lines to scavenge more bullets from fallen soldiers. Dodging fire, zigging and zagging, he resumed his perch on the knoll, caught an enemy platoon clawing its way uphill, and wiped it out.

From the rear, six colleagues from C Company suddenly appeared beside Knappie to join the fight. He continued spraying the field with automatic fire while his buddies plunked away with their M-1s. When the little crew finally ran out of ammunition, Knappie and company slid down the hill, backtracked to a field, and began searching for their unit. There was no unit. The 7 soldiers from the knoll were the only survivors from a 200 man company. Bold as their action had been, it failed to dislodge the Germans from Cisterna di Littoria. Nonetheless, Knappie had single-handedly disrupted an enemy attack, saved American lives, and provided a glimmer of hope in an otherwise disastrous offensive. It would take another four months for Allies to break through to Cisterna. When they did, they found the remains of numerous dead Germans around Knappie's knoll.[42]

"A one man army, that's what you are, a blasted one man army," Maj. Gen. Lucian K. Truscott Jr., 3rd Division commander, told Knappie after word of his performance raced through the ranks. The young Pennsylvanian had escaped the firefight with a single injury—a blistered heel. Whisked away for treatment in Naples, he found himself with a new assignment, baking doughnuts with Red Cross ladies. This kept him out of harm's way until Lt. Gen. Mark W. Clark, commander of the 5th Army, found time to drape the Medal of Honor around Knappie's neck. Cited for "conspicuous gallantry and intrepidity at the risk of his life above and beyond the call of duty," Knappie was a certified war hero. After just over two hours of fighting his war was ending and he was soon sailing for home.[43]

Nobody seemed more surprised—or less comfortable—about his elevated status than Knappie himself, who clammed up or stammered explanations when pressed to speak about his moment of glory. "Look it up in the Medal of Honor book," he told one interviewer. "I was scared the whole time I was over there," he told another. "You go in there and just try to get them guys before they get you."[44]

Shunning the spotlight and avoiding speeches, he quietly left the Army, disappeared into the Pennsylvania countryside, raised a family, went hunting, and spent the rest of his life trying to be profligately, unapologetically ordinary. Unlike millions of other veterans returning from the war, Knappie avoided further schooling, even though his education had ended in the fifth grade. He passed up big pay and supervisory positions for honest, menial work—driving trucks, working for paving companies, dabbling at farming. He enjoyed the pleasures of his hard-won peace, living with his wife, Hazel, in a trailer surrounded by woods, orchards, and wild turkeys, with a menagerie of dogs, cats, ponies, a rooster, a horse, a goose, a duck, and numerous grandchildren for company.[45]

He died of a heart attack at age eighty-four in 2008. After some debate within the family, Knappie was laid to rest at Arlington on January 31 of that year. It was a long way from Pennsylvania, but his loved ones thought it was time to give this reluctant hero the recognition he had evaded in life. So with his family gathered around the grave, attended by Army officers, a marching platoon, a military band, and a clutch of media, the one-man army was buried in Section 60 with full honors. The weather was suitable—a biting cold day that fell precisely sixty-four years after the morning in Italy when a frightened young private crawled up from the frozen ground to face the Germans alone.[46]

Like most American men and women who fought in the war, Knappie survived the great conflagration, which is thought to have claimed more than sixty million victims worldwide. Most of those deaths, perhaps thirty-nine million, were civilians. This gruesome metric made World War II unique: it was the first armed conflict in which civilian fatalities outstripped combatant deaths. The exact numbers—from death camps, bombings, collateral fire, starvation, displacement, and other causes—can only be guessed. Thousands of civilians simply disappeared. As in the Great War, the Soviet Union paid the biggest price, with an estimated thirteen million troops and sixteen million civilians killed.[47]

Poland, which counted more than 6.1 million wartime deaths, suffered the greatest proportion of losses—20 percent of its population.[48] This broke the heart of famed Polish pianist, composer, and statesman Ignace Jan Paderewski, who was forced to watch the dismemberment of his country from exile. Age eighty, he died in New York City in June 1941, just as Hitler unleashed his invasion of the Soviet Union. As the first prime minister of modern Poland and president of the wartime Polish parliament in exile, Paderewski was widely viewed as a symbol of patriotism and independence—a perception not lost on President Roosevelt, who gave the great musician temporary refuge at Arlington. There Paderewski was buried in a vault under the U.S.S. *Maine* Memorial until he could rest again in free Polish soil. Nobody, least of all Roosevelt, imagined that Paderewski would remain at Arlington for another fifty-one years, waiting for the war to end, then waiting for Eastern Europe to shake off domination of the Soviet Union. Paderewski's long exile finally ended in 1992, when he was brought out of the vault, carried through the hills of Arlington for the last time, and returned to a place of high honor at St. John's Cathedral in Warsaw.[49]

His presence at Arlington, like that of other foreigners interred there during the war years, helped make the national cemetery more international in character. This reflected a maturing outlook of the United States, which was less parochial, less isolationist, and more involved with global affairs as a result of its wartime experience. The conflict imposed new obligations on Americans, who, having been thrust onto the world stage by circumstances, remained prominently in that position.[50]

Compared to European and Asian nations, the United States paid a relatively small price for its role in the war,[51] sacrificing some 359,000 in combat, accidents, and other causes, while reaping economic benefits and international standing— one reason, perhaps, World War II is sometimes called the last good war.[52] Seen through the narrow lens of American history, however, the Second World War must be considered a national tragedy, coming second only to the Civil War in the number of lives it cost. This lesson is brought home at Arlington, where one walks among endless rows of graves of those who died at Anzio, Normandy, Iwo Jima, and other faraway battle zones, only to realize that they do not approach the toll from Fredericksburg, Chancellorsville, and other scenes of America's bloodiest conflict, which continues to haunt the old plantation.

The succession of wars led to improved methods for recovering and identifying the dead. As soon as the Second World War ended, thousands of specialists from the quartermaster's Graves Registration Service sifted through the battlefields of Europe, Africa, Asia, and the Pacific to find, identify, and concentrate the dead in 288 temporary cemeteries. There they remained until they could be shipped home or reburied in fourteen overseas cemeteries from the major theaters of war.[53] As in previous conflicts, families had the option of leaving their loved ones abroad or repatriating them to the United States. Some 97,000 war dead were brought home, many of them to Arlington.[54] By 1955, this influx of World War II burials pushed the number of graves in the cemetery from some 44,000 to 70,000. More space was needed, and Arlington grew from 400 acres to 600 acres. The new land came from South Post at Fort

Myer, where temporary wartime buildings were knocked down to make room for orderly rows of graves by the river—the very terrain General Somervell had coveted for his Pentagon.[55]

As in the Civil War, it took far longer to clean up from the Second World War than it took to fight it. Five years after the conflict ended, the Graves Registration Service was still recovering bodies. By this time, though, quartermaster squads had identified all but 3 percent of Americans killed in the war—an extraordinary achievement considering the breadth and violence of the conflict. The recovery campaign marked the most extensive reinterment effort in history, according to Steven E. Anders, historian for the Quartermaster Corps.[56]

Careful record keeping and the widespread use of dog tags made most identifications routine, but in a few cases some detective work was required. One badly mauled soldier was found with no dog tags or identifying marks, except for a ring he wore. What made it peculiar was that it came from a girl's school, which led army investigators to a roster of students, and eventually to a woman who provided the missing soldier's name. Dental evidence produced identities for many casualties; laundry marks or remnants of letters identified others.[57] Of the 359,000 Americans who died in World War II, investigators produced positive identification for 271,000; 10,000 more were classified as unknowns; 78,000 were missing in action. Of those missing, about half were determined to be "unrecoverable," lost at sea or entombed in shipwrecks.[58] To this day, specialty teams from the Pentagon's Joint POW/MIA Accounting Command continue searching for the 39,000 who never came home—with some success. Each year about fifty of the war dead are found at remote mountainside crash sites, in overgrown jungles, on isolated Pacific atolls, and sent home, beneficiaries of improved forensic methods, advances in DNA technology, and the government's commitment to account for all service members missing from all wars.[59]

Many are repatriated to Arlington, where they lie among thousands of fellow citizen-soldiers long since returned from the Second World War. Most are known only to the diminishing circle of family and friends who survive them. But a few others, whose names are incised on worn tombstones at Arlington, also hold prominent places in the national memory: Gen. George C. Marshall, who planned and directed the war and helped Europe climb out of the ruins; Gen. Omar N. Bradley, who led the First Army to victory in Europe; Adm. William D. Leahy, who offered FDR counsel through the war years; Adm. William F. "Bull" Halsey Jr., who won a hard-fought victory at Guadalcanal;

Gen. Henry H. "Hap" Arnold, who founded the modern Air Force; Lt. Gen. James Doolittle, who led daring B-25 bombing raids on Japan in 1942; Lt. Gen. Claire Chennault, who led the 14th Air Force in China; Brig. Gen. William "Wild Bill" Donovan, who organized the wartime Office of Strategic Services, forerunner to the CIA; Lt. Gen. Brehon B. Somervell, father of the Pentagon; Army Maj. Audie Murphy, one of the most decorated soldiers of World War II;[60] Marine Pfc. Lee Marvin, who stormed ashore at Saipan, got shot in the butt, and returned to civilian life as an actor; Pvt. Dashiell Hammett, who edited an Army paper in the Aleutian Islands; and Sgt. Joe Louis, the "Brown Bomber," who staged ninety-six exhibition matches for troops while serving in a segregated unit. Each earned his place at Arlington; each did his duty; each met the standard described by Lt. Gen. George S. Patton Jr. "Every little job is essential," Patton told his troops on the eve of D-Day in 1945. "Every man is a link in the great chain. Every man . . . plays a vital part."[61]

Patton, not always the most tolerant of officers, even admitted that black soldiers had a role to play. Originally skeptical of how African Americans would perform in combat, Patton changed his mind after watching his all-black tank battalion, the 761st, plowing across Europe and performing heroically. "I have nothing but the best in my Army," he crowed. "I don't care what color you are as long as you go up there and kill those Kraut sons-of-bitches."[62]

Patton's endorsement helped undermine the long and insupportable practice of segregation in the services. Returning veterans challenged their government to live up to its democratic ideals at home. President Harry S. Truman rose to the occasion, banishing racial discrimination in the services with a stroke of his pen on July 26, 1948. His Executive Order 9981 called for "equality of treatment and opportunity for all persons in the armed services without regard to race, color, religion, or national origin."[63] Truman's action, designed to help the living, also exalted the dead at Arlington, where segregated burials were soon consigned to the past.[64]

In the same month that Truman signed his historic order, the barriers of rank consciousness began to crumble at Arlington, thanks to a generous departing gesture from one famous old soldier, Gen. John J. Pershing, who had led American forces to victory in World War I. He watched from the sidelines as the next conflict ran its course, suffering from ill health when the Japanese surrender brought peace back to Washington. Seemingly forgotten by the public, lonely in his rooms at Walter Reed Army Hospital, the old hero had been relegated to the shadows, a relic of old wars and old ways. In better times, when the memory of his exploits was green in the public mind, he had been bombarded with hundreds of telegrams each Armistice Day. On his last one, in 1947, only ten arrived.[65]

Pershing began to contemplate his own funeral at Arlington, where he had seen so many comrades buried. It was a place as familiar to him as any home he ever knew. Always a stickler for details, Pershing took care of the particulars. Instead of erecting a lavish monument to himself, as so many officers had done since Civil War days, Pershing asked for the simple white government-issue tombstone available to any private. And, unlike officers who routinely commanded better real estate than those who fought under them, Pershing chose a burial site among enlisted men from the Great War. "Here let me rest among the World War veterans," Pershing is supposed to have told an officer who helped him select his gravesite. "When the last bugle call is sounded, I want to stand up with my soldiers."[66]

Age eighty-seven, he died in his sleep on July 15, 1948. Forgotten in life, he was remembered in death as few others are. Thousands of mourners, including President Truman and General Marshall, filed by his casket in the Capitol Rotunda, where the old general lay in state for twenty-four hours. Both Truman and Marshall had served under him; both had revered him; both solemnly marked his passing, as did some 300,000 ordinary citizens who crowded the sidewalks to watch Black Jack's caisson make its slow, stately progress to Arlington on July 19. The skies opened and the rains came down; the wet streets fell utterly, eerily silent, a sign of respect for the man crossing the brown Potomac on his last journey.[67]

Dutifully sloshing behind Pershing's caisson, two soldiers who had served under him debated whether to seek cover or get soaked that day.

"Brad, what do you think?" Gen. Dwight D. Eisenhower asked Gen. Omar N. Bradley, as they marched along.

"For Black Jack Pershing I think it would be proper if we walked in the rain," said Bradley.[68]

They marched on. Drenched by the time they arrived at Arlington, they joined a sodden khaki tide, which flowed unbroken down the crest of a hill on

Grant Avenue, accompanied by the dull thunder of artillery, the thump of muffled drums, and the memories of comrades sleeping in long rows all around.[69]

"The march of another soldier is ended," said Maj. Gen. Luther D. Miller, chief of Army chaplains: A few more words, a barking of rifles, the solace of Taps, and they lowered General Pershing into the ground, where he was surrounded by the simple tombstones of regular soldiers who still keep him company on the prominence now known as Pershing's Hill.[70]

11

THE NASTIEST
LITTLE WAR

Since his burial beneath the amphitheater terrace in 1921, the Unknown of World War I had held the heights of Arlington in undisputed solitude, representing the war to end all wars, as well as the hope that the first great clash of the twentieth century would be the last. It was not, of course, but merely a forerunner of worse to come.

After Japan's surrender in August 1945, belligerents emerged from the ruins of World War II, shook off the dust, and commenced the hard work of recovery. Maps were redrawn, armies of occupation marched into place, schools and factories were painstakingly rebuilt. War trials began, memorials were erected across Europe, and search parties went forth to find and retrieve the dead from distant lands. It was a time for contemplating the enormity of what had transpired, a time for setting things right again. In the United States, that meant welcoming returning veterans, heading back to work, starting families, and planning suitable honors for the unlucky ones who never made it home.

Following precedent from the First World War, legislation was introduced in September 1945 to have an unknown serviceman from World War II brought to Arlington, where he would rest beside his comrade from the earlier conflict. The measure, signed into law by President Harry S. Truman in June 1946, called for this Unknown to be installed at Arlington no later than May 30, 1951, for Memorial Day celebrations. Given the global reach of the recent hostilities and the devastation they produced, the secretary of war allowed five years for recovery missions, an act of devotion barely begun before it had to be called off.[1]

A new war had intervened, forestalling efforts to clean up from the last one. On June 25, 1950, some 90,000 North Korean troops plowed across the 38th parallel in a surprise assault on South Korea, a U.S. ally. The offensive against the Republic of Korea, encouraged by Soviet premier Joseph Stalin, raised fears in Washington that Communists intended to fill the Asian power vacuum created by the collapse of Japan.[2] This prospect caused President Truman to divert occupying troops from Japan, mobilize forces at home, ask for reinforcements from the newly established United Nations, and rush them to defend South Korea.[3]

Thus began the three-year conflict described by historian S. L. A. Marshall as "the century's nastiest little war," fought on forbidding mountain terrain, often in freezing conditions, against a numerically superior enemy. While keen to answer the Communist thrust in Asia, President Truman worried that all-out war in Korea might spark a larger conflict with the Soviet Union, which had just exploded its first nuclear weapons. He hoped for a short, limited war on the Korean peninsula—so limited, in fact, that he preferred not to use the three-letter word for armed conflict; the Korean intervention was not a war but a police action, Truman announced, embracing the polite language of the United Nations, even as he summoned thousands of Americans for combat.[4]

Whatever one called the Korean adventure, it proved costly: by the time a truce suspended hostilities in July 1953, more than 36,576 American service members had been killed,[5] along with 415,000 South Korean combatants and an estimated 1.5 million North Korean and Chinese soldiers.[6] Despite its steep cost in lives, the Korean war resulted in a stalemate: After North Korea's dramatic opening assault, which left UN forces and the 8th U.S. Army teetering on the southeastern edge of the peninsula, the allies rallied; in September 1950, they launched a daring amphibious assault behind enemy lines at Inchon, while the 8th Army broke out of the Pusan Perimeter and ground its way toward North Korea. By October 26, the allies had overrun Pyongyang; just before Halloween they reached the Yalu River on the Chinese border. Gen. Douglas

MacArthur, commanding the combined allied forces from headquarters in Tokyo, assumed that the war would end then and there. He was wrong.

By November 1950, China had joined the fight, sending hundreds of thousands of its soldiers into North Korea near Unsan. These forces, combined with those from North Korea, made up in numbers what they lacked in modern equipment. They pushed south, driving allied troops before them, regaining Pyongyang, overcoming fierce Marine resistance around the Chosin Reservoir, and breaking across the 38th parallel by the end of the year. They retook Seoul in January 1951.

Then the tide of war turned again: UN troops, reinforced from the United States, rallied, secured Seoul, fought their way north, and pushed enemy forces back across the 38th parallel. This time the line held, but to what end? Neither side could claim decisive victory: the North had been unable to unify the country as a Communist whole; the South had repelled the North, but had failed to make it part of a fledgling democracy; the border between the two countries remained essentially where it had been at the outset of hostilities, but with a demilitarized zone interposed between warring parties.

Summing up the Korean experience in *The Coldest Winter*, the late David Halberstam described the war as "a puzzling gray, very distant conflict, a war that went on and on and on, seemingly without hope or resolution."[7] Opposing armies advanced, retreated, reappeared, and melted away. Positions were overrun and abandoned, only to change hands again in the following months; some places shifted ownership two or three times in the course of the war, which not only changed the way the United States fought through the unsettled, oscillating conflict but also revolutionized how the nation cared for its war dead. In the two previous wars of the twentieth century, American forces had concentrated their fallen combatants in temporary cemeteries within allied lines, with the understanding that the graves would be opened, its occupants identified, and the dead properly reburied or repatriated as soon as the fighting stopped.[8]

This practice proved impossible in Korea. In some cases, enemy forces pressed forward so swiftly and in such overwhelming numbers that the allied dead had to be hurriedly abandoned where they had fallen. In another instance, workers in Inchon unearthed the UN cemetery, hustled more than 800 dead to a waiting ship, and steamed for Japan—and safety—just two hours before Chinese forces swooped down on the city. Living soldiers sometimes competed for space with the dead on evacuation transports, which were in short supply in the war's early stages. "When they ran out of truck-bed space, they laid the dead on fenders, across hoods, tied on the barrels of artillery pieces," a marine private recalled.[9] Even when circumstances allowed for orderly retreat and burial in temporary cemeteries, a number of these graveyards were overrun as North Korean and Chinese troops pushed south, stripping the dead of boots and other equipment as they went. Dog tags, taken as trophies of war, disappeared in the back-and-forth struggle for the Pusan Perimeter, where the number of unknowns soared as a result. As the first months of war drew to a close, it was obvious that the United States needed to rethink its recovery methods to meet realities in Korea.[10]

That rethinking, just under way as Christmas of 1950 approached, was jump-started by the sudden death of Lt. Gen. Walton H. "Johnnie" Walker, commander of the 8th U.S. Army, on December 23, 1950. As allied forces edged their way back toward North Korea that winter, the hard-charging Walker, known for racing around to check on his troops, had sped north of Seoul on icy roads. He urged his driver into a passing lane and into the path of an oncoming truck. The general's jeep swerved and flipped into a ditch, killing Walker—just in time to rescue his reputation.[11]

Although credited with leading UN troops on their breakout from the Pusan Perimeter that autumn, Walker was also blamed in part for the enemy's early success in Korea. Criticized for advancing too cautiously, he was second-guessed and undermined by MacArthur's command in Tokyo; indeed, in the weeks before his accident, Walker had been convinced that his days in Korea were numbered and that he would be relieved of command. When death released him from the war at age sixty-one, it not only silenced his critics but also earned him a hero's homecoming at Arlington.[12]

Promoted to four-star rank in death, Walker was showered with honors. A special Air Force Constellation was summoned to take the general's body to Washington. The lordly MacArthur turned out to pay respects when the funeral party stopped in Tokyo. Lt. Gen. James S. Van Fleet, commander of the 2nd Army, met the plane in Philadelphia, where Walker's widow came aboard and an honor guard of military police stood vigil. Uniformed pallbearers took up the general's flag-covered casket in Washington, bore him past a ceremonial guard of fifty soldiers with fixed bayonets, and saw him safely to Fort Myer on New Year's Eve, there to await services on January 2, 1951. That day broke clear and cold at Arlington, where many of Walker's old comrades came to see him off, their gathering constituting a who's who of World War II luminaries: Gen. Dwight D. Eisenhower, Secretary of Defense George C. Marshall, Chief of Staff Gen. Omar N. Bradley—all marched behind Walker's new four-star flag as his horse-drawn caisson creaked down McPherson Drive, past the Confederate Memorial, past the graves of men of the U.S.S. *Maine*, past the tombs of Moses Ezekiel, James Parks, Thomas Selfridge, and all the nameless ranks from the old wars. The procession came to a halt on Pershing's Hill in Section 34, where Eisenhower and the old lions filed into position, formed an honor cordon, and snapped off their salutes. Unseen howitzers, tucked away in the hills, pounded out a seventeen-gun tribute, just as an Episcopal priest prayed for permanent peace and Gen. Walton H. Walker was settled into the ground.[13]

Because of Walker's prominence and his recent promotion, his funeral was well covered by the press. Wire services had tracked the Constellation's progress from Korea. The *New York Times* prominently displayed a photograph of Eisenhower and other famous mourners at graveside.[14] All hailed Walker as a hero. Few begrudged the tribute, but his high-profile treatment touched a raw nerve among ordinary citizens whose wartime sufferings had passed without much notice. "I'd like to know if a soldier's high rank made him better to be brought home right away for a safe burial," a sergeant's widow wrote President Truman three days after Walker's funeral. "If I had my way, and could get to Korea, I'd accompany my husband's body home . . . I've been very bitter about all this, and there are a lot of others who feel this way . . . When I look around and see what little it matters to the big guys, that my daughters have lost a father, I can't help the bitterness."[15] More families chimed in, calling for the return of their loved ones. "I am one of the many mothers with a personal grudge toward you," Norma Potter wrote Truman from Cheboygan, Michigan. "My son is gone. I can do nothing about it," she wrote. "But I can and will find out somehow where his body is and if possible I will get his personal things."[16] Deara Eartbawey pleaded with Maj. Gen. Henry H. Vaughan, a military aide to Truman, to send her dead son from Korea. "I want my boy buried where he was born in Boston with his father," she wrote. "That's the least I could do is to give him a decent burial and that's the least the army could do to help me find my boy."[17] If the nation could bring a general home, families argued, it could do the same for the privates and sergeants dying in Korea.

Prodded by this outpouring of public sentiment and faced with combat conditions which made American cemeteries vulnerable in Korea, the United States quickly adopted a new policy of "concurrent return," which meant that the nation's war dead would be collected on the battlefield, transported to Japan, and shipped home for timely burial. This new policy, announced by George Marshall in March 1951, made the Korean conflict the first in which America's dead were repatriated during active hostilities, a practice continued with each subsequent war.[18] In time, the image of flag-covered caskets arriving at bases in the United States would become the symbol of unpopular wars, from Vietnam to Iraq and Afghanistan, but at midcentury the practice of concurrent return was lauded by the press and by families alike.

The return of dead sons and husbands helped loved ones adjust to the loss. President Truman, excoriated for the government's laggard response early in the war, now was praised for bringing relatives home for burial.[19] As the first funeral ships arrived in the port of Oakland in the spring of 1951, newspapers noted the historic nature of the moment with approval. Not only were the dead being returned in wartime, but their treatment reflected the multiplicity of America's fighting forces: the caskets of enlisted men and officers were stowed side by side on shipboard without regard to race or rank, proof that the nation had recovered its sense of democratic propriety, briefly undermined by the handling of General Walker's funeral.[20]

The Korean conflict, launched with broad public support, lost popular backing as the war of containment dragged on with no clear sign that success was at hand. In the days after Walker's funeral, a national survey showed that more than 60 percent of Americans favored withdrawal from the peninsula. It was not the sort of war the United States was accustomed to fighting. Truman's popularity sank, and Korea became known as the forgotten war, fought on obscure terrain under restrictive conditions. "It is murder to send boys to fight with their hands tied by your 'limited police action,'" the mother of a dead airman scolded the president in 1951. "Have you forgotten how America fights?"[21]

American servicemen had not forgotten. They fought with determination and distinction in Korea, even as patience faded on the home front and the first waves of war dead arrived at Arlington. Among those who joined Walker at Arlington were Marine Pfc. Walter C. Monegan Jr., who single-handedly took out two enemy tanks before he was gunned down near Sosa-ri; Army Sfc. Charles W. Turner, who dashed through hostile fire, took an exposed position on a tank, and repelled enemy troops until his platoon could safely regroup for a counterattack near Yongsan; Marine Staff Sgt. William G. Windrich, twice wounded and refusing evacuation near Yudam-ni, where he guided his platoon to a strong defensive position and held the ground until he lapsed into unconsciousness; Navy Hospital Corpsman Francis C. Hammond, who exposed himself to enemy fire while treating wounded Marines near Sanae-dong—all perished in the Korean fighting, all came to rest in the hills of Virginia, all earned the Medal of Honor for their heroism.[22]

They had not won the war, but they helped turn back the threat to South Korea, which finally made its uneasy truce with the North in 1953. When the shooting stopped, the army's identification specialists continued searching for the dead in South Korea, in due course recovering 30,425 American service members and identifying more than 29,500. The low proportion of unknowns—less than 3 percent of those recovered—was unprecedented, a tribute to the growing professionalism of the army's specialty teams. Identification experts established a modern laboratory near Yokohama, Japan, where they collected and collated information for each dead serviceman, including his dental profile, hair color, height, shoe size, skin pigmentation, and fingerprints. X-rays were taken for each of the dead, which revealed old injuries and helped identify some of them.[23] Another 8,100 combatants were listed as missing in action, presumed to be buried in North Korea or held as prisoners of war when the truce was declared.[24]

The few Americans who ended the war as unknowns—there were 848 in that category—were held at the allied mortuary near Yokohama. There they remained, stripped of their identities and unclaimed by loved ones until 1956, when officials began to cast about for a suitable burial site. The army, designated as the lead service for handling the dead from Korea, first proposed that the unknowns be interred at the United Nations cemetery near Pusan, South Korea. This idea was abandoned when the fragility of the truce was considered; North Korea had overrun the South in earlier fighting, and it might do so again. Officials next considered moving the unknowns to the Philippines, where the United States maintained a cemetery for the dead of World War II; this suggestion was discarded as a hard sale for the American public. The next proposal was to send the Korean unknowns—all of them—to Arlington, which proved unworkable; the cemetery was already cramped for space and it was thought that the mass interments of Korean war dead would detract from the Tomb of the Unknowns. With all other options exhausted, the Army finally decided to bury the Korean unknowns in the National Memorial Cemetery of the Pacific in Honolulu, an old volcanic crater known locally as the Punchbowl for its scooped-out topography. There, in May 1956, all of the unknowns from the Korean war were buried, taking their berths alongside more than two thousand unknowns from the Second World War.[25]

The uneasy truce along Korea's demilitarized zone allowed the United States to resume the unfinished business the conflict had interrupted—namely, the burial of an unknown serviceman from World War II at Arlington. In August 1955, responding to requests from veterans' groups, the secretary of defense asked the Army to find an unknown from the Second World War for Arlington honors; the next year, in August 1956, Congress authorized the burial of an unknown from the Korean conflict. To simplify matters, both would be repatriated in a joint ceremony at Arlington on Memorial Day 1958.[26]

Plans for the World War II Unknown had originally called for construction of a new sarcophagus on the amphitheater terrace. With two Unknowns scheduled for burial on the plaza in 1958, the Army revised its original plan, deciding instead to excavate crypts for the two newcomers at Arlington, each of whom would have his grave marked by a flat marble slab to be placed in the shadow of the World War I monument. While construction began at the amphitheater, specialty teams scattered overseas to exhume a number of nameless servicemen from both wars, reexamining each candidate for any identifying features or personal effects, and destroying all paperwork associated with the burials to guarantee the anonymity of the selection.[27]

For World War II candidates, the Army picked finalists from the transatlantic and transpacific theaters to ensure that the main regions of fighting were fairly represented. They exhumed thirteen of the dead from military cemeteries in North Africa and Europe; those thirteen were sent to the U.S. cemetery at Epinal, France, where one unknown candidate was chosen and shipped across the Atlantic on the U.S.S. *Blandy*, one of the Navy's newest destroyers, in mid-May 1958.[28]

While these proceedings went forward, a second candidate for World War II honors was chosen in ceremonies on May 16 at Hickam Air Force Base in Hawaii from unknowns exhumed at the Fort McKinley American Cemetery in the Philippines and from the Punchbowl on Oahu. The Pacific candidate joined the Korean Unknown, already designated on May 15, for the long flight to Guantánamo Bay, Cuba. From there the two servicemen were transferred to the U.S.S. *Boston*, which steamed northward for the Virginia Capes to complete the selection. The *Boston* met the *Blandy* offshore on May 26, when the Unknown from World War II was chosen by Hospital Corpsman 1st Class William R. Charette. Charette, a Medal of Honor winner from the Korean conflict, placed a wreath on one of the World War II caskets, saluted smartly, and stepped back. The runner-up was taken eight miles out to sea, wrapped in the traditional sailcloth shroud, and committed to the deep; he hit the water, slid under the waves, and disappeared to the sound of Taps.[29] With these rituals accomplished, the Unknowns remaining—one from Korea and one from the Second World War—were ready for the last phase of their journey. Side by side, their flag-covered caskets were settled onto the *Blandy* and, watched over by honor guards and with sailors lining the rails, motored up the Potomac for Washington, following the path their comrade from World War I had pioneered more than thirty-six years before.[30]

For three days thousands of citizens converged on the Capitol Rotunda to pay their respects. Foreign dignitaries brought flowers and expressions of thanks; comrades with gray hair filed through the echoing marble hall; hundreds of families still missing loved ones stood under the dome, stared at the flag-covered caskets, and allowed themselves to think that one of their own had returned home. They joined some one hundred thousand mourners who turned out to see the Unknowns bound for Arlington on Memorial Day, May 30, 1958.[31]

At precisely one P.M., just as the caskets were borne down the Capitol steps with the Unknown from World War II in the lead, an artillery battery at the Washington Monument commenced the booming salutes that would punctuate every minute until the Unknowns arrived at the amphitheater. Silent crowds gathered along the sidewalks with heads bared to watch the procession roll down Capitol Hill, along Constitution Avenue, around the Lincoln

Memorial, and over the river to Arlington. The matching black caissons, each draped in velvet and pulled by six gray horses from the Fort Myer stables, rode side by side, preceded by the national colors. At the cemetery gates, the procession halted, the World War II Unknown swung into the lead, and the cortege resumed its unhurried progress in a single column, ascending the green hills as twenty fighter jets and bombers rumbled overhead, each group flying the missing man formation.[32]

When the caskets were settled into the apse of the amphitheater and VIPs had filed into their seats, the nation's most prominent World War II veteran, President Dwight D. Eisenhower, took his place as chief mourner. The sun blazed high, raising the temperature to eighty-two degrees and sending waves of heat rippling up from the bowl of the white marble amphitheater. Several hundred spectators swooned, including an associate justice of the Supreme Court. For his part, President Eisenhower, dressed in a black suit and accustomed to state ritual, soldiered on through the heat and glare, impressing at least one reporter that afternoon.[33] "The President's capacity for standing at attention and sitting in prayerful attitude during the long ceremonies was notable," the *New York Times* reported. "Others fanned themselves with their programs. Many did not display the sixty-seven-year-old President's stamina."[34]

Looking cool and crisp, Eisenhower stepped across the stage to speak for the two honored warriors who had endured so much and traveled so far to reach Arlington: "On behalf of a grateful people I now present the Medal of Honor to these two Unknowns who gave their lives to the United States of America," he said, placing the first medal, mounted on a velvet board, atop the flag-covered coffin of his comrade from World War II; he followed suit for the Unknown from the Korean conflict. Then ceremonies moved onto the terrace, where hundreds of servicemen stood rigid in the sun, bayonets fixed, medals shining, young faces incongruously set and stony.[35] Casket teams lowered the Unknowns onto rails over their crypts and lifted the flags from each, holding them taut. Watching solemnly, President Eisenhower stood at the World War II Unknown's grave, while Vice President Richard M. Nixon took his place before the Korean Unknown. Chaplains from the Catholic, Protestant, and Jewish faiths stepped forward to read the burial service, each in his way and each in his turn. A battery from the Army's 3rd Infantry Regiment, positioned over the next hill, shook the warm afternoon with their twenty-one-gun salute, which was still reverberating when a firing party shouldered their rifles and delivered the traditional three-part volley. A lone bugler sounded Taps. Dusk eased down on Arlington, and workers lowered two honored warriors beneath the terrace.[36]

With their arrival, each of the century's major wars took its place on the amphitheater plaza, where three tombs symbolized a distinct phase of the nation's evolution—one from the era of Black Jack Pershing, biplanes, and doughboys; one from the time of Pearl Harbor, Ike, Normandy, and the mushroom-shaped cloud; and one from the false hope of Inchon and the confusion of night fighting, long retreats, and limited war. Having used the ultimate weapon at Hiroshima and Nagasaki in 1945, the United States could not easily unleash it again—nor, for that matter, could the growing number of nations in possession of that power. The specter of nuclear holocaust, hovering just over the horizon, ensured that the last wars of the century would be small, costly affairs of containment, limited in scope and unsatisfying in outcome, with few obvious winners.[37] Total war was unthinkable, the future uncertain.

That future, and all that the nuclear age implied, were made obvious at Arlington within three days of President John F. Kennedy's inauguration in 1961. That is when a C-54 transport touched down at Bolling Air Force Base in Washington at three thirty on the morning of January 23, taxied to a secure area, and rolled to a halt in the dark. Guards kept vigil around the plane until daylight, at which time the transport's cargo door heaved open and a forklift ventured across the tarmac. A bulky vault was removed from the plane and loaded onto a flatbed truck. The truck proceeded to Arlington, thirty minutes away, and stopped in front of a little-used chapel. Soldiers appeared there and gingerly took the vault inside, while a technician swept the truck's cab with a Geiger counter, detected a few harmless millirems of radiation, and sent the flatbed on its way. An Army guard was posted at the chapel's door, along with a health physicist from the Atomic Energy Commission. Nobody was allowed to approach the vault inside, which held the badly burned remains of Spec. Four Richard Leroy McKinley, twenty-six, a casualty of the nation's first nuclear accident. Saturated with radiation, McKinley was kept in isolation as he awaited burial, double-sealed in a lead-lined casket and concrete vault.[38]

McKinley, a career soldier who had survived the fight for Korea, was one of three technicians killed on January 3, 1961, while performing maintenance on the nuclear reactor known as SL-1, the Army's Stationary Low Power facility some forty miles west of Idaho Falls, Idaho. The small, isolated experimental station, a two hundred–megawatt plant, was the prototype for power plants the Army hoped to build for its remote radar outposts in the Arctic. But SL-1 had exploded when one of McKinley's comrades, Army Spec. John A. Byrnes III, had pulled the reactor's central control rod too far out of its seat, producing a power surge and explosion inside the containment vessel. Byrnes, standing over the reactor, was thrown onto the ceiling of the containment chamber and impaled there by the power rod. McKinley and another serviceman, Navy Electrician's Mate Richard C. Legg, were scorched and killed. Both were so thoroughly irradiated that rescue teams wearing lead-lined suits could handle the dead men for only a few minutes at a time. Legg and Byrnes were returned to their home states for burial—consigned, like McKinley, to lead-lined caskets inside sealed cement vaults.[39]

McKinley, a native of Ohio, was brought to Arlington at his wife's request to honor his service in Korea. Grave diggers excavated a special place for him in Section 31, just uphill from the cemetery's main entrance on Memorial Drive; following guidelines from the Atomic Energy Commission, they dug down to ten feet, more than a yard deeper than the regulation depth at Arlington, and lined the grave's interior with a foot of cement. On January 25, the day of McKinley's burial, family members were kept twenty feet away from the grave. His eight-minute service went quickly. When it was done and Taps was sounded, a truck brought more cement, which was poured into the grave before it was filled with earth. A few days later, the commander of the Military District of Washington issued a dire warning to the cemetery superintendent.[40]

"It is desired that the following remarks be placed on the permanent record DA [Department of the Army] Form 2122, Record of Interment," an assistant adjutant general wrote on January 31. "Victim of nuclear accident. Body is contaminated with long-life radio-active isotopes. Under no circumstance will the body be moved from this location without prior approval of the AEC [Atomic Energy Commission] in consultation with this headquarters."[41]

Covered with thick turf and softened by the decades, the tomb looks much like any other at Arlington today, but the warning remains on file in the superintendent's office.

PART III

THE NATION'S CEMETERY

12

"I COULD STAY
HERE FOREVER"

PAUL FUQUA, A YOUNG NATIONAL PARK SERVICE RANGER AND COLLEGE STU-
dent, was just settling in for his evening routine at the Lee mansion. It was
about four thirty P.M. on March 3, 1963, and the crowds were dispersing for
the day. He pulled up to a desk in the conservatory overlooking Mrs. Lee's garden and opened a book, relishing the prospect of some quiet time.[1]

Then the moment was shattered. A bald man in a suit dashed into the mansion, shouting: "The president is coming! The president is coming!" before racing
out among the tombstones. "Great," Fuqua thought, closing his book and slowly
rising to his feet. "I am going to spend the next three hours chasing this demented
little guy through the cemetery so I can run him down and turn him in."[2]

Fuqua followed the man outside, turned a corner, and ran into the most
familiar face in America. "Mind if we look around?" President John F. Kennedy
asked Fuqua, who straightened his Smokey Bear hat and came to his senses.
"No, of course not," he said. "I'd be happy to show you through the house."[3]

Thus began President Kennedy's first—and only—tour of the mansion, up
the stairs and through the bedroom where Robert E. Lee had written his letter
of resignation, through the parlor that had rung with laughter in happier times,

and finally up the narrow back stairs into the attic, where Fuqua pointed out the mortised beams and a little rectangular peephole that had allowed Union soldiers to keep an eye on the river below.[4]

"He tried the peephole," Fuqua recalled more than four decades later. "He was like a big kid looking through it—he thought it was really nifty. As a history buff, he knew all about Lee's place. He knew all about the Civil War. He was quite conversant with the Meigs story and all that."[5]

Dusk was approaching as Fuqua wrapped up the tour. The party—consisting of Kennedy, his friend the newspaper correspondent Charles Bartlett, and the bald fellow, whom Fuqua took to be an advance man or Secret Service agent—moved outside for a look at the grounds. It was an exquisite Sunday in late winter, with the sun slanting low through bare trees, over the beige hills, and across the river to the Lincoln Memorial, cast in pale evening light.[6]

"We stood over there," Fuqua said, walking to a point where the lawn begins to drop away from the crest of the hill, "and I explained how Memorial Bridge was built to link the Lincoln Memorial with the Lee mansion, symbolizing the reunification of the nation, and President Kennedy thought that was the neatest thing in the world! He really liked the idea. We were just looking across the river and talking quietly as we are now," Fuqua said.[7]

Kennedy drank in the scene. "I could stay here forever," he said.[8]

His words hung in the air until the sound of tires crunching on gravel announced that it was time for the president to go. Kennedy said his thanks and disappeared into a limousine. "And that was that," Fuqua said.[9]

Eight months later, on November 23, 1963, President Kennedy lay dead in the White House while his family, friends, and aides made hurried plans for a state funeral—the first since President Eisenhower had officiated at Arlington ceremonies for the Unknowns of World War II and Korea in 1958.[10] Kennedy's friends were still discussing whether to bury the president in Boston or Arlington on that dreary Saturday morning as hundreds of disbelieving citizens, not knowing where else to go, huddled under dripping umbrellas by the White House gates. Inside, an honor guard stood vigil around the president's casket in the candlelit East Room.[11] Just down the hall, Kennedy's brother-in-law Sargent Shriver took charge of funeral planning, sifting through thousands of suggestions and translating Jacqueline Kennedy's wishes into action.[12]

In the uncertain hours after the president's assassination, Mrs. Kennedy had developed some very specific ideas for his funeral—to walk behind her husband's caisson, to adopt President Lincoln's funeral as a model, and to march JFK's casket to the Capitol with no music, only muffled drums marking time.[13] But as of Saturday morning, she had still expressed no preference for a burial site. The most likely one, a family plot in Brookline, Massachusetts, was favored by Kenny O'Donnell, Larry O'Brien, and other insiders with strong ties to Boston.[14] Indeed, it was the place Kennedy himself expected to go; he had mentioned it on that afternoon at Arlington, where the subject of burials had arisen naturally. "Guess I'll have to go back to Boston," Kennedy had told Bartlett then.[15] Military planners also had Boston in mind on the day of Kennedy's death, when they made provisional arrangements to ship the president's body from Washington north by destroyer, by air, or by train, depending on the family's wishes.[16] But as funeral plans took shape, Kennedy's secretary of defense, Robert S. McNamara, jumped in with a surprise suggestion, proposing Arlington as a suitable alternative, given the cemetery's national prominence and the president's appreciation for the old Lee estate.[17]

The suggestion did not endear McNamara to O'Donnell and fellow members of the so-called Boston mafia, but others from Kennedy's inner circle embraced the Arlington idea. Bartlett was among them. "Bob McNamara was bold enough . . . to suggest to the family where the President should be buried," he recalled. "As soon as I heard Bob say this, why then of course I jumped in . . . and . . . said it was a beautiful place and it was something he loved and was part of the heritage he loved."[18] Bartlett reinforced McNamara's proposal, but the question remained unsettled that Saturday, like a myriad of shifting details: Gray horses or black ones for the caisson platoon?[19] Was there time to invite foreign leaders to Washington? Could the military band at the Capitol play "Hail to the Chief" in solemn adagio instead of regular time?[20] Was the Washington mass to be held at St. Matthew's Cathedral or the Shrine of the Immaculate Conception? And for burial, was it Boston or Arlington, Arlington or Boston? This last choice proved to be the most vexing of all, according to historian William Manchester, who credited the Arlington-Boston debate as a source of lingering friction between proponents for each site.[21] History was on the side of Boston: In the ninety-nine years of Arlington's existence as a national cemetery at the time of Kennedy's death, the only president entombed there was William Howard Taft, buried in 1930 barely a month after his retirement as chief justice of the Supreme Court.[22] No sitting president had ever been interred at Arlington. Almost every other one had gone home for final honors.[23]

While this discussion ran its course, John C. Metzler, Arlington's superintendent, slid into his car and began to prowl the rain-slicked roads of the cemetery about nine A.M. on Saturday. Like most others, Metzler assumed that the president was destined for Boston. But just in case Arlington won out, he wanted to be prepared; indeed, when the superintendent reviewed the standing plans for a presidential funeral, a document constantly updated by the Military District of Washington, he discovered that those plans called for him to prepare a list of prospective burial sites for the chief executive. "I toured the cemetery . . . closely observing all the possible locations for a President's burial," Metzler recalled. "I finally decided that only one location was worthy of consideration but two others should be mentioned and considered by the family."[24] Metzler finished his survey, returning to his office with three choices marked on a map. The first two had naval associations, in acknowledgment of Kennedy's wartime service: one, on the southern edge of Arlington by Dewey Circle, was near the grave of Rear Adm. Robert E. Peary, the Arctic explorer, while the second was to the west of the amphitheater, on the high ground near the U.S.S. *Maine* Memorial; the third had no naval connection but was the most prominent, situated just downhill from the Lee mansion overlooking the Lincoln Memorial and all of Washington—the very view Kennedy had enjoyed with Paul Fuqua and Charles Bartlett a few months before.[25]

Metzler was ready with these suggestions when the call came from the White House about ten thirty A.M. that Saturday: Attorney General Robert Kennedy was on his way to screen prospective burial sites with his sisters Eunice Shriver and Patricia Lawford, McNamara, and a contingent of aides. Metzler met them at the gates and the group drove around the cemetery in a downpour, getting out of their cars and sloshing through the hills to inspect the places on Metzler's list. They backtracked for a second look at the site near the Lee mansion, where they walked around and around, gazing back and forth at the old house, the river, and the gray city swirling in and out of the mists below. "Without any commitment they departed," Metzler said.[26]

Back at the White House, Robert Kennedy gave the former First Lady a favorable report for Arlington, backed up by his sisters.[27] Mrs. Kennedy, whose sense of the historic moment was stronger than any tribal ties she felt toward Boston, was inclined to bury her husband at Arlington "so that he would belong to the nation."[28] But she wanted to see the place for herself. So with Bobby Kennedy and a growing retinue of aides and friends, she was driven back across the river, where Metzler waited to greet the party about three thirty P.M. Since the attorney general had already written off the sites at Dewey Circle and the *Maine* Memorial, Metzler led the group toward the mansion.[29] They emerged from their cars and watched as Mrs. Kennedy, standing under a black cloud of umbrellas, stared silently at the slope where her husband would be buried. She did not budge for fifteen minutes. Then she nodded approval. William Walton, a family friend and artist with a good eye for proportions, stepped out from under the bank of umbrellas, climbed the hill, and pointed to the spot where the grave should go. All watched as Metzler pounded a stake into the soggy ground. The superintendent was told to prepare for a Monday funeral. The family drifted away.[30]

Metzler planned to summon his workers for duty the next day, a Sunday. A thick mat of fallen leaves had to be cleared from the site, security cordons laid out, mats spread over the wet earth, a press stand erected, and a presidential grave prepared.[31] McNamara returned to Arlington on Sunday morning with a crew of engineers who surveyed the president's six-hundred-square-foot plot. Their measurements showed that Metzler's stake was a mere six inches off the true axis running from the Lee mansion to the Lincoln Memorial; the marker was adjusted and twelve granite posts were set to establish boundaries.[32] Given Arlington's tangled real estate history, both McNamara and Bobby Kennedy took great pains to avoid future property disputes between the Army, which still controlled Arlington National Cemetery, and the National Park Service, which held the mansion and twenty-eight acres surrounding it.[33] The attorney general dispatched Justice Department lawyers to search the title to his brother's gravesite, which showed that the plot was situated entirely on Army property.[34] President Kennedy could rest in peace there.

With his burial site resolved, other funeral details fell into place. Kennedy would be conveyed from the White House to Capitol Hill on Sunday to lie in state in the Rotunda, as President Lincoln and other honored leaders had done. On Monday, he would be marched to the White House for a brief ceremony at the north portico before traveling to St. Matthew's Cathedral for a requiem mass; then he would make the traditional journey through the streets of Washington, past the Lincoln Memorial, over Memorial Bridge, and finally up the hill to Arlington.[35]

Following tradition, each leg of the president's passage would be made by caisson, the old fashioned, horse-drawn artillery wagon that had once carried ammunition to the battlefront and returned with war dead. Two such caissons, both of World War I vintage, had been salvaged for full honors ceremonies at Arlington. Stationed at Fort Myer, members of the Army's 3rd Infantry Regiment, also known as the Old Guard, operated the caissons and maintained a stable of some forty horses for funeral duty.[36]

After vacillating over whether to use matched grays or black horses for the president's caisson, Mrs. Kennedy declared in favor of grays on Saturday afternoon.[37] This sent Sgt. Tom Setterberg and other members of the Old Guard caisson platoon into high gear—pressing their dress blues, cleaning tack, polishing brass, picking hooves, and preparing to lead their commander in chief on one glorious last ride.[38]

Setterberg, designated leader of the platoon's White Horse Section, would ride Big Boy, a massive gray gelding who walked in front, unattached to the six matched horses pulling the caisson in harness: Count Chris and Skyline in the lead, followed by swing horses Blue and Blue Dare, and wheel horses Cap and Cloudburst. Setterberg would use Big Boy to guide other horses out of the familiar cemetery grounds and into the capital, where gathering crowds, snapping flags, and flashing cameras threatened to spook the animals.[39] The caisson would be followed by Black Jack, a spirited black gelding, age sixteen, designated as the riderless horse. Named for the famed World War I general, Black Jack was outfitted with riding boots reversed in the stirrups, a traditional symbol for a departed warrior facing no more battles. It was an honor accorded to former presidents, officers of colonel's rank or higher, and commissioned officers from one of the mounted services. Black Jack, who could be as strong-headed as his namesake, gained his own degree of fame during the weekend of Kennedy's funeral, dancing across millions of television screens, barely under control.[40]

While the lights burned in the Old Guard stables that Saturday night, a weary Sargent Shriver and presidential counselor Ted Sorenson drove out to the home of Patrick O'Boyle, archbishop of Washington, to discuss funeral services with him and Cardinal Richard J. Cushing, the Boston archbishop and family friend who would preside at Kennedy's mass, scheduled for Monday in Washington. Sorenson conveyed Mrs. Kennedy's wish that the service be kept as plain as possible. "Yes," Cushing said, grasping the point. "We'll leave him as a Jesuit."[41]

Such was the goal, but the funeral grew complex as new players arrived on stage, seating charts shifted, and fresh elements were cranked into the ceremonies. Prince Philip arrived to represent Britain; Emperor Haile Selassie flew in from Ethiopia; Gen. Charles de Gaulle, from France; President Eamon de Valera, from Ireland; King Baudouin, from Belgium, and scores of other leaders, each expecting a suitable place in the proceedings. Former presidents Dwight D. Eisenhower and Harry S. Truman signaled their intention to attend. Bobby Kennedy, recalling his brother's fondness for the Green Berets, summoned a delegation of Special Forces soldiers from Fort Bragg to march beside the president's caisson.[42] Mrs. Kennedy wanted the Old Guard's Colonial Fife and Drum Corps, dressed in their eighteenth-century knee breeches and tricornered hats, to participate, along with cadets from the Irish Guard, a silent drill team from the old country, and the Naval Academy Catholic Choir. Letitia Baldrige, Mrs. Kennedy's social secretary, tracked down bagpipers from the Black Watch of the Royal Highland Regiment, which happened to be touring the United States, and diverted nine of the kilted gentlemen to join the funeral march. More pipers were added at Arlington, where a special Air Force unit was recruited to play at interment services.[43]

These extra flourishes, which transformed the event into a made-for-television production, multiplied as the weekend progressed. It proved too much for one White House aide, who stalked off at the height of funeral preparations Saturday afternoon. "I got teed off and got out," he grumbled. "Things were getting out of control . . . I thought at any minute the Flying Wallendas would be called in." The aide disappeared, mastered his irritation, and returned to help with the burgeoning arrangements.[44]

Much to the relief of the Joint Chiefs of Staff, Mrs. Kennedy relented on her ambition to accompany the president's caisson on foot through the entire

two-day ceremony, from the White House to the Capitol to St. Matthew's to
Arlington. Walking this six-mile circuit would have taxed the endurance of the
military chiefs—all of whom were middle-aged, some of whom were over-
weight and out of shape. Their reluctance to make the forced march may have
encouraged Mrs. Kennedy to scale it back.[45]

Whatever the reason, when the president's body left the Executive Mansion
for the Capitol early Sunday afternoon, Mrs. Kennedy followed by car, with
the chiefs piled into limousines behind her. Black Jack led the motorcade, toss-
ing his head and jigging his way up Pennsylvania Avenue with Pfc. Arthur A.
Carlson hanging on to his reins. Silent crowds, ten to fifteen people deep, lined
both sides of the parade route, with some mourners scrambling into trees or
onto statues for a better view. It was the job of Carlson, an Old Guard from the
caisson platoon, to lead Black Jack through the funeral rites. The horse, high-
strung under the best of circumstances, had been badly spooked as the procession prepared to leave the White House, where a metal grate had fallen to the
pavement with a clang. "Black Jack went wild," Carlson recalled. "He stayed agitated for the . . . entire funeral." Carlson struggled to maintain decorum, even
after the horse contrived to stomp his escort's foot. Millions of television viewers, watching through that heartbreaking weekend, may have identified with
the horse, which seemed to recoil from all that had happened. Carlson held
him in check.[46]

In a time of turmoil, such rituals served an important purpose. "In the eyes
of the world we looked pretty shoddy, having our President assassinated in
Dallas," said Letitia Baldrige, who helped carry out Mrs. Kennedy's funeral
plans. "She wanted this to be done to absolute perfection exactly as the President would have done for someone he loved very much . . . I think the way the
funeral was handled, the way everybody acted, suddenly put Americans back
up again in the minds of the people around the world."[47]

Nobody worked harder at perfection than the Old Guard, whose members
devoted an immoderate amount of time to shining shoes, polishing medals,
and drilling for ceremonial duties at Arlington. They practiced earth-shaking
artillery salutes, folded flags until they could do it in their sleep, and tromped
the Virginia hills in marching platoons until the formation moved as a single

organism. Four times a year, they made dry runs for a presidential funeral, hauling weighted caskets up and down the steps of the National Cathedral in Washington to prepare for the death of President Hoover, President Eisenhower, or President Truman—nobody expected President Kennedy to go first.[48] When they were transported across the river for such ceremonies, the Old Guard made the trip standing—their buses were not equipped with seats because sitting would wrinkle one's sharply creased trousers. "We all stood erect," said 1st Lt. Edward M. Gripkey, who helped organize President Kennedy's funeral. "Once dressed in my trousers, I did not sit."[49]

The Old Guard was proud of its traditions, taking a dim professional view of comrades who devoted less attention to discipline and appearance. A few Old Guards, irked that Special Forces soldiers had been airlifted to Washington for the Kennedy funeral, took quiet delight when one of the Green Berets swooned under the unaccustomed strain of duty at Arlington. "When one of them 'took a knee' after standing in position for a long time, the ceremonial troops who saw him go down smiled as if they were amused at his misfortune," recalled Capt. Thomas F. Reid, the site officer initially in charge of planning the president's interment.[50]

The Old Guard not only furnished the caisson and horses for Kennedy's funeral; it also dispatched honor guards to stand watch over his casket, helped form security cordons for his funeral procession, and assigned one of its most promising young officers, 1st Lt. Samuel R. Bird, to oversee the joint services casket detail, which met their slain commander in chief at Andrews Air Force Base, stayed with him through the wee hours of Saturday morning, returned him to the White House, and moved him through the weekend ceremonies in fine military style. When it came time to see him across the river to Arlington, they did that too.[51]

On Sunday, arriving for rituals on Capitol Hill, some members of Bird's casket detail faced the long flight of stairs to the Rotunda with a sense of foreboding. Thirty-six shallow steps led from the Capitol Plaza to the Rotunda entrance. A stand of television cameras bristled at the top of the stairs and the Kennedy family filed into place at the bottom, with Bird's casket team in between. The whole world would be watching the nine men assigned to carry a mahogany casket weighing 1,300 pounds—about the heft of a thoroughbred horse—to the top. "I remember looking at the steep incline and thinking it looked more like a wall than steps," said Army Spec. Douglas A. Mayfield, one

of three soldiers, two marines, two sailors, one airman, and one coastguards-
man assigned to carry the president's casket that weekend.[52] With Lieutenant
Bird hovering behind, the team eased Kennedy from the caisson and slowly
began its ascent. As the casket detail did so, Bird sensed that the men were
having trouble balancing their load. He slipped behind the squad and lifted
the casket from its back corners to relieve the strain, which gave the pallbearers
a boost up the stairs. With each step the strain grew greater as they struggled
to keep the casket level and struggled to make it look as if they were not struggling. Those on the lower end had to hoist the casket shoulder high, while the
men in front tried to maintain their grip at waist level. With Bird close behind,
watching for any signs of slippage, the casket bearers inched up the stairs, followed by Mrs. Kennedy and her two children.[53] Down on the plaza, just as the
Coast Guard Band sounded the last strains of the Navy Hymn, "Eternal
Father, Strong to Save," the casket detail reached the top, moved out of the
bright sunlight, and disappeared into the darkened Rotunda. Under the dome,
they settled Kennedy onto President Lincoln's catafalque and stepped back.
Mrs. Kennedy, dressed in black with a long veil, emerged from the shadows,
clutching the hand of her daughter, Caroline. The pair of them strode forward
through the soaring chamber and knelt before the casket. As Mrs. Kennedy
did so, she stretched out one hand to touch the box. She leaned in to kiss the
flag, rose to her feet, and melted into the Rotunda again.[54]

Across the river at Arlington, soldiers and civilians made preparation for Monday's interment. John Metzler summoned Clifton Pollard, his best gravedigger,
to work that day. "Sorry to pull you out like this on a Sunday morning," Metzler told Pollard. "Oh, don't say that," the gravedigger told him. "Why, it's an
honor for me to be here." With Metzler watching, Pollard climbed aboard his
massive backhoe, revved the diesel engine, and began to bite great chunks of
earth from the hill below the Lee mansion. "That's nice soil," said Metzler, in-
specting the first shovelful with a practiced eye. "I'd like to save a little of it."
Some of the earth was taken away to grow new turf for the president's grave.
Pollard, operating his machine with surgical precision, resumed digging, making a tidy job of it.[55]

Shortly after Metzler became superintendent of Arlington in 1951, he had moved the cemetery into the automated age, replacing shovels, in use since the time of James Parks, with new earthmoving machines. It took a man with a shovel most of a day to dig a proper grave, while an experienced backhoe operator such as Pollard could complete the task in fifteen minutes.[56] Given the occasion, Pollard may have taken a bit longer, consulting with Metzler between scoops, at one point offering his own simple eulogy for Kennedy. "He was a good man," said Pollard. "Yes, he was," echoed Metzler. "Now they're going to come and put him right here in this grave I'm making up," said Pollard.[57]

The gravedigger went back to work, while Metzler wrestled with a challenging new request from Mrs. Kennedy, who wanted an eternal flame installed at her husband's grave. She had seen such a memorial in Paris at the Arc de Triomphe, while visiting the tomb of the *poilu inconnu* with the president in 1961. That experience now inspired her suggestion for Arlington. Her appeal, conveyed to Metzler about three P.M. on Sunday, allowed precious little time for designing, constructing, installing, and testing the device so that Mrs. Kennedy could safely light it on Monday afternoon—less than twenty-four hours away.[58]

What if the flame exploded? What if it failed to light? What if it set an archbishop on fire? "I advised them that such a construction and installation was beyond my capabilities," Metzler said, "and their answer was, 'Yes, we know but somehow get an eternal flame.' "[59] Metzler hung up, pondered the request, and reached for the receiver again. This time he phoned Lt. Col. Bernard G. Carroll, the post engineer at Fort Myer, to see if his shop could produce the required torch. Carroll thought he might be able to build the thing. While Carroll considered a workable design, he and Metzler pulled the Yellow Pages from the shelf and began phoning gas companies in Virginia and Maryland for equipment. The men discovered with a growing sense of anxiety that few businesses were answering their telephones that Sunday afternoon. Finally a contractor from Rockville, Maryland, took the call, listened with interest, and offered to help. A tank of propane gas and three hundred feet of quarter-inch copper tubing were soon on their way to Arlington. Carroll, meanwhile, consulted with fellow engineers for a simple but foolproof design, which combined one tank of gas, the length of copper tubing, one Hawaiian luau torch, and a custom-built wire basket to hold the burner eighteen inches off the ground. The apparatus would be neither pretty nor eternal but it might work until something better could be devised.[60]

While workers at Arlington dug a trench for the gas line, army engineers welded the basket and torch into a single unit. The device was delivered to the cemetery by nine P.M. Sunday and set in place at the head of Kennedy's grave. The gas tank, hidden in a thicket of bamboo near the Lee mansion, would be operated by an army sergeant, ready to open the valve on a signal from graveside.[61] Fresh-cut pine boughs were heaped around the burner to hide the unsightly contrivance. With all elements in place, the patchwork creation was ready for a test run. The sergeant turned the tap. Gas hissed from a valve by the president's grave. A burst of light flared on the dark hillside. The eternal flame was up and running by midnight.[62]

Exhausted soldiers from the Old Guard drifted back across the river as Sunday evening lengthened, but nobody got much rest that night, which was filled with shining shoes, pressing uniforms, poring over funeral plans, and drilling for the next day's duty. Just after dinner, Army Spec. Douglas Mayfield and others from the joint service casket team were summoned for flag-folding practice with Lieutenant Bird. The team was expected to retire the Stars and Stripes from the president's casket in the traditional, slow-motion manner, transforming the familiar rectangle into a tight blue triangle. Under Bird's watchful eye, the eight men folded and unfolded the flag for hours until the crew was performing flawlessly.[63]

"As good as each member was individually, it was critical that we practice together over and over . . . since two days before we had never met and didn't know each other," Mayfield recalled. "If just one member falters or the team's timing is off, the flag could be dropped, red and white stripes could be other than straight, and red could be showing in the triangular folded flag where only blue with white stars are supposed to be. We knew that we would be . . . scrutinized by millions of viewers and we wanted to give the impression that . . . operating in unison was second nature to us."[64]

By the time the flag folders had reached that benchmark, the clock was ticking toward midnight. But the casket men still had work to do. They filed onto a bus, rode through the empty cemetery, and emerged at Arlington's amphitheater, where the Tomb of the Unknowns was bathed in ghostly white light. Lieutenant Bird had ordered a practice casket—one of several the Old Guard kept to train recruits at Arlington—to be brought out for his men to carry up and down the long amphitheater stairs. He wanted to simulate the next day's most daunting challenge: bringing President Kennedy out of the Rotunda and down the Capitol stairs without slipping.[65]

"It appeared to me that very little consideration had been given to the tremendous weight of the casket during the planning stages of the funeral," Bird said. "It required every ounce of strength that all nine of us could muster to move the casket in an appropriate and respectful manner.[66] We knew it would be much harder to carry it down because they would lose me on the back as it came down," Bird recalled.[67] That night at Arlington, as Specialist Mayfield took his accustomed position on the front corner of the casket and lifted, he noticed that the practice box was heavier than usual—for good reason: Bird had stuffed it with sandbags to make the burden more realistic. The casket men hoisted their load, slow-marched it down the steps, and seemed to have little trouble. Thinking the box might still be too light, Bird clambered aboard to make it heavier, hanging on to the casket while his men carried him down the stairs. The exhausted team managed with aplomb, so Bird added more weight, this time in the person of a tomb sentinel who had been watching the trials from the sidelines. He joined the lieutenant as casket rider, while the body bearers wobbled beneath them, straining down the long stairs for the last time. With their hands blistered and their backs sore, they finally lost their grip, and Bird called a halt to the proceedings. "We've done all we can tonight fellas," he said. "We're just not going to make it . . . Don't worry about it. We'll get it in the morning."[68]

Crowds jammed the Rotunda that Sunday night, waiting in long lines to pay their respects to the slain president. A Democratic congressman from Michigan, Rep. Neil Staebler, wandered Capitol Hill at eight P.M. to find mourners patiently waiting to get inside, in ranks four abreast and ten blocks long. When he returned five hours later, thinking that the November chill and the late hour might have thinned the crowds, he was surprised to find that the multitude had grown—now the lines stood twelve abreast for fifteen blocks. "The people just had come to Washington to somehow be near the occasion and express themselves," Staebler said.[69] The masses were still there on Monday when the great bronze doors of the Rotunda heaved shut at nine A.M., leaving

12,000 mourners outside, still waiting for a glimpse of the president's casket. Officials estimated that some 250,000 passed through the Rotunda on Sunday and Monday.[70]

The crowds grew on Monday as Lieutenant Bird's bleary-eyed casket team filed onto a bus and drove across the river to Capitol Hill. Traffic choked the streets. The bus, blaring its horn, could not break through, so Bird and company jumped out and covered the last quarter mile on foot, arriving in time to huddle in a quiet corner of the Rotunda before their next moment in the spotlight.[71]

"Bow your heads," Bird ordered his men. The lieutenant prayed: "Dear God, please give us strength to do this last thing for the President." Bird opened his eyes and checked his watch. "Let's move," he said, leading them toward the Rotunda, where they collected Kennedy's casket and made for the steps.[72] They began to descend as the Coast Guard Band struck up the first chords of "O God of Loveliness."[73] They glided down to the plaza with no hint of trouble, keeping the casket level and making it look effortless. One of them later said it had seemed like a magic carpet ride.[74]

For the first time in its history, the whole nation watched a presidential funeral as it took place, the flag-draped caisson rattling through silent, brooding streets, the solemn ranks of warriors marching in strict columns, Black Jack skipping sideways up the White House drive, Mrs. Kennedy, standing tall and perfectly composed, striding out the drive for St. Matthew's, with Robert and Teddy Kennedy alongside. The Black Watch, in bristling bearskin hats and white spats, set the pace, their pipes wailing "The Brown- Haired Maiden" and "The Barren Rocks of Aden" under skeletal trees on a brilliant autumn day.[75] One of the president's friends said it was just the sort of New England weather Kennedy loved, along with the martial pageantry.[76] As noon approached, all lines converged on the sturdy Romanesque hulk of St. Matthew's, where world leaders, politicians, and family trudged up the steps and packed the pews inside. It was a crowded, disparate audience, including, among others, Dr. Martin Luther King Jr. and Gov. George C. Wallace, who settled in for the unyielding, comforting words of departure rendered in Latin, bathed in incense, promising better days.[77]

With the blessing, the crowd spilled out into the narrow streets, where three-year-old John-John snapped off the famous salute to his father, and Sgt. Tom Setterberg guided Big Boy into position to lead the president's caisson across the river.[78] There nervous Secret Service men made their last-minute checks at Arlington. One agent scrambled down into Kennedy's grave to look for bombs and had to be pulled out by a soldier.[79] Another checked for booby traps among the flowers Mrs. Kennedy's friends brought for the grave. All fretted over the eternal flame, which remained an object of suspicion. Grudgingly the Secret Service yielded, but only if the Army promised to drench the pine boughs around the torch with two buckets of water before it was lit.[80]

The funeral cortege inched toward Arlington, taking forty-five minutes to cover the three-mile march.[81] As the first columns approached and the national drama moved toward its dénouement, Army Sgt. William Malcolm watched from the hillside above the president's grave and felt an uncharacteristic twinge of stage fright.

"We could look out over the Memorial Gate and see them coming," said Malcolm, the officer in charge of the seven-man firing party that would provide the last salute for Kennedy. "I was shaking with fright, the way I shook when I came for my first funeral here. That was in January 1961 and I have attended some four thousand funerals since. I had not been frightened since my first funeral, but was with this one."[82]

Malcolm was not the only one feeling jittery that afternoon. Army Sgt. Keith Clark, assigned to play Taps for the president, had been standing on the hill since just after noon, feeling the chill seep into his bones as the hours ticked away. There was trouble brewing in the color guard, which had marched before the caisson all weekend, led by Army Platoon Sgt. James R. "Pete" Holder, who proudly carried the American flag, flanked by a marine and an airman. "By the time we reached the graveside," Holder recalled, "the Air Force guard complained that he could not stand up any longer, and he was going to pass out. I reassured him that he would be okay and cursed him, calling him a S.O.B. to get his adrenaline flowing, and make him mad enough to stay on his feet. He did not fall out, but it was close."[83] Black Jack continued to act up, jerking and jouncing across Memorial Bridge and threatening to break his weary handler, Pfc. Art Carlson. "I had to make a choice," Carlson recalled, "good posture or keep in step with the drumbeat. I chose keeping in step . . . I was getting desperately tired, especially my right arm, but knew that if that horse got away from me I would be walking ... around a radar station in Greenland before the week was out." Carlson held on for Arlington, where the arrival on home turf seemed to calm both horse and man.[84] Black Jack became an overnight sensation and a beloved character from the Kennedy funeral, but the beast was not universally admired by his coworkers. "I wanted to take him, sight unseen, to a very ... secluded place and hit that sonofabitch with a very big board right over the head," admitted Sergeant Setterberg, sorely tried by the horse's antics.[85]

At precisely two forty-two P.M., the caisson rolled to a halt in the cemetery, where the Air Force pipers launched into "Mist-Covered Mountain" and filed over the hills in a slow, majestic march. Lieutenant Bird and his casket team took the president from the wagon and marched him to the grave, easing his casket to rest on supports there. Squadrons of F-105 fighter jets streaked over the hill in the missing man formation, followed by the low-flying 707 Kennedy had known as Air Force One, which dipped its wings in final salute.[86]

The firing party, deployed above the president's grave, stiffened at Sergeant Malcolm's command, raised their M-1 rifles to port arms in one fluid motion, and swung into position for firing, executing a perfect three-round volley. The salute startled an infant, who shrieked disconsolately.[87]

The baby continued screeching as Sgt. Keith Clark stood to attention, pointed his bugle toward Kennedy's grave, and began to sound Taps. The song rang true until Clark hit the sixth note, which broke horribly. Everyone heard it. Some thought that Clark's broken note had been intentional, meant to emphasize the distress the nation felt, but it was nothing of the sort. Clark later said he had missed the note under pressure because his lips were numb and he had been deafened by muzzle blasts from the firing party, which had been uncharacteristically—and unwisely—placed directly behind him instead of off to the side[88] to give television cameras a better view.[89] Despite the cracked note, Clark finished Taps in good form, with the last crystalline tones lingering over the cemetery. A long moment of silence, and the Marine Band struck up the Navy Hymn, the signal for Bird's men to begin folding the flag.[90]

Without a wrinkle, the flag crisply passed down the line of eight men, resolved into a perfect blue triangle in the white-gloved hands of Specialist Mayfield. Clutching the ensign to his heart, Mayfield stepped smartly across the turf to John Metzler, who took the flag and held it while Cardinal Cushing blessed the eternal flame, still inert in its evergreen bed. When Cushing was done, Mrs. Kennedy stepped forward to accept the flag from Metzler, who offered it with these words: "Mrs. Kennedy, this flag is presented to you in the name of a most mournful nation." He felt a catch in his throat. "Please accept it." She took the ensign, her eyes filling with tears behind the black veil. "She did not speak," Metzler said. "I do not believe that she could at that moment."[91]

Army Maj. Stanley Converse stepped forward with a lighted taper, which he handed to Mrs. Kennedy with an admission: "This is the saddest moment of my life," he told her.[92] She touched the taper to the torch. The flame burned bright. The crowd stood silent. All of a sudden, there was nothing left to do. Metzler led Mrs. Kennedy and the family down to their waiting cars, which purred off in the late afternoon light, heading back across the river.[93]

When they were on the way, Metzler plodded up the hill, where visitors continued milling around the grave. "Practically all of the dignitaries were either filing by or just standing and looking at the casket as though in a trance," Metzler said. "Ever so slowly they began to move off as though they were reluctant to leave . . . The first sergeant of the Special Forces . . . stood quietly by the head of the grave, removed his hat and placed it on the frame of the eternal flame. He saluted and departed." Others spontaneously followed suit, leaving hats and medals by the grave.[94]

Workers prepared to lower Kennedy's casket into the earth. Metzler asked the remaining television crews to stop filming. They ignored him. So he ordered his groundsmen to halt work. Then he placed a call to the engineer at Fort Myer, who shut off electricity to Arlington at three thirty-four P.M. that day.[95] "Without power they packed their gear and departed," Metzler said.[96]

Crowds gone, light failing, Metzler watched his workmen slide Kennedy's casket into the ground, seal it in a vault, and cover it with the good earth of Arlington. The men erected a white picket fence around the plot to keep visitors from trampling it; inside the paling, they heaped the ground with flowers from well-wishers, tidied up the area, latched the gate, and called it a day. "Our task of burying the President was finished," said Metzler, who retired to his home in the cemetery that night with a sense of satisfaction—and with no inkling of the profound change the president's death was about to visit upon Arlington.[97]

★ ★ ★

The first sign that things would be different came on the morning after Kennedy's funeral. When the cemetery gates swung open that day, thousands of visitors poured up through the hills to pay their respects, a pattern which would repeat itself in the weeks and months ahead. Before Kennedy's funeral, about two million people visited Arlington annually; in the year after it, the number swelled to seven million. Citizens swarmed over the site—to sing hymns, to pray, to conduct obscure religious rites. One woman brought a bottle of holy water, shook it over the eternal flame, and watched in horror as the cap flew off and doused the fire. A soldier from the Old Guard, standing nearby, whipped out his Zippo, restarted the flame, and reassured the visitor. "There, Ma'am," he said. "And I won't tell if you won't tell."[98]

Day after day, mourners left mountains of flowers and trinkets, which had to be carried away by the truckload. Most came just to stand and stare at the simple grave before moving on. A few seemed to forget where they were, sitting on nearby headstones, picnicking, making too much noise, and complaining when they were admonished for it.[99] The never-ending stream of visitors tramped past the president's tomb at the rate of three thousand an hour, forming long lines down the hill from Lee's mansion. The crowds grew on weekends, when fifty thousand citizens routinely came to visit the new national landmark in the year following Kennedy's death.[100]

He had helped to put Arlington on the map again, transforming the place as events of the past had done—like Robert E. Lee's departure in 1861, the establishment of Freedman's Village in 1863, the creation of the national cemetery in 1864, the first Decoration Day in 1868, the return of the dead from the Spanish-American War in 1899, and the succession of all the wars since, each of which added new graves, new monuments, new traditions, and new layers of meaning to the nation's cemetery. After President Kennedy joined the ranks there, nothing would be the same.

The combination of foot traffic and autumn rains transformed the ground around the president's plot into a quagmire. Workers threw up stanchions to create waiting lanes and walkways, which were layered with tons of gravel. The gravel began to disappear, piece by piece, into pockets and handbags for souvenirs. More stone was trucked in; more vanished.[101] The Old Guard deployed sentinels to provide some semblance of order during regular cemetery hours, establishing a temporary command post and shelter for its soldiers in a school bus commandeered from Fort Myer.[102]

"Nobody was prepared for the increase in visitors," said John C. Metzler Jr., who took his father's old job as superintendent of Arlington in 1991. "Everything was trampled. There was no planning for traffic or crowd control. It took a few years to sort it out."[103]

Seeing that a permanent, well-planned gravesite was called for, the Kennedy family and Arlington officials began work on a new gravesite almost as soon as the president had been settled at Arlington. The new parcel, designed by architect John Carl Warnecke of Washington, covered a 3.2-acre plot incorporating a terrace carved from the hillside, with curving walkways and ample room for visitors. Located a few yards downhill from the original grave, the new site preserved the view the president had admired, on the axis between the Lee mansion and the Lincoln Memorial. Excerpts from Kennedy's speeches were chiseled into low-lying walls around the grave, which was outfitted with a new, re-engineered eternal flame. Fed by a permanent natural gas supply, the new torch was set in a five-foot disk of stone, framed by massive paving blocks of Cape Cod granite and equipped with a constantly renewed electrical spark to keep the fire burning through wind and rain. Work on the new site began in 1965 and was finished in July 1967 at a cost of $2.5 million; most of the money came from federal appropriations, but the Kennedy family contributed $632,000 toward the project. As construction neared completion, the president was quietly exhumed after cemetery hours and installed in his new resting place. There he joined two of his infant children, who had been reinterred previously from Boston and Newport, Rhode Island. His brother Robert, assassinated in 1968, came to rest on the terrace that year, his grave marked by a simple white cross.[104]

As years passed, the flood of tourists diminished but the Kennedy grave remained a magnet for pilgrims, drawing almost four million visitors annually—more than the Tomb of the Unknowns, the Robert E. Lee Memorial, or other popular sites at Arlington. Like other landmarks, the Kennedy tomb occasionally attracted the deeply troubled: a veteran who fatally stabbed himself while horrified onlookers watched in 1972; thieves who made off with the cross from Robert Kennedy's grave in 1981; an immigrant who drifted into the locked cemetery on a rainy night, fell into the eternal flame, and suffered a fatal heart attack in 1982; vandals who tried to dig up one of the paving stones from the terrace in 1997 but abandoned the venture when they realized that the rock, weighing 500 pounds, was too heavy a trophy.[105] These were the exceptions;

most visitors came in peace, pausing for reflection under the maturing locusts, hollies, and cherries sheltering the president's tomb before wandering off to explore other parts of Arlington.

Just as Kennedy inspired a new generation while he was alive, he also influenced thousands of Americans by his example in death. At the time of Kennedy's funeral, about four thousand people were buried at Arlington each year; afterward, demands for interment jumped to seven thousand annually.[106] Like the burials of Gen. Montgomery Meigs and distinguished Civil War officers in the previous century, Kennedy's widely watched funeral made Arlington a prestigious venue for final honors. The sudden increase in burial requests meant that Arlington would be full by 1988, with no space for new interments unless the cemetery tightened burial restrictions. After 1966, therefore, new interments were limited to those who died on active duty, retired with a disability or twenty years of service, or won high military honors—rules that still apply at Arlington. At the same time, Arlington planned for a columbarium to hold cremated remains and preserve space for traditional in-ground burials.[107] The cemetery proceeded to develop two hundred acres of land from South Post of Fort Myer, which would provide space for new burials well into the twenty-first century.[108]

"Kennedy's funeral prompted these changes," said John C. Metzler Jr. "It was a milestone, one of the most significant events in our history."[109]

That milestone not only shaped Arlington's development but also transformed the lives of many who participated in that memorable weekend of pageantry and loss.

For Capt. Michael Groves, twenty-seven, a popular officer who commanded the Honor Guard Company at Fort Myer, the stress of planning and staffing Kennedy's funeral proved too great a burden. Ten days after the president's interment, Groves collapsed at his dinner table, dying of a heart attack. Comrades from the Old Guard, already saddened by Kennedy's death, were stunned by the sudden loss of Groves, a respected young soldier who had betrayed no sign of ill health.[110] "We'd lost a popular President," said Pfc. William W. Morris, "but Mike Groves was one of us, a great leader, and a friend to many in the company." With other members of the Old Guard, Morris pressed his best uniform that December, polished his medals to a high sheen, and solemnly carried his young captain to the grave, in Section 30 of Arlington, long before such a funeral seemed reasonable.[111]

For John C. Metzler Jr., who had been a sixteen-year-old watching his father preside over President Kennedy's funeral, the occasion reinforced his decision to join the Army and serve in Vietnam. When he returned from overseas, Metzler went to work for the Veterans Administration, moved back to the superintendent's lodge, and oversaw another Kennedy funeral at Arlington—this time for Jacqueline, who was buried beside her husband in 1994. "Never in a thousand years did I imagine that I would come back to finish what my father started in 1963," said Metzler, standing on the hill above the grave.[112]

The fractious Black Jack continued his career as a riderless horse, serving with characteristic flair at services for Gen. Douglas MacArthur, President Herbert Hoover, and President Lyndon B. Johnson before retiring in 1973. The horse lived to the ripe old age of twenty-nine, dying in 1976. Comrades from the Old Guard buried him with honors on the broad turf of Summerall Field at Fort Myer, not far from the stables; his grave is marked by a bronze tablet and a horseshoe-shaped hedge.[113]

President Kennedy's death marked the end of one era and the beginning of another. In Vietnam, the escalating war would draw more American troops into the struggle, including some of the best officers from the Old Guard. Among those who eagerly joined the fight was fresh-faced, patriotic 1st Lt. Sam Bird, who had so ably headed the casket team for Kennedy's funeral. Promoted to captain, Bird led a combat company in fierce fighting until 1967, when his helicopter came under heavy enemy fire. Several rounds hit Bird, including one that blew away a quarter of his skull. By some miracle, Bird survived the brain injury, living another seventeen years. He was greatly diminished but still proud of the way his men had performed for President Kennedy in November 1963.[114]

13

THE LAST UNKNOWN

Memorial Day of 1984 broke hazy over Washington, with low gray clouds and weeping skies evoking the oppressive atmosphere familiar to so many who had served in Vietnam. "Mekong weather," recalled one veteran among the two hundred fifty thousand well-wishers who crowded the capital's streets to watch a flag-covered caisson make the familiar, measured journey down from Capitol Hill and across the river to Arlington for a state funeral.[1]

After more than a decade of uncertainty and bitterness, the nation was finally honoring the Unknown of the Vietnam War—the long, star-crossed conflict that continued to stir argument for years after the last U.S. troops had withdrawn from Southeast Asia. Some three thousand guests had taken their seats on the marble benches of the Arlington amphitheater, where President Ronald Reagan strode to the podium, squared his shoulders, and launched into an overdue tribute to the Vietnam Unknown and those who had served with him.[2]

"The Unknown soldier who has returned to us today . . . is symbolic of all our missing sons," said Reagan. "About him, we may well wonder as others have: As a child, did he play on some street in a great American city, did he work beside his father on a farm in America's heartland? Did he marry? Did he have children? Did he look expectantly to return to a bride? We may never know the answers to those questions about his life. We do know, though, why he died. He saw the horrors of war and bravely faced them, certain his own cause and his country's cause was a noble one . . . Today we pause to embrace him and all who served us so well in a war whose end offered no parades, no flags, and so little thanks."[3]

As Reagan spoke, a sultry breeze stirred American flags in the colonnade behind him. Before him sat reminders of the war's cost—a man with a black eye patch, a squadron of young veterans in wheelchairs, a scattering of others sitting with crutches or canes at the ready. Near the front of the arena a line of warriors occupied an honored place, some streaming tears that threatened to stain the pale blue ribbons around their necks, from which hung the Medal of Honor. Several hundred others in the audience had never served in Vietnam but nonetheless carried deep wounds from the conflict; their loved ones were among the twenty-five hundred men still missing in action,[4] eleven years after Americans ended their involvement in the war.[5]

To reassure this last group, Reagan promised that the government would continue searching for their lost brothers, fathers, and husbands, no matter how long it took or where it led. "An end to America's involvement in Vietnam cannot come before we have achieved the fullest possible accounting of those missing in action," he said. "Our dedication to their cause must be strengthened with these events today. We write no last chapters, we close no books, we put away no final memories."[6]

Coming full circle, Reagan turned back to the man of the hour, whose flag-covered casket occupied center stage. "Thank you, dear son," said Reagan, his voice cracking, "and may God cradle you in His loving arms." The president, tucking his speech cards in a pocket, crossed the stage and draped the Medal of Honor on a velvet stand at the foot of the Unknown's bier. Then the nameless hero of Vietnam was decorously borne away by eight white-gloved comrades who slow-marched him from the apse of the amphitheater and out onto the terrace overlooking Washington, where Reagan joined mourners for final honors. The muddled weather prevented a flyover by F-15 fighter jets that day, but this did not keep a joint services color guard from gliding across the terrace with battle ribbons streaming. Nor did it dampen the Old Guard's artillery battery, which uncorked a thundering twenty-one-gun salute that shook the earth and answered itself in echoes from the hills. The Army Band, all shining brass and gold braid, rolled the drums and sent a majestic version of "America, the Beautiful" sailing out over the cemetery. Pallbearers from the uniformed services lifted the Unknown's flag from his casket, tugged the ensign free of wrinkles, folded it into a taut triangle, and passed it to Maj. Gen. John L. Ballantyne III, chief of the Washington Military District, who in turn presented it to President Reagan. Accepting the flag as the Unknown's next of kin, Reagan nodded his thanks to General Ballantyne, entrusted the flag to Arlington's superintendent, and paused for a last look at the Unknown. Then Reagan turned for home, having put in a performance considered to be one of his most affecting.[7]

Later that evening, after the flags had come down and the crowds had dispersed, cemetery workers lowered the Unknown into the ground, where he would rest beside his comrades from World War I, World War II, and Korea. Just before midnight a marble slab was hoisted into place over the new crypt and sealed flush with the plaza; its simple inscription, "1958–1975," was a reminder that the undeclared conflict in Vietnam had been one of the longest wars in American history.[8]

Reagan's appearance at the cemetery helped smooth raw memories of Vietnam and reinforce the pride of those who served there. Since the time of his election in 1980, he had worked toward this symbolic moment at Arlington, which would bury not only an individual but also, with luck, the war's divisive legacy.[9] In 1973, as America withdrew the last of its forces from Vietnam, Congress authorized the entombment of an anonymous serviceman from the conflict,[10] and workers at Arlington readied a new crypt for him.[11] But the tomb remained empty as the years piled up, through the reunion of North and South Vietnam in 1976, through President Jimmy Carter's pardoning of Vietnam-era draft evaders in 1977, through President Reagan's dedication of the black-walled Vietnam Veterans Memorial on the National Mall in 1982.[12]

By this time the number of unidentified war dead had been whittled down to just four candidates out of more than 47,000 killed in combat.[13] Some specialists held out the hope that each of those remaining four could have their names restored by further investigation. Forensic medicine had developed to the point that science might render obsolete the nation's long tradition of honoring Unknowns from each war.[14]

Even though few suitable candidates from the Vietnam conflict were available for Unknown honors, veterans continued to press for a new tomb at Arlington, in part to justify their sacrifice in an unpopular conflict. "Vietnam veterans for the most part interpreted, in their accustomed way, the decade of delay in seeking and interring an Unknown comrade as yet another of the many real or imagined insults and omissions they have endured for their participation in our nation's first true bastard war," Joseph Rehyansky wrote in the *National Review*. Reagan sought to erase those insults, which set him on the path to that unforgettable Memorial Day of 1984.[15]

The journey might have ended then and there, with the Unknown resting in marble splendor "until the second coming of Christ," in the phrase of a Marine Corps chaplain who conducted prayers that day.[16] But just as the fighting for Vietnam was seldom predictable, so with the war's aftermath. Fourteen years after Reagan's appearance at Arlington, the unthinkable happened: the Tomb of the Vietnam Unknown was broken open, not to the rousing call of Gabriel's trumpet, but to the prosaic shriek of a diamond-tipped saw biting through granite. As the clock ticked toward midnight on May 13, 1998, workers made their way through ten-inch-thick paving stones and into the tomb, lifting the heavy marble marker away, prizing the lid from the Unknown's vault, and bringing his steel casket up into the night. When the chill morning of May 14 arrived, so did a military band, which struck up "Amazing Grace" to announce the next, wholly unexpected leg of the Unknown's journey. Covered in a new flag and bundled into a hearse, he was driven to Walter Reed Army Medical Center in Washington, where his meager remains were prepared for DNA testing. Much to the relief of one anguished family and the disappointment of others, those genetic tests provided a name: the Unknown was Lt. Michael J. Blassie, a twenty-four-year-old Air Force pilot shot down over An Loc, South Vietnam, in 1972.[17]

The final chapter of Blassie's story—from the Air Force Academy, to a jungle war zone, to years of limbo in mortuaries and forensic labs, to the ceremonial heights of Arlington, and finally home to his native St. Louis—is a narrative spanning more than a quarter century, with enough twists and turns to make his experience seem like a work of barely plausible fiction. It is a story confused by the fog of war, the loss of crucial evidence, the misreading of forensic data, and the well-meaning but poorly considered ministrations of a Reagan White House keen to enshrine an Unknown for political purposes despite the sketchiness of the evidence, the objections of service families, and the warning of a key forensics officer who worried that the Unknown was being rushed to the grave.

That forensics officer, Johnie E. Webb Jr., was a Vietnam veteran and a major commanding the army's Central Identification Laboratory in the early 1980s when his Pentagon superiors began squeezing him to find an Unknown. "There was a lot of pressure to get a Vietnam Unknown," recalled Webb, who still serves as a civilian in the Pentagon's Joint POW/MIA Accounting Command, which oversees operations of the Central Identification Laboratory at Hickam Air Force Base in Hawaii. "All the pressure was coming to bear on me," said Webb. "I was the guy who was not in agreement with what the White House was trying to do." He described his tug of war over Michael Blassie as the most trying period of his long military career.[18]

The chain of events that brought Blassie to Arlington was set in motion by the bleating of a Klaxon summoning pilots to duty at the Bien Hoa Air Base at dawn on May 11, 1972. Blassie rushed to his A-37 Dragonfly attack jet, strapped himself into the seat, and zoomed northwest toward An Loc in formation with Maj. Jim Connally, the flight commander who piloted an identical Dragonfly that morning. Each plane, known for its lightness and maneuverability, was equipped with a Gatling gun, fourteen rockets, and two five hundred–pound napalm bombs; the napalm was meant for enemy antiaircraft emplacements near An Loc, a strategically situated city of thirty thousand close to the Cambodian border and about sixty miles northwest of Saigon.[19]

Under siege by North Vietnamese ground troops for more than a month, An Loc stubbornly held off its attackers, in part with air support from pilots such as Blassie, a decorated veteran of 132 combat missions. Connally led the attack on May 11, whizzing in low over enemy guns, releasing one bomb, and pulling up to open the way for Blassie. When the ground debris cleared, Blassie put his jet into a dive and dropped toward the target, but he was intercepted by antiaircraft fire. His jet began spewing fuel, rolled over, and slammed into the earth with a tremendous explosion.[20] Connally circled and watched carefully. He saw no sign of a parachute, no sign of life on the ground below. He continued circling, swooping in to repel enemy ground troops, until Cobra helicopters arrived for search-and-rescue operations. "The team pulled out after determining that Mike indeed had gone in with the aircraft," Connally reported to Blassie's family shortly after the crash. "However, no attempts were made to pull anything out of the wreckage, because the helicopters were caught in a murderous hail of fire. I orbited over the crash site until the last hope faded and all other aircraft departed the scene."[21]

Fierce fighting around An Loc marooned Blassie's wreckage for more than five months, while his parents and four siblings in St. Louis pored through letters of condolence from friends and comrades, grieved over his disappearance, and hoped for some word regarding his fate. None was forthcoming. "We didn't hear a whole lot for a period of time," said Patricia S. Blassie, who was fourteen when her brother vanished. "They told us they couldn't recover him but they knew he was killed."[22]

Blassie's comrades waited for an opportunity to resume their search. Unable to reach An Loc by chopper, they finally dispatched allies from the Armed Forces of the Republic of Vietnam (ARVN), who disguised themselves as Viet Cong to comb through the area. Walking some thirty miles into the volatile An Loc region, a reconnaissance patrol from the 48th ARVN Regiment made their way to the coordinates of Blassie's crash and found what they described as an A-37 wreck on October 11, 1972. With it they found what remained of Michael Blassie—four ribs, one humerus, and part of a pelvis, or six of the 206 bones each of us is allotted in life. From the same site, the ARNV team recovered physical evidence—Blassie's military identification card with his picture, remnants of his flight suit, an ammunition pouch, a parachute fragment, a holster for a signal marker, a piece of his pistol holster, a life raft, a wallet, and a small amount of local currency.[23]

Packing the remains and evidence away, the ARVN patrol made its long return trek through the jungle to a remote rendezvous point, where Army Lt. Chris Calhoun and other American advisors were waiting to meet them. Calhoun, taking charge of the airman's remains and other evidence, was struck by an incongruity that day—how new Blassie's wallet looked considering what it had been through. Calhoun summoned a helicopter, which came beating in over the trees and dropped into the makeshift landing zone. Two bags were unceremoniously tossed aboard, one containing physical evidence, the other Blassie's remains. Army Capt. Richard S. Hess, another ARVN advisor on the scene that day, confirmed the inventory of recovered items and witnessed their transfer to the Tan Son Nhut Air Base in Saigon. In a later statement, Hess recalled verbatim the details from Blassie's ID card: "Name: Blaisse [*sic*], Michael Joseph, 1LT, 6 foot 200 lbs picture showed with mustache, dark hair." Hess's recollection would later prove to be a critical clue linking Blassie to the crash site.[24] The reason? At some point during Blassie's journey from An Loc to Saigon, his wallet, identification card, and money disappeared, never to be recovered.[25]

Thus began the St. Louis airman's long descent into limbo. There was enough evidence to form a reasonable hypothesis that the bones and other material from the crash were probably Blassie's, but not enough to support a positive identification. Reliable DNA testing, still decades in the future, was unavailable to those who took charge of Blassie's remains when they arrived at the Tan Son Nhut mortuary in November 1972. His case number reflected the ambiguity of his new status: "TSN 0673-72 BTB Blassie, Michael Joseph," military shorthand for Tan Son Nhut remains Believed To Be Blassie.[26]

Because mortuary specialists had insufficient evidence to provide an official identification, they kept Blassie's family in the dark. His parents, George and Jean Blassie, were not informed that remains had been recovered from their son's crash site, nor were they told about the lieutenant's new "Believed To Be" status.[27] George Blassie, a meatcutter in the Florissant suburb of St. Louis, kept his son's memory alive by furnishing a basement room with photographs, awards, and other memorabilia from Michael's military career. And each morning when the sun climbed out of the Mississippi River, George Blassie raised the Stars and Stripes in his front yard, dutifully reversing the ritual every evening.[28] He was proud of his son's service, an attitude reflecting Michael Blassie's own feelings about his assignment in Southeast Asia.

"Even with the protests at home, Michael wasn't tainted," his sister Pat recalled. "He really believed that the people needed us there. He wanted to keep flying as long as he could help." She produced a copy of her brother's last letter home, which arrived the same week his family received the telegram announcing his crash: "Why am I trying to live if I'm just living to die?" Michael wrote to his girlfriend. "I'll keep on living to fight as long as there is a fighting reason . . . for others to live."[29] By this time, most of the ground war had been transferred from the Army and Marines to ARVN units, with an enhanced role for those like Blassie, who took America's fight into the skies, even as peace talks between the United States and North Vietnam continued in Paris.[30]

With the conflict's end in sight, the military stepped up its withdrawal of remaining forces, along with the unidentified dead stored in wartime mortuaries. The Army, designated as the lead service for search, recovery, and identification of the war dead, transferred remains and case files from its in-country morgues at Tan Son Nhut and Danang to a newly opened Central Identification Laboratory at Camp Samae San in Thailand. Blassie's remains, evidence, and paperwork were transferred there in 1973. The St. Louis airman was moved again in 1976, a year after Saigon fell to Communist forces; this transfer took him to the Army's new forensic laboratory near Honolulu, a modern facility where scientists and investigators methodically worked through the war's backlog of unidentified servicemen—poring over after-action reports, interviewing witnesses, scrutinizing debris from crashes, and analyzing fragments of bone to reduce the number of unknowns to a handful. Blassie was part of that handful remaining on the shelf, not yet identified, not yet buried, awaiting the one scrap of evidence that would end their war.[31]

Instead of resolving Blassie's identity, though, investigators from the Hawaii lab sent his case deeper into the shadows as 1978 drew to a close. That is when Blassie's box was taken from the shelf and his bones were spread out on a stainless-steel table for inspection. Tadao Furue, a physical anthropologist with more than twenty years of forensic experience and a reputation for making osseous material yield its secrets, supervised the examination. Furue was famous in the forensic community for innovating a technique known as craniofacial superimposition, where he married a database of hundreds of thousands of photographs to the skulls of unidentified humans to produce a match—and a name; his technique is still solving cases today.[32] Since no skull was recovered from Blassie's crash, Furue relied on more traditional anthropological identification methods, measuring the airman's bones for comparison to averages derived from thousands of others to determine the likely age, height, and sex of the person on his table.[33]

Based on his analysis, Furue concluded that the bones labeled TSN 063-72 BTB Blassie did not match Michael Blassie's. Instead, Furue suggested, the remains belonged to a man who was between thirty and forty years of age. Blassie was twenty-four. Furue guessed the height of his subject to be between five feet six inches and five feet eleven inches—a possible match, since Blassie stood between five feet eleven and six feet, but at the outer limit of the average. Finally, Furue discovered a small, light brown body hair on a fragment of the flight suit recovered from Blassie's crash; this minuscule clue yielded another piece of evidence, fixing the dead man's blood as type O. Blassie's was type A. Based on these three findings, Furue recommended, in a memorandum dated December 4, 1978, that the remains previously associated with Blassie be reclassified as unidentified and that the airman's name be stripped from the accompanying case file.[34] Faced with this recommendation and the anthropological evidence before them, a military review board followed Furue's lead: on May 7, 1980, Blassie's remains were designated as unidentified and his Believed To Be status rescinded. His bones were assigned a new file number, TSN 0673-72 X-26. The X designation, which took the place of Blassie's name, pushed him one step closer to the Tomb of the Unknowns.[35]

With the benefit of hindsight it is easy to see flaws in Furue's analysis, which has been criticized as too pedantic, relying heavily on numerical averages with scant attention to the individual variations in bone size that make each human unique. Some people have long arms for their height; others have short arms and long legs, as was the case with Blassie. And while the wear and tear on bones is generally a good guide to the age of their owner, the method relies on guesswork and personal judgment and is therefore imprecise. If the dead person engaged in a lifetime of vigorous sports—as Blassie did—his bones would appear to be older than their true age, according to Robert Mann, deputy scientific director of the Central Identification Laboratory in Hawaii. "Some people's bones don't fit the expected pattern," he wrote in *Forensic Detective*, in which he reviews the handling of Blassie's case. "Although forensic anthropology is founded in science," Mann wrote, "there is still some art and subjective professional judgment to it. One always has to be aware of the limited degree of precision inherent in drawing conclusions about a dead person's biological profile based on skeletal features."[36]

As for the conflicting blood type produced by Furue's tests, such assessments, though considered reliable when they were made, have since been shown to be less than perfect, producing dependable results about 67 percent of the time.[37] Mann noted that the single hair provided for Blassie's blood test may have been compromised by five months' exposure to Vietnam's lashing rains and acid soil. If there was chemical degradation, Mann suggested, it could have produced a false reading for type O blood.[38] There was also a pertinent chain-of-custody question: when did the anomalous hair attach itself to the flight suit? If it was not Blassie's, it might have been picked up at almost any point on his peripatetic journey, from the jungle to the helicopter to Tan Son Nhut to Thailand to Hawaii. Finally, even if one accepted Furue's anthropological conclusion, what did the physical evidence from Blassie's crash contribute to his story? Furue did not say. At least eight other servicemen disappeared near An Loc and had not been found.[39]

One of these, Army Capt. Rodney Strobridge, crashed in an AH-1G Cobra helicopter near the site of Blassie's loss on May 11, 1972, the same day the St. Louis airman disappeared. This introduced another wrinkle into an already difficult case: Strobridge's physical profile matched Furue's analysis for height, age, and blood type. But other physical evidence from the wreck pointed to an A-37 Dragonfly, the only such aircraft that went down in the area and the only one equipped with a parachute and the distinctive one-man life raft like those found with Blassie's remains.[40] In his report, Furue dutifully listed the raft along with other recovered equipment, but he failed to consider their significance, or to invoke the testimony of witnesses such as Hess and Calhoun, who had seen Blassie's identification card before it disappeared.[41]

In the end, Mann concluded, Furue had too little evidence in 1980 to say whether the remains in the lab belonged to Blassie or to someone else, a state of affairs that should have kept the pilot's name associated with his remains and invalidated his candidacy as the Vietnam Unknown.[42] In fairness to Furue, who died in 1988, it should be noted that he thought the identity of X-26 could be established by further recovery missions in Vietnam, where new evidence might turn up.[43]

By the early 1980s, however, key officials of the Reagan administration evinced little patience for more investigation, having satisfied themselves that suitable remains were available if only the Central Identification Laboratory could be prodded to produce them. "President Reagan and Caspar Weinberger [secre-tary of defense] wanted to go forward with it, as a way to honor those who served and as a way to reach closure on the Vietnam era," recalled John O. Marsh Jr., who as secretary of the Army became Reagan's point man for the Vietnam initiative. "The process was held up because some of the people in the forensic area began to have second thoughts about it," said Marsh. The former con-gressman from Virginia had no such qualms. "It's what the American Legion, the VFW, the Congress, and President Reagan wanted to do, as a way to help heal the divisions from the war. My role was to jump-start the process."[44]

To that end, Marsh traveled to the Army's Hawaiian lab in 1982 to gather firsthand information about remains that might qualify for Unknown status. By this time the possible candidates were down to the last four—Blassie and three others recovered from Southeast Asia. Having borne more delay than he thought to be reasonable, Marsh made his move on June 16, 1982, declaring that the time had come to make the selection and bury the symbolic warrior from Vietnam.[45]

"We have remains which meet the legal requirements for the Unknown," Marsh told Weinberger that day. "After careful consideration, I have concluded that the interests of the Nation are served best by proceeding with the anony-mous selection and subsequent interment of a Vietnam Unknown from these candidates. This coming Veterans' Day, November 11, 1982, would be an ap-propriate date since the World War I Unknown was also interred on Armistice Day." In keeping with tradition from World War II, Marsh pro-posed that the three runner-up candidates be buried at sea to preclude their later identification.[46]

Marsh's proposal ignited howls of protest from the National League of Families of American Prisoners and Missing in Southeast Asia, who believed that the action was premature. "We are opposed to the interment of any re-mains now held," Ann Mills Griffiths, executive director of the league, wrote Weinberger in July. "Perhaps the Army should respond to Congressional in-quires with . . . a clear statement that qualified remains are not available and may never be due to technical expertise attained." She presciently warned against "interring an individual who may be identified at some point in the future."[47] Her note set off alarm bells in the Reagan White House, where Richard T. Childress, a Vietnam veteran and influential member of the National Security Council staff, sided with Mrs. Griffiths. Pointing out that the Unknown contenders might be identified in the future, he cautioned against rushing the process, which could be perceived as nakedly political. "We simply can't have the public believe we created an unknown for interment," Childress told William P. Clark, Reagan's national security chief.[48] Faced with these objections, Weinberger delayed the selection so that the forensics laboratory could narrow its list of Unknown candidates.[49]

While investigators in the Hawaii lab cranked up their review, a strange drama played out in Washington, demonstrating just how resentful some Vietnam veterans remained about their lack of recognition. At about five P.M. on March 23, 1983, as Arlington National Cemetery prepared to close for the day, a man in a business suit appeared at the Tomb of the Unknowns and stepped over chains separating the visitors' area from the amphitheater terrace. The tomb sentinel on duty, Cpl. Michael Kirby, challenged the visitor. The man produced a small-caliber pistol, identified himself as an Air Force veteran who had seen duty in Vietnam, and began railing about his treatment upon returning home. Kirby backed away. Other tomb guards appeared, jumped the gunman from behind, and pinned him to the ground. The distraught man, who turned out to be a thirty-six-year-old car salesman from Virginia Beach, Virginia, was taken to the hospital, confined for treatment, and later released. It was true that he had served in Vietnam. He had driven to Washington intent on killing himself at the nation's most famous military shrine. Tomb sentinels foiled his suicide, but the episode was a reminder of the war's unsettled legacy and Arlington's importance to those who still struggled with it.[50]

Burying a Vietnam Unknown would be an important sign of thanks from the nation, a sentiment that fueled the Reagan administration's drive to fill the tomb—and soon. But instead of producing prospects for Vietnam honors, the Central Identification Laboratory began eliminating them. The first candidate to be withdrawn was a serviceman killed in 1970 and labeled as X-15. Much to the consternation of Pentagon officials, Johnie Webb refused to certify this combatant for Arlington honors because Webb suspected that the man's identity would eventually be established. His skeleton was in the best condition of the four candidates—more than 90 percent complete. He had a full set of teeth, which would cinch identification if only his service records could be found in the coils and recesses of the military bureaucracy. Even without those files, X-15's bones carried a tantalizing clue to his identity: three steel pellets were imbedded in his right arm, put there not by enemy action but most likely by an American-made claymore mine he had tripped. It was almost certainly the cause of his death. But his remains could not be associated with any of the twenty-five hundred servicemen still listed as missing. Prodded by Webb, the Army eventually produced a name, which led to the man's dental records, which provided a perfect match with X-15's teeth. The soldier, who had been erroneously listed as honorably discharged, proved to be an eighteen-year-old Army private from Michigan who had gone AWOL near An Khe, where he made his fatal misstep on the fringes of Camp Radcliff. He won a long-delayed ticket home for burial in 1983, at which point the case of X-15 came off the list of prospective Unknowns.[51]

"We came that close to putting a deserter in the Tomb of the Unknown," Webb recalled, holding his thumb and finger a few millimeters apart. "We went on to the next three individuals."[52] The first of that trio, designated as X-32, turned out to be William McRae, an Army private killed in a helicopter crash near Long Binh in 1967 but misidentified in the chaos of that multi-fatality incident. Another victim from the same crash, thought to be McRae, was mistakenly sent home to McRae's family in Boston. Years later, when Webb and his associates received a shipment of badly decayed remains from Vietnam, they discovered McRae's dog tags in the box labeled X-32. The lab won permission to exhume the misidentified body from Boston, whereupon McRae took his rightful place in the cemetery at home. This closed the X-32 file, but it created a new mystery: who was the man mistaken for McRae? Until his identity could be established, scientists at the lab dubbed him "Boston Billy," a label that stuck until 2002, when investigators determined that he was Jerry Degnan, a civilian who trained helicopter pilots in Vietnam until 1967, when he died in the same Huey crash that killed McRae and jumbled their remains.[53]

With the mysteries of X-15 and X-32 settled, attention shifted to a third case, which involved a set of unidentified remains turned over to the United States by Laos. Since this recovery was, in the military argot a "unilateral turnover," with no Americans involved in collecting or transferring the remains, the chain of custody failed to meet basic requirements of the 1973 law.

"The pertinent law says that the remains must be an American fighting man who died in combat during this time period," Webb said. "Since it's a unilateral turnover, you have no information to meet the intent of the public law. My contention was that those remains did not meet the requirement. Won that argument. That brought us down to the fourth guy, the X-26 case. That one I lost."[54]

With all other candidates eliminated, on March 16, 1984, Caspar Weinberger informed President Reagan that the Pentagon was ready to bury X-26 as the Vietnam Unknown on Memorial Day. "In 1982 we began an intensive effort to determine whether any of the remains in our possession are qualified for the Vietnam Unknown," Weinberger reported. "We concluded that we have one set of remains which cannot be identified and which, although not as complete as we would like, meets the legal requirements for the Vietnam Unknown . . . The interment of a Vietnam Unknown is the highest honor our Nation can give to the Vietnam Veterans . . . I look forward to joining you in honoring those who faithfully served their Nation during those difficult times."[55]

Weinberger said nothing about lingering doubts over X-26, or the associations with Michael Blassie. "Reagan wanted his Unknown," said a historian at Arlington. "Nobody was going to stop it."[56]

In Hawaii, however, Johnie Webb made one last try. "These remains should be disqualified for selection as the Unknown because of past and present name associations," he wrote to Washington about the time of Weinberger's announcement. Webb sketched out the tangled story of X-26 in his memo. Without naming Michael Blassie, Webb reminded his superiors that his case had been linked to a particular pilot who had been formerly assigned "Believed To Be" status. He listed the evidence found with Blassie, including the one-man raft, the flight suit, the parachute, and the vanished identification card. For good measure, Webb also mentioned another unnamed casualty associated with the X-26 remains; he was referring to Capt. Rodney Strobridge, who matched the anthropological profile from Blassie's crash but not the other evidence from the site. Webb's note, sent to an assistant secretary of the army, was supposed to be forwarded up the chain to John O. Marsh Jr.[57] Marsh says he never saw the document. "If Johnie Webb had second thoughts, I never heard about it," Marsh said recently. "He should've said something." [58] For his part, Webb avows that he *did* say something—and that Washington ignored his warning. [59]

Within five days of Weinberger's letter to Reagan, Webb received orders to certify that X-26 could never be identified, an action that would clear the way for Blassie's entombment. [60] Against his better judgment, Webb produced the required document on March 21, 1984, certifying that the remains of TSN 0673-72 X-26 "failed to support a positive identification with any known casualty of Southeast Asia." He continued:

> All efforts since 4 November 1972 to establish a positive identification have proven negative. The portions of the recovered remains do not include the identification criteria that can be matched exclusively to an individual and it is highly improbable that continued identification processing would be successful. These remains are determined to be unidentifiable. [61]

Webb swallowed hard and signed his name. "I tried," he recalled recently, "but the political pressure was such that I wasn't going to win." [62] Webb told another interviewer that short of resigning under orders, he could do nothing further to prevent Blassie's designation as the Unknown. "I didn't have the horsepower . . . As an Army officer, my job was to advise. After the decision was made, I saluted and began carrying out the mission." [63]

Now his mission was to prepare Blassie for his trip to Washington. In keeping with the tradition of the Unknowns, the Pentagon ordered Webb to surrender all original files relating to Blassie and to destroy all copies to guarantee the anonymity of the tomb. [64] Webb dutifully obeyed the first part of this directive, but not the second: He kept copies of the Blassie dossier in the belief that they would be needed if the case was reopened. Webb was also asked to send the life raft and other physical evidence to Washington, where it would be destroyed with the original paperwork. Webb demurred, keeping all of the evidence with Blassie—which meant that man and artifacts would be buried together at Arlington. [65]

"These remains came in together with the material evidence," Webb recalled. "I wanted to make sure everything stayed together. If the remains were going into the tomb, the artifacts needed to go to the tomb so that at some point there was the historical perspective on what came in with these remains." Leaving nothing to chance, Webb monitored the preparation of Blassie's bones, which were folded into an olive drab army blanket with the life raft, the parachute fragments, and other physical evidence. Webb watched as the blanket was fastened shut all around with safety pins to form a woolen envelope. He saw it go into the polished steel casket. He saw the lid eased shut and heard the lock click in place. Blassie was ready for the next stage of his journey, which commenced on May 17, 1984.[66]

For all the indignities Blassie had suffered, his passage from Hawaii to Washington constituted a sort of restitution. At Pearl Harbor, he was presented with flowers by a Medal of Honor winner, eulogized by admirals and generals, and given a place of pride aboard U.S.S. *Brewton*, the naval frigate that conveyed him past all the ships in Pearl Harbor while all rendered passing honors. He sailed across the Pacific Ocean with a Marine honor guard watching over him night and day, and on May 24 they sailed under Golden Gate Bridge, past the gleaming hills of San Francisco, and into moorings at Alameda Naval Air Station, where further honors awaited: a twenty-one-gun salute, more eulogies, and fighter jets streaking overhead in the missing man formation. These rituals were but a warm-up for the round of state honors in Washington, where four days of tribute were planned, culminating with President Reagan's Memorial Day speech.[67] Among those who stood proudly with Reagan that day were Sen. Strom Thurmond of South Carolina and Rep. John P. Murtha of Pennsylvania, both of whom had worked tirelessly to win recognition for this forgotten war, which had finally earned its place at Arlington.[68]

This, at least, was the plan, and to a large degree it succeeded in calming the old ghosts of Vietnam. While Blassie slept in anonymity on the grand plaza of the amphitheater, dead comrades were found and restored to their families; an all-volunteer army replaced the draft; old enemies shook hands and made peace at home and abroad. New wars boiled up on the horizon. Reagan flew to California and disappeared into the shadowy world of Alzheimer's. George Blassie died in St. Louis never knowing that his son had come home. Jean Blassie carried on but found it impossible to speak about her son outside of her family. Pat Blassie took her brother's place in the Air Force and worked her way up the ranks, earning her captain's bars by 1994, when all of a sudden the ghosts of Vietnam came rumbling back.[69]

That year, for the first time since Michael Blassie's death in 1972, his family learned that the airman's remains had been found and, further, that he was most likely installed in the Tomb of the Unknowns at Arlington.[70] This revelation came from an unlikely source, a former Green Beret and Vietnam veteran named Ted Sampley, the scrappy publisher of *U.S. Veteran Dispatch* and founder of the Last Firebase Veterans Archives Project in Kinston, North Carolina. Rooting through his extensive files on POW/MIA cases, grilling sources, and poring over Pentagon documents, Sampley independently pieced together his own version of Michael Blassie's chronicle, publishing his findings in *Veteran Dispatch* on July 14, 1994.

Under the headline "The Vietnam Unknown Soldier can be Identified," Sampley described the recovery of Blassie's remains and identity card, the testimony of eyewitnesses, and the suggestive evidence linking Blassie with the Tomb of the Unknowns. "Many facts pertaining to 1 Lt. Michael J. Blassie's shootdown closely match those of the Unknown Soldier," Sampley reported. Noting recent advances in forensic technology, Sampley made a suggestion: "If the experts at CILHI [Central Identification Laboratory Hawaii] can identify American MIAs from minute tooth fragments . . . then they should be able to right this wrong by determining through DNA if the remains of 1 Lt. Blassie is [sic] in the tomb of the Vietnam Unknown Soldier."[71] Before publishing his article, Sampley telephoned St. Louis to share his discovery with Michael's mother. "She seemed grateful," Sampley recalled. "She had heard nothing since 1972." After his report was published, Sampley delivered a copy to the Pentagon a few days later—in person.[72]

Sampley's revelation stirred up old feelings for the Blassie family, who had to relive the anguish of Michael's death all over again. "It was shock and disbelief," Pat Blassie recalled. "I still marvel at it after all these years. They knew it was Michael. They didn't tell us because of the political expediency. They took his name away. Your name is your identity, the first thing you tell someone when you're introduced: "Hello, I'm so-and-so . . . They took that away from Michael. We felt betrayed."[73]

After discussing the situation with her mother, Pat Blassie approached colleagues in the Air Force casualty office, who informed her that Sampley's article could not be authenticated. They expressed no interest in reopening the case.[74] Discouraged and numbed, the family let the matter drop for two years.[75] Then Vince Gonzales, a producer from CBS News, read the *Veteran Dispatch* report, collected Sampley's extensive research files, and called the Blassie family for their cooperation.[76] The Blassies gathered in St. Louis. They talked for hours until Jean Blassie signaled that she had made a decision. The matriarch scanned the faces of her four children, one after the other, before speaking: "For twenty-six years, we have been told that Michael was never found. Yet he was found five months after he was shot down and then buried without our knowledge in the Tomb of the Unknowns. I want to bring my son home." The family rallied around.[77] Jean Blassie granted CBS access to her son's files. Pat Blassie agreed to speak on camera. Gonzales wrapped up a seven-month investigation and, with Eric Engberg narrating, *CBS Evening News* broadcast the results on January 19, 1998.

Blassie was "almost certainly" buried in the Tomb of the Unknowns, the report said. His identity had been known for decades, and the government had deliberately hidden this information from his family and the public, CBS reported.[78] Pat Blassie spoke for her family: "The trail of documents concerning Lt. Blassie leads to the Tomb," she said. "We want to know the truth. We want to bring Michael home." The family then asked the impossible: They wanted the tomb opened. They wanted the remains submitted for mitochondrial DNA testing, a relatively new procedure unknown at the time of Blassie's death.[79]

The CBS report sparked outrage from the Veterans of Foreign Wars and the American Legion—the same groups that had lobbied for selection of a Vietnam Unknown, now complaining that the Blassies threatened to violate the most sacred site at Arlington.[80] "It's not sacred if we know the name of the person you have there," Pat Blassie retorted.[81] "It's an honorable place to be, but not for a known soldier. That's not what the tomb was meant for . . . [82] Either put his name on the tomb or disinter him for DNA testing."[83]

Two powerful lawmakers from Blassie's home state, Sens. John Ashcroft and Christopher S. "Kit" Bond, asked for an explanation from William S. Cohen, secretary of defense under President Bill Clinton. At a Pentagon press briefing on the afternoon following the CBS story, the agency's spokesman was peppered with questions about Blassie. Why had he been hurried into the tomb? Would the grave be opened? When? Had others been misidentified? Faced with the family's high-profile appeal, the objections from veterans' groups, the outrage on Capitol Hill, and the prospect of a public relations disaster, the Pentagon did what it often does at such times: it ordered a study.[84]

Cohen named Rudy deLeon, the respected and cool-headed undersecretary of defense for personnel and readiness, to head up a senior task force investigating the matter. "The last thing we expected was that we were going to exhume the remains from Arlington," deLeon said recently. "That was the last resort."[85]

Instead, deLeon mounted a fact-finding mission with three goals: to establish that the casualty known as X-26 was indeed the man entombed at Arlington; to find a paper trail and evidence linking him to the 1972 crash in Vietnam; and to determine if new DNA testing could provide a foolproof identity if the grave was exhumed. DeLeon met privately with Johnie Webb, who helped fill gaps in the documentary record with the purloined papers he had copied in 1984. Webb also dropped the bombshell that he had placed the relevant physical evidence in Blassie's casket. From John Marsh, deLeon learned of the political pressures that had mounted within the Reagan administration as Unknown candidates fell by the wayside, leaving six tiny bone fragments to stand for all who fought and died in Vietnam.[86]

"In every other war," deLeon said, "there were so many sets of unidentified service members that you could just arbitrarily pick a set of remains and there was no history. With Vietnam, everything was different. There was difficulty in finding a set of remains that could not be identified. What we discovered in our task force was a full inventory of the flight materials recovered with this set of remains," deLeon said. "We got Captain Hess's memo from the preinterment period. We got information from all of the primary sources. When this was done, I felt that indeed all of the data we had on X-26 told us that those were the remains at Arlington. Then the next question was whether the DNA testing could be conclusive. We were satisfied that it could be." So on April 23, 1998, deLeon recommended that the tomb be opened, based on the following rationale:

> The Tomb is a national symbol in which the entire nation has a heartfelt interest. Unfortunately, the current controversy has raised questions concerning the integrity of this national symbol. It requires us to recon-

cile two competing interests—the sanctity of the Tomb and our national commitment to return unaccounted for servicemen to their families. By taking action to resolve this controversy, we can preserve the integrity of the Tomb and fulfill our responsibility to the families.[87]

A few weeks later, on May 14, 1998, the Unknown of the Vietnam War was exhumed. William Cohen presided at ceremonies, saying that the disinterment was taken "with profound reluctance" but for good cause. "If advances in technology can ease the lingering anguish of even one family, then our path is clear. We yield to the promise of science, with the hope that the heavy burden of doubt may be lifted from a family's heart."[88]

By this time, Pat Blassie had no doubt. "I knew it was Michael before they opened the tomb. I knew the DNA would prove it. It was the only conclusion you could reach based on the evidence."[89] By June 28, 1998, DNA tests confirmed a match for Michael Blassie.[90] He was flown home to St. Louis for a military burial with full honors at the Jefferson Barracks National Cemetery. This time, his name was inscribed on his tombstone.[91]

The story did not end there. A few weeks after Blassie's reburial in St. Louis, Cohen announced that he was withdrawing the airman's Medal of Honor, based on complaints from the American Legion and the Medal of Honor Society. "The Medal of Honor is something very, very special," said Phil Budahn, a spokesman for the Legion. "It simply was not awarded to this particular hero."[92] Cohen determined that the Legionnaires had a point, since President Reagan had presented the award to the Vietnam Unknown as a symbolic figure, not to Blassie as an individual; thus the medal remains at Arlington, where it is displayed in a glass case with other trophies overlooking the amphitheater terrace.[93] Out on the plaza, a marble slab covers the Tomb of the Vietnam Unknown, vacant since Blassie left it, but with a new inscription for all of those lost in Vietnam: "Honoring and Keeping Faith with America's Missing Servicemen, 1958–1975."[94]

Given the innovations in forensic science, improved record keeping, better recovery methods, and enhanced investigative techniques, it is almost certain that Michael Blassie will be the last of the Unknowns. Some of his comrades from Vietnam, scattered through four hundred boxes of unidentified remains, still occupy shelf space in the Hawaii laboratory, where experts hope that further sleuthing and new science will eventually provide names for other missing warriors.[95]

"Unidentified doesn't mean unidentifiable," said Johnie Webb, who still haunts the Central Identification Laboratory as a senior advisor to the commanding officer. "We've got DNA samples from most of them—we just haven't found a match yet."[96]

14

WAR COMES TO ARLINGTON

The big 757 came silently, and so low that it almost grazed the roof of the four-story Navy Annex building on the edge of Arlington National Cemetery. Darrell Stafford, the cemetery's interment foreman, watched in disbelief as the jet swooped toward him, head-on. "Look! Look! Look!" he shouted to three coworkers, who had just been discussing setups for the day's remaining funerals.[1]

"I know where he's going—it's the Pentagon," Stafford thought. In that instant of sinking recognition, he made a decision to run away from the Pentagon and toward the plane. "He goes over. He's pouring on the power. Then it's *Boom! Boom! Boom!* Everybody flattened on the ground. It was like somebody had just put a heat lamp on the back of your neck—the heat was that intense. I kind of peeked over my shoulder to see this big old ball of flame, hundreds of yards in the sky, just a big fireball."[2]

Stafford remembers the morning of September 11, 2001, with perfect clarity: a cool, sunny day carrying an intimation of autumn; the nose of the jet edging into view; the shining turbine blades whirling inside the engine cowlings; the bronze sheen of the fuselage lumbering into view; the blast, the heat, and the thick green cemetery turf showered with glass, plastic, and a million other bits of debris from the impact of American Airlines Flight 77 slamming into the west face of the Pentagon at 529 miles an hour.[3]

The day claimed the lives of 2,993 people in New York City, Washington, and Pennsylvania, plunging the nation into a messy period of conflict with multiple enemies, shifting battlefields, hit-and-run attacks, and no clear prospect of a traditional armistice to mark the end of hostilities, which continue to this day. It was not the "long twilight struggle" President Kennedy had foreseen in 1961, but the phrase seems eerily apt. However one characterizes this state of affairs—as a "global war on terror," which President George W. Bush termed it, as an "overseas contingency operation," in the preferred wording of President Barack Obama, or "asymmetric warfare," as Gen. David Petraeus and other professionals call it—the consequences of September 11 have been seen, felt, and heard at Arlington each day since the shadow of Flight 77 passed over the cemetery.[4] For months after the disaster, the sounds and dust of reconstruction drifted across Arlington from the charred black gap in the Pentagon's west face, even as men and women from the building's wreckage were identified, borne off, and buried in Section 64, within sight of the place where they died. Uniformed service members, sent off to fight in Iraq and Afghanistan, returned to lie in Section 60, where young families gathered to hear the sound of Taps, collect their folded flags, and sometimes to linger as Darrell Stafford's crews reverently close the earth over another grave.[5]

Now and then Stafford glances up from his work to track a jet's progress across the sky. "I look at things a little differently now," said Stafford, a lean, soft-spoken man in dark blue coveralls with his name on the pocket. He has worked at Arlington for twenty-seven years, in that time digging many a grave and watching the planes hustling in and out of the airport just downriver. "I'd see them in the wintertime when it was cold and I'd be like a kid thinking, 'I'll bet they're going to Florida where it's warm. Wonder where they're going while we're freezing?' You know? Now I wonder, 'Where is *he* going? Is he coming this way?' I'm very conscious of flight patterns and what doesn't look right in the sky. Maybe it bothers me more than I realize."[6]

★   ★   ★

Stafford had little time to reflect upon the events of September 11 before he was drawn into the investigation and its aftermath. Within minutes of the crash, a military police officer came by to search for clues. He collected Stafford for the short walk across Columbia Pike to the Pentagon, where a column of black smoke coiled into the sky, wounded workers staggered to aid stations, and FBI agents began interviewing any eyewitness they could grab. Stafford was one of them.[7]

"They wanted to know if I could see the pilot," Stafford recalled. "I told them all I saw was the plane coming in and that's when I started scrambling for my life. I wasn't looking to see who the pilot was." That seemed to satisfy the agents, who sent Stafford back across the road to Arlington, where he was soon busy with the morning's funerals, even as sirens wailed in the background and workers picked through the smoldering rubble a few hundred yards away. "Some of my guys were so scared they left right after the plane hit," Stafford said. "One jumped in his car and didn't stop until he got to North Carolina. But we continued to bury that day with the staff we had. We finished the last funeral about two or two-thirty that afternoon. That was just the beginning for us."[8]

For the next several months, Stafford and his colleagues at Arlington would be burying many of the victims of the Pentagon attack. Of 189 who died in the crash, 125 were uniformed service members, civilian workers, or contractors—all at their desks when the plane hit; the remaining 64 fatalities were passengers aboard Flight 77. In addition, five hijackers were killed. Before the end of September, Stafford's crews began peeling back the turf for the first Pentagon victims. More came in October, November, and December.[9]

Most of the Pentagon fatalities—sixty four—were laid to rest in Section 64, a low-lying part of the cemetery on its southeastern edge, affording a clear view of orderly white gravestones climbing the green hills all around, with the tan hulk of the Pentagon breaking the near horizon.[10]

"Normally, somebody dies, we don't know them and we weren't there," said Stafford. "But because of the crash, I felt connected to them. Everybody who came from there," he said, nodding toward the Pentagon, "I felt like I knew them. You recognize the name when you're burying them."[11]

Stafford helped bury Army Lt. Col. Kip Paul Taylor in Section 64 a month after the attack. The thirty-eight-year-old Michigan man, a major before his posthumous promotion, served as military assistant in the Office of the Deputy

Chief of Staff for Personnel, in the Pentagon's outer ring. Taylor's office took a direct hit from Flight 77, leaving very little of him or his personal effects intact. "There was nothing left of his office," his sister Ann Zaenglein told USA Today. But on the morning of the attack, Taylor left something that would be remembered by many in the days ahead, a string of e-mail messages to friends about his happy marriage to Nancy Melvin Taylor, their joy in their two-year-old son, Dean, and a father's great expectations for a second child, due in a month. Luke Taylor was born right on schedule, on October 25, just after his father was buried at Arlington.[12] While Nancy Taylor was hospitalized for Luke's birth, doctors discovered that she had cancer. She survived two more years before joining her husband at Arlington. Their sons, then ages four and two, were taken in by Kip's brother and his wife, who still care for them.[13]

The Taylors' grave is in a quiet, lonely part of the cemetery, placed well away from the heavily visited Kennedy memorial and the Tomb of the Unknowns. The Taylors lie among the graves of others killed in the Pentagon attack; surrounded by a wide swath of turf, their stones form a sort of island, standing together, just as they died together. A few steps away, near the intersection of Patton Drive and Marshall Drive, a black granite marker, notable for its understated dignity and modest height, lists the names of all who died at the Pentagon on September 11. Among those named are the five who could not be found, now represented by unidentified remains gathered into one casket and buried on September 12, 2002, beneath the five-sided memorial stone.[14]

The black stone in Section 64 was a reminder that this conflict was unlike traditional wars, in which forces faced enemies on more or less equal terms until one side got the upper hand and dictated peace terms. In the 9/11 attacks, a small, elusive enemy had struck indiscriminately at civilians and uniformed service members alike, sacrificing their own lives and exacting terrible bloodshed from an adversary of superior strength. The sneak attacks on Washington and New York were the most devastating since Pearl Harbor, but the asymmetric tactics were hardly unprecedented. Similar methods had been used by kamikaze pilots in World War II, by Viet Cong fighters in the Vietnam conflict, and most memorably by a terrorist attack on the Marine Corps barracks in Beirut on October 23, 1983.[15]

On that cool, crisp morning by the Mediterranean, a single suicide bomber crashed a yellow Mercedes-Benz truck laden with explosives into the Marine outpost near the city's airport, producing a blast that the FBI described as the largest non-nuclear explosion since World War II. Equivalent to 12,000 pounds of TNT, the discharge collapsed the barracks, killing 241 service members, all part of the multinational peacekeeping mission to Lebanon; another 58 victims, most of them from French military services, died in a similar attack minutes later. The Marines, lightly armed and forbidden to take the high ground surrounding their position for fear of sparking a larger conflict, had been sitting ducks for the terrorist assault that day. They suffered 220 fatalities, more single-day losses than at any time since their fighting on Iwo Jima in 1945. Calling the Beirut massacre the saddest day of his presidency, President Ronald Reagan withdrew the Marine battalion from Lebanon three months later.[16]

By that time, many of those killed in the bombing had been brought back to Arlington for burial. Most of them—nineteen Marines and two sailors—were laid to rest alongside one another near Eisenhower Drive in Section 59 of the cemetery, where they were seen off to the strains of the Navy Hymn, a flourish of swords, and the high-precision ceremony of which the Marines are justifiably proud. True to their motto, *Semper Fidelis,* "always faithful," the Marines have not forgotten the comrades lost in Beirut. A cedar of Lebanon, like the one depicted on that nation's flag, was planted in Section 59 a year after the bombings; now the tree spreads its arms over the graves of the fallen. And even after a quarter century, comrades, friends, and family return to Arlington each year on the anniversary of the attack to read the names of the dead, salute the fallen, and consider the long chain of events the 1983 attack set in motion. "This loss is not in vain and we will not break faith with them in the tasks we have ahead," said Marine Lt. Gen. Jan C. Huly, speaking at such a ceremony in 2003. "We did not know they would be the first casualties—among the first—in the war on terrorism."[17]

The tragedy in Beirut convinced Osama bin Laden, then unknown to the larger world, that the United States could not withstand a drawn-out fight with determined opponents. In an interview with ABC News in 1998, the al-Qaida founder pointed to the Marines' abrupt withdrawal from Lebanon as a sign of weakness in Americans "ready to wage cold wars but unprepared to fight long wars."[18] He was wrong about the Marines, who continue to suit up and go to work in a dangerous world, just as their comrades from other services have done since the Beirut bombing.

That suicide attack of 1983 set the pattern for the bloody years to follow—in the first bombing of the World Trade Center, which killed six in 1993; in the bombing of the Khobar Towers apartment building in Saudi Arabia, which killed twenty in 1996; in the coordinated bombings of U.S. embassies in Tanzania and Kenya, which killed 223 in 1998; in the bombing of the U.S.S. *Cole* in Yemen, which killed seventeen in 2000. All, except for the World Trade Center assault of 1993, produced new casualties for Arlington; all followed the same tactical model; all were prelude to the September 2001 attacks, which brought the reality of asymmetric warfare forcefully home and prompted the deployment of U.S. forces to Afghanistan and Iraq.

This strange new war—waged on two fronts, under harsh conditions, against a backdrop of tribal antipathies—was unlike any conflict the United States had known before, a state of affairs illustrated by the war's earliest combat casualty and the first to be honored at Arlington: not a uniformed soldier but a CIA officer, Johnny "Mike" Spann, killed in prison rioting in northern Afghanistan on November 25, 2001.[19]

Spann, a former Marine Corps captain, was a member of the CIA's paramilitary Special Activities Division. He had been questioning suspected Taliban terrorists at a temporary prison near Mazar-e Sharif when hundreds of inmates staged an uprising and seized weapons from an armory maintained by the Afghan Northern Alliance, allies of the United States. A fierce firefight ensued, raging for most of three days. By the time the melee ended, hundreds of inmates and dozens of Northern Alliance soldiers had been killed. Among the dead was Spann, thirty-two, shot in each temple. Official government reports attributed the agent's fatal wounds to the firefight, but after carefully examining his son's body in a Virginia funeral home, Spann's father believed that he had been dispatched execution-style. A detainee later transferred from Afghanistan to Guantánamo told FBI interrogators that Spann had sparked the rioting by shooting a prisoner who threatened him; another Guantánamo inmate suggested that Spann had been killed by friendly fire when the North Alliance sent in thousands of troops to quell the riot. Because of the confused struggle at Mazar-e Sharif and the spy agency's reluctance to reveal details of its operations, the truth may never be known.[20]

Whatever the exact cause of Spann's death, it was undeniable that he had fallen in the line of duty, which made him a candidate for hero status at home. Within the CIA his sacrifice is represented by a star carved into the marble wall of the agency's headquarters in Langley, Virginia, where Spann became the seventy-ninth officer so honored since the agency's founding in 1947.[21] And, despite the secrecy shrouding Spann's work in Afghanistan, he was treated to an outpouring of public gratitude in a nation still shattered by the 9/11 attacks and eager for a decisive response. "He Died a Hero," the *New York Post* proclaimed that November. "First Hero," the *New York Daily News* declared, welcoming the dead agent back to the United States.[22]

Special provision had to be made for Spann's funeral at Arlington, for, despite his eight years of Marine Corps service, he did not die in uniform and could not qualify for burial in the national cemetery. His family pressed for an exception. A home-state lawmaker, Sen. Richard Shelby of Alabama, ranking member of the Senate Intelligence Committee, took the request to the White House. George J. Tenet, director of Central Intelligence, endorsed the proposal, in part because the agent's identity had already become known, in part because the CIA needed a boost after its failure to predict the 9/11 attacks. President George W. Bush signed a waiver for Spann's burial at Arlington, where several hundred mourners gathered on December 10, 2001, to honor the first casualty of what promised to be a long and tangled conflict.[23]

"Those who took him from us will be neither deeply mourned nor long remembered," Tenet told the crowd at Arlington. "But Mike Spann will be forever part of the treasured legacy of free peoples everywhere—as we each owe him an immense, unpayable debt of honor and gratitude. His example is our inspiration. His sacrifice is our strength. For the men and women of the Central Intelligence Agency, he remains the rigorous and resolute colleague . . . the patriot who knew that information saves lives, and that its collection is a risk worth taking."[24]

When Tenet was through, the Marines of Bravo Company, resplendent in their dress blues and white gloves, carried their former comrade's flag-covered casket to the grave.[25] Used to doing more with less, the Marines deploy a six-man casket squad of body bearers to Arlington, three to a side, instead of the eight assigned to casket teams from the other services. On this frigid day, they made it look graceful, hoisting Spann's remains on their shoulders and marching him to a choice plot in Section 34, on the rolling knoll where Gen. John J. Pershing's simple tomb commands a fine view of the capital. The graveside service concluded, Spann's widow, Shannon, crossed over the grass, knelt by her husband's plot, and quietly spoke a few words to him. She kissed her hand and touched it to the cold wood. Her father-in-law followed in her wake, keeping his eye on the grave, holding the couple's six-month-old son, Jake, and speaking comfort to him, now fatherless and bundled against the December chill.[26]

Since Spann's arrival at Arlington in 2001, more than 5,000 Americans have been killed in the fighting for Afghanistan and Iraq, a conflict that has added hundreds of new graves to the cemetery's Section 60. It has been called the "saddest acre in America," occupied by young service members who died long before their time.[27] "You never get used to seeing the young ones die," said Tom Sherlock, a cemetery historian who has worked at Arlington for more than thirty years. "For the Greatest Generation, who account for most of our funerals, they've had the chance to live full lives. It's never easy, but it seems natural. When you see a young wife holding her infant, and the young friends and family with her, well, that's just a little harder. Like I say, you never get used to it."[28]

It was a fine day in early May and Sherlock was between funerals, setting out little American flags at the graves of four sailors in Section 60, just a few strides away from the tomb of Army Capt. Russell B. Rippetoe, twenty-three, the first combat fatality from Iraq to be buried at Arlington. Like scores of others resting in orderly rows there, Rippetoe was killed by a suicide car bomb—the terrorist's weapon of choice, along with the roadside bomb or improvised explosive device (IED). Manning a checkpoint near Hadithah, northwest of Baghdad, Rippetoe and other members of his company stopped a car on April 3, 2003, two weeks into the U.S. invasion. A woman emerged from the vehicle to plead for help: "I'm hungry and I need food and water!" Instinctively Rippetoe rushed toward her, just as a ball of fire exploded from her car. He and two other soldiers were killed in the blast, as were the woman and driver. Spec. Chad Thibodeau was knocked flat by the explosion that day, but he survived, drifting in and out of consciousness as he heard medics working over Rippetoe and the others, to no avail.[29]

Severely injured, Thibodeau was transferred for treatment at Walter Reed Army Medical Center in Washington. He was still in the hospital when he learned about Captain Rippetoe's funeral, scheduled for April 10, 2003. When the day arrived, Thibodeau scrambled out of bed, hitched a ride across the river, and found his way to Arlington, intent on paying homage to a respected officer. Laboriously maneuvering his wheelchair onto the soft ground in Section 60, Thibodeau got mired, struggled up from his chair, and limped the rest of the way to Rippetoe's grave, where he heard an Army chaplain offer up some particularly fitting scripture. "Be strong and of good courage," said Lt. Col. James May. "Be not afraid, neither be thou dismayed, for the Lord thy God is with thee whithersoever thou goest." The verse, from the first chapter of Joshua, had been well known to Captain Rippetoe, who had it engraved on the reverse side of his dog tag, which was found on his body and returned to his parents.[30]

The bombings would continue in Afghanistan and Iraq, setting others on the path to Arlington, where Sfc. Robert A. Durbin of the Army's Old Guard saw hundreds of men and women into their graves. Durbin, a career noncommissioned officer with fifteen years' experience, was leader of an honors casket team, one of the specialty squads contributing to Arlington's reputation for highly refined ritual. Durbin made sure that his squads carried their caskets on the level, that they folded their flags tight and straight, and that their final salutes were rendered with snap and precision—all antidotes, perhaps, to the messy circumstances of the outside world that had brought so many of the dead to Arlington.[31]

Durbin was all too familiar with the chaotic nature of life outside. Reassigned from his Old Guard duties, Durbin had been deployed—and redeployed—to Iraq as a sergeant in combat. He had learned to survive in the war zone, where random violence and sudden death were daily occurrences. But one particularly bloody episode from his third tour burned itself into Durbin's memory, setting him on what seemed like a quixotic one-man crusade to change the rules for honors ceremonies at Arlington.[32]

It happened on February 8, 2008. Four members of the 2nd Stryker Brigade Combat Team from the army's 25th Infantry Division were on patrol near Taji, a rural area in the volatile Sunni Triangle, northwest of Baghdad. The patrol's light armored vehicle hit a powerful IED buried under the road. It blew the vehicle apart in a shower of dust and debris. Called to the scene with members of his platoon, Durbin helped pull mangled soliders from the wreckage. He found Staff Sgt. Jerald Allen Whisenhunt, thirty-two, already dead. The dead man had entertained dreams of returning to Hawaii after the war, where he looked forward to watching the next Super Bowl with his wife, Betsy, and their daughter, Alyson.[33] "Tell Aly I will take her to the zoo and anywhere else she wants," Whisenhunt had written in a final e-mail message home.[34] Now he went into a body bag. Durbin stared into the dead soldier's eyes before they took him off, "a burning image that won't go away." A few days later, when Durbin learned that Whisenhunt was bound for a funeral at Arlington, he began to fume. "All I could think of was how his funeral would go."[35]

By all accounts, it was a beautiful service, conducted on February 21, 2008. A casket team soberly glided across the grass with Whisenhunt's casket held high; the firing party rendered a flawless three-volley salute; Betsy Whisenhunt tearfully accepted the folded flag from an officer; Taps settled over a knot of mourners in Section 60 to mark a young warrior's passing. Any outsider would have been moved and impressed by the standard-honors funeral, which was more memorable than the farewell most civilians received. But it was far less than Whisenhunt would have rated as an officer or an enlisted man of E-9 rank—and that was the distinction that ate at Durbin. As an old Arlington hand with years of funeral experience, Durbin believed that enlisted men such as Whisenhunt who died in combat deserved the same full-honors treatment that officers rated at Arlington, which included all of the standard honors (a casket team, a folded flag, a firing party, and a bugler) plus the treatment accorded only to officers and top-ranked enlisted personnel—a military band, a marching platoon, a color-bearer, and a caisson.[36]

"Honors rendered should be rendered fairly, based on actions, not rank," Durbin told *Military Times* newspaper, setting off a controversy that would simmer for months.[37] "This is flat out disgraceful," Durbin said. "A 2nd Lieutenant can die in a car accident 2 days after graduating Officer Candidate School and get a Full Honor Funeral, while a Master Sergeant in the Army, Air Force, Marine Corps, or Navy with 22 years of Service can die in Combat in Afghanistan or Iraq, receive a Silver Star for Valor, and receive a Standard Honor Funeral."[38] The unequal treatment at Arlington was a form of segregation, Durbin said, overlooking the cemetery's long tradition of isolating its graves by rank and race, a practice maintained until halfway through the twentieth century.

In a military culture where hierarchy was necessary and rank had its privileges, Durbin's plea on behalf of enlisted soldiers took more than a year to gain traction. After a blizzard of letters and e-mails to the president, senators, news outlets, veterans' groups, and military brass, Durbin's appeals finally reached the office of Pete Geren, secretary of the Army, who bought the sergeant's argument. Geren issued new regulations granting full-honors funerals for enlisted soliders killed in action. His directive, announced on December 12, 2008, took effect on January 1, 2009.[39]

"Arlington National Cemetery is an expression of our nation's reverence for those who served her in uniform, many making the ultimate sacrifice," Geren said. "Arlington and those honored there are part of our national heritage. This new policy provides a common standard for honoring all soliders killed in action."[40]

Geren's decision surprised and elated Durbin, who was still serving at Camp Tali in Iraq when the announcement came through. "First time in thirteen months over here I've had something to smile about," he told the officer who informed him of the policy shift.[41] It applied only to army personnel but set the precedent other services were expected to follow at Arlington, making the nation's cemetery a bit less rank-conscious and a bit less elitist, continuing the trend that General Pershing's arrival at Arlington had set in train more than half a century before.

The first soldier to be buried under the new rules was Army Spec. Joseph M. Hernandez, twenty-four, killed in Zabul Province of Afghanistan on January 9, 2009. The manner of his death was depressingly familiar: He and two other soldiers from the 1st Battalion, 4th Infantry Regiment, had been driving near Jaldak when their armored Humvee was blown up by a roadside bomb, killing all three in the vehicle.[42]

On the day this happened, his wife, Alison Hernandez, staying with relatives in Dyer, Indiana, sensed that something was wrong. Her husband phoned every other day from Afghanistan but had missed the last scheduled call. Feeling ill and fearing the worst, she was standing on the front porch when the two soldiers pulled up and emerged from a government car, looking grim. One of them was a chaplain. "I heard her scream from the porch," her father, Robert Gordon Jr., said. "I got up and she fell through the door. 'He's gone,'" she said.[43]

A few days later, on January 23, Alison Hernandez was sitting in the front row at Arlington by her husband's open grave with their sons, Jacob, two, and Noah, nine months. A cold wind whipped over Section 60 that day as more than a hundred mourners gathered for services. Hernandez was brought to his grave in a silver hearse, his widow having decided, for the sake of a timely burial, to forgo the horse-drawn caisson to which he was entitled but which would not be available for several weeks, because of a tightly packed funeral schedule. The weather also conspired against the family. Instead of a full military band, Hernandez was led to the grave by a single Army drummer, whose solemn cadence seemed all the more poignant for being solo. The subfreezing temperature, which iced up musical instruments, kept the Army band away from the service. Despite this, a single bugler, bundled in a heavy coat with his ear flaps deployed, stood tall among the white tombstones waiting for the last crack of the rifle salute for Specialist Hernandez. Then the bugler sent Taps ringing clear and true over the cemetery, at once lamenting the loss of a young warrior and welcoming a new recruit for Arlington.[44]

1 5

TAPS

When night came to Arlington, the crowds scattered, the cemetery gates clanked shut, and Old Glory was ceremoniously lowered in front of the Lee mansion. Silence settled over the dark hills. Yet the workday continued on the amphitheater plaza, where a lone sentinel marched slowly back and forth in the moonlight, keeping vigil at the Tomb of the Unknowns as Army guards have done since round-the-clock watches began in 1937.

Even though no spectators were present, the sentinel followed a painstaking routine, patrolling the terrace with soldierly precision. He marched twenty-one steps to the south, stopped, and pivoted to the east with a sharp click of his heels. Standing rigid, he held this position for a count of twenty-one seconds. Then, with another heel click, he wheeled a half turn, shifted his M-14 rifle from one shoulder to the other, and resumed patrol. He stepped exactly twenty-one paces to the north before turning and halting to face the capital once more. Back and forth he marched on a frosty December night, repeating the process until his one-hour duty was finished and another guard relieved him.[1]

Like other Arlington traditions, this one was steeped in symbolism. The sentinel's twenty-one-step pace and his twenty-one-count pauses were based on the twenty-one-gun salute, the highest honor the military can render. He wore heavy heel taps, which rang on the stone terrace, recalling the jangling spurs of cavalry troopers who once patrolled these heights. He kept his rifle facing away from the sarcophagus and toward the amphitheater on each pass. This showed that he was ready to defend the Unknowns from outside threats. He packed a 9 mm Beretta on his hip and looked prepared to use it. His face, devoid of expression, was as hard and cold as the granite under his feet.[2]

"Even out here at night it's hard mentally and it's hard physically," said Spec. Bruce Bryant, pausing to watch a fellow sentinel marching back and forth in Battle Dress Uniform (BDU), the camouflage fatigues guards wear during night patrol, saving their flawless dress blues for daytime duty. "Even with no one watching, it's very tense," Bryant said. "You hit your marks, you make your turns, you try for perfection—even if it's at three in the morning. You don't want to do anything to disgrace the Unknowns."[3]

"Why?" a visitor asks. "Who would know?"

"*He* would know," Bryant said quietly, nodding toward the sarcophagus. His comment, startling at first, proved to be not at all unusual for a Tomb Guard. Living with the Unknowns night and day, the sentinels soon speak of their dead comrades as if they were present. They imagine the faraway battles that brought them to Arlington. They develop a strong affection for the dead men they are meant to protect.[4] When Lt. Michael Blassie was removed from the Vietnam Unknown's crypt in 1998, one of those mourning his departure was Cpl. Mark Travis, a Tomb Guard who had spoken to the dead airman during night patrols and had taken time for a private goodbye before Blassie was disinterred and driven away. "I was just so sad to see him go. I miss him," said Travis, who left Arlington a few weeks after Blassie did.[5]

Tomb Guards spare no effort to honor the memory of those under their care. They keep to a firefighter's schedule, working twenty-four-hour shifts, eating, sleeping, and training in the tidy underground quarters beneath the amphitheater where they are billeted a few hundred feet from the Unknowns. In their subterranean warren, the guards practice their twenty-one-step walk to the beat of a metronome, stand in front of full-length mirrors to practice heel clicks and rifle drills, and spend hours polishing their shoes, steam-pressing their own uniforms, and measuring the alignment of their medals to $\frac{1}{64}$ of an inch. It would be unkind to suggest that their approach to work is obsessive-compulsive, yet far too mild to describe them as merely meticulous.[6]

When a sentinel suits up for a daytime appearance on the terrace, he or she is assisted by another sentinel, who functions as a dresser, making sure that the gold band on the duty guard's hat is perfectly parallel with the top of his head and that the yellow stripe of his trousers is exactly perpendicular to the floor.[7] His uniform must be free of lint and loose threads, which are dispatched with sticky tape and cigarette lighters, respectively. One young guard, preparing for a late afternoon patrol (which in the argot of sentinels is a BOLO, or to "be on the lookout"), blows fugitive dust from his shoes with a blast of air from a compressor, wriggles into a rubberized corset that flattens his stomach, pulls on a fresh white shirt, squares his tie exactly, slides into his coat (which the Army calls a blouse), and cinches himself in with a blue belt bordered with gold braid. The dresser yanks the sentinel's blouse down tight from behind, pulls it free of wrinkles, makes a final check for imperfections, and sends his comrade out to greet the public with a word of advice:

"Don't forget your dead-man's face!"

At that instant, an apple-cheeked youth becomes a marble man, gliding up the stairs from the catacombs and into the light, ready for his BOLO.[8]

"We take it one step further because we are so visible," said Staff Sgt. Adam L. Dickmyer, one of three relief commanders for the Tomb Guard. "Thousands of people see us every day—more come here than go to the Jefferson Memorial— so we want to make the best possible impression. And we want the guys who sacrificed everything to know that they are still remembered, that someone still cares. That's why we do it."[9]

Arlington remains the last refuge for these nameless warriors. Here their memories live on long after the guns have fallen silent and the smoke has cleared away. The cemetery also provides a home for the ones who once were lost but now are found.

Such was the case for Pvt. Francis Z. Lupo of Cincinnati, who had vanished without a trace near Soissons, France, in the summer of 1918. Lupo, twenty-three, a member of the Army's 18th Infantry Regiment, had fallen in the first day of fighting in the Second Battle of the Marne, which many consider to be the turning point of World War I. Hastily buried in a bomb crater, Lupo rested undisturbed there until 2003.[10]

Then a French archaeologist, conducting a salvage survey in advance of construction projects, discovered the bones of two people, recognized parts of old army uniforms from the Great War, and turned his find over to the Defense Department's Joint POW/MIA Accounting Command in Hawaii.[11]

One set of bones was so diminutive that anthropologists initially thought that they belonged to a woman. But when other clues were considered, they pointed to Lupo. The teeth matched most elements of Lupo's dental record; the private was short, probably less than the regulation height of five feet; and a tattered wallet had been recovered—with Lupo's name stamped on it. Part of a size 5½ army boot, undoubtedly Lupo's, was found with the bones. All suggested that a soldier presumed dead since July 20, 1918, might finally come home from the war. But what of the other combatant found with Lupo? To separate the remains, both sets of bones were subjected to mitochondrial DNA tests. One set of bones matched the mtDNA sample from Lupo's teeth, so those remains were collected into one group, while the others were retained for further investigation.[12]

With Lupo's identification in hand, the Army began searching for his next of kin, eventually locating Rachel Kleisinger, a niece born a dozen years after Lupo's death, in Kentucky. Although Mrs. Kleisinger had never laid eyes on her uncle, she had seen his picture, lit candles for him at church, and watched his mother, Anna Lupo, mourn his loss until the day she died in 1949. It was always the same: Mrs. Lupo, a tiny Sicilian woman in black, would open the window of her Cincinnati house and summon Francis: "Sciue-ducce! Sciue-ducce!" she shouted to the neighborhood, using the nickname for her "Sweet," as if she expected him to answer.[13]

Everyone who had known Private Lupo was dead by the time they brought him to Arlington for burial on September 26, 2006. Mrs. Kleisinger, then seventy-three and confined to a wheelchair, sat front and center at the Old Post Chapel of Fort Myer, accompanied by her daughter and grandchildren. Lupo's immediate kin had disappeared, but his military family remained. They turned out more than a hundred mourners to honor one of their own. Sgt. Maj. John Fourham, the ranking noncommissioned officer from the Army's 1st Infantry Division, Lupo's old unit, flew in from Fort Riley, Kansas, to pay his respects;

ordinary soldiers in working BDU fatigues crowded into the back pews, as did civilian scientists from the Armed Forces DNA Identification Laboratory, who had helped solve Lupo's case. Two officers from the French army filed down the aisle, shoulders squared and caps tucked reverentially under their arms, heel taps ringing on the chapel's red tiles.[14]

"I thought it was a mistake when I got the information about today's service," a priest admitted to the assembled mourners. "How could we be burying a soldier from World War I after all this time? The fact that we are here today, brothers and sisters, is a miracle. Now we know where he will be buried. Now we can say a little prayer at his graveside." This they did, following the priest and Lupo's flag-covered casket out into the sunlight and down through the hills to Section 66, just to the east of Eisenhower Drive, where a casket team from the Old Guard marched Lupo to the grave for the familiar rituals of parting. The priest opened his book and said a prayer; the firing party cracked out its salute; the casket team carefully folded the flag; Mrs. Kleisinger took it with her head held high. A few tears were shed for the private nobody knew but all remembered.[15]

"It is so amazing to know that this soldier was so young," said Sgt. Maj. Frederic Plautin, one of the French officers attending Lupo's service. "Many French died in battle with him the same way, but they were in France. This American soldier was not in his country. So we really wish to share the grief and express our thanks for what he has done."[16]

All around the Frenchman, the white tombstones stretched out of sight, up through the dappled hills and down to the shining river, thousands for Lupo's war, thousands more for all of the others. With the ravages of age and with new conflicts adding five thousand to six thousand new graves to Arlington each year, would the cemetery run out of space?[17] "We'll have room for another fifty years," said John C. Metzler Jr., the cemetery superintendent, who has overseen what is likely the last expansion of Arlington. Slated to take effect over the next decade, the extension will add more than 70 acres to the cemetery, bringing the total to some 680 acres, space enough for burials and inurnments into 2060.[18] "I won't be here," Metzler said. "But Arlington will be here."[19]

EPILOGUE

A<small>FTER THE FIRST EDITION OF THIS BOOK WAS PUBLISHED IN</small> 2009, <small>THE</small> Pentagon announced the results of a year-long investigation into poor management at Arlington National Cemetery, where the Army's inspector general found more than two hundred graves to be misidentified or unmarked, cremated remains improperly handled, record-keeping haphazard, and the cemetery's administration ineffective.[1]

"I deeply apologize to the families of the honored fallen resting in that hallowed ground who may now question the care afforded their loved ones," said John M. McHugh, secretary of the Army, who shuffled the cemetery's civilian management and called for stringent quality control and computerized burial files. He promised to restore the cemetery's reputation as a place of honor.[2]

"While the inspector general's team found that employees performed their jobs with dedication and to a high professional standard, they also found them hampered by dysfunctional management, the lack of established policy and procedures, and an overall unhealthy organizational climate," McHugh announced on June 10, 2010. "That ends today."[3]

McHugh forced the retirement of John C. Metzler, Jr., the cemetery superintendent who had grown up at Arlington and lived on the property for the last nineteen years. The Army placed Metzler's deputy, Thurman Higginbotham, on leave while investigators continue what is likely to be an open-ended probe into irregularities at the cemetery. "The new leadership team is going to reestablish the baseline of accountability, and they are going to take a hard look at every section [of the cemetery]," said Gary Tallman, an Army spokesman. The inspector general's team focused on irregularities in Sections 59, 65, and 66, where most of the burials are those of veterans who served from World War I through Vietnam; one misidentified grave was from the current wars in Afghanistan and Iraq. In the months to come, as investigators comb through old burial records and try to match the names on file with those on tombstones, more mistakes will undoubtedly come to light—a prospect that distresses those with loved ones and comrades buried at Arlington.[4]

"It is absolutely unacceptable that something like this would happen at America's most sacred burial ground," said Paul Rieckhoff, founder of Iraq and Afghanistan War Veterans of America. "We expect action from the Pentagon and the administration."[5]

Like other painful chapters from Arlington's history, this one will leave scars. But they will undoubtedly heal, and the nation's premier cemetery will be the stronger for it. "I am confident that we will learn from our mistakes and be able to restore the nation's confidence in our ability to be a responsible steward of this hallowed landmark," said McHugh.[6]

BENEDICTION

For all of the dead at Arlington,
Requiescant in pace.

For all of the living, a line of wisdom from an army chaplain
who has buried hundreds of comrades
at Arlington:
"Life is short. Live it well."

ACKNOWLEDGMENTS

The idea for this book came from my friend and agent Raphael Sagalyn, who is patient only up to a point. He listened to my long list of inappropriate and un-marketable ideas until he could stand it no longer. "Arlington National Ceme-tery!" he blurted. "Why don't you do a book on Arlington? It is a great subject."

Several years and many funerals later, here it is, Rafe, with thanks for the gift of a story peopled with so many memorable characters and so much historic in-terest that the great challenge has been to keep Arlington down to manageable size. Much has been cast to the wayside, but I trust that enough remains to do justice to a worthy subject.

If I have succeeded in this, it is because so many kind people have guided the way. They include: Laura Anderson, Karen Byrne Kinzey, Mary Troy, and Kendell Thompson of the National Park Service, which manages Arlington House, the Robert E. Lee Memorial, as a national historical site. Their library, situated across Sherman Drive from the old Lee mansion, is an outstanding repository of archival material on Arlington estate, the family who lived there, and the cemetery's tumultuous early years.

From the Army's Old Guard, the 3rd U.S. Infantry at Fort Myer, Virginia, thanks to Col. Robert Pricone, Sgt. Jason Cauley, Sgt. Brian K. Parker, and Sgt. Jeremy A. Kern for taking the time to educate me about their work at Arlington. Sfc. Robert A. Durbin, a former casket team leader for the Old Guard, answered my queries about Arlington and kept me apprised of his campaign to change fu-neral regulations while he was deployed to Iraq. Kenneth S. Pond and other re-tired members of the Old Guard provided a wealth of new material on the funeral of President Kennedy. I am also obliged to former and present sentinels who allowed me to keep vigil with them at the Tomb of the Unknowns by day and by night: Sgt. Bruce Bryant, Sgt. Christopher Moore, Staff Sgt. Stephen Kuehn, Staff Sgt. Adam L. Dickmyer, and Staff Sgt. Justin E. Bickett. Special thanks to Kim Bernard Holien, Army historian for Fort Myer and Fort McNair, who patiently and generously guided my research.

One seldom gets a chance to say this, but I was happy to be a taxpayer each time I went to the National Archives for research. Jill Abraham steered me to dusty boxes of papers from the Meigs era in Washington, D.C., while Timothy K. Nenninger, chief of modern military records at the facility in College Park, Maryland, proved that his reputation for being a knowledge-able and enthusiastic partner in research is well deserved. At the Library of Congress, thanks to Thomas J. Mann, reference librarian in the main read-ing room, and to Jeffrey M. Flannery, reference specialist in the manuscript division.

The story of Arlington often led to Capitol Hill, where historians helped me sort through the many-layered legislative history of my subject. Thanks to Beth Hahn, Chris Cochrane, and especially Zoe Davis of the Senate Historical Office; also to Ora Branch in the office of the clerk, House of Representatives, for providing documents and guidance.

I am also grateful to Judith Knudsen, manager of the Virginia Room, Arling-ton Country Public Library; E. Lee Shepard, director of manuscripts and senior archivist, Virginia Historical Society in Richmond, Virginia; Leith Johnson and Jennifer Miglus, special collections and archives, Wesleyan University Library, Middletown, Connecticut; Elizabeth Dunn, research services librarian, rare book, manuscript, and special collections library, Duke University, Durham, North Carolina; Rebecca Cooper, manager of reader services, Society of the Cincinnati, Washington, D.C.; Vaughan Stanley, research librarian, special col-lections, Washington & Lee University, Lexington, Virginia; Robert C. Peniston, archivist, Custis Lee Papers, Washington & Lee University; Kelly D. Barton, archivist, Ronald Reagan Library, Simi Valley, California; David Clark, archivist, Harry S. Truman Library, Independence, Missouri; Stephen Plotkin, reference archivist, John F. Kennedy Library, Boston, Massachusetts; Arthur Link III, act-ing director, library and archives, Woodrow Wilson Library, Staunton, Virginia; Luther Hanson, U.S. Quartermaster's Museum, Fort Lee, Virginia; Douglas V. Johnson II and Richard Sommers, U.S. Army Heritage and Education Center,

Carlisle, Pennsylvania; Bill McKale, director, 1st Infantry Museum, Fort Riley, Kansas; Andrew Woods, historian, 1st Division Museum, Wheaton, Illinois; and Michael Rhode, historian, Army Medical Museum, Walter Reed Army Medical Center, Washington, D.C.

The men and women of the Armed Forces Joint POW/MIA Accounting Command (JPAC) at Hickam Air Force Base in Honolulu deserve special praise for their efforts to locate, repatriate, and identify fallen service members from America's wars. In 2006, I joined them on a mission to Laos, where we recovered the remains of Capt. Michael J. "Bat" Masterson, an Air Force pilot missing since 1968. Since Masterson was not buried at Arlington, he does not appear in this book, but it was on that assignment that I met Troy Kitch, then deputy director of public affairs at JPAC, who subsequently helped me piece together the story of Lt. Michael J. Blassie in Chapter 14. Thanks to Troy and to his former JPAC colleagues Johnie Webb, Robert Mann, and Thomas Holland, all of whom contributed valuable insights and new information. Lieutenant Blassie's sister, Air Force Col. Patricia S. Blassie, unhesitatingly shared family documents and made time for a several interviews despite a busy schedule. Thanks also to Ted Sampley, publisher of the *U.S. Veteran Dispatch* in Kinston, North Carolina; to John O. Marsh Jr., former secretary of the Army; and to Rudy deLeon, who headed the Pentagon investigation of the Blassie case, leading to the airman's disinterment. DeLeon, now senior vice president for national security and international policy at the Center for American Progress in Washington, D.C., helped make sense of a tangled and often emotional piece of recent history.

For many years now, Arlington has set the standard for other cemeteries in the national system. Special thanks to Superintendent John C. Metzler Jr., who drove me around the cemetery, settled points of history, took time for interviews, and provided unfettered access to Arlington's employees. Two of these, Kaitlin Horst and Darrell Stafford, were especially helpful, despite the demands of their daily schedules.

Betsy Whisenhunt, whose husband was killed in Iraq and buried at Arlington in 2008, instantly and kindly answered my queries about the late Staff Sgt. Jerald Allen Whisenhunt, providing me with his last correspondence from the war zone. "Just let everybody know what a great guy he was," she explained.

To Carey Winfrey, editor-in-chief of *Smithsonian*, Thomas A. Frail, senior editor, and other colleagues at the magazine, thanks for the steady assignments—and for the friendship—that kept me going while this book was under construction.

I am indebted to Geoffrey C. Ward and Ernest B. Furgurson, faithful friends who read the manuscript and saved me from numerous mistakes and many embarrassments. Any flaws remaining are mine alone.

George Gibson, publishing director of Bloomsbury/Walker, understood the book's appeal from our first conversation and patiently prodded me forward. He never wavered in his support or enthusiasm. Sincere thanks to him and to his colleagues Jacqueline Johnson, Margaret Maloney, Jeremy Wang-Iverson, Peter Miller, and Mike O'Connor.

Finally, my greatest debt, thanks, and love to my wife, Suzie, who has heard enough Arlington stories for a lifetime but pretends to be hearing each one for the first time.

APPENDIX I

ARLINGTON CHRONOLOGY

JUNE 30, 1831 Mary Anna Custis marries Robert E. Lee at Arlington House.

APRIL 12, 1861 Confederates fire on Fort Sumter, precipitating the Civil War.

APRIL 17, 1861 Virginia convention votes to secede from the Union.

APRIL 18, 1861 Francis P. Blair Sr. offers Lee command of Union forces in the field.

APRIL 20–23, 1861 Robert E. Lee resigns from the Union Army, leaves Arlington, and accepts command of Virginia's military forces.

MAY 15, 1861 Mary Custis Lee leaves Arlington, leaving the keys to the mansion with Selina Gray a trusted slave and housekeeper.

MAY 24, 1861 Some 14,000 Federal troops cross the river to Virginia, taking control of Alexandria, bridge crossings, and the Lees' Arlington estate.

JUNE 1861 Virginia joins the Confederacy, which transfers its capital from Montgomery, Alabama, to Richmond, Virginia. Lee is given the rank of brigadier general and named as chief military advisor to Confederate president Jefferson Davis.

JULY 21, 1861 The first major battle of the Civil War takes place at Manassas, Virginia, where the Federals suffer 2,700 casualties, the Confederates

2,000. Because of the disappointing Union showing, Gen. George Mc-Clellan replaces Gen. Irvin McDowell as commander of the Army of the Potomac.

JANUARY 2, 1862 Secretary of War Simon Cameron assigns Union officers responsibility of feeding and clothing slaves on the Arlington estate.

APRIL 16, 1862 Congress emancipates all slaves in the District of Columbia. Primitive camps are established for freedmen in Washington.

MAY 31, 1862 When Gen. Joseph E. Johnston is wounded in the Peninsula Campaign, Robert E. Lee takes command of Confederate forces in Virginia.

JUNE 7, 1862 Congress passes an act to collect taxes from the "Insurrectionary Districts of the United States." Under the new law, the value of Arlington is assessed at $26,810. When Mrs. Lee fails to pay the tax of $92.07 in person, the property is purchased by the federal government at a tax sale.

JULY 17, 1862 War deaths mount at an unexpected pace, leaving the government poorly prepared to bury its fighting men. Congress creates a national cemetery system to accommodate "the soldiers who shall die in the service of the country." New cemeteries are established in Alexandria and the District of Columbia.

JULY 1862 During the bruising Peninsula Campaign below Richmond, Union Brig. Gen. Daniel Butterfield asks his bugler Oliver Wilcox Norton to change the standard lights out call, which results in a new tune, called Taps.

SEPTEMBER 17, 1862 McClellan batters Lee's forces at the Battle of Antietam, which costs the Federals 12,000 deaths and the Confederates a proportionate number. Five days after Antietam, President Lincoln announces a general Emancipation Proclamation freeing slaves in Confederate states. The new order is scheduled to take effect in January 1863.

JANUARY 1863 The Emancipation Proclamation brings a flood of black refugees to Washington, D.C., overwhelming the freedmen's camps established for them.

MAY 5, 1863 Lt. Col. Elias M. Greene proposes a new Freedman's Village at Arlington to accommodate former slaves. Formally dedicated in December, the village grows to a population of 1,500, reinforcing the federal presence at Arlington.

MAY 4, 1864 Gen. Ulysses S. Grant, determined to end the war, crosses the Rapidan River of Virginia to face Robert E. Lee in forty days of almost continuous fighting. Their bloody exchange creates more than 80,000 casualties. When cemeteries in the capital run out of space, the Union quartermaster, Brig. Gen. Montgomery C. Meigs, begins unofficially burying war casualties on Lee's Arlington estate

MAY 13, 1864 Pvt. William Henry Christman of the 67th Pennsylvania Infantry is the first soldier buried at Arlington, on the edge of the property near a small cemetery for slaves. With cemeteries overflowing and deaths mounting, Edwin M. Stanton, secretary of war, asks Meigs to recommend new national burial sites.

JUNE 15, 1864 Meigs proposes that 200 acres at Arlington should be taken for a national military cemetery. Stanton approves and Meigs orders burials around Lee's mansion to prevent the family's return to Arlington.

APRIL 9, 1865 Lee surrenders to Grant at Appomattox Court House.

FEBRUARY 1866 Robert E. Lee returns to Washington to testify before Congress but avoids visiting Arlington. He consults lawyers about reclaiming the property.

APRIL 1866 Meigs orders a huge pit dug in Mrs. Lee's garden and fills it with the remains of 2,111 unknown Civil War dead.

1868 Gen. John Alexander Logan, commander in chief of the Grand Army of the Republic, designates May 30, 1868, as "Decoration Day" to honor the Union war dead. It is, in effect, the first Memorial Day.

DECEMBER 25, 1868 President Andrew Johnson declares amnesty for all former Confederates.

1870 Robert E. Lee dies. Mrs. Lee immediately petitions the Senate to disinter thousands of those buried at Arlington and return the property to her. Her appeal is soundly defeated.

JUNE 1873 Mary Custis Lee returns to visit Arlington for the last time. She dies five months later.

1873 Congress approves a free white marble marker for each service member buried at Arlington.

1874 The Old Amphitheater, a bowl encircled by wooden colonnades, is dedicated at Arlington, where it is used for gatherings of veterans' groups.

1877 After unsuccessfully petitioning Congress to restore Arlington to his family, George Washington Custis Lee, Robert E. Lee's eldest son, goes to court to have Arlington returned to his family.

DECEMBER 4, 1882 The Supreme Court, holding that Arlington was seized illegally during the Civil War, rules in Custis Lee's favor. He sells the property to the government for $150,000, its fair market value.

DECEMBER 7, 1887 Residents of Freedman's Village are ordered to leave Arlington, where they have been living since the Civil War.

1888 Congress declares Memorial Day a national holiday.

1889 The cemetery annexes 142 adjoining acres, bringing the total acreage to 342.

1892 Montgomery C. Meigs is buried near the Lee mansion, where he is surrounded by the graves of family members and by prominent Union officers.

1892 The first Revolutionary War casualties are brought to Arlington National Cemetery, signaling a change in status for Arlington. It is becoming an important symbol for the nation.

1897 The cemetery annexes 56 acres, bringing Arlington's total to almost 400.

1898 The U.S.S. *Maine* explodes and sinks in Havana Harbor, killing 260 and precipitating the Spanish-American War.

1899 More than 160 of the dead from the *Maine* explosion are buried at Arlington under a mast salvaged from the ship.

1900 The last of the freedmen are turned out of Arlington. Their lands, scattered over 400 acres, are turned over to the Agriculture Department, which establishes an experimental farm.

1900 In the spirit of conciliation marking a new century, Congress approves a new Confederate Section at Arlington, where almost 500 Rebel soldiers are reburied from Washington.

1903 Arlington is up to 300 funerals a year. Burials total 19,000.

1905 Fourteen unknowns from the War of 1812 are reburied at Arlington; most are thought to be marines.

JANUARY 1906 Maj. Gen. Joseph Wheeler, a Confederate cavalry officer who later led Union troops in the Spanish-American War, is buried among Union officers at Arlington.

SEPTEMBER 1908 Lt. Thomas Selfridge ushers in the age of military aviation at Fort Myer, flying in a demonstration flight with Orville Wright. Selfridge dies when the plane crashes. The nation's first casualty of powered flight, he is buried at Arlington.

1909 Pierre Charles L'Enfant, veteran of the Revolutionary War and architect of Washington's original city plan, is exhumed and buried just in front of the Lee mansion, with a fine view of the capital he designed.

NOVEMBER 12, 1912 A cornerstone is laid for the new Confederate Memorial, where former enemies come together for a ceremony of reunion.

AUGUST 1914 World War I begins.

NOVEMBER 11, 1918 The Armistice ends World War I, which claims the lives of 116,516 Americans.

1920 Arctic explorer Rear Adm. Robert E. Peary is buried. The new Memorial Amphitheater, an imposing white marble bowl built to the south of the Lee mansion, is dedicated.

DECEMBER 21, 1920 Rep. Hamilton Fish, an Army officer who saw action in the war, introduces legislation to bring an unknown American soldier for burial in the United States.

NOVEMBER 11, 1921 With President Warren G. Harding officiating, the Unknown Soldier of World War I is buried under the plaza of the new Memorial Amphitheater at Arlington. The grave becomes a symbolic focus for the cemetery.

1924 Congress authorizes the transfer of 400 acres from the Agriculture Department's Experimental Farm to the Army, which holds the land for possible use at Arlington and Fort Myer.

1925 Congress authorizes the restoration of Arlington House, in part to recognize Robert E. Lee's role in reunifying the country after the Civil War.

1926 Robert Todd Lincoln, son of the president and a former secretary of war, is buried at Arlington.

1929 James Parks, former Arlington slave, is buried in special ceremonies at the national cemetery.

1930 William Howard Taft becomes the first president to be buried at Arlington.

JANUARY 16, 1932 Memorial Bridge, connecting the Lincoln Memorial with Arlington National Cemetery, is dedicated by President Herbert Hoover. The bridge, intended to link North and South symbolically, also unifies the city's landscape design.

1933 The National Park Service takes jurisdiction of the Arlington mansion and more than 20 acres of land surrounding it.

1937 The Tomb of the Unknown is placed under round-the-clock guard.

1939 Adolf Hitler invades Poland, triggering World War II.

1940 With war raging in Europe, plans advance for a massive new War Department building—the Pentagon—at Arlington. President Franklin Roosevelt moves the building to a less objectionable site after Secretary of the Interior Harold Ickes and others complain that the plans would spoil views from the Lee mansion. Burials reach 49,927 before the United States enters World War II.

DECEMBER 7, 1941 Japanese attack Pearl Harbor, drawing the United States into war.

1941 President Roosevelt gives Ignace Paderewski, the musician and Polish statesman, temporary burial at Arlington, in a crypt under the U.S.S. *Maine* Memorial.

1948 Gen. John J. Pershing is buried among the simple graves of men he commanded in World War I. His gravestone, a plain government-issue marker, sets an example for other officers at Arlington.

1948 President Harry S. Truman orders integration of the Army, which leads to desegregation of burial plots at Arlington.

1950 The total number of Arlington burials passes 70,000.

JANUARY 2, 1951 Lt. Gen. Walton H. "Johnnie" Walker, killed in a jeep accident in the Korean conflict, is promoted to four-star rank and given a prominent burial at Arlington. His prompt return to the United States leads to a new policy of "concurrent return," by which service members are sent home for burial during wartime.

1955 The Arlington mansion is designated as a national memorial to Gen. Robert E. Lee. The superintendent of Arlington, John C. Metzler Sr., orders the first trenching machines for digging graves at Arlington.

MAY 30, 1958 Unknowns from World War II and the Korean conflict are buried on the amphitheater plaza, with President Dwight D. Eisenhower officiating.

1959 Gen. George C. Marshall, five-star general, secretary of state, secretary of defense, and Nobel Prize laureate, is buried at Arlington. Interments reach 100,000 this year.

1961 One of the first to die in a nuclear accident in the United States, Spec. 4 Richard Leroy McKinley is buried at Arlington. His casket is lined with lead and sealed in concrete.

NOVEMBER 22, 1963 President John F. Kennedy is killed. His burial at Arlington, nationally televised, is the first for a sitting present at the cemetery.

After his death, visits to Arlington jump to 7 million a year. Requests for burial at Arlington also increase, necessitating a tightening of burial restrictions.

1966 Arlington plans to annex 200 acres from the South Post of Fort Myer, which will bring the cemetery's total acreage to more than 600 by the late 1970s.

1967 President Kennedy and two of his children are moved a few feet downhill to a permanent burial site, which becomes one of Arlington's key attractions.

1968 Robert F. Kennedy is buried next to his brother.

1970 Arlington is closed to car and truck traffic.

1971 Audie Murphy, the most decorated soldier from World War II, is buried near the Memorial Amphitheater.

1976 For Bicentennial ceremonies, the tombstones of Congressional Medal of Honor winners are given gold lettering. Emperor Hirohito of Japan, Queen Elizabeth of Britain, and King Juan Carlos of Spain visit Arlington for the occasion.

1977 Francis Gary Powers dies in a helicopter crash. The former CIA agent, captured when his U-2 plane is shot down over the Soviet Union, is buried at Arlington.

1980 With demand for burial space growing, the first of nine columbaria for cremated remains is established on the cemetery's southeastern corner. When completed, the columbarium will have space for some 45,000 remains. Robert E. Lee's citizenship is restored in ceremonies at his old home.

1980 Associate Justice William O. Douglas is buried near former Chief Justice Earl Warren. They are later joined on a hillside by Justices Harry Blackman and Potter Stewart.

1980 Three aviators from the aborted Iranian hostage rescue mission are buried. President Jimmy Carter attends.

1981 Omar N. Bradley, last of World War II's five-star generals, is buried at Arlington.

1981 Joe Louis, the heavyweight boxing champion, is buried. His funeral costs are paid for by Max Schmeling, whom Louis defeated in a closely watched title bout in 1938.

OCTOBER 23, 1983 Two hundred twenty marines and sailors are killed in a terrorist bombing in Beirut. Nineteen marines and two sailors are buried at Arlington.

MAY 28, 1984 The Unknown serviceman from the Vietnam conflict is buried.

1986 Adm. Hyman G. Rickover, father of the nuclear navy, is buried.

1986 Dick Scobee and Michael Smith, two casualties of the space shuttle *Challenger* explosion, are buried. The number of total burials at Arlington reaches 200,000.

1988 Matthew Henson, the black explorer who accompanied Robert Peary on two decades of Arctic travel, is reburied near his old associate.

1988 John Mitchell is buried. The former commander of JFK's PT boat unit and two-time Purple Heart recipient is also a former attorney imprisoned for conspiracy and obstruction of justice in the Watergate scandal.

1992 Ignace Jan Paderewski finally goes home fifty one years after his "temporary" burial at Arlington.

1993 Civil rights pioneer and Associate Supreme Court Justice Thurgood Marshall is buried. Burials reach 230,000 this year.

1994 Jacqueline Onassis is buried next to her husband and children.

1995 Cpl. Heather Johnson becomes the first female sentinel to guard the Tomb of the Unknowns.

1998 The Tomb of the Unknown from Vietnam is opened and the remains examined. DNA testing identifies Lt. Michael Blassie, an Air Force officer missing since being shot down over Vietnam on May 11, 1972.

SEPTEMBER 11, 2001 On the same day terrorists strike the World Trade Center in New York, hijackers crash American Airlines Flight 77 into the Pentagon, killing 189 people. Sixty-four, most of them uniformed service members killed in the attack, are buried at Arlington, near the crash site.

DECEMBER 2001 Johnny "Mike" Spann, a CIA officer, is buried at Arlington. He is the first casualty of fighting in Afghanistan.

2001 Members of the "Greatest Generation" from World War II die at the rate of 1,500 a day, increasing demand for new burial space at Arlington.

APRIL 10, 2003 Army Capt. Russell B. Rippetoe, the first Iraq War casualty to be interred at Arlington, is buried. The number of interments and inurnments approaches 300,000.

JANUARY 23, 2009 Army Spec. Joseph Hernandez, killed by a roadside bomb in Afghanistan, is buried in a full-honors ceremony at Arlington. He is the first enlisted man to be accorded such honors, extended to all service members killed in action. Full honors at Arlington include a bugler, a firing party, a casket team, a marching platoon, a military band, a caisson, and a folded flag.

FEBRUARY 2009 Arlington plans to expand to more than 680 acres by annexing adjacent land. This creates space for a total capacity of 400,000 burials and inurnments, ensuring that the cemetery will remain active until 2060.

APPENDIX II

REGULATIONS FOR BURIAL

Qualifying for Burial or Inurnment at Arlington

BURIAL
+ Current and former presidents of the United States
+ Any former member of the Armed Forces who served on active duty and held an elective office of the federal government or the office of chief justice or associate justice of the Supreme Court
+ Service members on active duty
+ Those with at least twenty years of active duty
+ Those on active reserve who qualify for pay upon retirement or retire at age sixty
+ Those retired for disability
+ Veterans honorably discharged with a disability of 30 percent or greater before October 1, 1949
+ Those who have received one of the following: the Medal of Honor, the Distinguished Service Cross, the Air Force Cross, the Navy Cross, the Distinguished Service Medal, the Silver Star, or the Purple Heart
+ Former prisoners of war
+ Spouses or unmarried minors of any of the above

INURNMENT
+ Any of those qualifying for in-ground burial
+ Any veteran whose last discharge was honorable
+ Spouses or unmarried minors of any of the above

EXCEPTIONS
+ The president can make exceptions to regulations on recommendation of the Secretary of the Army

For more detailed information, write to:
The Superintendent, Arlington National Cemetery, Arlington, VA 22211
or visit www.arlingtoncemetery.org

NOTES AND SOURCES

Any reader who has gotten this far knows that *On Hallowed Ground* reaches across a broad expanse of time and geography, far beyond the well-fenced borders of Arlington National Cemetery. For this reason, I am indebted to an army of writers who have gone before me, exploring parts of the Arlington story I had no hope of mastering to the extent they have done. I freely acknowledge my obligation to:

Ernest B. Furgurson and the late Margaret Leech, for their studies of Washington in the Civil War, *Freedom Rising* and *Reveille in Washington*, respectively, and to Margaret Leech for her book *In the Days of McKinley*, which treats the McKinley presidency and the Spanish-American War.

The best recent biography of Robert E. Lee is *Reading the Man*, brilliantly researched and written by Elizabeth Brown Pryor. Her book should be read in apposition to Emory Thomas's *Robert E. Lee*. Thomas judges his subject by what Lee *did*, Pryor by what Lee *said* or *wrote*. Both make for compelling reading. The most thorough study of Lee is the late Douglas Southall Freeman's four-volume *R. E. Lee: A Biography*, considered to be inexcusably old-fashioned and worshipful these days—but it is essential reading for anyone exploring the general's life. Murray H. Nelligan, a former historian for the National Park Service, has written the definitive study of the Lee family estate and its restoration in *Arlington House*.

No history of Arlington National Cemetery would be complete without attention to the clear-eyed work of Drew Gilpin Faust, whose book *This Republic of Suffering* examines American attitudes toward death at the time of the Civil War and recounts the nation's remarkable effort to recover, rebury, and honor those sacrificed to the conflict.

For much of the material on Washington's landscape design and Arlington's place in it, I leaned on *Grand Avenues*, an entertaining and diligently researched study of Pierre L'Enfant by Scott W. Berg. Jennifer Hanna's book *Cultural Landscape Report: Arlington House, The Robert E. Lee Mansion*, is a detailed study of how the people living and working at Arlington have shaped its character, from precolonial times to the present.

The late Barbara Tuchman provides a beautifully written and thoroughly documented account of conditions leading to World War I in *The Proud Tower* and in her magisterial *The Guns of August*. By far the best single volume on that conflict is John Keegan's *The World War*. To examine the traditions that inspired Americans to honor an unknown serviceman from World War I, see Neil Hanson's *Unknown Soldiers*, which takes place largely in Europe but includes an excellent chapter on the Unknown's path to Arlington.

Thomas B. Allen and Paul Dickson, two friends from Washington, D.C., documented the veterans' march on the capital following World War I in their book, *The Bonus Army*, which provided material for my treatment of the subject.

The late William Manchester's minute-by-minute account of President Kennedy's funeral, *The Death of a President*, was the starting point for Chapter 12. I benefited greatly from selected portions of Manchester's research files, which were generously made available to me by Wesleyan University. Recent oral histories gathered by Kenneth S. Pond and other members of the Army's Old Guard provided fresh perspectives on an exhaustively covered event.

Finally, I wish to acknowledge an enormous debt to Steve Vogel of The *Washington Post*. His recent book, *The Pentagon: A History*, is a marvel of painstaking research and fine storytelling, the bedrock on which my Chapter 10 was constructed.

Full citations for these references appear below.

To save space in the endnotes, I have employed these abbreviations:

ACL	ArlingtonCounty Public Library
AHA	Arlington House Archives, National Park Service
D-E Collection	DeButts-Ely Collection, Library of Congress
LOC	Library of Congress
NARA	National Archives and Records Administration
HSTL	Harry S. Truman Presidential Library
JFKL	John F. Kennedy Presidential Library
MCM	Montgomery C. Meigs Papers
RRL	Ronald Reagan Presidential Library
VHS	Virginia Historical Society
JW	Johnie Webb Papers
WUL	Wesleyan University Library
WWL	Woodrow Wilson Presidential Library

PROLOGUE

1. Thucydides, *History of the Peloponnesian Wars* (New York: Penguin Books, 1972) 143.
2. Caroline Alexander, "Across the River Styx," *New Yorker*, Nov. 25, 2004, 47
3. The three-rifle salute, which is rendered at all honors funerals, may be rooted in the ancient burial practices of Rome. Guided by a belief in numerology, Romans held the number three to be auspicious. When a friend or family member was buried, loved ones cast three handfuls of earth onto the coffin and called out the name of the dead three times to conclude the ceremony.

I: LEAVING ARLINGTON

1. Douglas Southall Freeman, *R. E. Lee: A Biography*, (New York: Charles Scribner's Sons, 1936), I: 440.

2. Ibid., 439.

3. Margaret Leech, *Reveille in Washington: 1860–1865* (New York: Harper & Brothers Publishers, 1941), 56-64.

4. Ibid.; Ernest B. Furgurson, *Freedom Rising: Washington in the Civil War* (New York: Alfred A. Knopf, 2004), 63-98.

5. Robert E. Lee to Mary Custis Lee, May 11, May 25, June 11, Dec. 25, 1861; Robert E. Lee to Mildred Lee, Dec. 25, 1862, D-E Collection, LOC; Robert E. Lee to G. W. C. Lee, Mar. 17, 1858, in Murray Nelligan, *Arlington House: The Story of the Lee Mansion Historical Monument* (Burke, VA: Chatelaine Press, 2005), 404.

6. Robert E. Lee to Martha Custis "Markie" Williams, Mar. 15, 1854, D-E Collection, LOC.

7. Of the 196 slaves Mrs. Lee inherited, 63 lived on the Arlington estate; the others worked on the White House and Romancock farms.

8. "Romancock" was renamed "Romancoke" by the Lee family; for the sake of clarity, I have retained the original name throughout.

9. Nelligan, 126; Godfrey T. Vigne, *Six Months in America* (London: Whittaker, Treacher & Co., 1831), 147.

10. Emory M. Thomas, *Robert E. Lee* (New York: W. W. Norton & Company, 1997), 144.

11. Ibid.

12. Nelligan, 359.

13. Robert E. Lee to W. H. F. Lee, Aug. 7, 1858, in Nelligan, 356.

14. Slaves also escaped when Custis was running the plantation. He offered a $50 reward for the return of a twenty-four-year-old named Eleanor. *Daily National Intelligencer*, Oct. 29, 1829, in AHA.

15. Records of Arlington County, Virginia, March 15, May 22, June 29, and July 23, 1858, in Will Book 7, pp. 485, 487, 488 in AHA.

16. Freeman, I: 390–94.

17. Robert E. Lee to G. W. C. Lee, July 2, 1859, in Freeman I: 392.

18. Robert E. Lee to E. S. Quirk, March 1, 1866, in Michael Fellman, *The Making of Robert E. Lee* (New York: Random House, 2000), 67.

19. Records of Arlington County, Virginia, Will Book 7, 485, 487, 488, 490 in AHA.

20. Robert E. Lee to Mary Custis Lee, Dec. 27, 1856, in Thomas, 173.

21. Robert E. Lee to G. W. C. Lee, July 2, 1859, in Nelligan, 359.

22. Robert E. Lee to Edward C. Turner, Feb. 12, 1858, in Nelligan, 354.

23. Robert E. Lee to Anne Lee, August 27, 1860, in Thomas, 184.

24. Freeman, I:428–29.

25. Robert E. Lee to W. H. F. Lee, Dec. 3, 1860, in Thomas, 186.

26. Thomas, 187.

27. Diary of Robert E. Lee, March 1, 1861, D-E Collection, LOC.

28. Clifford Dowdey and Louis H. Manarin, eds., *The Wartime Papers of R. E. Lee* (New York: Bramhall House, 1961), 3.

29. Doris Kearns Goodwin, *Team of Rivals* (New York: Simon & Schuster, 2005), 350, quoting from William Ernest Smith, *The Francis Preston Blair Family in Politics* (New York: The Macmillan Company, 1933), II:17. Douglas Southall Freeman was skeptical of the quotation attributed to Lee, which was based on the secondhand testimony of Montgomery Blair, the son of Francis Preston Blair. While the sense of the quotation is plausible, Freeman doubted that Lee would have expressed reluctance to draw his sword upon Virginia on April 18, 1861, when he did not yet know that Virginia had seceded. Freeman, I: 633–35.

30. J. William Jones, *Personal Reminiscences, Anecdotes, and Letters of General Robert E. Lee* (New York: D. Appleton & Co., 1875), 141.

31. Thomas, 145.

32. Freeman, I: 437.

33. Robert E. Lee to Sydney Smith Lee, April 20, 1861, *Wartime Papers*, 10.

34. Freeman, I: 439.

35. Agnes Lee to Mildred Lee, April 18, 1861, D-E Collection, LOC.

36. George L. Upshur, *As I Recall Them: Memories of Crowded Years* (New York: Wilson-Erickson, Inc. 1936), 16.

37. Grace H. Sharp, "Colored Servant of Adopted Son of George Washington," *Christian Science Monitor*, Sept. 24, 1924. The slave James Parks was born at Arlington, spent most of the war there, and continued to work there as a laborer after the war. Reporters and historians describe him as an honest witness who never exaggerated his role and admitted it when he could not provide answers. Although his memory was generally reliable, he confused a few facts in old age—but not many. I have quoted him accurately, but in the interest of clarity, I have translated into standard English the stereotypical dialect ascribed to him.

38. Freeman, I: 442.

39. Robert E. Lee to Simon Cameron, April 20, 1861, in *Wartime Papers*, 9.

40. Robert E. Lee to Winfield Scott, April 20, 1861, in *Wartime Papers*, 8–9.

41. Robert E. Lee to Sydney Smith Lee, April 20, 1861, in *Wartime Papers*, 10–11.

42. Robert E. Lee to Mrs. Anne Lee Marshall, April 20, 1861, in *Wartime Papers*, 9–10.

43. Goodwin, 351.

44. Freeman, I:434.

45. W. W. Scott, "Some Reminiscences of Famous Men," *Southern Magazine*, July 1894.

46. Robert E. Lee, "Speech to the Virginia Commission Upon Acceptance of Command of Virginia Forces," April 23, 1861, and Robert E. Lee, "General Orders, No. 1," April 23, 1861, both in *Wartime Papers*, 11.

2: OCCUPATION

1. Mary Custis Lee, "Manuscript Statement," Sept. 1866, in Murray Nelligan, *Arlington House: The Story of the Lee Mansion Historical Monument* (Burke, VA: Chatelaine Press, 2005), 393.

2. Nelligan, 393; Karen Byrne Kinzey, interviewed by author, March 7, 2006.

3. A few weeks after his warning to Mrs. Lee, Orton Williams resigned from the Union Army, joined the Confederates, and saw several years of fighting. Captured behind Union

lines in 1863 while disguised as a federal officer, he was accused of spying and hanged the next day.

4. Nelligan, 393–94.

5. Mary Custis Lee to B. J. Lossing, May 1, 1861, D-E Collection, LOC.

6. Mary Custis Lee to Robert E. Lee, May 9, 1861, D-E Collection, LOC; see also Jennifer Hanna, *Arlington House, The Robert E. Lee Memorial, Cultural Landscape Report* (Washington D.C.: National Park Service, 2001), 65.

7. Robert E. Lee to Mary Custis Lee, April 26, 1861, in *The Wartime Papers of R. E. Lee*, ed. Clifford Dowdey and Louis H. Manarin (New York: Bramhall House, 1961), 13.

8. Robert E. Lee to Mary Custis Lee, April 30, 1861, in *Wartime Papers*, 15.

9. "Encampment of the Fire Zouaves," The *New York Daily Tribune*, May 10, 1861, in AHA.

10. The *New York Daily Tribune*, May 17, 1861, in AHA.

11. Robert E. Lee to Mary Custis Lee, May 11, 1861, D-E Collection, LOC.

12. Thomas, 194.

13. *Wartime Papers*, 20, 22, 23, 27–28.

14. The *New York Daily Tribune*, May 9, 1861, in AHA.

15. Ernest B. Furgurson, *Freedom Rising: Washington in the Civil War* (New York: Alfred A. Knopf, 2004), 89.

16. David W. Miller, *Second Only to Grant* (Shippensburg, PA: White Mane Books, 2000), 89–90.

17. Miller, 95.

18. Furgurson, 52.

19. Mary Custis Lee to Mildred Lee, May 11, 1861, D-E Collection, LOC.

20. Mary Custis Lee to Mildred Lee, May 5, 1861, D-E Collection, LOC.

21. Nelligan, 396.

22. Douglas Southall Freeman, *R. E. Lee: A Biography* (New York: Charles Scribner's Sons, 1936), I: 508.

23. *The War of the Rebellion: a compilation of the official sources of the Union and Confederate Armies* (Washington: Government Printing Office, 1880), Series I, Vol. 2, 39–41, hereafter O.R.; Margaret Leech, *Reveille in Washington: 1860–1865* (New York: Harper & Brothers, 1941), 80.

24. Grace H. Sharp, "Colored Servant of Adopted Son of George Washington," The *Christian Science Monitor*, Sept. 24, 1924, in AHA.

25. Richard H. Schneider, *Taps: Notes from a Nation's Heart* (New York: William Morrow, 2002), 5–12.

26. O.R., Series I, Vol. 2, 39–42; "The Seventh In Virginia Friday," The *New York Times*, May 28, 1861; *Frank Leslie's Illustrated Weekly*, New York, June 1, 1861; Furgurson, 93–94.

27. Maj. Gen. S. P. Heintzelman to Lt. Gen. Winfield Scott, July 29, 1863, in O.R., Series I, Vol. 2, 39–42.

28. O.R., Series I, Vol. 2, 39–42; Brig. Gen. Irvin McDowell to Mrs. R. E. Lee, May 30, 1861, O.R. Series 1, Vol. 2, 655.

29. The *New York Times*, May 27–28, 1861; O.R., Series I, Vol. 2, 39–42; Edward W. Emerson, *Life and Letters of Charles Russell Lowell* (Boston: Houghton, Mifflin & Co., 1907), 207.

30. Robert E. Lee to Mary Custis Lee, June 9, 1861, *Wartime Papers*, 45; Emory M. Thomas, *Robert E. Lee* (New York: W. W. Norton & Co., 1997), 198.

31. O.R., Series I, Vol. 2, 39–42; *Pictorial War Record*, Jan. 28, 1882.

32. *Frank Leslie's Illustrated Newspaper*, June 15, 1861, AHA.

33. Nelligan, 407.

34. Mary Custis Lee to Maj. Gen. Charles W. Sandford, May 30, 1861, VHS.

35. Robert E. Lee to Mary Custis Lee, May 25, 1861, *Wartime Papers*, 36.

36. Robert E. Lee to Mary Custis Lee, June 24, 1861, *Wartime Papers*, 53.

37. Robert E. Lee to Mary Custis Lee, June 11, 1861, D-E Collection, LOC.

38. Thomas, 196.

39. Mary Custis Lee to Maj. Gen. Charles W. Sandford, May 30, 1861, VHS. Mrs. Lee's "my boy Billy" is Billy Taylor, one of two slaves who stayed with her throughout the war. The author can find no record of the slave Mrs. Lee called Marcellina; perhaps she is referring to Magdalena Parks, one of Lawrence Parks's nine children. Robert E. Lee took slaves with him too—among them was a man named Meredith, otherwise unidentified; George Parks, a cook; and Perry Parks, a valet. George and Perry Parks, brothers of James Parks, continued working for Lee after their emancipation, at which point they were paid for their labors.

40. Brig. Gen. Irvin McDowell to Mary Custis Lee, May 30, 1861, in O.R. Series I, Vol. 2, 655.

41. The *New York Daily News*, July 9, 1861, AHA.

42. The *National Republican*, July 12, 1861, AHA.

43. War Department, "Arlington House," interview with Mrs. Emma Syphax and Mrs. Sarah Wilson, Dec. 16, 1929, AHA.

44. Diary of Maj. Gen. S. P. Heintzelman, May 26, 1861, in Nelligan, 401; Karen Byrne Kinzey, interviewed by author, March 7, 2006.

45. Sketch by anonymous Union soldier, c. 1863, AHA.

46. Karen Byrne Kinzey, "The Remarkable Legacy of Selina Gray," *CRM* 4, (1998), 22.

47. Furgurson, 105–6.

48. Furgurson, 116; Leech, 86.

49. Brig. Gen. Irvin McDowell to Lt. Col E. D. Townsend, July 21 and July 22, 1861, in O.R. Series I, Vol. 2, 316.

50. Furgurson, 122–3.

51. Mrs. Annice Baker, daughter of Selina and Thornton Gray, The *Evening Star*, Washington, D.C., Dec. 11, 1950, in Virginia Room, ACL.

52. Leech, 102.

53. Furgurson, 121.

54. Leech, 107.

55. William T. Sherman, *William Tecumseh Sherman: Memoirs of General W.T. Sherman* (New York: Library of America, 1990), 199.

56. Leech, 112–13.

57. Alan T. Nolan, *The Iron Brigade: A Military History* (Bloomington: Indiana University Press, 1994), 31–32.

58. Robert E. Lee to Mildred Lee, Nov. 15, 1861, *Recollections*, 38.

59. Robert E. Lee to an unidentified daughter, Dec. 1861, in *Personal Reminiscences, Anecdotes, and Letters of General Robert E. Lee*, ed. J. William Jones (New York: D. Appleton & Co., 1875), 385.

60. Robert E. Lee to Mary Custis Lee, Dec. 25, 1861, *Wartime Papers*, 95–96.

61. Robert E. Lee to Gen. Samuel Cooper, Jan. 8, 1862, *Wartime Papers*, 101–2.

62. Robert E. Lee to Mary Custis Lee, Jan. 28, 1862, *Wartime Papers*, 107–8.

63. Robert E. Lee to Mary Custis Lee, Oct. 7, 1861, *Wartime Papers*, 79.

64. The author has included family names for the Lee slaves when they appear in the record, but some, such as Daniel the coachmen, are referred to only by their Christian names in official documents. Many of the Lee slaves who lived long enough to be emancipated had their full names recorded in the deed of manumission, signed by Robert E. Lee, Dec. 29, 1862, and recorded in the Office of the Court of Hustings, Richmond, Virginia, Jan. 2, 1863. AHA.

65. Martha Custis William to Mary Custis Lee, June 13, 1861, July 25, 1862, AHA.

66. Furgurson, 102.

67. Nolan, 33.

68. Ibid.

69. Leech, 141–42.

70. Adj. Gen. Lorenzo Thomas to Col. J. P. Taylor, Jan. 2, 1862, NARA RG 92, Office of the Quartermaster General.

3: "VAST ARMY OF THE WOUNDED"

1. Letitia Jones to Mary Custis Lee, undated, Mary Custis Lee Papers (1835–1917), Mss 1 L5144a-1334-1336, VHS.

2. Mary Custis Lee to Mrs. E. A. Stiles, March 8, 1862, AHA.

3. Edwin M. Stanton to Charles A. Dana, Feb. 2, 1862, in Benjamin P. Thomas and Harold M. Hyman, *Stanton: The Life and Times of Lincoln's Secretary of War* (New York: Alfred A. Knopf, 1962), 146.

4. Robert E. Lee to Mary Custis Lee, April 4, 1862 in *The Wartime Papers of R .E. Lee*, Clifford Dowdey and Louis H. Manarin, eds., (New York: Bramhall House, 1961), 142.

5. Emory M. Thomas, *Robert E. Lee* (New York: W. W. Norton & Company, 1997), 230.

6. Douglas Southall Freeman, *R. E. Lee: A Biography*, (New York: Charles Scribner & Sons, 1936), II: 594.

7. David W. Miller, *Second Only to Grant: Quartermaster General Montgomery C. Meigs* (Shippensburg, PA: White Mane Books, 2000), 139.

8. Shelby Foote, *The Civil War: A Narrative* (New York: Random House, 1958), I:418.

9. Miller, 137.

10. Maj. W. Roy Mason, C.S.A., "Origins of the Lee Tomatoes," in Robert Underwood Johnson and Clarence Buel, eds., *Battles and Leaders of the Civil War*, (1887–88; reprint: Secaucus, NJ: Castle, 1982), II: 277; Freeman, II: 252–55.

11. Thomas and Hyman, 217.

12. Freeman, II: 254.

13. Foote, I: 516.

14. Jari A. Villanueva, "24 Notes That Tap Deep Emotions," www.west-point.org/taps/ Taps.html; Richard A. Schneider, *Taps: Notes From a Nation's Heart* (New York: William Morrow, 2002), 8–15. Accounts differ regarding the artillery exchange that produced the first military funeral at which Taps was played. Most sources agree that the shots were fired from Battery A of the 2nd Union Artillery; others credit Battery B, 3rd Artillery.

15. Brig. Gen. Montgomery Meigs to Charles Meigs, July 8, 1862, MCM Papers, LOC.

16. Richard Wheeler, *Sword Over Richmond* (New York: Harper & Row, 1986), 344.

17. Brig. Gen. John W. Ames, U.S.V., "In Front of the Stone Wall at Fredericksburg," *Battles and Leaders*, III:123–24.

18. Thomas, 271.

19. Robert E. Lee to Mildred Lee, Dec. 25, 1862, *Wartime Papers*, 381.

20. Lt. Col. Richard B. Irwin, U.S.V., "The Administration in the Peninsular Campaign," *Battles and Leaders*, II:436.

21. Robert E. Lee to George W. Randolph, July 12, 1862, *Wartime Papers*, 231.

22. Ernest B. Furgurson, *Freedom Rising: Washington in the Civil War* (New York: Alfred A. Knopf, 2004), 191.

23. "Requests Relating to Missing Soldiers, 1863–76," NARA RG 92, Office of the Quartermaster General.

24. Furgurson, 190–92; Margaret Leech, *Reveille in Washington: 1860–65* (New York: Harper & Brothers, 1941), 204–16.

25. Walt Whitman, *Prose and Poetry* (New York: Library of America, 1982), 720–21.

26. Constance McLaughlin Green, *Washington: Village and Capital, 1800–1878* (Princeton: Princeton University Press, 1962), 261; Whitman, 737. "Every family has directly or indirectly some representative among this vast army of the wounded and sick," Whitman wrote in The *New York Times*, "Our Wounded and Sick Soldiers," Dec. 11, 1864.

27. Eastern Branch is known today as the Anacostia River. The Washington Canal, filled in long ago, now forms the northern edge of the national mall.

28. Walt Whitman to his mother, Louisa Van Velsor Whitman, June 7, 1864, in John Burroughs, *Whitman: A Study* (Boston and New York: Houghton Mifflin Co., 1904), X:43.

29. Leech, 207–8.

30. As the war progressed, military hospitals improved.

31. General Orders No. 75, War Department, Sept. 11, 1861, cited in "History and Development of the National Cemetery Administration," Department of Veterans Affairs, National Cemetery Administration, Feb. 4, 2006, 1.

32. Capt. James M. Moore to Brig. Gen. Montgomery C. Meigs, "Extract from annual report of Capt. J. M. Moore, assistant quartermaster, U.S. Army, for the year ending June 30, 1865," in The *War of the Rebellion: a compilation of the official sources of the Union and Confederate Archives* (Washington, D.C.: Government Printing Office, 1880), Series III, Vol. 4, 317–22.

33. Dog tags, more formally known as identification tags, did not come into widespread use until 1913, when the Army published its first regulations requiring them. All U.S. combat soldiers were wearing aluminum identity disks by 1917; the tags took on the familiar oblong shape—and the canine associations—by World War II.

34. Untitled notes in NARA RG 92, Office of the Quartermaster General.

35. Capt. Richard W. Wooley, "A Short History of Identification Tags," *Quartermaster Professional Bulletin*, Dec. 1988.

36. Furgurson, 192–93.

37. Whitman, 714. "The wounded men often come up broke," wrote Whitman, who gave patients gifts they could not otherwise afford—apples, writing paper, candy, tobacco, and sometimes small sums of money, "bright new ten-cent and five-cent bills . . . about the best thing I could do to raise their spirits, and show them that somebody cared for them." Whitman, 749–50.

38. Leech, 207.

39. Furgurson, 192–93.

40. R. B. Bonteene to Capt. J. M. Moore, Jan. 10, 1865, "Requests for Information Relating to Missing Soldiers," NARA RG 92, Office of the Quartermaster General.

41. Leech, 207; Montgomery C. Meigs to Edwin M. Stanton, June 16, 1864, NARA RG 92, Office of the Quartermaster General.

42. The first permanent cemeteries on foreign soil were established in 1850, for burial of U.S. soldiers from the Mexican War. Brig. Gen. Monro MacCloskey, *Hallowed Ground: Our National Cemeteries* (New York: Richards Rosen Press, 1968), 19–20.

43. Ibid.

44. "History and Development of the National Cemetery Administration," Department of Veterans Affairs, National Cemetery Administration, Feb. 4, 2006, 1–3.

45. "Cemeteries—Cypress Hills National Cemetery," U.S. Department of Veterans Affairs, June 30, 2006.

46. Furgurson, 189.

47. Furgurson, 189–90; Doris Kearns Goodwin, *Team of Rivals: The Political Genius of Abraham Lincoln* (New York: Simon & Schuster, 2005), 454–55; Leech, 302–3.

48. Green, 277.

49. Felix James, "The Establishment of Freedman's Village in Arlington, Virginia," *Negro History Bulletin*, 33, 4 (April 1970). Lincoln's 1863 order did not apply to slaves living in Maryland or other border states for political reasons; it was feared that such action might drive border states to join the rebellion. In addition, Lincoln's authority for the order arose from his claim of extraordinary wartime powers, which applied only to those states at war with the Union.

50. "Jubilee Among the Contrabands," The *Evening Star*, Washington, D.C., Jan. 1, 1863, Virginia Room, ACL.

51. Robert E. Lee to Mary Custis Lee, Dec. 21, 1862, *Wartime Papers*, 378–79.

52. Robert E. Lee, Deed of Manumission, Dec. 29, 1862, Robert E. Lee Papers, Museum of the Confederacy, Richmond, Virginia.

53. Robert E. Lee to Mary Custis Lee, Dec. 21, 1862, *Wartime Papers*, 378–79.

54. Casualty estimates from the Battle of Gettysburg have been closely examined and debated since Civil War days. It would appear that Lee underestimated his losses, gauging them at about 20,000; in the years since, historians have adjusted the figure upward, suggesting that Confederates lost as many as 28,000, with Union casualties at 22,000.

55. James, 5.

56. *The National Freedman*, March 1, 1865, 60; Green, 276–78.

57. James, 5.

58. Green, 278.

59. Lt. Col Elias M. Greene to Maj. Gen. S. P. Heintzelman, May 5, 1863, NARA RG 92, Office of the Quartermaster General.

60. Ibid.; Jennifer Hanna, *Arlington House: The Robert E. Lee Memorial* (Washington, D.C.: National Park Service, 2001), 80.

61. Maj. Leavitt Hunt, General Orders No. 28, May 22, 1863, NARA RG 92, RG 92, Quartermaster General's Office.

62. "General Plans No. 9 and No. 10 VA" for Freedman's Village, Department of War, Office of the Quartermaster General, AHA.

63. "Freedman's Village, Arlington, Virginia," *Harper's Weekly*, May 7, 1864.

64. Lt. Col. Elias M. Greene to Charles Thomas, Dec. 17, 1863, NARA RG 92, Office of the Quartermaster General.

65. Mary C. Ames, The *Independent* (Washington, D.C.), January 6, 1867.

66. Lt. Col. Elias M. Greene to Brig. Gen. Montgomery C. Meigs, July 22, 1862, NARA RG 92, Office of the Quartermaster General.

67. "Report to the Executive Committee of New England Yearly Meeting of Friends upon the Condition and Needs of the Freed People of Color in Washington and Virginia," Nov. 10, 1864; see also Roberta Schildt, "Freedman's Village: Arlington, Virginia, 1863–1900," *Northern Virginia Heritage*, Feb. 1985, 11–23, Virginia Room, ACL.

68. James, 6.

69. "Addresses and Ceremonies at the New Year's Festival to the Freedmen of Arlington Heights and Statistics and Statements of Educational Condition of the Colored People in the Southern States, and Other Facts," 1867, 16, Virginia Room, ACL.

70. Furgurson, 257.

71. Enoch A. Chase, "The Arlington Case," *Virginia Law Review* XV, 3 (Jan. 1929): 207–33.

72. The *National Republican*, Jan. 12, 1864.

73. Chase, 207–33.

74. Robert E. Lee to Mary Custis Lee, Feb. 6, 1864, *Wartime Papers*.

75. Robert E. Lee to Mary Custis Lee, Jan. 24, 1864, *Wartime Papers*.

76. Robert E. Lee to Jefferson Davis, March 30, 1864, *Wartime Papers*.

77. Maj. Gen. Alexander S. Webb, "Through the Wilderness," *Battles and Leaders*, IV:152–69.

78. Foote, III: 268, 316. As the Forty Days' Campaign was starting, Gen. George Meade is supposed to have expressed apprehension about the coming fight. According to John Hay, President Lincoln's secretary, Meade worried that the Confederates would "make a Kilkenny cat fight of the affair." In Hay's account, General Grant told Meade: "Our cat has the longer tail." John Hay, *The Complete Civil War Diaries* (Carbondale: University of Illinois Press, 2006), 143.

79. Leech, 322–23.

80. Capt. James M. Moore, "List of papers Accompanying the Report of the Quartermaster General, 1864," *O.R.*, Series III, Vol. 4, 874–904.

4: FIRST BURIALS

1. H. J. Conner to Frederick L. Fishback, June 23, 1923, for Robert R. Dye, Superintendent, Arlington National Cemetery, with selected reports from *Medical and Surgical History of the War of the Rebellion*, Part III, Vol. I, AHA.

2. Enoch A. Chase, The *Sunday Star*, (Washington, D.C.), Nov. 4, 1928, 5.

3. Capt. James M. Moore, Extract No. 3, in annual report of the operations of the Quartermaster General's Department, Brig. Gen. Montgomery C. Meigs to Edwin M. Stanton, Nov. 3, 1864, *The War of the Rebellion: a Compilation of the Official Sources of Union and Confederate Armies* (Washington: Government Printing Office, 1900), Series III, Vol. 4, 874–905.

4. Conner.

5. Conner.

6. Brig. Gen. Montgomery C. Meigs to Edwin M. Stanton, April 11, 1873, NARA RG 92, Office of the Quartermaster General.

7. George W. Dodge, "The Rose Garden at Arlington House," The *Arlington Historical Magazine*, Arlington Historical Society, Oct. 1990, 20–21.

8. Dodge, 20–29.

9. Capt. James M. Moore to Brig. Gen. D.H. Rucker, Dec. 11, 1865, NARA RG 92, Office of the Quartermaster General; MCM Papers, LOC.

10. Dodge, 20–29.

11. Brig. Gen. Montgomery C. Meigs, Diary, June 9, June 10, 1864, MCM Papers, LOC.

12. J. Howard Avil, "United States National Military Cemetery, Arlington, Virginia," 1903. Other versions of Avil's account were repeated in subsequent publications, including the *Sunday Star*, May 27, 1923, and the book *Washington, City and Capital*, from the WPA American Guide Series, 1937. These accounts, and others based on them, erroneously record Confederate Pvt. Levi Reinhardt as Arlington's first military burial.

13. Roberta Schildt, "Freedman's Village: Arlington, Virginia, 1863–1900," *Northern Virginia Heritage*, Feb. 1985, 17; "First Interment in Arlington National Cemetery," copy of memorandum, Quartermaster General's File CMGME-C 687, June 16, 1959, AHA

14. Meigs makes no note of visiting Arlington with President Lincoln, nor does the quartermaster credit him as coauthor of the idea for a national cemetery—both of which Meigs would have been likely to mention in his wartime journal or his voluminous correspondence. Lincoln first enters the Arlington story after Meigs's death, when the general's granddaughter recalls a conversation between the two men. Lincoln supposedly asked Meigs about Arlington's fate, and Meigs is said to have replied: "The ancients filled their enemies fields with salt and made them useless forever but we are a Christian nation, why not make it a field of honor?" (MCM Papers, LOC).

15. Brig. Gen. Montgomery C. Meigs to Edwin M. Stanton, June 15, 1864, NARA RG 92, Office of the Quartermaster General.

16. Edwin M. Stanton, June 15, 1864, NARA RG 92, Office of the Quartermaster General.

17. "A Great National Cemetery," The *Washington Morning Chronicle*, June 17, 1864.

18. Brig. Gen. Montgomery C. Meigs to Brig Gen. D. H. Rucker, June 15, 1864, NARA RG 92, Office of the Quartermaster General.

19. Brig. Gen. Montgomery C. Meigs to Edwin M. Stanton, April 12, 1874, NARA RG 92, Office of the Quartermaster General. Meigs, a naturally industrious man, kept a furious pace throughout the war, providing his army not only with burial services but also with horses, shoes, food, overcoats, ammunition, and warships. He accomplished this with admirable efficiency and little evidence of waste or corruption. A man in a hurry, Meigs dashed off his orders with few pauses for punctuation, a style I have retained when quoting his correspondence.

20. Brig. Gen. Montgomery C. Meigs to Edwin M. Stanton, June 16, 1864; Brig. Gen. D. H. Rucker to Brig. Gen. Montgomery C. Meigs, July 8, 1864, NARA RG 92, Office of the Quartermaster General.

21. Brig. Gen. Montgomery C. Meigs to Edwin M. Stanton, June 16, 1864, NARA RG 92, Office of the Quartermaster General.

22. Ibid.

23. Brig. Gen. D. H. Rucker to Brig. Gen. Montgomery C. Meigs, July 8, 1864, NARA RG 92, Office of the Quartermaster General.

24. Dodge, "The Rose Garden at Arlington House," *Arlington Historical Magazine*, Arlington Historical Society, Oct. 1991, 57–59.

25. Ibid.

26. At least two other enlisted men found their way into Mrs. Lee's garden, but their presence can be explained. Pvt. Monroe Bradley of the 187th New York Infantry, buried in the garden on Dec. 5, 1864, was put there by accident—someone had mistaken him for a lieutenant; when the error was discovered, he was allowed to stay. Pvt. Adolph Ahrens, killed in the Battle of Second Manassas on Aug. 29, 1862, was buried near the battlefield and later exhumed to rest by his brother, Lt. Louis Ahrens, 4th New York Cavalry, buried in the garden in April 1866, after the war. Dodge, Oct. 1990, 44; Oct. 1991, 54.

27. Dodge, Oct. 1990, 20–50.

28. Capt. James M. Moore, in O.R., Nov. 3, 1864, 902–5.

29. MCM Papers, Oct. 3, 7, 11, 1865, LOC; David W. Miller, *Second Only to Grant: Quartermaster General Montgomery C. Meigs* (Shippensburg, Pa.: White Mane Books, 2000), 95, 241–42.

30. Douglas Southall Freeman, *R. E. Lee, A Biography*, (New York: Charles Scribner's Sons, 1936), IV:155–64; Emory M. Thomas, *Robert E. Lee: A Biography* (New York: W. W. Norton & Company, 1995) 368–69.

31. Allen Johnson and Dumas Malone, eds., *Dictionary of American Biography* (New York: Charles Scribner's Sons, 1930) 5:130.

32. Jefferson Davis was never brought to trial. After two years in jail, he was released in May 1867 on bond. He lived another twenty two-years, dying at age eighty-two. He never asked for a pardon. Johnson and Malone, eds., *Dictionary of American Biography*, 5:130.

33. Freeman, IV: 202–03.

34. MCM Papers, April 11, 1865, LOC; Miller, 253.

35. Wesley Norris's account of the whipping, published by the *National Anti-Slavery Standard* on April 14, 1866 (AHA), came seven years after the event, but it gives details of his

escape from Arlington with a sister, Mary Norris, and an unnamed cousin, in 1859. He recounted that Lee hired an Alexandria County constable named Dick Williams to capture all thee runaways and return them to Arlington, which is confirmed by Alexandria County records. What cannot be independently verified is that Lee ordered Norris and his cousin to be whipped and brine poured into their wounds as Lee watched. Before the war, when the original charge appeared in the anti-slavery *New York Tribune*, Lee told one of his sons that he would not dignify the report with a response; after the war, when Wesley Norris's firsthand account was published, Lee indignantly denied that he had ever mistreated slaves or soldiers, but did not say whether he considered whipping runaway slaves to be mistreatment. In her excellent biography of Lee, *Reading the Man* (New York: Viking, 2007) Elizabeth Brown Pryor makes a strong argument, though not a conclusive one, that Norris's charges were credible. "Wesley Norris gave his interview after he was freed, when he had nothing to hide, gain or fear," she writes. But there was one motive for Norris's testimony—retribution against his former owner, at a time when Lee was recently defeated and legally vulnerable. What can be verified is that Lee punished Norris by hiring him out to a plantation farther from freedom in Hanover County; that Norris escaped to the North in January 1863; that he worked for Union troops during the war; and that he returned to Arlington after the war, where he worked as a laborer in the new national cemetery.

36. Robert E. Lee to Gov. John Letcher of Virginia, undated, in *Recollections and Letters of General Robert E. Lee*, ed., Robert E. Lee Jr. (McLean, VA: IndyPublish.com, 2002), 112.

37. Lee was covered by President Johnson's general amnesty declaration of December 25, 1868, which allowed treason charges against Lee and other Confederates to be dropped on Feb. 15, 1869; Thomas, 370–71; Freeman, IV, 203–07.

38. Cynthia Gorney, The *Washington Post*, Aug. 6, 1975.

39. Cornelia Jones to Mary Custis Lee, May 15, 1865, Mary Custis Lee Papers, VHS.

40. Mary Custis Lee to Philip Fendall, undated, in Elizabeth Brown Pryor, *Reading the Man: A Portrait of Robert E. Lee Through His Private Letters* (New York: Viking, 2007), 445–46.

41. Philip Bigler, *In Honored Glory, Arlington National Cemetery: The Final Post* (St. Petersburg, FL: Vandamere Press, 1999), 29.

42. Mary Custis Lee to Emily Mason, April 20, 1866, K. M. Rowland Letters & Autographs, Museum of the Confederacy, Richmond, VA.

43. Robert E. Lee to J. S. Black, Jan. 13, 1869, D-E Collection, LOC.

44. Robert E. Lee to Smith Lee, Jan. 4, 1866, Robert Carter Lee Papers, VHS.

45. Thomas, 374–75.

46. Lee, *Recollections*, 140.

47. Mary Custis Lee to Florence Marshall, June 27, 1868, AHA.

48. Pryor, *Reading the Man*, 445–46.

49. Mary Custis Lee (daughter) to Mary Anna Custis Lee (Mrs. Lee), Dec. 9, 1865, Mary Custis Lee Papers, VHS.

50. Robert E. Lee to Smith Lee, Jan. 4, 1866, Robert Carter Lee Papers, VHS. Smith Lee's letter has not been found, but it is clear from Robert E. Lee's letter, and from Mary Custis Lee's letter of Dec. 9, 1865, that Smith had provided new details about Arlington.

Robert E. Lee joked about the clandestine nature of his brother's mission: "Your former letter enclosing an account of your visit to Arlington, would have been before acknowledged but I understand you had no P.O. nearer than 'Alias.'"

51. Capt. James M. Moore to Brig. Gen. D. H. Rucker, Dec. 11, 1865, NARA RG 92, Office of the Quartermaster General.

52. Moore to Rucker, Dec. 11, 1865, NARA RG 92, Office of the Quartermaster General.

53. *Frank Leslie's Illustrated Newspaper*, July 17, 1865.

54. Meigs placed the number of officers in the garden at forty-five—not the sixty reported by the *Philadelphia Press*. Brig. Gen. Montgomery C. Meigs to Edwin M. Stanton, June 10, 1867, NARA RG 92, Office of the Quartermaster General.

55. The *Philadelphia Press*, Dec. 28, 1865 in NARA RG 92, Office of the Quartermaster General.

56. Brig. Gen. Montgomery C. Meigs to Edwin M. Stanton, Feb. 23, 1866, NARA RG 92, Office of the Quartermaster General.

57. Capt. John R. Meyers to Col. M. J. Ludington, March 23, 1866, NARA RG 92, Office of the Quartermaster General.

58. Mark C. Mollan, "Honoring Our War Dead: The Evolution of the Government Policy on Headstones for Fallen Soldiers and Sailors," *Prologue*, 35, 1 (Spring 2003). As soon as the war ended, Meigs issued an order on July 3, 1865, for Army and Navy officers to provide him a list of all servicemen buried during the war. The directive was largely ignored in the rush of demobilization and shrinking of troop strength. Meigs reissued it in February 1866.

59. Mollan.

60. Confederates made a similar effort to find and rebury their war dead, but lacking funds, soldiers, and government authority, their reinterment programs were organized by volunteer groups—and were far less effective than the Union endeavor.

61. "History and Development of the National Cemetery Administration," Department of Veterans' Affairs, National Cemetery Administration, Feb. 4, 2006, 3.

62. Drew Gilpin Faust, *This Republic of Suffering: Death and the American Civil War* (New York: Alfred A. Knopf, 2008), 236.

63. *Annual Reports of the Quartermaster General for the Year 1870* (Washington, D.C.: Government Printing Office, 1870), 68; Edward Steere, "Genesis of American Graves Registration, 1861–1865," *Military Affairs*, 12, 3 (Autumn 1948): 149–61.

64. Faust, 211.

65. Brig. Gen. Montgomery C. Meigs to William W. Belknap, Aug. 5, 1871, NARA RG 92, Office of the Quartermaster General.

66. Mollan.

67. Faust, 256. Faust writes that after 1903, the Compiled Military Service Records were expanded to include Confederate as well as Union casualties, eventually reaching 30 million entries for Union veterans, 6 million for Confederates.

68. "A Sad Day at Arlington: Funerals for the Victims of the Disaster of Friday," June 11, 1893, newspaper unidentified, www.arlingtoncemetery.net/victims-of-ford's-theater-disaster-1893.htm.

69. Col. M. I. Ludington to Brig. Gen. Montgomery C. Meigs, Sept. 21, 1866, NARA RG 92, Office of the Quartermaster General.

70. The *National Intelligencer*, in Bigler, *Honored Glory*, 30.

71. Brig. Gen. Montgomery C. Meigs to Edwin M. Stanton, Oct. 13, 1866, NARA RG 92, Office of the Quartermaster General.

72. The original sarcophagus was later replaced by a plainer one, without guns or round shot, but with the inscription retained.

73. Miller, 63–67, 273–77, 287. Work on the Capitol dome continued in fits and starts through the war until Dec. 3, 1863, when Freedom was finally hoisted into place, to the accompaniment of cannon salutes from every fort in Washington. Constance McLaughlin Green, *Washington: Village and Capital, 1800–1878* (Princeton: Princeton University Press, 1962), 268.

74. Pryor, 314.

75. David C. Sloane, *The Last Great Necessity: Cemeteries in American History* (Baltimore: Johns Hopkins University Press, 1991), cited in *Arlington National Cemetery: Master Plan, 1998*, U.S. Army Corps of Engineers, Baltimore District, 36.

76. George W. Dodge, *Arlington National Cemetery* (Charleston, S.C.: Arcadia Publishing, 2006), 49; see also James Edward Peters, *Arlington National Cemetery: Shrine to America's Heroes* (Bethesda, MD: Woodbine House, 2000); Philip Bigler, *In Honored Glory*.

77. Brig. Gen. Montgomery C. Meigs, memorandum, April 22, 1877; Meigs to Capt. A. F. Rockwell, Oct. 3, 1874; Meigs, memorandum and sketch, "Menu for Arlington Rostrum," May 17, 1881; Meigs, undated memorandum, all NARA RG 92, Office of the Quartermaster General.

78. Brig. Gen. Montgomery C. Meigs to Gen. R. N. Batchelder, Sept. 11, 1885, NARA RG 92, Office of the Quartermaster General.

5: A QUESTION OF OWNERSHIP

1. Douglas Southall Freeman, *R. E. Lee: A Biography* (New York: Charles Scribner's Sons, 1936), IV: 256–57.

2. "Reconstruction Evidence," The *New York Times*, Mar. 28, 1866, 1; Freeman, IV: 256–57. Lee's reservations about black suffrage were soon made obsolete by ratification of the Fifteenth Amendment, which guaranteed African Americans the right to vote. The amendment was ratified March 30, 1870, a few months before Lee's death. Virginia was the eighteenth of the twenty nine states to accept it.

3. "Gen. Lee's Testimony," *Chicago Tribune*, Mar. 30, 1866, 2.

4. Freeman, IV: 257.

5. Although Lee avoided a return visit to Arlington, this did not keep one creative *New York Tribune* reporter from imagining that the general had been spotted there in the dusk, "a lonely figure standing at the foot of a tree . . . It was Robert E. Lee standing in the street that passes through the middle of his old estate." Reprinted in *The National Intelligencer*, Feb. 22, 1866.

6. Under the terms of her father's will, Mrs. Lee retained a life interest in the Arlington Estate, which then passed to her son G. W. C. Lee upon her death.

7. Lee, *Recollections*, 291–92. Gen. Lee does not refer specifically to Arlington in his account of the July 1870 meeting with Francis L. Smith, but a son reports that this was the object of their conference and the reason for Gen. Lee's pessimistic assessment in his letter of July 15, 1870. About the same time, Gen. Lee makes oblique reference to his Arlington deliberations in a letter to his eldest son, G. W. C. Lee. "I will tell you what I have been able to accomplish in reference to ... Arlington when we meet," he wrote on July 22, 1870. "It is not much but would take me too long to write." Robert E. Lee to G. W. C. Lee, Robert E. Lee Papers, Duke University.

8. Lee's old heart condition, probably complicated by arteriosclerosis, killed him. Contrary to his wartime predictions, Lee did not die as a pauper. He owned no real estate, but his other assets were worth $88,000, a substantial sum in those days. Freeman IV: 394.

9. When Union and Confederate forces clashed at the Battle of First Manassas, John Logan was one of the few congressmen who grabbed a musket and rushed to support Federal troops. He subsequently raised a volunteer regiment from Illinois, was twice wounded in the war, and served with distinction until removed from command near the end of hostilities. Allen Johnson and Dumas Malone, eds., *Dictionary of American Biography* (New York: Charles Scribner's Sons, 1930), 11: 363–64.

10. John A. Logan, commander in chief, Grand Army of the Republic, General Orders No. 11, May 5, 1868, in "Memorial Ceremonies at the National Cemetery, Arlington Virginia," May 30, 1868, (Washington, D.C.: McGill & Witherow, 1868), 5–6.

11. The Rev. C. B. Boynton, prayer and benediction, in "Memorial Ceremonies," 19–20.

12. Ibid, 8–12, 18–19.

13. Ibid, 8–12.

14. Ibid, 8–12.

15. Ibid. While General John Logan's May 5, 1868, designation of Decoration Day is generally considered to be the first national memorial event, David W. Bright, in *Race and Reunion* (Cambridge, MA: The Belknap Press, 2001), 65–70, suggests that Decoration Day had its origins in Charleston, SC. There, on May 1, 1865, some 10,000 citizens, most of them former slaves, marched through the war-battered city and spread flowers on the graves of 257 Union soldiers buried at the site of a Confederate prison camp. Like other Rebel camps, this one was infamous for inhumane conditions—most Union deaths there were caused by exposure, neglect, or disease.

16. Michelle A. Krowl, "In the Spirit of Fraternity: The United States Government and the Burial of Confederate Dead at Arlington National Cemetery, 1864–1914," *The Virginia Magazine of History and Biography* 111, 2 (2003): 151–186; see also Frederick Kaufman to E. D. Townsend, May 3, 1872, NARA RG 92, Office of the Quartermaster General; Frederick Kaufman, "Report to Quartermaster General," January 1884, NARA RG 92, Office of the Quartermaster General; "Dead of the Old North State," The *Washington Post*, Oct. 4, 1883; "The North Carolina Dead," The *Washington Post*, Oct. 15, 1883, 1; "Laid in Their Native Earth," The *Washington Post*, Oct. 18, 1883, 2; "The Arlington Dead," Historic Oakwood Cemetery, Raleigh, http://www.historicoakwoodcemetery.com/stories_arlington.asp.

17. Edward Steere, "Shrines of the Honored Dead: A Study of the National Cemetery System," *Quartermaster Review*, 1953–1954, 19; Monro MacCloskey, *Hallowed Ground: Our*

National Cemeteries (New York: Richard Rosen Press, Inc. 1968), 39–41; Erna Risch, *Quartermaster Support of the Army: 1775–1939* (Washington D.C.: Center of Military History, 1989), 466–67.

18. Risch, 466–67.

19. J. A. Kimmer to Capt. James Moore, Feb. 6, 1866, NARA RG 92, Office of the Quartermaster General.

20. Brig. Gen. Montgomery C. Meigs to William W. Belknap, Aug. 2, 1871, NARA RG 92, Office of the Quartermaster General.

21. Ibid; An influential veterans' group, the Grand Army of the Republic, renewed the request to integrate U.S. Colored Troops with white burials around the mansion in 1873. Meigs recommended against it and the proposal was rejected for the second time. G. E. Corson, secretary, executive committee, Grand Army of the Republic, to Quartermaster General, April 9, 1873, NARA RG 92, Office of the Quartermaster General.

22. In recent times, the graves of a few U.S. Colored Troops have been sprinkled around the cemetery proper, just to the west of the Lee mansion, but most remain in the Lower Cemetery, where they were initially buried.

23. Nelligan, 429.

24. *Congressional Globe*, Dec. 12, 1870, 41st Congress, 3rd Session, 53. One can imagine that, had he been alive, Robert E. Lee might have deflected his wife's foray into the highly charged political atmosphere of the day.

25. *Congressional Globe*, Dec. 13, 1870, 41st Congress, 3rd Session, 73–74.

26. Ibid, 77.

27. During the war, Sumner had made it clear in Senate debates that he believed secessionist states had relinquished all constitutional rights.

28. *Congressional Globe*, Dec. 13, 1870, 41st Congress, 3rd Session, 79.

29. Ibid., 77–78.

30. Ibid., 73–82.

31. Capt. James A. Moore to Brig. Gen. D. H. Rucker, April 28, 1865, NARA RG 92, Office of the Quartermaster General.

32. Jennifer Hanna, *Arlington House: The Robert E. Lee Memorial, Cultural Landscape Report* (Washington D.C.: U.S. National Park Service, 2001), 91–92.

33. Report from the Quartermaster General's Office, May 16, 1881, NARA RG 92, Office of the Quartermaster General.

34. "History of Government Furnished Headstones and Markers," U.S. Department of Veterans Affairs, April 12, 2008, http://www.cem.gov/cem/hist/hmhist.asp; Mark C. Mollan, "Honoring Our War Dead: The Evolution of the Government Policy on Headstones for Fallen Soldiers and Sailors," *Prologue*, 35, 1 (Spring 2003); Steere, 16–17; MacCloskey, 37–39; Risch, 467.

35. Ibid.

36. Steere, 17.

37. Ibid. The system of national cemeteries, numbering fourteen when the network was created in 1862, greatly expanded in the postwar years. By 1870, some 300,000 soldiers, sailors, and marines were buried in national cemeteries.

38. James Gall Jr. to Col. A. L. Rockwell, Oct. 5, 1877, NARA RG 92, Office of the Quartermaster General.

39. Roberta Schildt, "Freedman's Village: Arlington, Virginia, 1863–1900," *Northern Virginia Heritage*, Feb. 1985, 10.

40. Enoch A. Chase, The *Sunday Star* (Washington, D.C.), Nov. 4, 1928.

41. "Annual Report of the Secretary of War," 1866, Virginia Room, ACL

42. William Syphax to President Andrew Johnson, NARA, General Records of the Department of Justice, Papers of the Attorney General, in AHA.

43. "Washington Custis Head of 16 Syphax Families," *Washington Afro-American*, April 22, 1939, Virginia Room, ACL.

44. *Frank Leslie's Illustrated Newspaper*, Nov. 18, 1865, AHA.

45. Hariette C. Gillem Robinet, "Interview with Martha Gray Gillem," 1963, AHA.

46. Elizabeth Brown Pryor, *Reading the Man* (New York: Viking, 2007), 448; Thomas 383.

47. Ibid.

48. Ibid.

49. One account of Mrs. Lee's last visit to Arlington ends with Selina Gray bringing her a drink of water from the Arlington spring—most probably an apocryphal story, in the view of Karen Byrne Kinzey, former historian for the Robert E. Lee Memorial, National Park Service. "It makes a nice story, but there is no evidence for it," says Mrs. Kinzey.

50. "Mrs. Mary Lee Revisits Her Old Home," *Alexandria Sentinel*, reprinted June 8, 1874, in The *New York Times*, AHA.

51. Mary Custis Lee, June 5, 1873, to an unknown correspondent, in Nelligan, 429.

52. Freeman, I:178.

53. Bernice-Marie Yates, The *Perfect Gentleman: The Life and Letters of George Washington Custis Lee*, (Longwood, FL: Xulon Press, 2003) I: 245.

54. Washington College was renamed after Lee's death.

55. While Custis was at West Point, several months before his father was appointed superintendent, a case of liquor was found in his room—a violation of the rules, which might have resulted in his expulsion. Custis swore that the alcohol had been brought to his quarters without his knowledge; he was given eight demerits and survived the incident. Emory M. Thomas, *Robert E. Lee: A Biography* (New York: W. W. Norton & Co., 1995) 150–52. Before and after this occasion, Custis's father lectured him on the importance of temperance. About the same time, Custis revealed to his father that he suffered from dark moods and "melancholy." The older man encouraged his son to "shake off those gloomy feelings. Drive them away. Fix your mind & pleasure upon what is before you . . . All is bright if you will think it so." Robert E. Lee to G. W. C. Lee, March 28, 1852, Robert Edward Lee Papers, VHS.

56. "Memorial of G.W. Custis Lee, of Virginia," April 6, 1874, Miscellaneous Senate Document No. 96, 43rd Congress, 1st Session.

57. Ibid.

58. Ibid.

59. Brig. Gen. Montgomery C. Meigs to Secretary of War, Jan. 8, 1875, NARA RG 92, Office of the Quartermaster General.

60. Brig. Gen Montgomery C. Meigs to Secretary of War, June 10, 1876, NARA RG 92, Office of the Quartermaster General.

61. G. W. C. Lee to Capt. J. J. White May 4, 1876, in Yates, II:120.

62. William W. Belknap to Sen. John J. Patterson, May 25, 1874, NARA RG 92, Office of the Quartermaster General.

63. Maj. Oscar A. Mack to Mrs. C. P. Culver, Jan. 18, 1875, reprinted in The New York Times, Jan. 29, 1875.

64. Johnson and Malone, eds., Dictionary of American Biography, 8:446–51.

65. Charles R. Williams, Diary and Letters of Rutherford B. Hayes, III:24, in AHA.

66. Enoch A. Chase, "The Arlington Case," Virginia Law Review, XV, 3 (January 1929): 207–33. While President Rutherford Hayes sympathized with the Lees, he had the good sense to let the Arlington case proceed through the judicial system without White House interference. Robert Hughes, a native Virginian and originally a Buchanan Democrat favoring states' rights, detested Confederate president Jefferson Davis and, as a prominent newspaper editor in Richmond, suggested that Virginia consider negotiating a separate peace. After the war, he became editor of the Republic, the first postwar Republican newspaper in Virginia, attended the Democratic National Convention of 1868, and ran as a Republican for Congress and governor—unsuccessfully—before President Grant appointed him as a federal judge in 1874.

67. Chase, 215.

68. Ibid., 217.

69. Ibid, 219–20.

70. United States v. Lee, 106 U.S. 196 (1882).

71. Chase, 218–19.

72. Ibid., 200.

73. Ibid., 219.

74. Prior to the sale of Arlington in 1883, the Secretary of War asked Gen. William T. Sherman, then in charge of the U.S. Army, about the military value of the estate. Sherman replied with characteristic bluntness: "Respectfully submitted to the Hon. Sec. of War with expression of my judgment that the Arlington Estate is not of the least military value to the U.S." William T. Sherman to Robert Todd Lincoln, Jan.12, 1883, NARA RG 92, Office of the Quartermaster General.

75. One begins to suspect a curse on the Lee family. With the ownership question resolved after twenty years, Custis Lee transferred Arlington's title to the federal government in 1883, paying a required $150 tax to Alexandria County—a sum promptly embezzled by the clerk of the Alexandria County Court and not discovered until three years later. The clerk was sent to jail. Memorandum, George A. Mushbach, attorney for Alexandria Board of Supervisors, to Lt. Col. R. N. Batchelder, April 26, 1883, NARA RG 92, Office of the Quartermaster General.

76. Chase, 232–33.

77. The estimates of the population of Freedman's Village vary considerably, from a high of 1,500 to some 100 in the initial colony. The only official figures come from the quartermaster's census in 1888, when 173 families were counted in a population of 763.

78. G. A. Wheeler to Gen. C. H. Howard, undated, but likely c. 1867, in Roberta Schildt, "Freedman's Village: Arlington, Virginia, 1863–1900," *Arlington Historical Magazine* VII, 4 (1984): 51.

79. J. S. Roberts to Lt. Col. William Bube, Jr., Jan. 8, 1867, in Schildt, 49.

80. Lt. Col. A. C. Card, deputy quartermaster, report to Quartermaster General, March 27, 1888, AHA.

81. The *Washington Post*, Dec. 7, 1887.

82. John B. Ellis, *Sights and Secrets of the National Capital* (New York: United States Publishing Company, 1869), 499–500.

83. Edgar S. Horner, principal clerk, Quartermaster General's office, to Col. Charles G. Mortimer, superintendent of Arlington National Cemetery, undated but at least 1895, AHA. Mortimer described payments to laborers Cornelius Syphax, who worked at the cemetery from 1870 through 1895, and to his brother Ennis Syphax, who worked from 1872 through 1891. Cornelius received as little as $1 per day and as much as $1.75; Ennis was paid $1 per day.

84. In July 1872, Secretary of War William W. Belknap declared all of Arlington, including the cemetery, Freedman's Village, and Fort Whipple (later Fort Myer) a national military reserve. This might have been an attempt to forestall Mrs. Lee's recovery of Arlington—then controversial and much in the news. Although Belknap's action failed to discourage the Lee family, it provided a pretext for evicting freedmen from the military reservation fifteen years later.

85. William Syphax to Sen. Algernon S. Paddock, Aug. 15, 1888, AHA.

86. Anonymous letter to the Hon. John A. Rollam, May 10, 1869, NARA RG 92, Office of the Quartermaster General.

87. Ibid.

88. Brig. Gen. J. C. McFerran, report to Quartermaster General, May 11, 1869, NARA RG 92, Office of the Quartermaster General.

89. J. A. Commerford to Lt. Col. George B. Dandy, deputy quartermaster, Nov. 12, 1887, NARA RG 92, Office of the Quartermaster General.

90. Brig. Gen. Samuel B. Holabird to William C. Endicott, Nov. 17, 1887, NARA RG 92, Office of the Quartermaster General.

91. Ibid.; see also *Alexandria Gazette*, Dec. 6, 1887; The *New York Herald*, Dec. 8, 1887; The *Washington Post*, Dec. 7, 1887.

92. The *Washington Post*, "The Eviction of the Squatters From Freedman's Village," Dec. 7, 1887.

93. The *New York Herald*, Dec. 8, 1887.

94. *Alexandria Gazette*, Dec. 6, 1887.

95. John B. Syphax, born a free man, was the son of Maria and Charles Syphax of Arlington. According to family tradition, Maria was the daughter of George Washington Parke Custis.

96. John B. Syphax to William C. Endicott, Jan. 18, 1888, NARA RG 92, Office of the Quartermaster General.

97. Brig. Gen. Samuel B. Holabird to Lt. Col. A. C. Card, Dec. 23, 1887, NARA RG 92, Office of the Quartermaster General.

98. Lt. Col. A. C. Card to Brig Gen. Samuel B. Holabird, March 27, 1888, with "Valuation of Property in Freedman's Village, 1888," NARA RG 92, Office of the Quartermaster General. The "contraband tax" was long an annoyance for freedmen at Arlington, where each was assigned a job, paid $10 per month, and assessed $5 per month to help former slaves unable to work. The tax was suspended in 1868 when the Freedmen's Bureau was dissolved.

99. Brig. Gen. Montgomery C. Meigs to F. T. Hodgdon, Feb. 18, 1881, in Risch, 490.

100. Brig. Gen. Montgomery C. Meigs to William W. Belknap, Aug. 5, 1871, NARA RG 92, Office of the Quartermaster General.

101. David W. Miller, *Second Only to Grant: Quartermaster General Montgomery C. Meigs* (Shippensburg, PA: White Mane Books, 2000), 272.

102. Ibid., 272–90.

103. The *Boston Daily Globe*, Jan. 3, 1892.

104. "Former Custis Slave to Sleep in Death in Arlington Estate," The *Evening Star* (Washington, D.C.) Aug. 22, 1929.

105. The *New York Times*, Jan. 3, 1892; The *Washington Post*, Jan. 4 and 5, 1892; Miller, 261–90; Pryor, 314–15.

106. Stanley P. Hirshson, *The White Tecumseh: A Biography of William T. Sherman* (New York: John Wiley & Sons, Inc., 1997), 388.

107. "It took a war to heal the scars of war; attack upon a foreign power to bring unity at home," wrote Edmund Morris in *The Rise of Theodore Roosevelt* (New York: Modern Library, 2001), 654.

6: "A SPLENDID LITTLE WAR"

1. Barbara Tuchman, *The Proud Tower: A Pportrait of the World Before the War, 1890–1914* (New York: The Macmillan Company, 1966), 55–56.

2. Margaret Leech, *In the Days of McKinley* (New York: Harper & Brothers, 1959), 168.

3. Ibid.,168. Roosevelt, disgusted by McKinley's dithering, famously declared that the president had "no more backbone than a chocolate éclair." Leech, 169.

4. Morris, 631–33; Leech, 168–69; A. C. M. Azoy, *Charge! The Story of The Battle of San Juan Hill* (New York: Longmans, Green and Co., 1961), 24–25.

5. Allen Johnson and Dumas Malone, eds., *Dictionary of American Biography*, (New York: Charles Scribner's Sons, 1930) 20: 50–52. Sherman, an admirer of Wheeler's fighting abilities, is reported to have said after the Civil War that Wheeler should be given a command in any future conflict. The *New York Times*, April 27, 1898.

6. Tennant S. McWilliams, "New Southerner Abroad: General Joe Wheeler Views the Pacific and Beyond," *Pacific Historical Review* 47, 1 (Feb.1978): 123–27.

7. Sam Hanna Acheson, *Joe Bailey, The Last Democrat* (Manchester, NH: Ayer Publishing, 1970), 91.

8. Leech, 228–29; Johnson and Malone, eds., *Dictionary of American Biography* 20: 51.

9. More than a century after the *Maine*'s sinking the cause of the ship's explosion remains uncertain. An official investigation by the late Adm. Hyman Rickover reported in 1976 that spontaneous combustion in the vessel's coal bunker probably set off an adjoining magazine; a later study, commissioned by *National Geographic* magazine, relied upon before and after

computer models in its study of the *Maine*, but the journal's report, in February 1998, did little to solve the mystery, concluding that it was possible—but not provable—that the explosion was sparked by an external source. Not enough evidence has appeared since to draw a definitive answer in either direction.

10. Leech, 228–40; Morris, 626–44; Joseph Wheeler, *The Santiago Campaign*, 1898 (Boston: Lamson, Wolffe and Company, 1898), 3–4.

11. Like other distinguished cavalry officers—among them J. E. B. Stuart, Philip Sheridan, and Fitzhugh Lee—Joe Wheeler was a West Point cadet when Robert E. Lee was superintendent there. Graduating in 1859, Wheeler was brevetted as a second lieutenant, served the Army for two years, and resigned his commission in 1861 when the Civil War began.

12. Wheeler, 4.

13. Leech, 162–93.

14. The *Indianapolis News*, June 28, 1898.

15. The *New York Tribune*, "Old Glory's Leaders," quoted in The *Atlanta Constitution*, May 7, 1898, with similar stories praising the appointment of Wheeler and Fitz Lee from The *Philadelphia Times*, The *Brooklyn Citizen*, The *Newark Advertiser*, and The *Philadelphia Inquirer*; see also The *New York Times*, April 27, 1898.

16. Wheeler, 13–38; Morris, 665–75; Azoy, 82–95.

17. Azoy, 95. Wheeler's war cry has been rendered several ways. The *Washington Post*, quoting him seven years after the event, has Wheeler saying: "Give the Yanks hell, boys! There they go!" The *New York Times*: "Give it to 'em boys! The Yankees are on the run!" Either way, the sentiment is the same.

18. Morris, 668.

19. Azoy, 139.

20. Despite the gallantry of African American troops in the Civil War, the Indian Wars, and the Spanish-American War, the armed forces remained determinedly segregated through World War II, reflecting the status of race relations in many parts of the United States.

21. John Hay to Theodore Roosevelt, July 27, 1898, *Bartlett's Familiar Quotations*, 16th ed. (Boston: Little, Brown and Company, 1992), 536.

22. Ernest R. May, *Imperial Democracy: The Emergence of America as a Great Power* (Chicago: Imprint Publications, 1991), 242–43.

23. Erna Risch, *Quartermaster Support of the Army: 1775–1939* (Washington, D.C.: Center of Military History, 1989), 465–67.

24. Monro MacCloskey, *Hallowed Ground: Our National Cemeteries* (New York: Richards Rosen Press, Inc., 1968), 46.

25. Under the congressional statute of July 8, 1898, the secretary of war was given discretionary authority to repatriate the war dead from overseas; relatives could leave loved ones abroad, have them returned for private burial, or have them buried in a national cemetery. About half of those repatriated from the Caribbean went to national cemeteries. Most received in San Francisco were taken by friends and relatives for private interment.

26. Edward Steere, "Shrines of the Honored Dead: A Study of the National Cemetery System," *Quartermaster Review*, 1954, 22–23.

27. *Annual Reports of the War Department for the Fiscal Year Ended June 30, 1899* (Washington, D.C.: Government Printing Office, 1899), 187. While Ludington was correct in suggesting that repatriation of overseas war dead was unprecedented in U.S. history, the practice had antecedents in ancient Greece.

28. Ibid.,184–85. It is likely that burial details provided the bottles with names inside, a means of identifying the dead adapted from Civil War days. "Bringing Home The Heroic Dead," *Boston Daily Globe*, May 28, 1899, 31.

29. Ibid.

30. Ibid.

31. Steere, 24.

32. Brig. Gen. M. I. Ludington, *Annual Report of the Quartermaster General to the Secretary of War, 1900* (Washington, D.C.: Government Printing Office, 1900), 40.

33. Michael Sledge, *Soldier Dead: How We Recover, Identify, Bury & Honor Our Military Fallen* (New York: Columbia University Press, 2005), 220.

34. MacCloskey, 46; Steere, 24; Sledge, 36.

35. The *New York Times*, Dec. 15, 1898.

36. Ibid.; Leech, 349–50.

37. Ibid.

38. The *Atlanta Constitution*, Dec. 15, 1898.

39. The *New York Times*, Dec. 15, 1898. Margaret Leech, 646, quoting correspondence between Clark Howell and H. Kohlsaat, credits Howell for McKinley's conciliatory gesture regarding Confederate graves. Howell was editor of The *Atlanta Constitution* at the time of McKinley's visit.

40. Leech, 353-360.

41. "Soldier Dead At Rest," The *New York Times*, April 7, 1899.

42. William McKinley, Executive Order, April 3, 1899, from John T. Woolley and Gerhard Peters, The American Presidency Project, University of California, Santa Barbara, http://www.presidency.ucsb.edu/ws/?pid&equals$69321; "Soldier Dead At Rest," The *New York Times*, April 7, 1899.

43. Ludington, *Annual Reports of the War Department, 1899*, 31; *Annual Report of the Quartermaster General, 1900*, 40; "*Maine* Dead Receive The Nation's Homage," The *New York Times*, March 24, 1912.

44. "*Maine's* Dead At Rest," The *Washington Post*, Dec. 29, 1899.

45. Ibid. While most victims from the *Maine* eventually came to rest at Arlington, not all did. The two ship's officers killed in the blast were sent to their hometowns and buried in private cemeteries. Twenty-five injured men were shipped to Key West, where they died and were buried. The rest were never found.

46. After the Confederate section was established at Arlington, Sen. John B. Foraker, a Union veteran from Ohio, delivered on President McKinley's pledge to assume the care of other Confederate graves. Foraker introduced legislation in 1903 to locate all Confederate

graves in the North and mark them with new headstones like those authorized for Arlington. The bill was finally enacted in 1906. Six years later, a federally appointed commissioner had placed new headstones at 30,000 Confederate graves around the country. Michelle A. Krowl, "In the Spirit of Fraternity: The United States Government and the Burial of the Confederate Dead at Arlington National Cemetery, 1864–1914," *Virginia Magazine of History and Biography*, 111, 2, (2003): 171–73.

47. Confederate Memorial Associations from Virginia, North Carolina, and South Carolina had previously won permission to disinter and rebury several hundred soldiers from Arlington National Cemetery; nonetheless, some were overlooked at Arlington and elsewhere. AHA.

48. Krowl,161–63.

49. Ibid.

50. Although Marcus Wright was well known for spearheading the drive to rebury Confederates at Arlington National Cemetery, his contribution as a Civil War historian earned him wide respect in his lifetime. Appointed by the War Department to gather official Confederate records from the Civil War, Wright spent decades on the project, which provided thousands of pages of authentic documentary material for *Official Records of the War of the Rebellion*, the 128-volume history published by the federal government from 1880 through 1901.

51. Krowl, 163–65.

52. "Letter from the Acting Secretary of War Transmitting A Report of the Commissioner for Marking Confederate Graves, Together with Recommendation for Further Continuance of Said Act, and Reasons Therefor," 64th Congress, 1st Session, House of Representatives Document No. 795," 2–3; Krowl, 164–66.

53. Krowl,170–71.

54. "Tribute Paid in New York," The *Washington Post*, Jan. 29, 1906;"Gen. Wheeler's Coffin Passes 'Mid Thousands," The *New York Times*, Jan. 29, 1906; "President to Attend Gen. Wheeler's Funeral," The *New York Times*, Jan. 27, 1906.

55. Ibid.

56. "Dead Lying in State," The *Washington Post*, Jan. 29, 1906;"Home to South They Brought Joe Wheeler," The *Atlanta Constitution*, Jan. 30, 1906;"Gen. Joseph Wheeler Buried in Arlington," The *New York Times*, Jan. 30, 1906;"Atlanta Vets Go To Funeral," The *Atlanta Constitution*, Jan. 28, 1906.

57. "Sleeps in Arlington," The *Washington Post*, Jan. 30, 1906.

58. "Ex-Confederates Angry," The *New York Times*, Jan. 29, 1906. Wheeler's obelisk, a copy of the Washington Monument, is forty five-feet tall.

7: l'enfant's grand view

1. James Dudley Morgan, "Major Pierre Charles L'Enfant, the Unhonored and Unrewarded Engineer," *Records of the Columbia Historical Society of Washington, D.C.*, 2 (1899): 118–157; see also Wilhelme B. Bryan, *Records of the Columbia Historical Society*, 2 (1899): 111–117; and Arthur H. Codington, "Major Charles Pierre L'Enfant at Last Honored by Republic," The *Atlanta Constitution*, April 26, 1909.

2. Ibid.

3. Washington concluded that L'Enfant had an "untoward disposition." Report No. 4595 to accompany S. 7081, "Grave of Maj. Pierre Charles L'Enfant," 58th Congress, 3rd Session, House of Representatives, Feb. 11, 1905.

4. Richard W. Stephenson, *A Plan Whol[l]y New: Pierre Charles L'Enfant's Planning the City of Washington* (Washington, D.C.: Library of Congress, 1993), 34.

5. Allen Johnson and Dumas Malone, eds., *Dictionary of American Biography* (New York: Charles Scribner's Sons, 1933), 11: 169.

6. Codington.

7. Codington; Johnson and Malone, eds., *Dictionary of American Biography* 11:169; Scott W. Berg, *Grand Avenues: The Story of the French Visionary who designed Washington, D.C.* (New York: Pantheon, 2007), 244. Berg writes that L'Enfant had claims pending against the federal government at the time of his death; sixteen years later, the War Department awarded L'Enfant's estate $92.80 for his work on Fort Warburton, later called Fort Washington; see also Jean Jules Jusserand, *With Americans of Past and Present Days* (New York: Charles Scribner's Sons, 1916), 190.

8. Burnham, who helped raise a new Chicago from the ashes of the 1871 fire, is often credited for saying, "Make no little plans; they have no magic to stir men's blood." Whether Burnham actually said it has been disputed, but there is no doubt that Burnham lived by the credo, which has been embraced by generations of architects since his time.

9. After the British torched the White House in 1814, President James Madison and his family took refuge in the Octagon House a few blocks away. It served as the White House until the president's mansion could be restored.

10. Sara A. Butler, "The Monument as Manifesto: The Pierre Charles L'Enfant Memorial, 1909–1911," *Journal of Planning History*, 6, 4 (Nov. 2007): 283–310.

11. Many of the architects and artists contributing to the McMillan Commission later served on the Council of Fine Arts, a federal committee appointed by President Theodore Roosevelt's order of January 19, 1909. The council was charged with reviewing plans for buildings, statues, or parks in Washington to provide for orderly and aesthetic development. Although Roosevelt's order was later revoked by President William Howard Taft, Congress reestablished the panel in 1910 as the United States Commission on Fine Arts, which continues to pass judgment on all plans for buildings and parks in the federal city to this day.

12. *Report of the Senate Committee on the District of Columbia on the Improvement of the Park System of the District of Columbia*, U.S. Senate Report No. 166, 57th Congress, 1st Session (Washington, D.C.: Government Printing Office, 1902).

13. Ibid.

14. Ibid.

15. Butler, 293–94; see also Henry B. F. Macfarland to Luke E. White, Dec. 28, 1908, NARA RG 92, Office of the Quartermaster General.

16. Berg, 274; see also *Congressional Record—Senate*, 61st Congress, 1st Session, March 25, 1909, 263–64; "Removal of the Remains of Pierre Charles L'Enfant," House of Representatives Document No. 214, Jan. 11, 1905, 58th Congress, 3rd Session; *Congressional Record—Senate*, Feb. 8, 1905, 58th Congress, 3rd Session, 2060.

17. Macfarland to White, Dec. 28, 1908.

18. Murray Nelligan, *Arlington House: The Story of the Lee Mansion Historical Monument* (Burke, VA: Chatelaine Press, 2005), 143. The quote is not direct but as related by G. W. P. Custis, who was standing with Lafayette at Arlington when the Frenchman is supposed to have said it.

19. Capt. E. H. Humphrey Jr. to D. H. Rhodes, April 11, 1909, NARA RG 92, Office of the Quartermaster General.

20. D. H. Rhodes to Maj. F. W. Matteson, June 10, 1930, AHA. According to Rhodes's account of L'Enfant's reburial, the cedar that had marked his grave did not go to waste. After the Frenchman's disinterment, Rhodes wrote, the tree "turned out to be a boon to those most interested, in that it furnished wood for souvenirs that were made into mallets, etc."

21. "L'Enfant Disinterred," The *Washington Post*, April 23, 1909.

22. Rhodes to Matteson, June 10, 1930.

23. "L'Enfant Disinterred."

24. "Memorial or Funeral Services in the Capitol Rotunda," U.S. Senate Historical Office, 2005.

25. "Taps for L'Enfant," The *Washington Post*, April 29, 1909

26. Ibid.; see also "Bacon Placed Pin In L'Enfant Coffin," The *Atlanta Constitution*, April 29, 1909.

27. Ibid.

28. According to Rebecca Cooper, manager of reader services in the library of the Society of the Cincinnati, L'Enfant misjudged the market for the new medals. Having run through the funds provided him to commission medals, L'Enfant dipped into his own pocket and ended up with more badges than he could sell—a precursor of the fiscal exuberance that would finally be his undoing. Author interview, Washington, D.C., July 7, 2008.

29. "Taps for L'Enfant." As with other controversies in L'Enfant's eventful life, there is confusion regarding his reburial in 1909. The *Washington Post* account has Sen. Bacon giving his Cincinnati medal to L'Enfant at the Arlington graveside; an account from The *Atlanta Constitution*, also printed on April 29, 1908, has Bacon transferring the medal during ceremonies at the Capitol Rotunda. The *Post*'s account contains more detail and seems more credible, but either version may be correct.

30. Col. George Ruhlen, assistant quartermaster, to Jacob M. Dickinson, secretary of war, Nov. 16, 1910, NARA RG 92, Office of the Quartermaster General.

31. Butler, 299–300.

32. Butler, 301–303.

33. Ruhlen to Dickinson, Nov. 16, 1910.

34. Ibid.

35. "Honor to L'Enfant," The *Washington Post*, May 23, 1911.

36. Butler, 300. In his ill-fated design, submitted in March 1909, William Welles Bosworth correctly listed L'Enfant's birth year as 1754; this was changed to 1755 during the process of review and revision.

37. Butler, 305.

38. "American Revolutionary War Veterans Interred at Arlington National Cemetery," Arlington National Cemetery, www.arlingtoncemetery.org; see also "Interim Special Report: Revolutionary War Veteran Gravesites in Virginia," Joint Legislative Audit and Review Commission of the Virginia General Assembly, House Document 91, Feb. 15, 2000.

39. Although the War of 1812 occurred long before the creation of Arlington National Cemetery, it provided new burials for the nation's graveyard. Working at the Marine Barracks in Washington in 1905, a construction crew discovered a mass grave containing the remains of fourteen unidentified sailors and marines from the War of 1812. All were reburied under a stone tablet in Section 1.

40. Ella Loraine Dorsey, "A Biographical Sketch of James McCubbin Lingan, one of the Original Proprietors," *Records of the Columbia Historical Society of Washington, D.C.*, 13 (1910): 1–48; Johnson and Malone, eds., *Dictionary of American Biography*, 11: 107–8; Anthony S. Pitch, *The Burning of Washington: The British Invasion of 1814* (Annapolis: The Naval Institute Press, 1998), 1–12.

41. Ibid.; James Edward Peters, *Arlington National Cemetery: Shrine to America's Heroes* (Bethesda, MD: Woodbine House, 2000) 126–28.

42. Ibid.

43. Ibid.

44. "Honors to Peary," *National Geographic*, January 1907.

45. Edmund Morris, *Theodore Rex* (New York: Random House, 2001), 8.

46. Peary's North Pole claim, controversial in his own time, has since been questioned by scholars who suggest that he came very close to his goal but provided insufficient proof to validate his claim.

47. Johnson and Malone, eds., *Dictionary of American Biography*, 10:183–88. Some mystery still hovers over the remains General Porter recovered in 1905. Following a documentary trail to a tiny Protestant cemetery outside of Paris, Porter cracked open three lead-lined coffins before he found one with no identifying plaque. He was convinced that Jones, preserved in alcohol, was in this coffin. Using a forensic technique familiar to modern scientists, Porter compared the high cheekbones, arched eye, and other features of the corpse to contemporary likenesses of Jones and pronounced a match. Subsequent investigators are less confident of Jones's identity. Joseph E. Callo, "Sea Power Visionary," *Military History*, July/Aug. 2008.

48. Robert M. Poole, *Explorers House: National Geographic and the World It Made* (New York: The Penguin Press, 2004), 65–66.

49. "Removal of the Remains of Pierre Charles L'Enfant," House of Representatives Document No. 214, Jan. 11, 1905, 58th Congress, 3rd Session; *Congressional Record—Senate*, Feb. 8, 1905, 58th Congress, 3rd Session, 2060.

50. Rhodes to Matteson, June 10, 1930; see also Jennifer Hanna, *Cultural Landscape Report: Arlington House, The Robert E. Lee Mansion* (Washington, D.C.: National Park Service, 2001), 120–22.

51. "History of Government Furnished Headstones and Markers," Department of Veterans Affairs, July 9, 2008, www.cem.va.gov/cem/hist/hmhist.asp.

52. 1st Lt. Frank P. Lahm, Chief Signal Officer, U.S. Army, "Proceedings of the Aeronautical Board for the Purpose of Investigating and Reporting on the Cause of the Accident to the Wright Aeroplane Which Resulted in the Death of First Lieutenant Thomas E. Selfridge, First Field Artillery," Sept. 18, 1908; Dr. George A. Spratt, "Proceedings of the Aeronautical Board," Appendix 1, Sept. 18, 1908; "Fatal Fall of Wright Airship," The New York Times, Sept. 18, 1908; "Airship Falls: Lieut. Selfridge Killed, Wright Hurt," The Washington Post, Sept. 18, 1908; "Aviation: From Sand Dunes to Sonic Booms: Fort Myer Historic District," The National Park Service, July 28, 2008, www.nps.gov/history/nR/travel/aviation/ftm.htm.
53. Ibid.
54. Ibid.
55. Ibid.
56. Ibid.
57. Ibid.
58. Ibid.
59. Ibid.
60. Ibid.

8: KNOWN BUT TO GOD

1. John Keegan, A History of Warfare (New York: Vintage Books, 1994), 362; Keegan, The Second World War (New York: Penguin Books, 2005) 17–18; Barbara Tuchman, The Proud Tower (New York: The Macmillan Company, 1996), 235–236.
2. Caroline Alexander, "Faces of War," Smithsonian, February 2007.
3. Tuchman, 235–236.
4. Keegan, A History of Warfare, 360–361.
5. Woodrow Wilson, "Abraham Lincoln: A Man of the People," in Abraham Lincoln: The Tribute of a Century 1809–1909, Nathan William MacChesney, ed. (Chicago: A. C. McClurg & Co., 1910), 14.
6. Allen Johnson and Dumas Malone, eds., Dictionary of American Biography, (New York: Charles Scribner's Sons, 1933), 20:353.
7. "Address of President Wilson at Arlington," May 30, 1914, WWL.
8. Davis's birthday was actually June 3, so the Confederates celebrated a day late.
9. Laura Wheeler, "Confederate Dead Are Still Remembered at Arlington," The Washington Post, June 14, 2007.
10. "Gray and Blue Join," The Washington Post, June 5, 1914; "Address of President Wilson Accepting the Monument in Memory of the Confederate Dead at Arlington National Cemetery," June 4, 1914, WWL.
11. Barbara Tuchman, The Guns of August (New York: Macmillan Publishing Co., 1988), 174.
12. Geoffrey Barraclough, ed., The Times Atlas of World History (Maplewood, NJ: Hammond Incorporated, 1979), 252–53.
13. Edward J. Renehan Jr., The Lion's Pride: Theodore Roosevelt and His Family in Peace and War (New York: Oxford University Press, 1998), 97; Barbara Tuchman, The Zimmermann Telegram (New York: Macmillan Publishing Co., 1966) 118–19.

14. John Keegan, *The First World War* (New York: Alfred A. Knopf, 1999), 136.

15. John Laffin, ed., *Letters from the Front 1914–1918* (London: J. M. Dent & Sons, 1973), 8.

16. Renehan, 97–98.

17. *Letters*, 24–25.

18. Ibid., 31–32. Chapin's letter was written on September 24, 1915, two days before he died in battle.

19. "United States Must Act at Once on *Lusitania*, Says Colonel Roosevelt," The *New York Times*, May 10, 1915.

20. Renehan, 104.

21. Even though Wilson pulled back from war after the *Lusitania* sank, the stern tone of his diplomatic note to the Germans was too much for Vice President Bryan, who felt that it threatened the nation's neutral stance. He resigned.

22. "Address of President Wilson at Philadelphia," May 10, 1915, WWL. Germany rationalized its attack by saying *Lusitania* had been armed, which made it a warship. In addition, it was later established that the ship had been carrying contraband—4,200 cases of Remington rifle cartridges, 1,250 cases of shrapnel shells, and 50 cases of explosive powder.

23. Edgar E. Robinson and Victor J. West, *The Foreign Policy of Woodrow Wilson, 1913–1917* (New York: Macmillan Publishing Co., 1918), 329–330.

24. Tuchman, *Zimmermann*, 195–97.

25. "Address of the President of the United States, Delivered at a Joint Session of the two houses of Congress," April 2, 1917, WWL.

26. Keegan, *First World War*, 372.

27. Donald Smythe, *Pershing: General of the Armies* (Bloomington: Indiana University Press, 1986), 33–34. Colonel Stanton's quote, "Lafayette, we are here!" is often misattributed to Pershing.

28. Ibid.

29. Keegan, *First World War*, 372–77.

30. Ibid., 373.

31. All of Roosevelt's sons felt duty-bound to enter the war. Ted junior became a major of infantry, Archie served as an infantry captain, and Kermit as an artillery captain. Both Ted junior and Archie were severely wounded in the fighting.

32. Paul Duggan, "World War I Soldier Repatriated at Long Last," The *Washington Post*, Sept. 25, 2006.

33. Combat deaths were staggering, with Germany losing 1.95 million men; France, 1.8 million; Russia, 1.7 million; Austria-Hungary, 1.05 million; Britain, 1 million; Italy, 533,000; the Ottoman Empire, 325,000; Belgium, 41,000; Serbia, 322,000; and others some 200,000. Most of the 116,516 American combatants who died were victims of the great influenza epidemic of 1918 and 1919, which claimed some 60,000 U.S. troops and killed 20 million to 40 million worldwide.

34. Michelle May, "He Died Fighting," *Aviation History*, January 2008; Renehan, 193–94; Andrew E. Woods, "World War I Soldier Repatriated After 88 Years," Cantigny First Division Foundation, Wheaton, IL.

35. Jeremiah M. Evarts, *Cantigny: A Corner of the War* (New York: The Scribner Press, 1938), 85–96.

36. Woods; Duggan.

37. Duggan; "A Doughboy Killed in Action is Home at Last," The *New York Times*, Sept. 24, 2006.

38. Florence Cannon, "Our Honored Dead," *Quartermaster Review*, May-June 1952.

39. "Lieut. Roosevelt Falls in Air Fight; Believed Killed," The *New York Times*, July 18, 1918.

40. Renehan, 198.

41. Ibid., 5–6.

42. Ferdinand Cowle Inglehart, *Theodore Roosevelt: The man as I knew him* (New York: The Christian Herald, 1919), 271; "A Solution Perhaps Acceptable," The *New York Times*, Jan. 1, 1919. After resting near Chamery for almost three decades, Quentin Roosevelt's body was removed to the American cemetery at Saint-Laurent-sur-Mer in 1945, when he was buried beside his brother Brig. Gen. Theodore Roosevelt Jr., who died of a heart attack after the Normandy invasion of 1944. Ted junior was posthumously awarded the Medal of Honor. Renehan, 239–40.

43. Margaret MacMillan, *Paris 1919: Six Months That Changed The World* (New York: Random House, 2002), 3–4.

44. Erna Risch, *Quartermaster Support of the Army, 1775–1939* (Washington, D.C.: Center of Military History, 1989), 599–694; Edward Steere, "National Cemeteries and Memorials in Global Conflict," *Quartermaster Review*, Dec. 1953, 23–25; statement of Brig. Gen. Peter C. Harris, House Committee on Military Affairs, Feb. 1, 1921.

45. According to ancient tradition, Athenians carried their honored warriors home for burial, but they made an exception after the great battle at Marathon, where Thucydides wrote that the dead "were interred on the spot where they fell . . . for their singular and extraordinary valor." This was the standard Theodore Roosevelt cited for leaving his son Quentin buried in Europe.

46. Memorandum of Adj. Gen. Robert C. Davis for the Commander in Chief, GHQ, 4th Section, G.S., May 6, 1919, NARA RG 407, File 293.8 to 293.9. Testifying at congressional hearings in February 1921, Maj. Gen. John A. Lejeune, commandant of the Marine Corps, provided stark testimony about the dehumanizing effect of battle conditions. After the fight for Soissons in July 1918, "a number of men killed could not be identified," he told the House Committee on Military Affairs. "This was due to several causes, the most frequent being the rending apart of men's bodies by high explosive shells, so that in many instances only small bits or pieces or fragments of a body could be found. In one case, I remember particularly, a man was wounded and left in a shell hole and when they went to find him there was nothing there but some small pieces of flesh. A shell had made a direct hit and torn the body into a thousand pieces."

47. Ibid.

48. Memorandum of Brig. Gen. Peter C. Harris, June 4, 1919, NARA RG 407, Box 566, File 293.8 to 293.9.

49. Letter from Maj. Gen. Frank McIntyre for War Department News Bureau, July 25, 1919, NARA RG 407, Box 566, File 293.8.

50. Mrs. L. Mantel to Secretary of War Nelson A. Baker, Dec. 10, 1919, NARA RG 407, Box 565, File 293.8.

51. G. Kurt Piehler, "The Dead and the Gold Star: American Commemoration of the First World War," in John R. Gillis, ed., *Commemorations: The Politics of National Identity* (Princeton: Princeton University Press, 1994), 174.

52. Ibid.; Neil Hanson, *Unknown Soldiers: The Story of the Missing of the First World War* (New York: Alfred A. Knopf, 2006), 241.

53. Brig. Gen. Peter C. Harris, adjutant general memorandum of Oct. 29, 1919, NARA RG 407, Box 565, File 298.8. Undertakers would harvest their profits from these private burials, which accounted for more than 40,700 of the nation's 46,520 stateside reinterments.

54. In March 1920, France relented on its objections to the removal of Americans from their soil.

55. A few individual World War I servicemen have been returned in the years since mass repatriations were finished in 1922.

56. Enoch A. Chase, "Fame's Eternal Camping Ground," *National Geographic*, Nov. 1928.

57. Risch, 693–95.

58. B. C. Mossman and M. Warner Stark, *The Last Salute: Civil and Military Funerals 1921–1969* (Washington, D.C.: Center of Military History, 1971), 3–4; Hanson, 331. For more on General March, see Edward M. Coffman's excellent biography, *The Hilt of the Sword: The Career of Peyton C. March* (Madison: The University of Wisconsin Press, 1966).

59. Hanson, 260–327. Italy, Belgium, and Romania also established tombs for their unknown war dead; tiny Portugal honored two anonymous soldiers in its shrine.

60. Marie M. Meloney to Gen. Peyton C. March, Nov. 13, 1920, NARA RG 407, Box 563, File 293.8.

61. Ibid.

62. Ibid.

63. The *New York Times*, Dec. 9, 1920.

64. Fish was a captain of Company K, 15th Infantry Regiment, New York National Guard, when World War I broke out. The regiment, composed of African Americans commanded by white officers, was restyled the 369th Infantry when assigned to France. There its members fought under French leadership. Known as the Harlem Hellfighters, the 369th took part in the bloody action at Château Thierry and Belleau Wood, had one-third of its men killed, and served 191 days of combat, longer than any other American unit. It was the first Allied unit to reach the Rhine—and one of the few black outfits allowed to fight in France. Most African American soldiers were assigned to work as laborers and stevedores. Fish, promoted to major in 1919, was awarded the Silver Star and the French Croix de Guerre.

65. H.J. Resolution 426, 66th Congress, 3rd Session, Dec. 21, 1920, NARA RG 407, Box 562, File 293.8.

66. Mossman and Stark, 3–4.

67. "Leaders for Honor to Unknown Dead," The *New York Times*, Feb. 2, 1921.

68. Ibid. Petyon March, whose relationship with Pershing was uneasy, was nowhere to be seen during congressional hearings on the Unknown Soldier. Pershing, triumphant in victory, would replace March as the Army's chief of staff in May 1921.

69. Ibid.

70. The *New York Times*, June 12, 1921.

71. "Leaders for Honor." When Rodman Wanamaker spoke, patriotic audiences listened: he had purchased more war bonds than any other individual in World War I.

72. Hanson, 332–33.

73. Brig Gen. William Lassiter, memorandum to Army chief of staff, Sept. 8, 1921, NARA RG 407, Box 563, File 293.8.

74. Mossman and Stark, 4–8; Hanson, 335.

75. Hanson, 335–36; Mossman and Stark, 5–8.

76. Ibid.

77. "A Stillness at Arlington," *Time*, Nov. 21, 1955; "Our Soldier Unknown," Army Quartermaster Museum report, 1937; Hanson, 337–39.

78. Mossman and Stark, 5–8; Hanson, 337–40.

79. Edwin L. James, "Unknown Soldier Chosen in France," The *New York Times*, October 25, 1921.

80. "Our Soldier Unknown"; Mossman and Stark, 7–8; Hanson, 339.

81. Mossman and Stark, 8–9; Hanson, 340–41.

82. After his native Lorraine region was overrun and occupied by Germans, André Maginot vowed to make France's eastern borders impregnable to future invasions. As war minister in the 1920s and early 1930s, he proposed a line of fortifications, which came to be known as the Maginot Line when completed. German forces swept around the line and later occupied it in World War II, by which time Maginot was dead.

83. Maj. Gen. Henry T. Allen, Dec. 11, 1921, to Adjutant General's Office, including letters and speeches from ceremonies at Le Havre and Châlons, NARA RG 407, Box 563, File 293.8.

84. Mossman and Stark, 8–9; Hanson, 340–41; U.S.S. *Reuben James* continued in service until Oct. 31, 1941, when she was sunk by German submarines in the North Atlantic, the first American warship to be lost in World War II.

85. "Arlington National Cemetery Tomb of the Unknowns Monument Repair or Replacement Project," June 1, 2006, Arlington National Cemetery.

86. NARA RG 407, Box 564, File 293.8.

87. Ibid.

88. Ibid.

89. Ibid.

90. H. Allen Griffith to Nelson D. Baker, April 17, 1920, NARA RG 407, Box 563, File 293.1.

91. Brig. Gen. William Lassiter, acting chief of staff, memorandum, "Distribution of bodies returned from Europe," Oct. 9, 1921, NARA RG 407, Box 563, File 293.8.

92. Ibid.

93. "Body of the 'Unknown Soldier' Arrives Home," Associated Press, Nov. 9–11, 1921; Mossman and Stark, 9–16; Hanson, 342–57.

94. Ibid.

95. Ibid.

96. Ibid.

97. Ibid.

98. Gillis, 11–13; "Bereaved Mothers Grateful, She Says," The *Washington Post*, Nov. 12, 1921.

99. Piehler, 175.

100. "Body of Unknown Hero, Under Guard, Lies in State At the Capitol," The *Washington Post*, Nov. 10, 1921; Associated Press, Nov. 9–11, 1921.

101. Associated Press, Nov. 9–11, 1921; Mossman and Stark, 9–16.

102. Ibid.

103. Ibid.; "Solemn Journey of the Dead," The *New York Times*, Nov. 12, 1921.

104. Ibid.

105. "Millions to Pray For Peace Today," The *New York Times*, Nov. 11, 1921. Flights were banned during President Harding's address at Arlington on the recommendation of Earl Godwin, broadcast technician for C&P Telephone Co. "The noise of an aeroplane would be carried into the amplifier magnified through the projectors until it would sound like the roar of Niagara Falls," Godwin wrote to Col. George Penrose of the quartermaster's office on Oct. 12, 1921. Penrose took the advice.

106. Associated Press, Nov. 9–11, 1921; "President Harding's Address at the Burial of an Unknown American Soldier," The *New York Times*, Nov. 12, 1921; "Solemn Journey."

107. "Solemn Journey."

108. Ibid.; Associated Press, Nov. 9–11, 1921; Mossman and Stark, 9–16.

9: A TIME TO BUILD UP

1. "Bereaved Mothers Grateful, She Says," The *Washington Post*, Nov. 12, 1921. Mrs. Digney's son, Lt. Louis Freeman Plummer, was killed in the crash of a training plane.

2. "Whittlesey Talked About War On Ship," The *New York Times*, Nov. 30, 1921. Based on testimony from a fellow passenger, investigators estimated that Whittlesey went overboard just after midnight on Nov. 26, 1921. Donald Smythe, *Pershing: General of the Armies* (Bloomington: Indiana University Press, 1986), 205. Press reports on the travails of the "Lost Battalion" embellished the story, reporting that Maj. Whittlesey had refused the German invitation to surrender with a curt "Go to hell!" In fact, Whittlesey revealed, he made no response at all, believing that silence was his best answer. See also Neil Hanson, *The Unknown Soldier: The Story of the Missing of the First World War* (New York: Alfred A. Knopf, 2006), 352.

3. Ibid.; B. C. Mossman and M. Warner Stark, *The Last Salute: Civil and Military Funerals 1921–1969* (Washington, D.C.: Center of Military History, 1971), 14.

4. The *New York Times*, Nov. 30, 1921.

5. "The Second World War was the continuation of the first, and indeed it is inexplicable except in terms of the rancours and instabilities left by the earlier conflict," writes John Keegan in *The First World War* (New York: Alfred A. Knopf, 1999), 423. Yet historian Margaret MacMillan argues that Versailles gets too much credit for spawning World War II. It has become commonplace, she writes, "to blame everything that went wrong in the 1920s and 1930s on the peacemakers and the settlements they made in Paris in 1919 . . . That is to ignore the actions of everyone—political leaders, diplomats, soldiers, ordinary voters—for

twenty years between 1919 and 1939." Margaret MacMillan, *Paris 1919: Six Months That Changed the World* (New York: Random House, 2002) 493.

6. "The Washington Naval Conference, 1921–1922," U.S. Department of State, Bureau of Public Affairs, Office of the Historian, http://www.state.gov/r/pa/ho/time/id/88313.htm.

7. Smythe, 278.

8. "The Washington Naval Conference."

9. Jennifer Hanna, *Arlington House: The Robert E. Lee Memorial* (Washington, D.C.: National Park Service, 2001) 132–33; Frank Luther Mott, *A History of American Magazines* (Cambridge, MA: The Belknap Press, 1968), 5:134.

10. Hanna, 132–33.

11. "Restoration of Lee Mansion," hearing before the Joint Committee on the Library, Congress of the United States, Pursuant to H.J. Res 264, May 28, 1924, 2–3.

12. "Report on S. 3189," Sen. Porter H. Dale, Committee on Military Affairs, Feb. 17, 1926, 69th Congress, 1st Session, AHA; "Porter Hinman Dale (1867-1933)," *Biographical Directory of the United States Congress, 1774–Present*, http://bioguide.congress.gov/scripts/biodisplay.pl?index=D000009.

13. Constance McLaughlin Green, *Washington: Capital City, 1879–1950* (Princeton: Princeton University Press, 1963),141–42; Hanna, 132–36.

14. Hanna, 133; "Restoration of Lee Mansion," 4–7.

15. H.J. Resolution 264, 562, "Joint Resolution Authorizing the Restoration of the Lee Mansion in the Arlington National Cemetery, Virginia," 68th Congress, 2nd Session, Chapter 562, March 4, 1925, 1356.

16. The *New York Times*, Oct. 13, 1929, in AHA.

17. Maj. L. M. Leisenring, "The Restoration of Arlington House," *Quartermaster Review*, March-April 1934.

18. Ibid.; Lt. Col. Charles G. Mortimer to Gen. Louis H. Bash, Nov. 16, 1929, including memorandum of L. M. Leisenring's interview with "Uncle Jim Parks," AHA.

19. "Monument Honors Custis' Ex-Slave," The *Sunday Star* (Washington, D.C.), March 2, 1930; Mortimer to Bash.

20. Mortimer to Bash.

21. Ibid.

22. "Former Custis Slave To Sleep In Death In Arlington 'Estate,'" The *Evening Star* (Washington, D.C.), Aug. 22, 1929.

23. Ibid.

24. "Monument Honors Custis' Ex-Slave." While special recognition was given to James Parks at Arlington, he was by no means the only former slave buried in the national cemetery. Many who worked for the quartermaster's department during and after the Civil War were also interred there.

25. Hanna, 144.

26. Leisenring, "The Restoration of Arlington House." The administration building was raised on the site of Arlington's old stables, originally a smaller version of the main mansion. The stables burned in 1904, were rebuilt in 1907, and were refitted to accommodate cemetery administrators in the early 1930s.

27. Mabel S. Brown to Gen. John J. Pershing, Feb. 15, 1923; Maj. Gen. R.H. Fletcher to Adjutant General, Sept. 27, 1922, both from NARA RG 407, Box 565, file 293.8.

28. Ibid.

29. John W. Weeks to Mrs. Kathryn Chamberlain, Dec. 2, 1922, NARA RG 407, Box 565, file 293.8.

30. Brig. Gen. H. H. Bandholtz to the Adjutant General, Oct. 23, 1922, NARA RG 407, Box 565, file 293.8. Brig. Gen. Bandholtz failed to predict the popularity of the Tomb of the Unknowns, which attracts many of the 4 million people who visit Arlington each year. One reason they do, of course, is to watch the changing of the guard, which might never have come into being if Bandholtz's view had prevailed.

31. Ibid.

32. William H. Hart to Deputy Chief of Staff, Aug. 30, 1923, NARA RG 407, Box 565, file 293.8.

33. Secretary of War to Commanding General, District of Washington, "Establishment of an armed guard at the tomb of the Unknown Soldier in Arlington Cemetery," March 24, 1926; Capt. David G. Barr to Lt. Col. John Millikin, 3rd Cavalry, "Guard at Tomb of Unknown Soldier," July 1, 1937, both from Society of the Honor Guard, www.tombguard .org/formation.html.

34. "Annual Report of the Commission on the Erection of Memorials and Entombment of Bodies in the Arlington Memorial Amphitheater for the fiscal year ended June 30, 1925," Jan. 5, 1926, Committee on the Library, House of Representatives, 69th Congress 1st Session, AHA; "The Unknown Solider—Ten Years After," The *New York Times Magazine*, Nov. 8, 1931.

35. Lt. Donald R. Neil, "Nature Honors The Unknown Soldier," *Quartermaster Review*, Jan.–Feb. 1932; "Tomb of the Unknowns Monument, Repair or Replacement Project," June 1, 2006, Arlington National Cemetery.

36. Ibid.

37. Ibid.

38. "Arlington Memorial Bridge," George Washington Memorial Parkway, National Park Service, July 8, 1998, www.nps.gov/archive/gwmp/memorial_bridge.htm.

39. T. H. Watkins, *The Hungry Years* (New York: Henry Holt and Company, 1999), 131–141; Paul Dickson and Thomas B. Allen, *The Bonus Army: An American Epic* (New York: Walker & Company, 2004), 105–83; William Manchester, *American Caesar: Douglas MacArthur* (Boston: Little, Brown and Company, 1978),145–56.

40. Dickson and Allen, 123–24.

41. Manchester, 150.

42. Dickson and Allen, 168–174.

43. Dickson and Allen, 171.

44. Dickson and Allen, 173.

45. MacArthur's action in the BEF incident, in which he overstepped President Hoover's orders, predicted his behavior in the Korean conflict. President Harry S. Truman removed him for exceeding his authority there.

46. Dickson and Allen, 173–81.

47. A grand jury investigation cleared police officers in the deaths of Hushka and Carlson, who were said to have provoked the shots that killed them.

48. Dickson and Allen, 168–70, 192.

49. Manchester, 152.

50. Dickson and Allen, 184.

51. Dickson and Allen, 193.

52. "Riot Report," *Time*, Sept. 19, 1932.

53. Dickson and Allen, 201.

54. Harris B. Hull, "Formal Dedication of Soldier Tomb Is Planned On Friday," The *Washington Post*, Nov. 6, 1932.

55. James Cullinane, "Reverent Vets Walk Out As Hurley Speaks," The *Washington Herald*, Nov. 12, 1932.

56. Ibid.

57. Ibid.

58. "Vets Propose Walkout on Hurley Talk," The *Washington Herald*, Nov. 10, 1932.

59. "Reverent Vets."

60. Ibid.

61. Dickson and Allen, 252–61.

10: "WE ARE ALL IN IT—ALL THE WAY"

1. "The War Department and the Pentagon," http://www.arlingtonvirginiausa.com.html.

2. "Arlington Goes Green," http://www.arlingtonva.us/Departments/Libraries/history/LibrariesHistoryBackPages0032007.aspx.

3. Steve Vogel, *The Pentagon: A History* (New York: Random House, 2007), 31.

4. Ibid.

5. Ibid., 32.

6. Ibid., 39.

7. Ibid., 33.

8. Ibid., 71.

9. Ibid., 48.

10. *Congressional Record*, July 28, 1941, 6363-75.

11. Ibid.

12. Vogel, 49.

13. Jennifer Hanna, *Arlington House: The Robert E. Lee Memorial, Cultural Landscape Report* (Washington, D.C.: National Park Service, 2001), 153–154.

14. Ibid.

15. Vogel, 80.

16. Ibid., 65.

17. Ibid., 80.

18. Jean Edward Smith, *FDR* (New York: Random House, 2007), 498–502.

19. Vogel, 74.

20. Ibid., 80.

21. Ibid., 85.

22. Ibid., 82–83.

23. Ibid., 89–90.

24. Ibid., 93–97.

25. Ibid.

26. Ibid., 101–103

27. Ibid.

28. Ibid.

29. Ibid., 295–96.

30. Ibid., 127–28.

31. Ibid., 138–39.

32. Smith, 540–41.

33. Smith, 467; Douglas Brinkley and Michael E. Haskew, eds., *The World War II Desk Reference*, (Edison, NJ: Castle Books, 2004), 383.

34. Churchill scrupulously credited the boiler quote to Lord Edward Gray, Britain's foreign minister during World War I.

35. John Keegan, *The Second World War* (New York: Penguin Books, 2005), 11.

36. Brinkley and Haskew, 188.

37. Watertender First Class Elmer Charles Bigelow, Medal of Honor citation, from the website of the Medal of Honor Society, http://www.cmohs.org/recipient/2641/bigelow-elmer-charles.php.

38. Marine Cpl. Anthony Peter Damato, Medal of Honor citation, http://www.cmohs.org/recipient-detail/2702/damato-anthony-peter.php.

39. Army Tech Sgt. Forrest L. Vosler, Medal of Honor citation from the website of the U.S. Air Force National Museum, http://www.nationalmuseum.af.mil/factsheet_print.asp?fsID&equals$1440. Vosler survived the war and worked for the Veterans Administration until his retirement. He died in 1992 and is buried at Arlington.

40. C. L. Sulzberger, "The Doughboys' Grim Road to Rome," The *New York Times*, Feb. 20, 1944.

41. Army Pfc. Alton W. Knappenberger, Medal of Honor citation, http://www.lcmohs.org/recipient-detail2831/krappengerger-alton-w.php. David Venditta, "Farm boy won WWII fame, sought a return to obscurity," *Allentown Morning Call*, May 31, 2004; Adam Bernstein, "Alton Knappenberger, 84, Won Medal of Honor," The *Washington Post*, June 28, 2008; Rick Atkinson, *The Day of Battle: The War in Sicily and Italy, 1943–1944* (New York: Henry Holt and Company, 2007), 359–97.

42. Ibid.

43. Ibid.

44. Ibid.

45. Ibid.

46. Ibid.

47. Brinkley and Haskew, 432–34.

48. Keegan, 591.

49. Allan Kozinn, "Paderewski to Go Home, 51 Years After His Death," The *New York Times*, June 25, 1992; "Background of Ignace Jan Paderewski at Arlington National

Cemetery," http://www.arlingtoncemetery.org/hisorical_information/jan_paderewski
.html; Wanda Wilk, "Polish Composers: Ignace Jan Paderewski," http://www.usc.edu/
dept/polish_music/composer/padrewski/html.

50. More than sixty foreign nationals are buried at Arlington, many of them from the
Second World War. The best known is Field Marshal Sir John Dill, wartime chief of the
British Military Mission in Washington. Less prominent are the prisoners of war who
died before they could return home: Anton Hilberath of Germany; Mario Batista of Italy,
and Arcangelo Prudenza of Italy. Each year on All Souls' Day, officials from the Italian em-
bassy visit Arlington to leave flowers at the graves of their countrymen. "62 Foreign Nationals Interred at Arlington National Cemetery," http://www.arlingtoncemetery.org/
historical_information/foreign_nationals.html.

51. Keegan, 595.

52. World War II is also the last war to be officially declared by Congress, which helped
galvanize the nation for the conflict.

53. Steven E. Anders, "With All Due Honors," *Quartermaster Professional Bulletin*, Au-
tumn/Winter 1994.

54. Ibid.

55. *Arlington National Cemetery* (Washington, D.C.: Department of the Army, Office of the
Chief of Support Services, n.d., 17.

56. Anders. There were more deaths in the Civil War than in World War II, but the reinterment program from the Second World War was far broader in scope, ranging from the
Aleutian Islands, across the Himalayas, to the shores of the Mediterranean and up through
Europe. Some 280,000 Americans were recovered and reinterred during the six-year campaign.

57. "Graves Registration," *Quartermaster Review*, May/June 1946.

58. Anders.

59. Robert M. Poole, "Lost Over Laos," *Smithsonian*, August 2006.

60. Murphy's standard-issue tombstone was too small to list all of his 28 decorations, foreign and domestic.

61. Gen. George S. Patton Jr., speech to his troops before D-Day, in Douglas Brinkley,
ed., *World War II: The Allied Counteroffensive, 1942–1945* (New York: Times Books, 2003)
168–70.

62. Ibid., 171.

63. "Executive Order 9981," http://www.trumanlibrary.org/9981a.html.

64. It took until 1953 for Truman's order to take effect. But the military led the way for the
rest of society. By banning discrimination through executive order instead of legislation, Truman shrewdly short-circuited the political process in Congress, where southerners stalled or
defeated most civil rights measures.

65. Donald Smythe, *Pershing: General of the Armies* (Bloomington: Indiana University Press,
1986), 302–9.

66. Ibid. Like other statements attributed to Pershing, this one may be mythical, but the sentiment is genuine.

67. Ibid.; B. C. Mossman and M. Warner Stark, *The Last Salute: Civil and Military Funerals 1921–1969* (Washington, D.C: Center of Military History, 1971), 28–44.

68. Smythe, 302–9.

69. Mossman and Stark, 28–44.

70. Ibid.

II: THE NASTIEST LITTLE WAR

1. B. C. Mossman and M. Warner Stark, *The Last Salute* (Washington, D.C.: Center of Military History, 1971), 93; "Tomb of the Unknown Soldiers," *Quartermaster Review*, Jan.–Feb. 1964, 1.

2. John Keegan, *The Second World War* (New York: Penguin Books, 2005), 594.

3. David Halberstam, *The Coldest Winter: America and the Korean War* (New York: Hyperion, 2007), 1.

4. Ibid., 1–2.

5. Bradley Lynn Coleman, "Recovering the Korean War Dead, 1950–1958: Graves Registration, Forensic Anthropology, and Wartime Memorialization," 38, John A. Adams '71 Center for Military History and Strategic Analysis, Virginia Military Institute.

6. Halberstam, 4.

7. Halberstam, 2.

8. Lt. Col. John C. Cook, "Graves Registration in the Korean Conflict," *Quartermaster Review*, March-April 1953, 1–11; Coleman, 1–10.

9. Coleman, 8–9.

10. Ibid., 6.

11. Halberstam, 486–87.

12. Ibid.

13. "Walker Is Buried In Arlington Rites," The *New York Times*, Jan. 3, 1951; "Gen. Walker's Body Reaches Washington," The *New York Times*, Dec. 31, 1951; "Rites For Gen. Walker Tuesday," The *New York Times*, Dec. 29, 1950; "Hero's Rites For Walker: General's Body at Arlington—To Be Buried Near Pershing," The *New York Times*, Jan. 1, 1951; "4 Stars Voted Walker," The *New York Times*, Jan. 2, 1951.

14. "A Final Salute For Commander Of Forces in Korea," The *New York Times*, Jan. 3, 1951.

15. Shirley Young to President Truman, Jan. 5, 1951, Office File 471-B, Box 1351, HST Papers, HSTL.

16. Norma Potter to President Truman, June 26, 1951, Office File 471-B, Box 1351, HST Papers, HSTL.

17. Deara Eartbawey to President Truman, Jan. 31, 1952, Office File 471-B, Box 1351, HST Papers, HSTL.

18. Coleman, 11.

19. Ibid., 22.

20. Ibid.

21. Madelaine C. Smith, telegram to Sen. Ernest W. McFarland for President Truman, May (n.d.) 1951, Office File 471-B, Box 1305, HST Papers, HSTL.

22. Congressional Medal of Honor Society, http://www.cmohs.org/recipient. The Medal of Honor was awarded to 133 men from the Korean conflict, with 95 of the medals given posthumously. No other conflict approached it in proportion for posthumous awards, 74 percent. In the Second World War, 464 Medals of Honor were awarded, 266 of them posthumously.

23. Col. John D. Martz Jr., "Homeward Bound," *Quartermaster Review*, May-June 1954, 3.

24. During the past decade, North Korea allowed specialty teams from the United States to recover a few missing American servicemen from their country under carefully controlled conditions. The unsettled relations between the United States and North Korea has sharply limited such recovery missions.

25. Coleman, 39–40; Martz, 4–5.

26. Mossman and Stark, 93.

27. "Tomb of the Unknown Soldiers," *Quartermaster Review*, Jan.-Feb. 1964, 1–17.

28. Ibid.

29. The Navy had long buried its dead at sea, but this was the first time a candidate for Unknown honors had been committed to the deep. This form of burial not only gave the Navy an important role in the ceremonies of 1958 but also ensured the serviceman's anonymity.

30. "Tomb of the Unknown Soldiers," *Quartermaster Review*, Jan.-Feb. 1964, 1–17; Jack Raymond, "Unknown Soldier of World War II Is Selected at Sea," *The New York Times*, May 27, 1958; Mossman and Stark, 98–99.

31. Jack Raymond, "Unknowns of World War II And Korea Are Enshrined," *The New York Times*, May 31, 1958; Mossman and Stark, 105–24.

32. Ibid.

33. Ibid.

34. "Unknowns of World War II," *The New York Times*, May 31, 1958.

35. Ibid.

36. Ibid.; Mossman and Stark, 120–24.

37. John Keegan, *A History of Warfare* (New York: Vintage, 1994), 379–80.

38. Simon LeVay, *When Science Goes Wrong* (New York: Plume, 2008), 152–159; William McKeown, *Idaho Falls: The Untold Story of America's First Nuclear Accident* (Toronto: ECW Press, 2003), 143–44.

39. Ibid.

40. Ibid.

41. 2nd Lt. Leon S. Monroe II, assistant adjutant general, Headquarters Military District of Washington, to John C. Metzler, superintendent, Arlington National Cemetery, Jan. 31, 1961, "Interment of Radioactive Remains," http://www.arlingtoncemetery.net/mcknl.htm.

12: "I COULD STAY HERE FOREVER"

1. Paul Fuqua, interviewed by author, Nov. 1, 2006.

2. Ibid.

3. Ibid.

4. Ibid.

5. Ibid.

6. Ibid.; Charles Bartlett, interviewed by Fred Holborn, Feb. 20, 1965, JFKL. Bartlett credits Kennedy with another aside from that day at Arlington. "Wouldn't this be a fine place to have the White House?" the president asked Bartlett.

7. Fuqua.

8. Ibid.

9. Ibid.

10. John C. Metzler Jr., superintendent of Arlington National Cemetery, interviewed by author, Oct. 15, 2008; B. C. Mossman and M. Warner Stark, *The Last Salute: Civil and Military Funerals 1922-1969* (Washington, D.C.: Center of Military History, 1971), 188.

11. "Funeral Services of President Kennedy 23–25 November 1963," DVD, JFKL.

12. Ralph Dungan, interviewed by William Manchester, April 15, 1964, "William Manchester Papers," Special Collections and Archives, Wesleyan University Library, 79–82, hereafter WMP.

13. Nancy Tuckerman and Pamela Turnure, interviewed by Mrs. Wayne Fredericks, n.d., JFKL.

14. Rep. Hale Boggs, interviewed by Charles T. Morrissey, May 10, 1964, JFKL; William Manchester, *The Death of a President* (New York: Harper & Row, 1967), 448, 490–91.

15. Bartlett.

16. Paul C. Miller, interviewed by William Manchester, April 30, 1964, WMP.

17. Bartlett; Boggs.

18. Bartlett.

19. Dungan, WMP, 79–80. Jacqueline Kennedy, an accomplished horsewoman, used the technically correct nomenclature for gray horses, which the rest of the world, including the caisson platoon at Fort Myer, Virginia, calls white horses. The author follows Mrs. Kennedy's example.

20. Manchester, 539.

21. Ibid., 490–91.

22. Mossman and Stark, 19; John C. Metzler Jr., interviewed by author, Oct. 15, 2008.

23. Woodrow Wilson, who died in 1924, was buried in the National Cathedral in Washington.

24. John C. Metzler Sr. notes on the Kennedy funeral, undated, WMP. Metzler makes no mention of touring the cemetery with Robert McNamara, but Manchester has the secretary of defense visiting Arlington to inspect sites at the time of Metzler's survey, which suggests that they made at least one tour together.

25. Ibid.

26. Ibid.

27. Manchester, 492–95.

28. Ted Sorensen, *Counselor* (New York: Harper, 2008), 365.

29. Metzler, WMP.

30. Manchester, 495–96; Metzler, WMP.

31. Metzler, WMP.

32. Manchester, 496–97.

33. Fuqua.

34. Thomas A. Hughes to Ramsey Clark, "John F. Kennedy Plot in Arlington National Cemetery, Virginia," Nov. 27, 1963, WMP.

35. Samuel R. Bird, "After Action Report, Joint Casket Team—State Funeral, President John Fitzgerald Kennedy," Dec. 10, 1963, WMP.

36. Sgt. Keith Mann and other members of the caisson platoon, author interview, Fort Myer, VA, June 29, 2005; Tom Setterberg in Kenneth S. Pond et al., eds., *Farewell to the President, Personal Memoirs of the State Funeral of President John F. Kennedy* (privately published, 2008) 19:1–4 .

37. Dungan, WMP, 81.

38. Setterberg, 19:1–4.

39. Ibid.

40. Arthur A. Carlson, in *Farewell to the President*, 2: 1–4.

41. Sorensen, 366.

42. Manchester, 421; Thomas F. Reid, in *Farewell to the President*, 16:2.

43. Letitia Baldridge Hollensteiner, interviewed by Mrs. Wayne Fredericks, April 24, 1964, JFKL.

44. Confidential interview by William Manchester, WMP.

45. Louis W. Odom, in *Farewell to the President*, 14:4.

46. Carlson, 2:1–4.

47. Hollensteiner.

48. Kenneth S. Pond, in *Farewell to the President*, 15:4–5.

49. Edward M. Gripkey, in *Farewell to the President*, 7:3.

50. Thomas F. Reid, in *Farewell to the President*, 16:2. Sgt. Gary Rogers, a member of the Old Guard who helped form an honor cordon along the funeral route, notes a similar clash with the Green Berets: "I . . . remember the arrogance of the Special Forces Colonel who wouldn't allow his men to mess with our troops as they were too elite. Later we noticed some of the Special Forces guys faint as they stood at attention along the parade route. They may have been tough troopers, but they didn't know how to stand at attention for long periods of time." in *Farewell to the President*, 18:1–2.

51. Sam Bird was placed in charge of the president's casket team because the Army, as the nation's oldest military service, had seniority over other services contributing members to the casket detail.

52. Douglas A. Mayfield, in *Farewell to the President*, 10:3.

53. Samuel R. Bird, interviewed by William Manchester, April 30, 1964, WMP.

54. "Funeral Services of President Kennedy 23–25 November 1963," DVD, JFKL.

55. Jimmy Breslin, "Digging JFK Grave Was His Honor," The *New York Herald Tribune*, Nov. 26, 1963.

56. Philip Bigler, *In Honored Glory: Arlington National Cemetery* (St. Petersburg, FL: Vandamere Press, 2004), 86.

57. Breslin.

58. Metzler, WMP. Another possible inspiration for Arlington's eternal flame is the Eternal Light Peace Memorial at Gettysburg National Military Park. President and Mrs. Kennedy visited the memorial in March 1963 during the centennial year of the Civil War battle.

59. Metzler, WMP.

60. Ibid.; Manchester, 552.

61. Fuqua.

62. Manchester, 552.

63. Mayfield in *Farewell to the President*, 10:2.

64. Ibid.

65. Ibid.

66. Bird, "After Action Report," WMP.

67. Samuel R. Bird, interviewed by William Manchester, April 30, 1964, WMP.

68. Annette Bird and Tim Prouty, *So Proudly He Served: The Sam Bird Story* (Wichita: Okarche Books, 1993) 87; Samuel R. Bird, interviewed by William Manchester, April 30, 1964, WMP.

69. Rep. Neil Staebler, interviewed by Howard Cook, Dec. 4, 1964, JFKL.

70. Manchester, 570.

71. Mayfield, in *Farewell to the President*, 10:4.

72. Sam R. Bird, interviewed by William Manchester, April 30, 1964, WMP.

73. Irving Lowens, "Accurate Listing of Funeral Music," The *Washington Star*, Dec. 1, 1963.

74. Bird and Prouty, *So Proudly*, 89–90.

75. "Funeral Services of President Kennedy 23–25 November 1963," DVD, JFKL.

76. Mary McCrory, "He Would Have Liked It," The *Boston Globe*, Nov. 26, 1963; Lowens, "Accurate Listing of Funeral Music."

77. Michael J. McNamara in *Farewell to the President*, 12:6; Louie W. Odom in *Farewell to the President*, 14:3; Manchester, 560.

78. Setterberg, in *Farewell to the President*, 19:3.

79. Reid, in *Farewell to the President*, 16:3.

80. Ibid.

81. Pond, in *Farewell to the President*, 15:5.

82. William Malcolm, interviewed by William Manchester, April 30, 1964, WMP.

83. James R. Holder, in *Farewell to the President*, 8:2.

84. Carlson in *Farewell to the President*, 2:3.

85. Setterberg in *Farewell to the President*, 19:4.

86. "Funeral Services of President Kennedy 23–25 November 1963," DVD, JFKL; "Actual Time Sequence, State Funeral for President John F. Kennedy, 25 November 1963," WMP.

87. Malcolm, WMP; Manchester, 599.

88. Richard Goldstein, "Keith Clark, Bugler for Kennedy, Dies at 74," The *New York Times*, Jan.17, 2002.

89. Reid in *Farewell to the President*, 16:12; Manchester, 599–600.

90. "Funeral Services of President Kennedy 23–25 November 1963," DVD, JFKL.

91. Ibid; Metzler, WMP.

92. Manchester, 601.

93. Metzler, WMP.

94. Ibid.

95. Manchester, 605.

96. Metzler, WMP.

97. Metzler, WMP.

98. Michael J. McNamara in *Farewell to the President*, 12:5.

99. Woodrow T. Blair in *Farewell to the President*, 1:2.

100. Reid in *Farewell to the President*, 16:7; "Arlington National Cemetery—Comprehensive Plan," Washington, D.C., U.S. Army Corps of Engineers, 1978, 17; "Arlington National Cemetery—Master Plan," Washington, D.C., U.S. Army Corps of Engineers, 1998, 8–9.

101. Blair in *Farewell to the President*, 1:1–2.

102. Reid in *Farewell to the President*, 16:7.

103. John C. Metzler Jr., interviewed by author, Oct. 15, 2008.

104. "Robert F. Kennedy Memorial," Arlington National Cemetery, http://arlington cemetery.org/visitor_information/Robert_F._Kennedy.html.

105. Tom Sherlock, historian of Arlington National Cemetery, in "Tribute to Arlington National Cemetery," George J. Wilson Jr., CombatVets.net, Feb. 28, 2007. A new cross replaced the one stolen from Robert Kennedy's grave; the thieves were never found.

106. "Arlington National Cemetery—Master Plan," Washington, D.C., U.S. Army Corps of Engineers, 1998, 8–9.

107. Arlington's columbarium, a complex of marble courts where cremated remains are preserved in small niches, was opened in the early 1980s. Eight of nine courts have been completed, with capacity for some 5,000 inurnments in each court. Because the columbarium uses so little space, qualifying regulations for inurnment are less stringent for inurnment than those for interment.

108. "Arlington National Cemetery—Master Plan," Washington, D.C., U.S. Army Corps of Engineers, 1998, 8–9.

109. Metzler Jr., Oct. 15, 2008.

110. Samuel R. Bird, interviewed by William Manchester, April 30, 1964, WMP.

111. William W. Morris in *Farewell to the President*, 13:5.

112. Metzler Jr., Oct. 15, 2008.

113. "1/3 Battalion HHC Caisson Platoon," www.army.mil/oldguard/specplt/caisson.htm.

114. B. T. Collins, "The Courage of Sam Bird," *Reader's Digest*, May 1989, 49–54; Bird, "After Action Report," WMP.

13: THE LAST UNKNOWN

1. Ken Ringle, "Honored Symbol: Vietnam War's Unknown Buried In Arlington Tomb," The *Washington Post*, May 29, 1984.

2. "President's Speech at Arlington Cemetery," DVD, Video Control No. 06270-4T-W308-G52, RRL; William M. Hammond, *The Unknown Serviceman of the Vietnam Era* (Washington, D.C.: Center of Military History, 1985), 11–14.

3. Ibid.

4. All American women who died in Vietnam had been accounted for by this time.

5. "President's Speech," DVD G-50, G-52, G-53, RRL.

6. Ibid.

7. Ibid.; Ringle, "Honored Symbol"; Hammond, 11–14; Robert D. Hershey Jr., "One of 58,012 Vietnam Dead Joins the Unknowns," The *New York Times*, May 29, 1984.

8. Hammond, 14; "Secretary of Defense Approves Recommendations Concerning The Vietnam Unknown," Department of Defense Press Release No. 296–99, June 17, 1999. Fearing a spreading Communist threat, President Eisenhower sent the first American advisors to Vietnam in 1958; the war ended with the fall of Saigon in 1975.

9. John O. Marsh Jr. to Caspar W. Weinberger, June 16, 1982, "Unknown Serviceman from the Vietnam Era—Action Memorandum," Folder "POW/MIA—Tomb of the Unknown (4)," Box 924089, Richard Childress Files, RRL.

10. S. 49, "A bill to amend title 38 of the United States Code in order to establish a National Cemetery System within the Veterans' Administration, and for other purposes," June 18, 1973, Library of Congress.

11. James T. Wooten, "Arlington Crypt Vacant, Awaiting Vietnam 'Unknown,'" The *New York Times*, May 1, 1976.

12. Milton J. Bates et al., eds., *Reporting Vietnam* (New York: The Library of America, 1998), 2:793–99.

13. *Reporting Vietnam*, 2:798. More than 58,000 military personnel from the United States died in Southeast Asia between 1959 and 1973; some 47,000 of these deaths were the result of hostilities.

14. Rudy deLeon, former undersecretary of defense, interviewed by author, July 11, 2008; Wooten, "Arlington Crypt"; Caryle Murphy, "'Unknown' Was Hard to Find," The *Washington Post*, May 28, 1984.

15. Joseph Rehyansky, "The Unknown Soldier of the Vietnam War," *National Review*, June 29, 1984.

16. "President's Speech," DVD, Video Control No. 06270-4T-W308-G50, G52, RRL.

17. Robert Mann, *Forensic Detective: How I Cracked The World's Toughest Cases* (New York: Ballantine Books, 2006), 110–20; Department of Defense Briefing, "The Vietnam Unknown Soldier," May 7, 1998, www.arlingtoncemetery.net/unk-vn33.htm.

18. Johnie E. Webb Jr., interviewed by author, June 20, 2008, July 3, 2008; Col. Patricia S. Blassie, interviewed by author, July 5, 2007, June 17, 2008, Oct. 8, 2008.

19. "Now-Identified Vietnam Vet Was 'A Natural,' Fellow Soldiers Recall," The *Washington Post*, June 30, 1998; Department of Defense News Briefing, "Tomb of the Unknown Soldier," April 27, 1998, www.arlingtoncemetery.net/unk-vn46.htm.

20. "Now-Identified Vietnam Vet Was 'A Natural.'"

21. Maj. Jim Connally to Mr. and Mrs. George Blassie, n.d., in Col. Patricia S. Blassie, "Air Force Airman Selected As The Vietnam Unknown Soldier—The Truth And Its Consequences," thesis, Jan. 17, 2005, Air War College, Maxwell Air Force Base, Alabama, Appendix 2, hereafter "Blassie thesis." One of the Cobra pilots who tried to recover Blassie's remains on the day of his crash testified to the intense enemy fire. "I will never forget that day," he told Charles Cragin, acting assistant secretary of defense for reserve affairs. The pilot said he had fired 52 rounds of 17-pound rockets while trying to inspect Blassie's crash

site—and limped back to base with his helicopter's hydraulic system badly damaged. Blassie's plane, the pilot testified, was in "itty-bitty pieces." Department of Defense News Briefing, "Tomb of the Unknown Soldier," April 27, 1998, www.arlingtoncemetery.net/unk-vn46.htm.

22. Col. Patricia S. Blassie, interviewed by author, Oct. 8, 2008.

23. Maj. Donald E. Lunday, "Memorandum for Record: Body Recovery," Oct. 31, 1972, and Lunday "Memorandum for Record: Phonecon with Mr. Rogers, USA Mortuary, TSN," Nov. 5, 1972, in Blassie thesis, Appendixes 15 and 14; Rudy deLeon, action memorandum to Secretary of Defense William S. Cohen, "The Vietnam Unknown in the Tomb of the Unknown Soldiers," April 23, 1998, RdL Papers; Department of Defense News Briefing, "Tomb of the Unknown Soldier," April 27, 1998, www.arlingtoncemetery.net/unk-vn46.htm.

24. "Certificate," Capt. Richard S. Hess, n.d., detailing delivery of remains of Michael Blassie and evidence to Sgt. First Class Malcolm R. Biles, at Tan Son Nhut mortuary, Nov. 2, 1972, JW Papers.

25. DeLeon, action memorandum, April 23, 1998, RdL Papers.

26. John C. Rogers, skeletal chart, "BTB Blassie, Michael Joseph," Central Identification Library, Hawaii, n.d. in Blassie thesis, Appendix 16.

27. Col. Patricia S. Blassie, interviewed by author, Oct. 8, 2008; Mann, 98.

28. Mann, 95.

29. Col. Patricia S. Blassie, interviewed by author, Oct. 8, 2008.

30. *Reporting Vietnam*, 2:793.

31. Johnie E. Webb, Jr., interviewed by author, June 20, 2008; Mann, 96–98; Joint POW/MIA Accounting Command, "History," www.jpac.paccom.mil/index.php?page= mission_overview.

32. Robert B. Pickering and David Charles Bachman, *The Use of Forensic Anthropology* (Boca Raton: CRC Press, 1987), 5.

33. Tadao Furue, "Special Anthropological Narrative: Processing of TSN 0673-72, Dec. 4, 1978, in Blassie thesis," Appendix 16; Mann, 96–98.

34. Ibid.

35. Armed Services Graves Registration Office, "TSN 0673-72 BTB Blassie, Michael Joseph," May 7, 1980, Blassie thesis," Appendix 20.

36. Mann, 96–98.

37. DeLeon, action memorandum, April 23, 1998.

38. Mann, 98.

39. DeLeon, action memorandum, April 23, 1998.

40. Ibid.; Rudy deLeon, interviewed by author, July 11, 2008.

41. Furue, Dec. 4, 1978, in Blassie thesis.

42. Mann, 98, reports: "From the information available, scientists could neither prove nor disprove that the remains were Blassie's."

43. Blassie thesis, 30. New evidence was not to be found. The United States dispatched investigative teams from Hawaii in 1992 and 1994 to interview witnesses and search for clues in Blassie's case. They found nothing—except for a practical-minded farmer using what was likely the plane's impact crater as a watering hole. DeLeon, action memorandum, April 23, 1998.

44. John O. Marsh Jr., interviewed by author, July 21, 2008.

45. John O. Marsh Jr. to Caspar W. Weinberger, June 16, 1982, Folder "POW/MIA—Tomb of the Unknown (4)," Box 92409, Richard Childress Files, RRL.

46. Ibid.

47. Ann Mills Griffiths to Caspar W. Weinberger, July 26, 1982, Folder "POW/MIA—Tomb of the Unknown (2)," RAC Box 92409, Richard Childress Files, RRL.

48. Richard T. Childress to William P. Clark, Aug. 26, 1982, www.nationalalliance.org/Blassie/b820826.htm.

49. Caspar W. Weinberger to William P. Clark, Aug. 23, 1982, Folder "POW/MIA—Tomb of the Unknown (3)," RAC Box 85, Executive Secretariat, National Security Council: PA: Subject File: Records, RRL.

50. Carrie Brunosi, *The Sentinel*, 3, 3 (Aug.-Oct. 2001); logbook, March 23, 1983, Tomb of the Unknowns, Arlington National Cemetery.

51. Johnie E. Webb Jr., interviewed by author, June 20, 2008; Mann, 102–4. I have withheld the name of X-15 because there is still debate about whether he was AWOL when killed. In deference to his family, the Army fixed his time of death on July 27, 1970, the day before he was reported as a deserter. This allowed him to be buried with honors—but some investigators remain convinced that he was, in truth, a deserter.

52. Johnie E. Webb Jr., interviewed by author, June 20, 2008.

53. Ibid; Mann, 104–6; deLeon, action memorandum, April 23, 1998.

54. Johnie E. Webb Jr., interviewed by author, June 20, 2008; deLeon, action memorandum, April 23, 1998.

55. Caspar W. Weinberger to Ronald Reagan, March 16, 1984, Folder "Vietnam (April 1981–Sept. 1984)," RAC Box 11, Executive Secretariat, NSC: Records: Country File, RRL.

56. Karen Byrne Kinzey, historian, Arlington House, The Robert E. Lee Memorial, interviewed by author, April 16, 2006.

57. Johnie E. Webb Jr., undated memorandum "TSN 0673-72 (X-26)" to Army Personnel Command, JW Papers. In an e-mail to the author July 22, 2008, Webb says that the memo was sent to Washington in March 1984 and that it went up the chain of command to John O. Marsh Jr., secretary of the Army.

58. John O. Marsh Jr. interviewed by author, July 21, 2008.

59. Webb's warning note about the Vietnam Unknown, from JW Papers, appears below in its entirety:

TSN 0673-72 (X-26)

1. These partial remains consisting of approximately 9 % of the skeletal frame were recovered by Army Recon Team 1/48 from a plane crash site at Grid Coordinates UTM XT 716-904. Allegedly the team also recovered the ID card for the pilot of this one man aircraft. However, the ID card did not accompany these remains to the US Army Mortuary, the fate of the ID card has never been recovered.

2. The remains delivered to the Saigon Mortuary in a Believed to Be (BTB) status as those of the pilot were accompanied by "cut" remnants of a nomex flight suit, one man inflatable raft, one ammo pouch, remnants of a pistol holster, empty signal

marker pouch, and remnants of a parachute. Attempts to identify these remains has [sic] resulted in disassociation with the BTB name. Research has led to disassociation with all but two unresolved casualties. Further research has resulted in passive association with a single casualty. Further physical anthropological evaluation for personal identity is not feasible due to the absolute paucity of key skeletal elements.

3. These remains should be disqualified for selection as the Unknown because of the past and present name associations.

60. Johnie E. Webb Jr., interviewed by author, June 20 and July 3, 2008.

61. Johnie E. Webb Jr., memorandum of certification "Remains of TSN 0673-72 (X-26)" March 21, 1984, JW Papers.

62. Johnie E. Webb Jr., interviewed by author, June 20, 2008.

63. Blassie thesis, 28–30.

64. Johnie E. Webb Jr., "Memo for Record: Documents to Be Removed from X-26 File and Placed in the Blassie File," from Webb's telephone conversation with Lt. Col. David Peixotto, Office of the Assistant Secretary of the Army for Civil Works, April 4, 1984, JW Papers.

65. Johnie E. Webb Jr., interviewed by author, June 20, 2008.

66. Ibid.

67. At the time of ceremonies for Blassie, the U.S.S. *Brewton* was classified as an ocean escort; it was later designated a missile frigate.

68. "President's Speech," DVD, Video Control No. 06270-4T-W308-G52, RRL.

69. Pat Blassie is now an Air Force colonel working in the Pentagon as executive officer to the chief of the Air Force Reserve.

70. Col. Patricia S. Blassie, interviewed by author, July 5, 2007 and Oct. 8, 2008.

71. Ted Sampley, "The Vietnam Unknown Soldier can be Identified," *U.S. Veteran Dispatch*, July 14, 1994. A POW/MIA activist, Sampley is not known for journalistic restraint. While his reporting on the Blassie case has held up, he sometimes sees conspiracies where others do not. During the 2008 presidential election, for example, he happily spread the discredited rumor that Barack Obama was a secret Muslim and, in a demonstration of his non-partisanship, he expressed the opinion that Sen. John McCain was a Manchurian candidate controlled by Communists. Jim Rutenberg, "The Man Behind the Whispers About Obama," The *New York Times*, Oct. 12, 2008.

72. Ted Sampley, interviewed by author, June 15, 2007.

73. Col. Patricia S. Blassie, interviewed by author, Oct. 8, 2008.

74. Ibid.; George E. Atkinson, "Memo for Record," Dec. 20, 1994, in Blassie thesis, Appendix 11.

75. Mann, 108.

76. Ted Sampley, interviewed by author, June 15, 2007. Although much of the CBS report was based on research Sampley had shared with the network, CBS did not credit Sampley's contribution.

77. Blassie thesis, 18–19.

78. "Update: Unknown No Longer," CBS News, www.cbsnews.com/stories/1998/04/07/national/printable6793.shtml.

79. Blassie Thesis, 19.

80. Ibid.

81. Col. Patricia S. Blassie, interviewed by author, Oct. 8, 2008.

82. "Vietnam Unknown May Be Air Force Pilot," Jan. 20, 1998, www.arlingtoncemetery .net/unk-vn04.htm.

83. Col. Patricia S. Blassie, interviewed by author, Oct. 8, 2008.

84. Rudy deLeon, interviewed by author, July 11, 2008; deLeon, action memorandum, April 23, 1998.

85. Rudy deLeon, interviewed by author, July 11, 2008.

86. Ibid.; deLeon, action memorandum, April 23, 1998.

87. DeLeon, action memorandum, April 23, 1998. The task force did not try to fix responsibility for the Reagan administration's handling of the Blassie case, which the CBS report described as a politically motivated cover-up. The case might be more fairly characterized as an instance of good intentions gone awry. As political pressure mounted, Unknown candidates fell off the list, and Pentagon appointees failed to heed the warning signs in their zeal to deliver an Unknown for President Reagan and Vietnam veterans. Keeping to the high road, deLeon's task force gave John Marsh and other Pentagon officials the benefit of the doubt. "We have no reason to question the decisions reached in 1984 concerning the selection of Vietnam War remains for interment in the Tomb," the report said. "Given the limited technology at the time and the information available, the X-26 remains were at that point unidentifiable." The escape clause, of course, is "at that point," which did not allow for the possibility that Blassie might be identified at some future time; this distinction was the basis for Johnie Webb's objection.

88. Mann, 112.

89. Col. Patricia S. Blassie, interviewed by author, Oct. 8, 2008.

90. Jean and Pat Blassie provided blood samples for the DNA testing, which matched the mitochondrial DNA sequence from Michael Blassie's bones. At the time the tests were done, in 1998, the method was relatively new, having been approved only in 1995 as a reliable clinical means of legal identifications. DeLeon, action memorandum, April 23, 1998.

91. "Remains of Vietnam Unknown Identified," The Washington Post, June 29, 1998.

92. "Veterans Groups Oppose the Attempt by Blassie Family to Obtain Top Medal," Aug. 8, 1998, www.arlingtoncemetery.net/unk-vn61.htm.

93. The Blassie family fought to keep the Medal of Honor for their kinsman, arguing that the award was given to him as the Vietnam Unknown, a position in which he served for fourteen years. Bonnie Edwards, "U.S. Stripped Medal of Honor from Unknown Vietnam Soldier," U.S. Veteran Dispatch, June-Oct. 1998.

94. Jim Garramone, "Vietnam Unknown Crypt at Arlington to Remain Empty," American Forces Press Service, June 17, 1999.

95. Tom Holland, scientific director of the Central Identification Laboratory, cautions that the 400 boxes do not represent 400 sets of remains. Of 1,000 boxes in the lab, about 40 percent are Vietnam War–related cases. M.E. reports:

One box might contain 4-5 individuals; conversely, one individual might be in 5–6 boxes. In addition our 1,000 boxes include several hundred unidentified Asians. We also have boxes of remains turned over by governments (such as the 208 boxes turned over by the N Koreans, which probably represent the commingled remains of 400-plus Americans), or private citizens that have defied identification attempts. Many of these will never be identified, but some will—each year we identify 1–2 of these 20-year-old cases. That's what makes coming up with a number so vexing.

The boxes do not represent a backlog, Holland says.

Every box has been analyzed and everyone that we can identify has been identified. The reasons the boxes are still on the shelves are varied: we haven't completed the excavation, we're awaiting DNA results, we're awaiting a family reference sample, we've already identified the man [and] are waiting on the family to decide disposition, or we're simply stymied and are awaiting new information or a breakthrough in technology. Bottom line, we analyze every case as soon as it comes through the door. E-mail to author from Tom Holland, July 3, 2008.

96. Johnie E. Webb Jr., interviewed by author, June 20, 2008.

14: WAR COMES TO ARLINGTON

1. Darrell Stafford, interviewed by author, April 1, 2009.
2. Ibid.
3. Ibid.; Steve Vogel, The Pentagon: A History (New York: Random House, 2007) 449.
4. Scott Wilson and Al Kamen, "Global War on Terror Is Given New Name," Washington Post, March 25, 2009.
5. Stafford interview; "Presidential Address to the Nation, Oct. 7, 2001," http://georgewbush-whitehouse.archives.gov/news/releases/2001/10/20011007-8.html; Guy Raz, "Defining the War on Terror," All Things Considered, National Public Radio, Nov. 1, 2006; John Judis, "What is the War on Terror?" New Republic Online, June 5, 2006; William Safire, "On Language: Asymmetry," The New York Times, Oct. 21, 2001.
6. Stafford interview.
7. Ibid.
8. Ibid.
9. Jim Garamone, "Remains of Pentagon Attack Victims Buried at Arlington," American Forces Press Service, Sept. 12, 2002; Connie Cass, Associated Press, "Ceremony Honors Pentagon Victims," Sept. 13, 2002.
10. Ibid.
11. Stafford interview.
12. "Kip Paul Taylor," http://arlingtoncemetry.net/kiptaylor.html.
13. Joseph L. Galloway, "Family Tragedy Ends in Arlington Cemetery," undated article, Knight Ridder Newspapers.

14. Garamone, "Remains"; Cass, "Ceremony."

15. Fifteen servicemen and one servicewoman killed in Operation Desert Shield and Desert Storm, more popularly called the Persian Gulf War of 1990–91, are buried at Arlington. Another nine, whose remains could not be identified but who are known to have died, are honored with headstones in the cemetery's memorial section. Of all the conflicts in which the United States has been involved since World War II, the 1990–91 Gulf War was one of the most conventional, with a clear, narrowly defined objective, an overwhelming deployment of forces, and a relatively low number of fatalities. Out of some 340,000 Americans sent to fight, 293 were killed, 148 of those in battle.

16. Rick Hampson, "Fallout from 1983 Barracks Bombing Is Still Being Felt," USA Today, Oct. 22, 2008.

17. "Terrorist Bombing of the Marine Barracks, Beirut Lebanon," Oct. 23, 2008, http://arlingtoncemetery.net/html.

18. Hampson, "Fallout."

19. Richard A. Serrano, "Detainees Describe CIA Agent Slaying," Dec. 8, 2004, and "Driven by a Son's Sacrifice," April 7, 2005, The Los Angeles Times ; James Risen of The New York Times, interviewed on The News Hour with Jim Lehrer, PBS, Nov. 29, 2001.

20. Ibid. Moments before he died, Spann had been interrogating John Walker Lindh, a Californian arrested with Taliban fighters and taken into federal custody. Lindh avoided trial by pleading guilty to aiding the Taliban and carrying explosives, for which a U.S. District judge sentenced him to twenty years in prison. Lindh told the judge that he had no role in Spann's death, although members of Spann's family believed that the Californian had been complicit. Richard A. Serrano, "Detainees."

21. "CIA Honors Slain Officers at Annual Ceremony," May 31, 2002, CIA press release.

22. Serrano, "Detainees"; Serrano "Driven"; The New York Post, Nov. 29, 2001; The New York Daily News, Nov. 29, 2001.

23. Ibid.

24. "DCI Remarks at the Funeral of Johnny Micheal Spann," Dec. 10, 2001, CIA Speeches and Testimony, http://www.cia.gov/news-information/speeches-testimony/2001/dci-speech-12102001.html.

25. The Marine body bearers of Bravo Company, attached to the Marine Barracks at Eighth and I Streets in Washington, D.C., spend hours pumping iron to stay in condition for their work. Their unofficial motto: "World Famous Body Bearers, the Last to Let You Down."

26. http://www.arlingtoncemetery.net.

27. Karen Meredith, "Gold Star Mom Speaks Out: Section 60, the Saddest Acre in America," Oct. 11, 2008, http://gsmo.blogspot.com/2008/10/section-60-saddest-acre-in-america.html.

28. Tom Sherlock, interviewed by author, May 17, 2005.

29. Michael A. Cottman, "Pride, Sorrow Mingle in Maryland Couple's Loss," The Washington Post, April 8, 2003; Annie Gowen, "Fallen Soldier Honored in Arlington: He's the First Combat Death in the War to Be Buried at National Cemetery," The Washington Post, April 10, 2003; Eileen Putman, "Nation Buries War Dead at Arlington," Associated Press, April 11, 2003; Clay Latimer, "A Heart Laid Bare," The Rocky Mountain News, April 3, 2004.

30. Ibid.

31. Robert Allen Durbin, "Die in combat—receive full honors," The *Winchester Journal Gazette*, March 31, 2008; Sfc. Robert A. Durbin, e-mails to author, Sept. 17, Dec. 12, Dec. 22, 2008, Jan. 17, 2008; John C. Metzler Jr. to Sen. Richard G. Lugar, Nov. 28, 2007; Sen. Richard G. Lugar to Pete Geren, April 4, 2008; Pete Geren to Sen. Richard G. Lugar, April 30, 2008.

32. Durbin to author, Sept. 17, 2008.

33. Ibid.

34. Staff Sgt. Jerald Allen Whisenhunt e-mail to Betsy Whisenhunt, Feb. 5, 2008.

35. Durbin to author, Sept. 17, 2008.

36. William H. McMichael, "Should Arlington honors go beyond rank?" *Military Times*, April 2, 2008.

37. Ibid.

38. Durbin, "Die in Combat."

39. Pete Geren, memorandum for Assistant Secretary of the Army for Manpower and Reserve Affairs, "Funeral Honors at Arlington National Cemetery (ANC) for Enlisted Soldiers Killed in Action," Dec. 12, 2008, Department of Defense; William H. McMichael, "All enlisted KIAs to get full Arlington honors," *Military Times*, Dec. 15, 2008; Jeff Schogol, "Army extends honors to enlisted soldiers," *Stars and Stripes*, Dec. 17, 2008.

40. Mark Berman, "Full Military Honors Honor a Soldier's Full Sacrifice: First Enlisted Soldier Buried Under New Arlington Policy," The *Washington Post*, Jan. 24, 2009.

41. Confidential communication, Durbin e-mail to an officer, Dec. 12, 2008.

42. "Joseph M. Hernandez, Specialist, United States Army," U.S. Department of Defense Immediate Release No. 022-08, Jan. 12, 2009; Vanessa Renderman, "Hammond soldier killed in Afghanistan," The *Northwest Times*, Jan. 13, 2009.

43. Lolly Bowean, "Indiana soldier, father of 2, killed in Afghanistan," The *Chicago Tribune*, Jan. 16, 2009; Lu Ann Franklin, "Hammond soldier returns home," The *Hammond Times*, Jan. 16, 2008.

44. Berman, "Full Military Honors"; Mary Louise Kelly, "Enlisted Man Gets Burial Once Reserved for Officers," *All Things Considered*: National Public Radio, April 21, 2009.

15: TAPS

1. Daytime duty, which is limited to half-hour patrols, is even more rigorous for tomb sentinels because they must pay strict attention to the appearance of their dress uniforms and to the presence of millions of Arlington's visitors, for whom the Tomb of the Unknowns is a popular attraction.

2. Spec. Bruce Bryant, Staff Sgt. Stephen Kuehn, Pfc. Adam Boutross, Sgt. Christopher Moore, Pfc. Kyle Obrosky, sentinels interviewed by author, Dec. 4, 2006; Staff Sgt. Justin E. Bickett, interviewed by author, Nov. 28, 2006. Despite the Tomb Guard's stern appearance, no sentinel has carried live ammunition since 1948, when a jumpy guard heard a noise in the night and fired two warning shots into the air. One of the shots whizzed over the cemetery and pierced the leg of a woman in an apartment building at Arlington Farm, some 500 yards away. Beulah Irene Coslett survived the incident but lost the use of her left foot. She

sued the government, won a $50,000 settlement, and changed the policy for arming Tomb sentinels. "Shot By Shrine's Guard: Woman Is Hit By Stray Bullet," The *Washington Post*, Nov. 28, 1948.

3. Spec. Bruce Bryant, interviewed by author, Dec. 4, 2006; Bryant has since been promoted to sergeant.

4. Ibid.

5. Lisa Hoffman, "Guard Feels Bond With Vietnam War Soldier," July 7, 1998, The *St. Louis Dispatch*. Although upset by Blassie's departure from Arlington, the guard was happy that the airman's remains had been returned to his family.

6. Bryant and others, interviewed by author, Dec. 4, 2006; Staff Sgt. Adam Dickmyer, interviewed by author, Nov. 20, 2006.

7. The first woman sentinel was awarded the Tomb Guard badge in 1996. Three others have since received the badge, which is the Army's rarest award. Fewer than 600 have been given since 1957.

8. Bryant and others, Dec. 4, 2006.

9. Dickmyer, Nov. 20, 2006.

10. Thomas D. Holland, scientific director, memorandum to commander, Joint POW/MIA Accounting Command, "Identification of CIL 2004-101-1-01," Oct. 17, 2005; Paul Duggan, "WWI Soldier Comes Home at Long Last," The *Washington Post*, Sept. 25, 2006; Andrew E. Woods, "World War I Soldier Repatriated After 88 Years," 18th Infantry Annual Meeting, Aug. 9, 2007, St. Louis, MO.

11. Ibid.

12. Ibid.

13. Duggan, "WWI Soldier."

14. Author's notes and interviews, Sept. 26, 2006.

15. Ibid.

16. Duggan, "Long-Lost Soldier Remembered," The *Washington Post*, Sept. 27, 2006; Spec. Stephen Baack, "1st Division Soldier Identified, Laid to Rest," Oct. 26, 2006, army.mil/news; Steven Donald Smith, "Longtime-Missing WWI Soldier Buried at Arlington National Cemetery, American Forces Press Service, Sept. 26, 2006.

17. Rudi Williams, "Arlington National Cemetery Gains 70 Acres of Land," American Forces Press Service, May 27, 2005.

18. Kaitlin Horst, Arlington National Cemetery, e-mail to author, April 28, 2009.

19. John C. Metzler Jr., interviewed by author, Oct. 15, 2008. Most of Arlington's new space will come from the Navy Annex, a World War II–era building sitting on 44 acres and slated for demolition in 2010. Another 17 acres will be absorbed from adjoining Fort. Myer. Twelve more will be taken from a wooded area near the Lee mansion, much to the dismay of the National Park Service, which had previously controlled the parcel and considered it an important buffer of historical importance. Because one acre of land typically provides space for 600 to 800 graves, the additional 70 acres could hold as many as 56,000 graves; in addition, Arlington is developing another 40 acres of land it already controls within the cemetery, which could provide space for 36,000 new graves and inurnment sites. Thus Arlington's total capacity could approach 400,000 graves by 2060.

EPILOGUE

1. John M. McHugh, "Army Directive 2010–04 (Enhancing the Operations and Oversight of the Army National Cemeteries Program)," June 10, 2010.

2. Yeganeh June Torbati, "Inquiry Finds Arlington Errors," The *New York Times*, June 11, 2010.

3. Julian E. Barnes, "Arlington National Cemetery's Top Supervisors Ousted in Mismanagement Case," The *Chicago Tribune*, June 11, 2010.

4. Torbati; Christian Davenport, "More burials will be checked," The *Washington Post*, June 12, 2010.

5. Barnes.

6. John M. McHugh, letter of reprimand to John C. Metzler, Jr., June 10, 2010.

INDEX

A NOTE ON THE AUTHOR

Robert M. Poole is an editor and writer whose assignments for *Nation graphic* and *Smithsonian* have taken him around the world. He is the aut *Explorers House*: National Geographic *and the World it Made*, and a contribu editor at *Smithsonian*. He lives in Virginia.